Viatcheslav Vetrov

The Linguistic Picture of the World

Viatcheslav Vetrov

The Linguistic Picture of the World

Alice's Adventures in Many Languages

ERGON VERLAG

Cover illustration:
Viatcheslav Vetrov

The Deutsche Nationalbibliothek lists this publication in the
Deutsche Nationalbibliografie; detailed bibliographic data
are available on the Internet at http://dnb.d-nb.de.

First published 2021

Printed on age-resistant paper
Cover layout: Jan von Hugo

www.ergon-verlag.de

ISBN 978-3-95650-749-6 (Print)
ISBN 978-3-95650-750-2 (ePDF)

For Iwan and Svetlana

Babies are illogical;
Nobody is despised who can manage a crocodile;
Illogical persons are despised.
Therefore no babies can manage crocodiles.

Lewis Carroll, *Symbolic Logic*

Do not ask if a hare is literally mad in March but not in May.

Warren Shibles, *Wittgenstein: Language and Philosophy*

Mrs. Malaprop: I would by no means wish a Daughter of mine to be a Progeny of Learning; I don't think so much Learning becomes a young Woman – But at the same time, I would not have her so inarticulate in her Ideas as you mention. – For instance, I would never let her meddle with Greek, or Hebrew, or Simony, or Fluxions, or Paradoxes, or such inflammatory branches of Learning. Neither would it be necessary for her to handle any of your Mathematical, Astronomical, Diabolical Instruments; but, Sir Anthony, I would send her at nine years old to a Boarding School, in order to learn a little Ingenuity and Artifice; then, Sir, she should have a supercilious knowledge in Accounts – and, as she grew up, I would have her instructed in Geometry, that she might have something of the contagious Countries – But, above all, Sir Anthony, she should be Mistress of Orthodoxy, that she might not mis-spell and mis-pronounce words so shamefully as Girls usually do.

Richard B. Sheridan, *The Rivals*

Contents

Preface

This is an unbirthday book. The date of its publication coincides with neither Carroll's nor *Alice's* anniversary and yet it has grown out of my courses on *Alice* given at the Sinology department of Heidelberg University and at the ILAS Institute of Kyoto University (Kyōdai) that incidentally began in 2015, i.e. exactly when the world was celebrating 150 years of *Alice*. And so, even if the study you are about to read does not share the honor of such monumental birthday books as *The Annotated Alice: 150th Anniversary Deluxe Edition* and *Alice in a World of Wonderlands: The Translations of Lewis Carroll's Masterpiece*, it is a great comfort to me to think that it originates in the same year when they were first published to celebrate Carroll's heroine.

In our courses, we investigated the reasons for the immense quantity of *Alice*-translations in the languages that we speak, the extension of the original plot through translation-languages, questions concerning the extent to which our thinking is guided by different linguistic categories and the relation of translator's creative individuality to the power of the collective picture of the world. As a matter of fact, for discussing these issues Warren Weaver's *Alice in Many Tongues* (1964) deserved special attention. In this pioneering study on *Alice*-translations, Weaver analyzed an excerpt from Chapter VII "A Mad Tea-Party" that had been retranslated on his request from fourteen foreign languages into English and the primary goal of examining these back-translations was to elucidate the following question: "How good a translation does this seem to be when examined by an English-speaking person?...does this translation capture and convey those aspects of the original which seem important to us?"[1] When reading his book, I was not so much interested in this particular question as in the theoretical implications of this analysis with its basic assumption that back-translations from one single foreign version may be regarded as enough evidence to pass a judgment on the language in question as a whole. One of the conclusions at which Weaver arrived following his method was the following general impression about the Japanese language:

1 Warren Weaver, *Alice in Many Tongues*, p. 77.

"The Japanese version both puzzles and intrigues me. The three retranslations we have, all being made from exactly the same Japanese passage, differ so much, one from another, that it seems clear that translation back and forth between English and Japanese must be a rather loose and vague business. Could, for example, two excellent Japanese scholars translate into their language two different books by an American or English author in such a way that a third Japanese scholar would recognize the similarity of style?... Japanese ... seems to suffer from the fact that this language communicates in a way which is really substantially different from English."[2]

This conclusion seems to suggest that it is possible to speak about a specific national vision of a classic which is formed by the language of a given nation. The 'suffering' of Japanese was in his eyes evident, e.g. when he compared idiomatic expressions in the back-translations with those of the original: since "murdering time" was rendered in them as "wasting time" (Weaver, p. 97) Weaver took it as a deficit peculiar to the semantics of Japanese in general. A similar observation was made when discussing Nabokov's Russian rendition of "muchness" as "not enough of" (Weaver, p. 102.) Although Weaver did not use the term 'the linguistic picture of the world', in order to arrive at his conclusions, he must have been guided by the idea of an insurmountable impact imposed by languages on their speakers.

By contrast, the present study argues that no language imposes on its speakers something like a national interpretation of a literary work, that is, a reading of a text or even of some details in it that would be shared by the whole of the respective language community. In my analysis I was working with *Alice*-translations into six languages (Chinese, French, German, Italian, Japanese, and Russian.) The range of languages under discussion is thus rather limited, yet, I believe, it is broad enough for a comparative investigation into translation practice.

Each of the six target-languages offers a great number of *Alice*-versions. In my study, I have drawn on only a small portion of them. Nonetheless, even a cursory reading of these texts is enough to see that the situation which Weaver observed in his back-translations from Japanese is actually common in all the languages under study: Chinese readings prepared by Zhao Yuanren and Ma Teng display a wide variety of differences in grammar, semantics, strategy of reproducing puns, parodies, etc. The same thing holds good for the Russian versions by Nabokov and Demurova, for the German *Alices* by Zimmermann and Teutsch, etc. Some of the translators whose renditions have been analyzed in this book are themselves either famous writers (Vladimir Nabokov) or scholars (Zhao Yuanren.) I could not provide the book with detailed biographical and bibliographical infor-

2 Warren Weaver, *Alice in Many Tongues*, pp. 107–108.

mation on the translators and discussed all of them on the same basis, i.e. as creative individuals who in the course of their lives felt inspired to produce a personal version of Carroll's book.

Readers who would like to learn more about their lives can gain much relevant information from the above mentioned monumental work by John A. Lindseth (Ed.), *Alice in a World of Wonderlands: The Translations of Lewis Carroll's Masterpiece* (2015.) Although its compilation was largely inspired by Warren Weaver's study and was dedicated to him, in one particular point it is markedly different to *Alice in Many Tongues*: its numerous contributions pay much more attention to the general diversity characteristic of individual renditions of Carroll. As an example, in discussing Chinese versions, Feng Zongxin has laid great stress on the particular philosophical, literary and linguistic mastery of Zhao Yuanren, that is, the first translator of the book who has not been surpassed by any later translators of the book into Chinese[3].

Yet in one specific aspect this work is similar to that of Weaver: every language is discussed separately, as if it were hermetically sealed off from other languages. It hardly pays any attention to the mutual interaction of languages, their systematical convergence in certain areas and to the work of translating individuals against the background of these inter-linguistic phenomena. Both of these aspects will take central stage in the present study: For one thing, it will deal with *language that speaks* (*die Sprache spricht*) and more or less automatically steers its users in a particular direction which will be carefully examined from a number of perspectives (e. g. countability, gender, number, tense, aspect, etc.) and, for another, all language findings made by the translators under discussion will be regarded as products of their individual ability of linguistic seeing. The book begins with a discussion of these individuals. Chapter I introduces the translator in his/her visibility, i.e. as a creative speaker who, having produced his/her version of *Alice*, leaves behind a unique legacy for the rest of the world. Each of the subsequent chapters will keep an eye on their impressive resourcefulness in dealing with words, yet the focus will be put on a theoretical investigation into different linguistic problems.

---

3 Feng Zongxin, "*Alice* in Chinese Translation", in: John A. Lindseth (Ed.), *Alice in a World of Wonderlands: The Translations of Lewis Carroll's Masterpiece*, 3 Volumes, New Castle: Oak Knoll Press 2015, Vol. 1, pp. 187–198, here pp. 197–198. For translators of *Alice* into other languages under discussion see the following contributions in this volume: Isabelle Nières-Chevrel, "The French Translations of *Alice*: From an Ambivalent Literary Reception to a Masterpiece of Universal Literature" (Tr. by Justine Houyaux), pp. 239–248; Emer O'Sullivan, "Miss Zimmermann and Her Successors: German Versions of *Alice in Wonderland*", pp. 259–269; Momma Yoshiyuki, "*Alice* in Japanese: Named One of 'The Best 100'", pp. 316–319; Adele Cammarata, "Italians Love *Alice*!", pp. 310–315; Liudmila I. Skuratovska, Maria I. Isakova, "*Alice* in Russian: A Metamorphosis", pp. 461–466.

I would like to express special thanks to my students in Heidelberg and Kyoto with whom I could share my interest in all these issues: Fei Ruqing, Liliane Ronge, Patricia Slawek, Vera Hugler, Fabian Schmid, Paula Kuls, Sophie Boschan, Rebecca Yeh, Andreas Wagner, Minna Hon, Lydia Rachel, Fumi Sugimura, Ikumi Oe, Sae Suwamoto, Hiroki Goto, Marino Kato, Nao Hirai, Emi Shozui, Mayako Tsukamoto, Jose Manuel Dabat, and all the others. I have learned a great deal from our mutual discussions. Many thanks to Gotelind Müller-Saini, Hirata Shoji, and Kurata Shoko for their kind help with organizing my lectures at Kyoto University.

Heidelberg, August 2021

Viatcheslav Vetrov
svet@fengxingcaoyan.com

I. The Translator's Visibility

I.I

As is well known, translation studies represent a field of humanities that, over the past few decades, has been heavily influenced by political concerns. At least since 1978, when Edward Said, partly inspired by Michel Foucault, first published his study on the mental colonialization of the Orient by the West, scholars writing on translation have become acutely aware of the inherent powers of discourse and have pursued a thorough democratization of translation practice, i.e. paying close attention to the translator's dependency on the current political power relations and trying to liberate translations from any sort of hegemony. Lawrence Venuti's monograph *The Translator's Invisibility* (1995) is one of these works: it is imbued with the idea of a strong public commitment and has been conceived as a critique of different kinds of inequalities characteristic of translation practice in the English-speaking world. One of the book's chief concerns is the exact nature of the relation between the translator and the foreign author: according to Venuti, translation studies offer practically no theoretical criteria for differentiating between the authorial presence of an author and his/her translator in a given translated text. Among practical issues resulting from this theoretical deficit, Venuti observes a general expectation that a good translation should be a fluent one. Yet fluency is normally achieved by means of a thorough domestication of a foreign text to the target-language culture, so that, paradoxically, the translator's personality disappears in the shadow of the domesticated author, in other words, the translator becomes invisible. Venuti proclaims that the primary aim of his book is to combat this sort of invisibility. He addresses both translators and their reading public: Whereas translators, when working on their texts, should weigh up the possibilities of an effective foreignization by which to reduce domestication to a minimum, their readers are called to be attentive to the translator's culture and historical situation. In Venuti's eyes, these would be practicable measures against ethnocentrism, racism, and the hegemony of the English language in the globalized world and this, in turn, would ensure a political success of democracy[4]. The point is introduced as follows:

4 Lawrence Venuti, *The Translator's Invisibility: A History of Translation* (1995), London/New York: Routledge 2008, p. 16: "I want to suggest that insofar as foreignizing translation seeks to restrain the ethnocentric violence of translation, it is highly desirable today, a strategic cultural intervention in the current state of world affairs, pitched against the hegemonic English-language nations and the unequal cultural exchanges in which they engage their global oth-

To point out these implications is not to argue that the translator should be seen as comparable to the foreign author: translations are different in intention and effect from original compositions, and this generic distinction is worth preserving as a means of describing different sorts of writing practices. The point is rather that the precise nature of the translator's authorship remains unformulated, and so the notion of authorial originality continues to stigmatize the translator's work.[5]

Whereas the overall political motivation of Venuti's endeavor and his interest in elucidating the problems which he addresses in the above quote are quite plausible, having read his book, I do not really understand what he means by differences in intention and, first of all, in effect that he observes between an original and a translated work, as hardly anyone would expect a translator to produce by his rendition an effect that would be different from that of the original. On the other hand, it is not entirely correct that the nature of the translator's authorship remains unformulated. Among works on translation that have raised exactly this issue, Walter Benjamin's essay "Die Aufgabe des Übersetzers" ("The Task of the Translator", 1921) deserves being particularly mentioned at least for the following reasons: First, it offers a serious minute discussion of this theoretical problem and, second, it is conceived not as a political critique but rather, on the contrary, its focus is put on humanity as an uninterrupted continuum, i.e. the man and his language beyond history and therefore also beyond any political interest.

It is also worth bearing in mind that Benjamin's essay was first published as a Foreword to his translations from Charles Baudelaire's poetry, that is, it discusses the arguably most difficult sort of texts to be translated. The exact relation of the translator's words to those of the original is among the central issues of the essay and, although Benjamin also mentions differences in intention between the translator and the foreign author, he is much more concerned with affinities between them. On the differences, he says:

die des Dichters ist naive, erste, anschauliche, die des Übersetzers abgeleitete, letzte, ideenhafte Intention. Denn das große Motiv einer Integration der vielen Sprachen zur einen wahren erfüllt seine Arbeit.[6] (The intention of the poet is spontaneous, primary, graphic;

ers. Foreignizing translation in English can be a form of resistance against ethnocentrism and racism..."

5 Lawrence Venuti, *The Translator's Invisibility* p. 6.

6 Walter Benjamin, "Die Aufgabe des Übersetzers" (1921), in: Walter Benjamin (Tr.), Charles Baudelaire: *Tableaux Parisiens*, Heidelberg: Verlag von Richard Weissbach 1923, pp. V–XVII, here p. XIII.

that of the translator is derivative, ultimate, ideational. For the great motif of integrating many tongues into one true language is at work.[7])

In Benjamin's theory, the fundamental connection between an author and his translator is represented by the pure language which incorporates all that is being meant by the speakers of any natural language: the *meant* (*das Gemeinte*) may be interpreted as the activity of the spirit so that the principal task of the translator is to capture the movements of the spirit, its subtle manifestations that in their essence are the same in all natural languages. Having captured this essential meaning, the translator is to seek for an appropriate way of rendering it in his/her target-language. By transmitting the original message, he/she reveals one of the main characteristics of the pure language, namely, that all individual languages of the world naturally converge in it with each other, that they are *not foreign to each other* ("einander nicht fremd.") It is at this point that the concepts of 'kinship' (*Verwandtschaft*) and 'similarity' (*Ähnlichkeit*) begin to come into play: whereas the translator (by this word Benjamin, of course, refers to really great masters of this profession) makes visible the inner kinship of his/her own language, his/her meaning in it with that of the original, kinship is not to be confused with similarity which, in translation as in the nature of things, is not a necessary attribute of kinship. Kinship rather suggests the translator's congeniality with the original author and the translator's task is, therefore, the following:

> Jene reine Sprache, die in fremde gebannt ist, in der eigenen zu erlösen, die im Werk gefangene in Umdichtung zu befreien, ist die Aufgabe des Übersetzers. Um ihretwillen bricht er die morschen Schranken der eigenen Sprache: Luther, Voß, Hölderlin, George haben die Grenzen des Deutschen erweitert.[8] (It is the task of the translator to release in his own language that pure language which is under the spell of another, to liberate the language imprisoned in a work in his re-creation of that work. For the sake of pure language he breaks through decayed barriers of his own language. Luther, Voss, Hölderlin, and George have extended the boundaries of the German language.[9])

The extension of the boundaries of one's language through the contact with the meaning of the original is not understood as arising from the fidelity to the words of the original. In Benjamin's view, the translator has to realize that a literal reproduction, i.e. one that seeks to find for each foreign expression an exact

7 Walter Benjamin, "The Task of the Translator", in: *Illuminations*, Harry Zohn (Tr.), Hannah Arendt (Ed.), New York: Harcourt Brace Jovanovich 1968, pp. 69–82, here pp. 75–76.

8 Walter Benjamin, "Die Aufgabe des Übersetzers", p. XVI.

9 Walter Benjamin, "The Task of the Translator", p. 79.

semantic equivalent in the target-language, is not possible. This impossibility is explained by the fact that, although the meaning (*das Gemeinte*) of a spiritual message is in all languages the same, it is not so with the material form that it is given in different languages. These differences in the way to mean (*die Art des Meinens*) may be observed even in such seemingly identical expressions as 'Brot' (*bread*) in German and 'pain' (*bread*) in French.[10]

The crucial point of this theory is, I believe, that in the process of intercultural communication through translation the translator's personality cannot be but visible, which is basically due to his/her ability to capture that what is meant (*das Gemeinte*) in the original, to liberate it by his/her own language with all individual ways to mean peculiar to it. The intentions of these different languages run together within the pure language, nonetheless the material form taken on by these intentions is never one and the same. Visibility thus implies vital affinities in the perception of the spirit's movements, yet, on the other hand, it also necessarily arises from differences between speaking individuals and across cultures.

"Das Fortleben des Originals" (*the afterlife of the original*) counts among the central ideas of Benjamin's essay. There is both a positive and a negative side to this concept since it addresses a life of an original work when its existence in the initial linguistic form is over, i.e. as a continuation in the translation languages with all their different ways to mean. This unique dialectic of both understanding and moving away may be taken, I believe, as an alternative approach to the opposition of *domestication* and *foreignization* that are so common in translation studies (e.g. in the earlier mentioned study by Venuti.)

In the light of this theory, domestication loses its usual negative connotations and the translator whose task is to ensure the afterlife of the original automatically appears fully visible in front of his/her readers. The readers, in turn, contrary to the requirements suggested for them by Venuti[11], need not necessarily be informed about the translator's cultural and historic background in order to perceive the unity of the essential meaning of the original and that of the translated text. I would like to turn now to some of my observations on Carroll's translations in order to illustrate this.

In general, translations of *Alice in Wonderland* offer a rich variety of examples for both domestication and foreignization and it is by no means axiomatic that

10 Walter Benjamin, p. XI.

11 Cf. Lawrence Venuti, *The Translator's Invisibility*, p. 124: "Today, however, both elite and popular readers must learn how to read a translation, not as a simple communication of a foreign text, but as an interpretation that imitates yet varies foreign textual features in accordance with the translator's cultural situation and historical moment. Without such a reading practice, translation will remain invisible – regardless of the translator's discursive strategies or of the reader's knowledge and interests."

domestication forces translators to become invisible. Consider, e.g. two Japanese renditions of the text, one from Chapter IX in which Alice suddenly discovers a mysterious rule that explains to her some fundamental correspondences between language and psychology, among other things, that children who eat *barley-sugar* get *sweet-tempered*[12]. In Shōno Kōkichi's version (p. 133) *barley-sugar* is rendered as 水あめ (*mizuame-sirup, mizuame-sweet.*) The translator thus explicitly refers his readers to a specialty of Japanese cuisine and this detail will, of course, not be lost on the readers who would instantly see the translator's signature and recognize in the word a part of their own indigenous culture. Now consider another episode from Chapter IV in which the White Rabbit imagines how furious the Duchess will be for its coming late:

> The Duchess! The Duchess! Oh my dear paws! Oh my fur and whiskers! She'll get me executed, as sure as ferrets are ferrets![13]

Yamagata Hiro'o offers in his rendition of this scene a good example of foreignization by "translating" *ferrets* in katakana as フェレット (*feretto*), i.e. he marks the word as a loan and expects his reader not only to recognize what kind of animal it is, but also why the White Rabbit has to think about it in its panic. However, this word does not reveal anything about the author's intention, that is, without any comment provided by the translator it is highly unlikely to set off any associations with English culture. The reader would thus certainly stumble over this word, yet this kind of the translator's visibility is one that impedes successful communication between cultures. This last example will be discussed in greater detail in the chapter on Nonsense. Here it is called to demonstrate that the translator's visibility in itself is not a beneficial quality.

By the way of contrast, cases of an obvious assimilation of the original to the realities of the translator's culture (e.g. *barley-sugar* vs. *mizuame*) do not necessarily deserve criticism: the *mizuame* example may be regarded as controversial (who knows, maybe some Japanese readers will interpret this word as a sign of Carroll's great intimacy with Japanese cuisine), yet there seems to be no doubt about the latter example: if any translator of the text into, e.g. Russian had proceeded here as Yamagata Hiro'o (p. 49) and rendered the animal name by the corresponding Russian noun (*chorjok*), the words of the White Rabbit would make no sense at all and the only choice left here for the translator would be to provide a comment on why the Rabbit uses this particular word (incidentally, even in the edi-

12 *Alice*, p. 94.

13 *Alice*, p. 39.

tion of the original by Martin Gardner, the noun has been given an extra comment[14]) or to assimilate the word to the realities of the target-language culture.

Another point which, according to Venuti, should help the translator's personality become visible is the reader's familiarity with the translator's cultural and historical background: the more information the reader has at his/her disposal, so Venuti, the more visible the translator becomes in his text. Yet this is not always the case. The present study draws on a number of translations that have been issued chronologically in roughly the same period and within the same language communities, e.g. all of the seven Chinese renditions under discussion have been produced within the same culture, so that the problem of the translator's visibility cannot be reduced here to cultural and historical differences. The same is true of the various Japanese, French, German, etc. versions. All these mutually competing individuals who were working on their versions of *Alice* within more or less the same chronological and cultural context were hardly guided in their efforts by the desire to combat ethnocentrism, racism, the hegemony of English language in the globalized world, or by any other political motive. The merging of meaning which Benjamin suggests in his essay, i.e. the fundamental realization of one's resonance with the original message which again and again inspires Carroll's interpreters to prepare new versions of an already universally known classic, seems to be a far more plausible reason for the never ceasing process of recreating the story.

Every chapter in this book will provide numerous examples of differences between individual renditions of *Alice*, revealing the translators' visibility in both their understanding of the original meaning and in the ways to mean it in their target-languages. Some very special parts of *Alice*-versions in which the translators' visibility is probably most obvious are often overlooked in discussions on translation theory, namely, the paratexts. I would like to introduce here two of them, i.e. Prefaces by Boris Zachoder (1983) and Zhao Yuanren (1921.)

Zachoder's *Alice* begins with a chapter entitled as "Глава никакая, из которой тем не менее можно кое-что узнать" (pp. 33–38, lit.: *A chapter that in effect is no chapter, but is nonetheless revealing in some respects.*) This ironic title of a chapter that in effect is no chapter but a Preface to the book has been written for children. Carroll is introduced to them by the translator as an extraordinarily witty person whose most impressive ability was to play with words:

14 *Alice*, p. 39.

> Особенно он любил и умел играть…словами. Самые серьезные, самые солидные, самые трулные слова по его приказу кувыркались, и ходили на голове, и показывали фокусы, и превращались одно в другое – словом, бог знает что выделывали! И еще он умел переделывать старые, надоевшие стишки – переделывать так, что они становились ужасно смешными. Это, как вы знаете, называется пародиями. (p. 36)
> His great love and very special skill was to play with…words. He made most serious, solid, and difficult terms somersault, walk upside down, show tricks and turn into each other, in short, do really odd things! What's more, he could remake old hackneyed poems so that they became very funny. As you know, such remakes are called parodies.

Here, the discussion of Carroll's way of dealing with words is accompanied by the translator's adopting quite a special psychological attitude: by focusing on Carroll's ability to make most solid, difficult, awe-inspiring expressions become funny he actually anticipates one of the key motives of the book, i.e. the heroine's passionate love for strange complicated terms that are always a source of great joy to her (e.g. *to suppress an attempt at applause*, *the jurors*, etc.), even if sometimes she forgets their correct form (cf. *antipathies* vs. *antipodes* in Chapter I.) This love is constantly echoed by the author who equally enjoys observing words and playing with their meanings. Discussing this particular love of puns in his Preface, Zachoder himself begins playing with words, for example, when he touches upon unfathomable difficulties faced by anyone who wishes to translate Carroll's story (p. 37): "только я успел убедиться, что, пожалуй, легче будет … перевезти Англию." (lit: "I realized that it would probably be easier to transport England (than to translate *Alice*.)" In this phrase, the translator is playing with the homophones *perevesti* (*to translate*) and *perevezti* (*to transport*), thus providing a pun that is quite in the spirit of Carroll. This word-play provides the Preface with the prevailing mood of the original and, again, prepares the reader for facing another important motive of the book, i.e. self-estrangement: by telling his story, Carroll the mathematician actually moves away from the strict laws of mathematics as well as from the earnest self-perception of a solid scholar, and as far as his heroine is concerned, the journey through Wonderland turns for her into a series of metamorphoses of her own self, which may be considered the source of the strangest wonders in the whole story. Hence, the translator shows himself in his Preface as a most attentive reader of the book who recognizes psychology as its key motive. This is also revealed in the passage in which he describes why, in spite of all the difficulties of the book, he in the end decided to prepare a new personal reading of it. According to Zachoder, the most important stimulus to translate the book was gained by him when he was reading the following passage by Carroll in which the author depicts how exactly he imagined his heroine when writing the book:

> Stand forth, then, Alice, the child of my dreams… What wert thou, dream-Alice, in thy foster-father's eyes? How shall he picture thee? Loving, first, loving and gentle: loving as a dog (forgive the prosaic simile, but I know no earthly love so pure and perfect), and gentle as a fawn: then courteous—courteous to all, high or low, grand or grotesque, King or Caterpillar, even as though she were herself a King's daughter, and her clothing of wrought gold; then trustful, ready to accept the wildest possibilities with all that utter trust that only dreamers know; and, lastly, curious—wildly curious, and with the eager enjoyment of Life that comes only in the happy hours of childhood, when all is new and fair, and when sin and sorrow are but names—empty words signifying nothing![15]

These lines made the translator understand that the most important in Carroll's story was not the logic, not the puns, and not the wit, but the heroine with all the traits peculiar to her in Carroll's above description. In Zachoder's words (p. 37), it was Carroll's great love of his protagonist that turned tricks into wonders and made the author appear as a magician since only a magician is able to present a little girl with a life that would last for centuries. The translator's visibility is revealed in his congeniality with the author, in his sure perception of the book's spiritual essence and the ability to express his resonance with it. His final aim is to make the Russian readers recognize that the story about Alice deals first of all with the inner motives of human actions and all the complexities pertaining to the human nature.

Most works on *Alice in Wonderland* address nonsense as one of its focal issues. Quite an unusual – and therefore fairly visible – way of dealing with Carroll's nonsense is represented in Zhao Yuanren's Preface to his translation. Zhao not only introduces the basic qualities of nonsense (humor, paradoxes, etc.) to his readers but, similarly to Zachoder, uses his Preface to join Carroll's nonsense-game, which is clearly displayed already in its opening passage:

> 会看书的喜欢看序，但是会做序的要做到叫看书的不喜欢看序，叫他越看越急着要看正文，叫他看序没有看到家，就跳过了看底下，这才算做序做得到家。我既然拿这个当做作序的标准，就得要说些不应该说的话，使人见了这序，觉得它非但没有做，存在，或看的必要，而且还有不看，不存在，不做的好处。[16] (Those who read

15 Lewis Carroll, "Alice on the Stage", in *The Theatre* (1887) cited after: Harold Bloom (Ed.), *Lewis Carroll's Alice's Adventures in Wonderland* (*Bloom's Modern Critical Interpretations*), New York: Chelsea House Publications 2006, p. 52.

16 Zhao Yuanren, *Yi zhe xu* 译者序 ("Translator's Preface"), pp. 7–10, here p. 7.

books love reading prefaces. Yet those who write prefaces want to write them in such a way that the readers of the book would not like reading the preface, but get increasingly eager to read the book itself, so that before they have read the preface up to the end, they would jump over to what comes next. Only this can count as the real mastery of composing prefaces. And as far as I consider this a norm for writing prefaces, I will have to say here some unnecessary words and make the readers of this preface feel that it is quite unnecessary for the preface to be composed, to exist and to be read and, what's more, that it would be better if it had not been read, had not been written and had not existed at all.)

By pronouncing these words, the translator basically aims at achieving the same kind of self-estrangement that is characteristic of both Carroll and his heroine, that is, the whole passage above may be paraphrased by the question which Alice has to ask herself in the course of her journey: "Who in the world am I?" In other words, by asking himself what task he actually intends his Preface to perform and at the same time acknowledging that any Preface is superfluous, he is approaching the subject of the relativity of sense and touches upon one of the central themes of the book. It is exactly due to this ironic approach to his own position as translator and the writer of the Preface that the sense that has been critically questioned at the beginning becomes reestablished in its rights, not didactically, not by the authority of a learned man, but playfully and ironically, thus again anticipating the general mood of Carroll's story. This detached ironic position is kept throughout the Preface. Consider, for example, how it is concluded:

翻译的书也不过是原书的附属品之一，所以也不必看。既然不必看书，所以也不必看序，所以更不必作序。（不必看书这话，其实也是冒着一个"不通"的险说的，因为在序的第一段里，我就希望看序的没有看到这里早已跳过了去看正文，看到入了迷，看完了全书，无聊地回过头来翻翻，又偶尔碰到这几句，那才懊悔没有依话早把全书丢开了不念，给译书的上一个自作自受的当呢！）[17] (A translation is only an appendage to an original work, for this reason it is not necessary to read a book in translation or a preface to it and even less so – to write a preface. (However, saying that it is not necessary to read the book is also a risky thing which comes close to nonsense, because at the very beginning of this preface I expressed my hope that the reader would not read the preface up to the end but skip it and as soon as possible jump over to reading the book itself, get fascinated and read it through. And then, being bored because the reading is over, he would once more thumb through the book and accidentally hit upon these lines of the preface again. Then he would really regret that he

17 Zhao Yuanren, *Yi zhe xu*, p. 10.

did not listen to my advice earlier and did not put the book aside, because by doing so he would have avoided an obvious trap which has been set him by the translator!))

Here, the translator introduces himself as a cunning person calculating how to trap his reader and make him/her feel bored. And, again, much irony is at work in these words: the reader is supposed to feel bored not because the book is boring but, exactly the other way round, because, excited by the reading of the translated book he/she would feel sad about the reading being over and turn to reading it from the very beginning, thus getting back to the Preface which, as Zhao playfully puts it, is unnecessary, superfluous, meaningless, etc. Thus, as Zhao demonstrates in his Preface, a translation of *Alice* is first of all expected to puzzle and enjoy, which is also regarded by him as a key quality of Carroll's nonsense. Zhao explains his understanding of Carroll's Nonsense as follows:

> 第二，所谓‘没有意思’就是英文的 Nonsense，中国话就叫“不通”。但是，凡是不通的东西未必尽有意味。假如你把这部书的每章的第一个字连起来，成‘阿越这来那她那靠他阿’十二个字，通虽不通了，但是除掉有‘可做无意味不通的好例’的意味以外，并没有什么本有的意味在里头。“不通”的笑话，妙在听听好象成一句话，其实不成话说，看看好象成一件事，其实不成事体。[18] (Second, what we call "meaningless" corresponds to "Nonsense" in English and "obstruction" (*bu tong*) in Chinese. However, not everything that is obstructed is necessarily of interest. For example, if we string together all the initial characters from every chapter of the *Alice* book, we get a line of twelve characters "A yue zhe lain na, etc." Although it does not make any sense, it has no other significance than being a good example of gibberish or uninteresting nonsense. The subtlety of nonsense jokes is that hearing and reading them one becomes the impression that they make sense, whereas in reality they do not.)

In the chapter dealing with Nonsense, I will provide different standpoints concerning its nature. Among other things, it will be shown that the entertaining qualities associated with in Zhao's mind are often accompanied by much more gloomy ones, e.g. calculated violations of logic, arbitrariness, rudeness, physical and verbal violence, etc. Here, Zhao's theoretical exposition on Carroll's Nonsense is drawn on to explain what effect he wishes to achieve by his direct play with the reader. His Preface that basically shuns any theory is conceived as an attempt to convey to his reader how amusing it actually can be to hit against the borderline that divides nonsense from sense, to feel an illusion of sense in a situation in which none is to be found. Here, again, the translator's visibility is

18 Zhao Yuanren, *Yi zhe xu*, pp. 7–8.

revealed by his congeniality with the author and by the desire to join the Nonsense-game as soon as possible, already before the story begins.

I.II

The power of the linguistic picture of the world seems to become particularly great in the cases of association chains that are extremely difficult to reproduce by the lexical machinery of other languages. Linguistic pictorialness represents an area that mirrors the immense potential of human imagination and there are hardly two individual languages in the world whose speakers use exactly the same set of idiomatic expressions. During my courses in Heidelberg and Kyoto, one of my first questions to the students would be whether, in their opinion, Alice's fall through the Earth is in any way linguistically motivated. This question turned out to be rather difficult since the expression which I had in mind when asking it has not even been used by Carroll directly. However, it has been suggested by a dense net of such other expressions as *feeling tired, sleepy, pop down, dip down, falling down, falling very slowly*, etc. I was thinking about 'falling asleep', i.e. a phrase which is so common in English and which has been enacted by Carroll as a most significant event in the *Alice*-story. Although the word is not used directly, its semantics pierces through the whole action of the story and, ironically, only few languages allow the use of similar expressions to suggest the idea of the original. *In slaap vallen* in Dutch and *nemurikomu* 眠り込む in Japanese are rare exceptions. Thus, the event of Alice's falling asleep is part and parcel of all the numerous Alice-versions under discussion, yet most of them fail to reproduce that solid bridge connecting the story to the language and this is a really huge loss, considering how fundamental the idea of language is to the general conception of the book.

Having to abandon such an important picture at the very beginning of the story is in many respects similar to the situation that is well-known to any translator of Walter Benjamin's above mentioned essay, for *Aufgabe* in its title (*Die Aufgabe des Übersetzers*) has the meaning of 'task' but at the same time also that of 'surrender'/'capitulation', which is, again, a fixed combination of meanings in one word that symbolically, like a motto, reproduces the main idea of the whole essay and stubbornly defies direct translation into other languages. In similar situations, most translators hit against the limits of their language that does not offer adequate semantical means to suggest the idea of the original. Neither domestication nor foreignization can be here of any help to the translator and the only way to become visible in such a case is by providing a comment on the peculiarity of the given foreign idiom.

Admittedly, expressions like *falling asleep* in English and *Aufgabe* in German represent rather rare cases and in what fallows I would like to draw on an example from Chapter I in various translations in order to illustrate how the translator's in/visibility can result directly from a definite translation strategy and not from the limits imposed on the translator by his/her language. Falling through the Earth, Alice does not miss the opportunity to display her love of strange complicated words and says:

> "I wonder if I shall fall right *through* the Earth! How funny it'll seem to come out among the people that walk with their heads downwards! The antipathies, I think –" (she was rather glad there *was* no one listening, this time, as it didn't sound at all the right word.)[19]

As her sure linguistic intuition tells her, something is wrong with the label *antipathies*, yet she cannot remember the correct noun when pronouncing the phrase. The form used by Alice is thus a hybrid of *antipathy* and *antipodes* and anyone who knows the context of this episode will see that she is actually thinking about *antipodes* in the literal geographical sense of this word. Now consider the following Russian rendition of this passage by Zachoder (p. 41):

> А вдруг я буду так лететь, лететь и пролечу всю землю насквозь? Вот было бы здорово! Вылезу – и вдруг окажусь среди этих…которые ходят на головах, вверх ногами! Как они называются? Анти…Антипятки, что ли? (What if I will fly this way right through the Earth? That would be great! And when I come out I would suddenly be among those who…who are walking on their heads, upside down! What are they called? Anti…Anti-heels, I guess.)

A comparison of this passage with the original reveals two significant differences. The first of them is the semantics of the fall which has been rendered by Zachoder as a flight, although he could have reproduced here the original exactly without any loss of sense (cf. Nabokov, p. 7 *provaljus' skvoz' zemlju* (lit.: *I will fall through the Earth*), the same in Olenič-Gnenenko, p. 26.) I believe, the translator has preferred here a different verb, because in Russian *flying* is much closer to the semantics of *dreams* than *falling*, e.g. quite common is the expression *letat' vo sne* (*to fly in the dream*.) By contrast, *padat'* / *provalit'sja* 'to fall' that in theory can also accompany *vo sne* (*in the dream*) is not as natural and cannot suggest anything reminiscent of *falling asleep* in English.

19 *Alice*, p. 13.

Zachoder's image of *flight* does not evoke the idea of *falling asleep* either, yet the choice of the word can still be interpreted as arising from the wish to recreate – at least in part – the missing bridge between language and the plot of the story (cf. Demurova, p. 80, Ščerbakov, p. 32 both of whom have equally rendered Alice's *fall* as a *flight* by 'proleču' – 'will fly through'.) The second difference between Zachoder's rendition and the original concerns the pun (*antipathies*.) What is particularly remarkable about Zachoder's *anti-heels* is not so much that it is a coinage that may suggest the meaning of *antipodes* and that it sounds like a word of a child. From the point of view of translatability, still more striking is the fact that the target-language offers here an exact equivalent for the original word-play: *antipathy* (*antipatija*) and *antipodes* (*antipody.*) *Antipatii* (*antipathies*), i.e. a direct rendition of the pun has been provided in Russian by Nabokov (p. 7): *Antipatii*, Olenič-Gnenenko (p. 26): *antipatijami*, Demurova (p. 80) – *Antipatii*, the same direct rendition may be found in most French (e.g. Berman (p. 29): *les Antipatiques*), Italian (Pietrocòla-Rossetti (p. 5): *le Antipatie*) and German renditions (Zimmermann (p. 4) *Antipathien*; Enzensberger (p. 11): *Antipathien*; Hansen (p. 9): *die Antipathischen*.) The coinage of a new word can, I believe, be explained by Zachoder's decision not simply to reproduce Carroll's text but to be congenial with him by creatively playing with words, even if this causes the translator to move away from some of the original expressions. In other words, this kind of visibility with which the translator emerges from his text is entirely due to his personal intention to ignore the obvious possibilities that his language offers him for an exact reproduction of the original.

By the way of contrast, the visibility issue is different in languages that do not offer equally direct lexical means of translation, e.g. in Chinese and Japanese, so that the translator has to choose which word to use as a source of the corresponding word-play (i.e. either *antipathy* or *antipodes*) and to look for another expression in his/her language that would sound similar. As is suggested by the original context, the translator would have to prefer here *antipodes* (in the geographical sense) to *antipathy*. Zhao Yuanren (p. 7), for example, is playing here with an explicitly geographical term:

> 我倒不知道会不会一直掉穿了地球嘞，那怎么呢？掉到那边，遇见了许多倒着站的人，一定很好玩儿！叫倒猪世界，不是吗？——她这回倒觉得幸亏没有人听着，因为她想不起来书里那个“倒足世界”的名字，又觉 “倒猪世界”又不大象。(I don't know if I shall fall right through the Earth, what will happen then? When I come out, I will see many of those who are standing upside down. That will be funny! This is called the world of reversed pigs, isn't it? This time, she was glad there was no one lis-

tening, as she could not remember the way it was called in the books (lit: "the world of reversed feet") and felt that "the world of reversed pigs" did not sound correct.)

In this rendition, Zhao Yuanren made himself no less visible than Zachoder, for he resorted in it to a creative word-play that, as far as I know, has not been reproduced in any other Chinese rendition. Hence, he is also fairly congenial with Carroll, which becomes particularly evident by comparing his text with versions that reproduce the word, but do not provide any pun, e.g. in Chen Fuan (p. 7) *fanmian ren* 反面人 *(negative people)*, the translator refers to *fanmian renwu* 反面人物 (*a negative character*), that is, he decides to reproduce *antipathy* rather than *antipodes* and fails to come up with a word-play of his own; cf. a similar, yet not exactly the same rendition by Zhu Hongguo (p. 8), who has translated the word as *duili de ren* 对立的人 (*antagonist.*) Another similar version in Japanese has been provided by Shōno Kōkichi (p. 16) who has linked *hantai* 反対 (*oppose*) and *jin/nin* 人 (*man/people.*) In Zhao Yuanren's version the translator appears visible since he produces exactly the same effect as the original and provides a humorous transformation of a scholarly term, making it walk upside down, as Zachoder put it in his *Preface*. Thus, again, the translator's visibility results from a vivid linguistic imagination and is not imposed upon him by his language.

II. Gender and Style

II.I

In a great number of natural languages, gender represents a firm semantic and grammatical category which in the eyes of the native speakers may be quite natural and therefore not deserve much attention, yet some particularly sensible theoreticians of language take it to belong among crucial factors that directly affect human thought and action. The exact kind of this influence is occasionally made object of meticulous investigations with different focus areas as well as clearly different emotional attitudes towards the role attributed to linguistic gender. Consider, as an example, an Italian study *The Philosophy of Grammar* (*Verso la filosofia della grammatica*) which was produced by Edoardo Tinto and published by Rome University in 1953. Gender figures quite prominently among the preoccupations of its author who seems to be firmly rooted in the tradition of the *Port-Royal Grammar* (1660) and tries to produce evidence for the claim that the basis of gender is logic and that this category lies in the very nature of things. The distribution of logical (and natural) roles between masculine and feminine genders is introduced as follows:

> Il principio sostanza-forma che esiste nella natura delle cose ed è espresso dal bisogno genere-specie, domina dunque la morfologia grammaticale, come domina tutto l'ordine naturale.[20] (The substance-and-form principle which lies in the nature of things and which arises from the necessity (to differentiate between) kinds and species dominates grammar morphology just as it dominates the whole natural order.)

The masculine is taken to be the substance and the feminine – the form. The masculine is said to express the idea of singularity (*l'unico*), to refer to the absolute, original, and independent. By the way of contrast, the feminine is believed to suggest the idea of a plural (*il plurimo*) and to refer to what is relative and dependent:

> L'indipendente perciò è sempre generico e quindi maschile, il dipendente è sempre specifico, e quindi femminile.[21] (The independent is always generic and therefore masculine, the dependent is always specific and therefore feminine.)

---

20 Edoardo Tinto, *Verso la filosofia della grammatica*, Roma: Libreria Editrice Universitaria 1953, p. 13.

21 Edoardo Tinto, *Verso la filosofia della grammatica*, p. 71.

Although Tinto projects his considerations concerning the logic of grammatical gender onto all languages of the world and, by doing so, makes quite a universalistic claim, the evidence which he produces is almost completely limited to the semantics and the morphology of Italian, e.g. the plural morphology of the feminine noun *eco* (*the echo*) which represents an exception as it ends in *-o* and which is said to support the idea of its masculine original essence: its plural form is namely exactly the same as that of most masculine nouns (*echi.*) That the singular of this name is feminine is explained by the idea according to which the language has preserved in it a personal name from Greek mythology, i.e. that of a nymph who fell in love with Narcissus. Since there is hardly something more specific and therefore more distanced from the generic than a personal name, this name is taken as a perfect illustration of the feminine dependency on the masculine gender, in both language and the nature of things[22]. That the same principle governs most nouns and not solely rare exceptions like *eco*, is demonstrated as follows:

> Per la stessa ragione i nomi: *canto, orgoglio, destino*, non possono essere che maschili, mentre i nomi: *canzone, superbia, sorte* non possono essere che femminili... *Pane, vino, lavoro* sono nomi maschili perchè si possono concepire nel loro valore sostanziale. *Pagnotta, acqua, fatica* sono nomi femminili perchè, essendo specifici, si possono concepire soltanto come oggetti formali.[23] (For the same reason, the nouns *canto (singing), orgoglio (pride), destino (destiny)* cannot but be masculine, whereas the nouns *canzone (the song), superbia (arrogance), sorte (fate)* cannot but be feminine... *Pane (bread), vino (wine), lavoro (work)* are masculine nouns because they can be conceived of in their substantial value. *Pagnotta (loaf), acqua (water), fatica (labour/hard work)*, on the other hand, are specific and can be conceived of only as formal objects.)

In the above quote, every feminine noun is interpreted as a derivation from the masculine, the original, the substantial, the generic: *canzone* (fem.) as a kind of *canto* (masc.), *superbia* (fem.) – a kind of *orgoglio* (masc.), *fatica* (fem.) – a kind of *lavoro* (masc.), etc. There are, of course, lots of objections which may be raised against this theory: for one thing, the semantic distribution of genus is in different languages only seldom the same, e.g. whilst the opposition between *Stolz* (masc., *pride, orgoglio*) and *Arroganz* (fem., *arrogance, superbia*) displays the same pattern in terms of gender in German as it does in Italian, it is not so in Russian where both nouns share the same gender semantics: *gordost* (fem., *orgoglio*) and *nadmennost* (*superbia*.) On the other hand, an attentive reader will easily come up with lots of examples of masculine nouns in Italian that are equally derived

22 Edoardo Tinto, *Verso la filosofia della grammatica*, p. 36.

23 Edoardo Tinto, *Verso la filosofia della grammatica*, p. 77.

of other masculine nouns and thus display conceptual delimitation, e.g. *il panettone* (masc.) vs. *il pane* (masc.)

However, this is not the place to discuss the validity of Tinto's theory and it is drawn on here primarily as a historical document of a particular approach to gender which is anything but self-explanatory. His description of the above mentioned concepts such as the substance-and-form principle which is said to *dominate* logic and nature or of the natural and logical dependency of the feminine on the masculine can by no means be taken as part of a critical and detached discussion of grammatical gender. Quite on the contrary, these concepts represent vital ingredients within a theory that is imbued with traditionalism and is openly put forward as an apology of the masculine. It was only a few decades later, in the course of the feminist movement, that linguistic gender, i.e. all fixed semantical and morphological markers of gender in natural languages, came to be generally discussed in a much more critical manner. Consider, as an example, a short essay by the German writer Luise F. Pusch "Von Frauenflüchtlingen und Männerleichen" ("On Female Refugees and Male Corpses"[24] (1999) which discloses all the political and reformist dimensions of this critique.

In the eyes of its author, German is a language which is strictly speaking not really designed for women. Whereas it reserves for feminine gender unattractive concepts like *Leiche* (*corpse*) – the "male corpses" in the essay's title being in fact a feminine compound noun –, it is impossible to find in its lexicon a feminine noun for *female refugees*, since the corresponding word *Flüchtling* (*refugee*) as any other noun containing the suffix *-ling* is masculine. At the formal level, masculinity cannot be levelled even in the modern coinages like *Frauenflüchtling* that have been introduced to denote *female refugees*. This particular coinage is found to belong to a great number of *frauenwidrige Sprachverrenkungen* (*women-unfriendly linguistic distortions*) *imposed* by language on its users[25]. *Imposed* (*zwingt*) with an exclamation mark put after it provides a most critical counterpart for the benevolent treatment of the *masculine dominance* in Tinto's discussion of linguistic gender: the *imposition* (*der Zwang*) has now become a huge challenge as it makes visible a great injustice towards women which is deeply engrained in German and the writer takes it as a personal duty to increase the awareness of her language community of this fact.

The essay by Luise F. Pusch may also be interpreted as a document within a long history of man's (and women's) coming to terms with linguistic gender. Its goal is, perhaps predictably, not a philosophical speculation on the subject

24 Luise F. Pusch "Von Frauenflüchtlingen und Männerleichen", in: Luise F. Pusch, *Die Frau ist nicht der Rede wert*, Frankfurt am Main: Suhrkamp, 1999, pp. 195–196.

25 Luise F. Pusch "Von Frauenflüchtlingen und Männerleichen", p. 195.

but rather a declaration of war to gender, i.e. an extremely emotional and critical presentation of it as part of a political program which the author shares with lots of other contemporary thinkers. The key-word within this program is the equality of genders. It stands for a global movement against all those traditionalist sexist perceptions that much more often than not are corroborated by semantics and grammar of natural languages. Now language, of course, is not the only subject of criticism. Within the global movement toward gender democracy, a large proportion of works has been specifically dedicated to children's literature and to the evaluation of sexist stereotypes contained in it. Two following essays may serve as good examples: Janice McCabe, Emily Fairchild, Liz Grauerholz (et al.), "Gender in Twentieth-Century Children's Books: Patterns of Disparity in Titles and Central Characters"[26] and Emily Sigalow, Nicole S. Fox, "Perpetuating Stereotypes: A Study of Gender, Family and Religious Life in Jewish Children's Books."[27] Both works perceive a strong inequality in the treatment of male and female characters in children's books: male figures are found to be qualitatively much more present than female characters. Furthermore, compared to females, males are usually given stronger and more active roles, which is said to testify to a symbolic annihilation of women and girls:

> The disparities we find point to the symbolic annihilation of women and girls, and particularly female animals in the twentieth-century children's literature, suggesting to children that these characters are less important than their male counterparts.[28]

Of the numerous studies on children's literature that have been either directly produced within the feminist movement or have been written independently of it but nevertheless clearly reflect its goals and principles, the most relevant to the present study are those that focus both on gender as a social issue and on linguistic gender and, at the same time, investigate the question as to how the distribution of male and female roles manifests itself in the language of the books under discussion and whether the observed sexist stereotypes, e.g. the male dominance, the female subjugation, the above mentioned symbolic annihilation of women and girls, etc., are also in any way reflected in their language. One study

---

26 Janice McCabe, Emily Fairchild, Liz Grauerholz (et al.), "Gender in Twentieth-Century Children's Books: Patterns of Disparity in Titles and Central Characters", in: *Gender and Society*, Vol. 25, No. 2, 2011, pp. 197–226.

27 Emily Sigalow, Nicole S. Fox, "Perpetuating Stereotypes: A Study of Gender, Family and Religious Life in Jewish Children's Books", in: *Journal for the Scientific Study of Religion*, Vol. 53, No. 2, June 2014, pp. 416–431.

28 Janice McCabe, Emily Fairchild, Liz Grauerholz (et al.), *op. cit.*, p. 218. Cf. Emily Sigalow, Nicole S. Fox, op. cit., pp. 417–418.

that has been dedicated exactly to this problem is a monograph by Alessandra Levorato, *Language and Gender in the Fairy Tale Tradition: A Linguistic Analysis of Old and New Story Telling* (2003.) In this book, the focus is put on a long tradition in the development of the tale about the Little Red Riding Hood, from a medieval oral version and the well-known literary versions of it produced by Charles Perrault and the brothers Grimm up to some modern productions from the 20th century. While in the traditional versions the author observes two contrasting sets of vocabulary, one that is markedly childlike and feminine (naïve, sweet, endangered) and one that clearly mirrors male qualities (referring to predatory, beastly, aggressive behavior)[29], which fits neatly into the traditional gender stereotypes, the language of modern versions is different and displays a considerable transformation in the understanding of gender roles, e.g. the female language ranges from depicting practical and fearless girls up to laying great stress on "the necessity for women to recognize the wolfish side of femininity, their sensuality, and that they should be proud, rather than fearful, of their connection to nature and wilderness."[30]

A less optimistic view of the issue of gender language in children's literature is held by Donald G. MacKay and Toshi Konishi in their essay "Personification and the Pronoun Problem" (1980.) The authors investigate sexist stereotypes in children's books and try to find possibilities for overcoming them in literary productions of the future. This study is much broader in scope as it draws on a large number of works from a general anthology by Johnson et al. *Anthology of Children's Literature* (5th Ed., 1977.) The authors focus attention on the distribution of pronouns referring to personified figures in children's books and try to interpret these pronouns in terms of whether they are conceived as neutral, positive or negative ones. In the end, they reach the conclusion that in the works under study the masculine usually dominates the feminine, that is, the traditional sexist stereotypes feature quite prominently in children's literature and thus necessarily affect children's self-consciousness, their understanding of roles which the society expects them to play in the future, of traits which they have to cultivate in themselves, etc. The solutions proposed by the authors in the end are the following:

> One frequently suggested solution is to use *it*. However, the present data indicate that *it* carries connotations of distance and non-involvement which makes it an especially poor solution in children's literature...For the immediate future the best prescription seems to be role reversal: to personify stereotypically female animals e.g. *cats* as male

29 Alessandra Levorato, *Language and Gender in the Fairy Tale Tradition: A Linguistic Analysis of Old and New Story Telling*, Basingstoke: Palgrave Macmillian 2003, p. 119.

30 Alessandra Levorato, *Language and Gender in the Fairy Tale Tradition*, p. 10.

and stereotypically male animals e.g. *dogs* as female; and to assign stereotypically-male traits such as courage, strength and wisdom to female protagonists, while assigning stereotypically-female traits such as prettiness, niceness, and sweetness to male protagonists. We are of course not advocating changing existing literature. What is needed is new literature to balance the old. ...to break free of the sexist stereotypes and literary conventions of the past... For the long range future, balanced portrayals will be needed, involving some mixture of traditionally stereotypic traits for both male and female protagonists.[31]

In the light of this discussion, the work by Carroll deserves being mentioned for several reasons. For one thing, the protagonist of his books is a girl who possesses courage, endurance and clear mathematical thinking, i.e. qualities that are usually associated with males. There are no central male characters in these books who would be assigned a role similar to that of Alice. More than that: figures that are introduced by Carroll explicitly as male characters in most cases appear as reversals of what might be regarded as stereotypically male traits: they are fearful, petty, mournful, and powerless. Consider, e.g. the King who hides behind Alice while talking to the Cheshire-Cat (Chapter VIII), the Knave who – in stark contrast to Alice – lacks both the power and the courage to resist the irrational forces of the royal trial (Chapters XI and XII), the sighing and sobbing Mock Turtle (a character whose masculinity is constantly emphasized by the author in Chapters IX and X), the snorting boy from Chapter VI, etc. Although there are also some female figures in the story whose behaviour does not make the feminine gender appear in a favourable light (the ugly Duchess, the hysterical Queen, the violent-tempered cook, etc.), yet, on the one hand, none of them is given the protagonist role and, on the other, they are by far outnumbered by the characters that are introduced into the story as males and are systematically ridiculed by the author for their obvious lack of 'stereotypically male' features. This general disproportion in the psychological design of male and female characters is particularly striking in the first of the *Alice*-books. Since in the course of its development Alice is much more often confronted with male figures and has to prove her strength, logic and courage before them, it seems not too far-fetched to speak about a double reversal of sexist stereotypes in this work: first, in most situations she proves superior to male inhabitants of Wonderland (the feminine prevails upon the masculine, the masculine is exposed to ridicule) and, second, she is not only a female but also a child that proves superior to adult figures. In one of the later chapters of the present book, childhood will be treated

31 Donald G. MacKay, Toshi Konishi, "Personification and the Pronoun Problem", in: *Women's Studies Int. Quarterly* 1980, Vol. 3, pp. 149–163, here p. 162.

separately in detail. For the present, it is worth pointing out that this particular quality of the protagonist as a child significantly increases the psychological value of all those 'stereotypically male' traits that she possesses in contrast to most male characters of the book.

One further aspect which directly concerns the interaction between the feminine (the childish) and the masculine in Carroll's work and which could make the book all the more attractive for theoreticians of gender studies is its linguistic design. It is well known that compared to Old English, present-day English or Modern English in which it is written has only few traces of the category of gender so that some scholars even believe that it has no gender category at all.[32] Carroll's manner to employ personal and possessive pronouns nonetheless displays quite a regular pattern of meaning and lets the interaction between the masculine and the feminine become not only a major subject of its plot (i.e. the reversal of traditional stereotypes, the ridicule, the grotesque, etc.) but also figure among the constant stylistic devices at the formal level. The first question which arises in view of his usage of pronouns is how to interpret the high proportion of male personifications, relative to their female counterparts. Recalling in this regard the earlier mentioned studies that took the prominence of male animals (personifications) in children's books and the relative sparsity of female ones to be a sure sign of a symbolic annihilation of women and girls, a similar purely statistical approach to the gender issue is hardly applicable to the *Alice*-book. Female personifications like the old Crab (the mother) and the young Crab (the daughter) at the end of Chapter III are namely an exception from the general rule. By the way of contrast, male ones are quite common and, as already pointed out, they are normally figures that lack 'stereotypically male' traits, such as strength, courage and intelligence, that is, their masculinity appears as a consistently stylized one, which is contrasted with Alice's qualities. Therefore, it deserves particular attention what qualities in Carroll's text are characteristic of those figures that are introduced by masculine personal, possessive and reflexive pronouns (*he/him/his/himself.*) As a matter of fact, this question is basically the same as that discussed in the essay by Donald G. MacKay and Toshi Konishi: how, if at all, the pronouns and the gender of personified animals and things can be interpreted in terms of sexist stereotypes. In Carroll's text, there are three basic recurrent patterns in the distribution of relevant pronouns: the first is marked by switches between *it/its* and *he/him/his/himself* (as well as the respective form of address "Sir") referring

32 For a review of the debating positions concerning the category of gender in modern English, see, for example, Chapter III "Gender in English – a short overview" in the doctoral dissertation by Susanne Wagner, *Gender in English Pronouns: Myth and Reality* (PhD Dissertation) Freiburg im Breisgau 2003, pp. 35–50.

to one and the same character, the second is when a figure appears as a predominantly male one and the pronouns referring to it are correspondingly from the male group, the third is to make a figure appear predominantly in neuter and to make use only of *it/its/itself* to refer to it. Consider the following examples:

Type I (switches between *it/its/itself* and *he/him/his/himself*):

The Mouse (Chapter II and III)

p. 27 "We, indeed!" cried the Mouse, who was trembling down to the end of **its** tail.
p. 37 ...half hoping that the Mouse had changed **his** mind, and was coming back to finish **his** story.

The White Rabbit (Chapter IV)

p. 38 ...and she heard **it** muttering to itself, "The Duchess! The Duchess! Oh my dear paws! Oh my fur and whiskers!"
p. 38 "He took me for **his** house-maid," she said to herself as she ran. "How surprised **he**'ll be when **he** finds out who I am. But I'd better take **him his** fan and gloves – that is, if I can find them."

Bill (Chapter IV)

p. 44 (Alice) waited till she heard a little animal (she couldn't guess of what sort **it** was) scratching and scrambling about in the chimney close above her...
p. 44 "Catch **him**, you by the hedge!...Hold up **his** head – Brandy now – Don't choke **him**.."
p. 45 The poor little Lizard, Bill, was in the middle, being held-up by two guinea-pigs, who were giving **it** something out of a bottle.

The Caterpillar (Chapter V)

p. 48 "I ca'n't explain myself, I'm afraid, **Sir**," said Alice.
p. 51 "I'm afraid, I am, **Sir**"
p. 54 "Well, I should like to be a little larger, **Sir**.."
p. 54 "It is a very good height indeed!" said the Caterpillar angrily, rearing **itself** upright as **it** spoke (**it** was exactly three inches high...)

The Cheshire-Cat (Chapters VI, VIII)

p. 66 The Cat only grinned when **it** saw Alice. **It** looked good-natured, she thought: still **it** had very long claws and a great many teeth, so she felt that **it** ought to be treated with respect.
p. 91 The Queen had only one way of settling all difficulties, great or small. "Off with **his** head!" she said without even looking round.

The Dormouse (Chapter VII)

p. 72 a Dormouse was sitting between them, fast asleep, and the other two were using **it** as a cushion, resting their elbows on **it**, and talking over **its** head.
p. 79 "One, indeed!" said the Dormouse indignantly. However, **he** consented to go on.

The Gryphon (Chapters VIII, IX)

p. 103 "So he did, so he did," said the Gryphon, sighing in **his** turn…
p. 104 …said the Gryphon, and **it** set to work shaking him and punching him in the back.

Type II (*he/his/him*)

The Fish-Footman (Chapter VI)

p. 61 "Oh, there's no use in talking to **him**," said Alice desperately: "**he**'s perfectly idiotic!"

Time (Chapter VII)

p. 75 "If you knew Time as well as I do," said the Hatter, "you wouldn't talk about wasting *it*. It's ***him***."

Seven (Chapter VIII)

p. 83 "Yes, it is **his** business!" said Five. "And I'll tell **him** – it was for bringing the cook tulip-roots instead of onions."

The Mock Turtle (Chapters IX–X)

pp. 99–100 They had not gone far before they saw the Mock Turtle in the distance, sitting sad and lonely on a little ledge of rock, and, as they came nearer, Alice could hear

him sighing as if **his** heart would break. She pitied **him** deeply. "What is **his** sorrow?" she asked the Gryphon, and the Gryphon answered very nearly in the same words as before: "It's all **his** fancy, that: **he** hasn't got no sorrow, you know. Come on!"

Type III (*it/its/itself*)

The Lory (Chapter III)

p. 30 ...and, as the Lory positively refused to tell **its** age, there was no more to be said.

The Dodo (Chapter III)

p. 31 "In that case", said the Dodo solemnly, rising to **its** feet, "I move that the meeting adjourn..."

The Magpie (Chapter III)

p. 37 ...one old Magpie began wrapping **itself** up very carefully...

The Canary (Chapter III)

p. 37 And a canary called out in a trembling voice, to **its** children: "Come away, my dears! It's high time you were all in bed!"

The Pigeon (Chapter V)

p. 56 ...a large Pigeon had flown into her face, and was beating her violently with **its** wings.

p. 58 "Well, be off, then!" said the Pigeon in a sulky tone, as **it** settled down in **its** nest.

The above illustrations clearly suggest that the predominant gender of personifications in the book is the masculine. During my research I could find only very few commentaries concerning the gender of Carroll's personifications and those that I have read do not discuss gender throughout the whole book but are rather limited to mentioning some separate episodes from it as, for example, Warren Shibles whose philosophical commentary to *Alice* mentions the episode from Chapter VII in which the Hatter insists that Time must be understood as a male person. This leads Shibles to the question as to what gender can be assigned to time in reality:

> The table is turned here on Alice. She objects to riddles, but by talking of time as if it could be wasted, she creates her own puzzles. Is time neuter? Why not a male time? To take expressions like "Can you beat time?" literally would land Alice in difficulty. The problem is similar with the term "God." What gender is God?[33]

In the course of similar speculations, Shibles arrives at the conviction that time does not possess reality and therefore questions regarding its gender cannot be particularly illuminating, at least not from the standpoint of philosophy. One further study by Lecercle invites the readers to turn their attention to another episode from Chapter VIII in which the King and the Queen are talking about the Cheshire-Cat: the King is referring to the Cat as *it*, the Queen – as *he* (*his head.*) In so doing, the King is said to refuse to treat the Cat as a person and the Queen is said to be "more frank, because her violence is physical rather than strictly verbal."[34] Admittedly, this line of thought is not so easy to follow. In the course of her adventures Alice herself refers mentally to many of her conversation partners as *it/its* (e.g. in Chapter II, while thinking about the Mouse: "Perhaps it doesn't understand English.") Not less frequent is the use of the pronouns *it/its* by the author (e.g. whenever he comes to speak about the Lory, the Dodo, the Magpie (Chapter III), the Pigeon (Chapter V), the Cheshire-Cat (Chapters VI, VIII.) *It/its* must therefore be considered as natural a way to refer to personified figures as *he/his* and cannot be taken as a refuse to accept them as persons. Nor does the Queen's use of *his* really suggest any peculiar characteristics pertaining to her violence. This interpretation may be little persuasive because it regards the switch from *it* to *his* as an isolated incident whereas it actually represents one of the recurrent patterns in the pronoun usage throughout the story. Somewhat different is the discussion of the gender issue in a study by Monica Barretta who pays attention to regular switches between *it/its* and *he/his* in the book. In her opinion, these switches indicate the position of the respective figures, i.e. whether they are depicted as staying *within or outside of the magical garden* (*dentro al giardino incantato o fuori.*) and that occasionally they also refer to the figures' mental states, e.g. the Dormouse in Chapter VII is said to be neuter when sleeping and masculine when talking (*il Ghiro è in genere it quando dorme o sonnecchia, he*

33 Warren Shibles, "A Philosophical Commentary on *Alice's Adventures in Wonderland*", in: Warren Shibles, *Wittgenstein: Language and Philosophy*, pp. 14–45, here pp. 27–28.

34 Jean-Jacques Lecercle, *The Violence of Language*, London: Routledge 1990, pp. 252–253.

quando è sveglio e partecipa alla conversazione.)[35] However, this way of reading the text raises more questions than it answers: Given that all personifications met by Alice in the story are equally located within Wonderland, the opposition of *within/outside* does not make much sense. Nor do the mental states of different figures seem to be in any way related to whether they are addressed by neuter or masculine pronouns. Much more plausible would be to assume a connection between Carroll's choice of pronouns, his construction of certain psychological portraits and the perception of this psychology by Alice, i.e. her own interpretation of the linguistic behaviour of the figures that she meets in Wonderland.

At least purely hypothetically, it could be assumed that personal, possessive and reflexive pronouns in the text are to be understood as signals that correspond with some particular attitude of the protagonist (and of the author) to the conception of gender. One possible way to interpret the pronoun groups *it/its/itself*, *he/his/himself* and *she/her/herself* in the story would be by drawing comparisons between pronoun switches in Carroll's text, other works of children's literature, and the usual emotional attitude to pronoun switches in modern English. Regarding the comparison with children's literature in general, the above mentioned essay by Donald G. MacKay and Toshi Konishi provides some fruitful observations. Consider the following passage:

> One factor that seems to characterize all 19 pronoun switches is personal involvement. That is, the use of *he* or *she* seems to signal personal involvement or empathy for the referent in the case of a protagonist reflecting on its own personal situation, an owner of an animal, someone who is emotionally attached or values the referent, a protagonist taking an active part in a situation, or someone attached to a specific animal. By the way of contrast, the use of *it* seems to signal lack of involvement or empathy with the referent…[36]

Hence, on the one hand, the use of the pronoun groups *he/she* in children's literature normally demonstrates a much more positive emotional attitude towards the respective antecedents than that of *it/its/itself*. On the other, psychological portraits of males must appear particularly appealing to the reader compared to those of females since males are consequently depicted as displaying stronger, more active and more courageous behavior.[37]

---

35 Monica Berretta, "Problemi testuali della traduzione: casi di ambiguità anaforica in Alice nel paese delle meraviglie", in: Daniela Calieri, Carla Marello (Eds.), *Linguistica Contrastiva*, Publicazioni della Società di Linguistica Italiana 20, Roma: Bulzoni 1982, pp. 229–254, here p. 238.

36 Donald G. MacKay, Toshi Konishi, "Personification and the Pronoun Problem", p. 155.

37 Donald G. MacKay, Toshi Konishi, "Personification and the Pronoun Problem", p. 154.

Basically the same pattern of preference is described in Susanne Wagner's study on the usual practices of indicating the gender of animals (e.g. of pets) in modern English:

> As some degree of personal involvement is usually present when speakers talk about animals, neuter pronouns are the least expected forms. Pets will be *it*s only derogatorily or when talking about them in a detached manner, while the status of wild animals depends to a large extent on the speaker's "civilization" background.[38]

Now a rapid glance at the usage of pronouns in Carroll's text reveals considerable differences with the situations described in the above studies. There is nothing whatever derogatory about the use of *it/its/itself* in *Alices*. This is shown by the fact that Alice uses this pronoun group quite naturally alongside the pronouns *she/her/herself* to refer to her pet Dinah and to the terrier from her neighbourhood. Consider the following passages from Chapter II:

> Dinah: p. 14: She …had begun to dream that she was walking hand in hand with Dinah, and was saying to **her**, very earnestly: "Now, Dinah, tell me the truth: did you ever eat a bat?"; p. 36: "Dinah's our cat. And she's such a capital one for catching mice, you ca'n't think. And oh, I wish you could see **her** after the birds!" p. 37: "Nobody seems to like **her**, down here, and I'm sure **she**'s the best cat in the world!"; p. 39: "Only I don't think that they'd let Dinah stop in the house if **it** began ordering people about like that!"

> The terrier: p. 27: "There is such a nice little dog, near our house, I should like to show you! A little bright-eyed terrier, you know, with oh, such long curly brown hair! And **it**'ll fetch things when you throw them, and **it**'ll sit up and beg for **its** dinner, and all sorts of things – I ca'n't remember half of them – and **it** belongs to a farmer, you know, and he says **it**'s so useful, **it**'s worth a hundred pounds! He says **it** kills all the rats…"

Both animals meet with much sympathy here. Alice refers to Dinah by the pronouns *she/it* and to the terrier – consistently by *it*. In the latter passage, the masculine pronoun is used only to denote the dog-holder, not the dog itself, therefore this instance of usage is not relevant to the present study. In view of all this, it can be clearly seen that Carroll's way of employing pronouns so as to indicate Alice's personal involvement toward animals contrasts sharply with the cases observed by MacKay/Konishi and Wagner, i.e. it is expressed equally by *it/its* and by *she/her*. Therefore, whenever *it* is used in the text to refer to personified animals this pronoun cannot be interpreted as a sign of detachment or aversion.

38 Susanne Wagner, *Gender in English Pronouns: Myth and Reality*, pp. 126–127.

By contrast, switches between *it* and *he* signal a much more cautious attitude towards the respective personified figures, as, for example, those that are introduced into the story by the neuter *it* but later are either mentally referred by Alice as *he/his/him* or addressed by her directly as *Sir*. Among the first of these switches is her reaction to the footsteps she hears at the end of Chapter III: "she looked up eagerly, half hoping that the Mouse had changed his mind, and was coming back to finish his story."[39] In the conversations that precede this episode, the Mouse shows itself to be a fearful, easily offended and quick-tempered figure. The author provides a comprehensive set of attributes characteristic of its behaviour which helps the reader clearly understand its psychological portrait, e.g. the following traits:

> quivering all over with fright (p. 26), crying in a shrill passionate voice (p. 26), bristling all over (p. 27), trembling down to the end of its tail (p. 27), (speaking) in a low trembling voice (p. 28), frowning (p. 31), reply(ing) rather crossly (p. 31), sighing (p. 34), say(ing) severely (p. 35), cried the Mouse, sharply and very angrily (p. 36), only growled in reply (p. 36), only shook its head impatiently (p. 36.)

Attributes referring to Alice are equally numerous and they regularly contrast with those of the Mouse. Consider the following examples:

> Alice – afraid that she had hurt the poor animal's feelings, speaking in a soothing tone (p. 26), call(ing) softly after it, "Mouse dear!" (p. 27), half afraid that it would be offended again (p. 34), say(ing) very humbly (p. 36), looking anxiously about her (p. 36.)

Whereas the Mouse, in spite of being trembling and fearful, insists on its authority and promptly reacts whenever it feels that Alice or others do not take it in earnest, Alice appears as a patient conversation partner who is intelligent enough to understand the reasons for the Mouse's anger. Her "soothing tone" and her being afraid that she might offend the animal are clear signs of understanding and compassion. Hence, it is at least arguable that Alice's referring to the Mouse as a male at the end of Chapter III may be interpreted as a sign of comprehending and of accepting what is among the main propelling forces of its behavior, i.e. its desire to exert authority over others.

The textual environment of this particular switch from *it* to *he* is also quite meaningful in terms of gender semantics: shortly before the Mouse gets offended and leaves the scene, Alice pictures to herself its history in the form of the Mouse's *tail*. Here, the author is playing with the homophones *tale* and *tail* by

39 *Alice*, p. 37.

making their meanings merge and by using the history (the *tale*) to explain to his heroine why the Mouse hates not only cats but also dogs. In this tale, a cunning dog Fury makes appearance to judge the Mouse and to sentence it to death. This particular dog is introduced explicitly as a male person (p. 35): "Fury said to a mouse, That **he** met in the house, etc." It is worth pointing out that by saying "'I'll be judge, I'll be jury / said cunning old Fury'" to the Mouse the dog insists upon his absolute power over it, thus displaying basically the same authoritarian traits as the Mouse in the main *Alice*-story. And it also deserves attention that within the extremely short tale about Fury it is addressed by the Mouse as *Sir*, thus its masculinity which is introduced as pertaining to a brutal, arbitrary and aggressive character is mentioned twice and is therefore a rather prominent feature of the tale.

A marked resemblance between both male characters is that they claim authority over others. And it is exactly this trait which they share with a further character that appears immediately after Alice's mentally addressing the Mouse by the pronoun *his*. Contrary to her expectations, the little pattering of footsteps she hears at the end of Chapter III does not come from the Mouse but from the White Rabbit whom she suddenly meets again in Chapter IV. Seeing Alice, the Rabbit mistakes her for a servant and instantly orders that she fetch him his fan and gloves. In this episode, once again, Alice reacts to the order by mentally referring to the character by a switch from *it* – which is used by the author in his introduction of the White Rabbit at the beginning of Chapter IV – to *he*: "'He took me for his housemaid,' she said to herself as she ran. 'How surprised he'll be when he finds out who I am! But I'd better take him his fan and gloves – that is, if I can find them.'"[40]

The density of employing the pronouns *he/his* and the form of address *sir* with which the three figures are conceptualized as males at the beginning of the story may bear out the assumption that from the aesthetical standpoint gender does not represent a neutral category and that pronouns are used here to serve definite stylistic aims. The masculine is not merely – naturally – contrasted with the feminine but is consistently invested with negative connotations, which is also true of all other male personifications in the story. Among a broad range of negative qualities there are, e.g. the coarseness and indifference of the Caterpillar, the vulnerability of Time in the Hatter's story, the helplessness and clumsiness of Bill the Lizard, the sentimentality and arbitrariness of the Mock Turtle. The general negative picture of masculinity is also demonstrated in the only instance of depersonalization in the book, i.e. in the episode from Chapter VI in which

40 *Alice*, p. 39.

a grunting boy turns into a pig, which is observed by Alice with great relief. Her reaction to this wonderful transformation is rendered as follows:

> So she set the little creature down, and felt quite relieved to see it trot away into the wood. "If it had grown up," she said to herself, "it would have made a dreadfully ugly child: but it makes rather a handsome pig, I think."[41]

Compared to other instances of pronoun switches, the difference is here in that *he/his* is used first (to refer to *the boy*, e.g. in "'Oh, there goes his *precious* nose!'"[42]) and is thereafter succeeded by *it* which in the above passage refers both to *the pig* (*to see it trot away*) and to *the child* (*if it had grown up*, etc.) Thus, in the depersonalization act gender semantics meets the same stylistic purpose as in the depiction of male personifications: an ironic presentation of the masculine as flawed, ridiculous and unattractive.

When observing the textual distribution of pronouns and interpreting the predominantly negative stylistic connotations pertaining to textual markers of masculinity it is also necessary to pay attention to the frequency with which they are used as well as to the number of different perspectives from which a figure is reflected upon as a male. Consider in this connection two extreme examples: the Cheshire-Cat and the Mock Turtle. Chapter VIII contains the only instance in the whole book in which *his* is used referring to the Cat: "The Queen had only one way of settling all difficulties, great or small. 'Off with **his** head!' she said without even looking round."[43] The easiness with which the Queen's phrase is produced as well as her refusal to look at the Cat, to which the author explicitly directs the reader's attention, strongly suggest that this particular instance of using a masculine possessive pronoun has nothing whatever to do with the psychological portrait of the Cat who, different to other male figures, is described by Carroll as quite an amiable character. Consider, by contrast, the plurality of perspectives which reflect the masculinity of the Mock Turtle: he is introduced into discourse by the Queen as a male ("...take this young lady to see the Mock Turtle and to hear **his** history", p. 99), Alice perceives him equally as a male throughout the related chapters ("'What is **his** sorrow?'", p. 99; "'I don't see how **he** can ever finish, if **he** doesn't begin.'", p. 100), the Gryphon consistently makes use of masculine pronouns to refer to him ("'It's all his fancy'", p. 100; "'Same as if **he** had a bone in his throat'", p. 104), and the author also employs the same pronouns to make his masculinity explicit ("The Mock Turtle sighed deeply, and drew the

41 *Alice*, p. 66.

42 *Alice*, p. 63.

43 *Alice*, p. 91.

back of one flapper across **his** eyes. **He** looked at Alice and tried to speak, but, for a minute or two, sobs choked **his** voice." (p. 104.) The frequency of these textual markers of masculinity is striking and it underscores the peculiarity of this character, his difference from both of his conversation partners, i.e. from Alice as well as from the Gryphon who is only in few instances denoted by the author as a male, the majority of pronouns that refer to the Gryphon being from the neuter *it/its/itself* group. That means that the Mock Turtle's masculinity should be associated with traits that make him appear different to both Alice and the Gryphon and this is primarily his excessive bent for sobbing and sighing which makes him fit perfectly into the whole series of male figures in the book who are depicted as constantly *sighing* (the Mouse, p. 34), *sobbing/howling/snorting/grunting* (the boy, pp. 62–65) and *squeaking* (Bill, p. 44, p. 115.)

Other than the boy and Bill the Lizard who are portrayed as small, pesky and helpless the Mock Turtle rather appears to be of an impressive physical size (Tenniel has provided a telling illustration of it, p. 101), so that the tears that he is incessantly shedding contrast both with his stature and with the high-handed ways he shares with the Mouse and the White Rabbit. Owing to his inclination to verbal arbitrariness, he will be discussed contrastively in more detail in the Chapter "Through the Eyes of a Child." This particular quality which openly opposes logic and rationality is one that Alice cannot comprehend or tacitly accept. It can be regarded as the highest possible progression of masculinity in Carroll's stylization, i.e. the ultimate stage in manifesting both the desire to maintain the strictest control over others and the sheer inability to tolerate disagreement.

By systematically providing his male characters with negative connotations, Carroll may well be considered to upset all those earlier mentioned sexist stereotypes which are critically questioned at the present time. It would, of course, be to too far-fetched to label him a feminist writer or a pioneer of some political movement. He rather seems to represent the same humanistic vision which some hundred years before his time made another thinker recognize the essence of real beauty in overcoming all those set qualities ('stereotypes' as they are termed today) with which men and women tend to be associated owing to their nature.[44] Carroll seems to make the same point whenever he contrasts the courage and logic of Alice with her male counterparts who either are literally shown as weak and helpless (the boy, Bill the Lizard) or are conceived as negative reversals of masculinity (the Mock Turtle.) At the formal level, Carroll's use of personal, possessive and reflexive pronouns proves to be an effective means for car-

44 Wilhelm von Humboldt, Über die männliche und die weibliche Form (1795), in: Wilhelm von Humboldt, *Werke*, Albert Leitzmann (Ed.), Berlin: B. Behr's Verlag 1903, Vol. I, pp. 335–369

rying out this humanistic idea and one of the paramount questions that arise in studying various renditions of his work is how attentive translators are to these signals of style which are constantly sent to the reader in the English original.

All the six target-languages under discussion provide translators with definite means for marking a textual interaction between genders, even though they represent quite different development stages of the category of gender: in the case of Chinese, gender is made visible merely at orthography level (by the characters *ta* 她 (fem., *she/her*) /*ta* 他 (masc., *he/him*) /*ta* 它 (neut., *it*)); in Japanese, apart from a great many semantical and grammatical markers of male and female language[45], gender is also denoted in distinct personal pronouns (cf. *kanojo* 彼女 (*she*), *kare* 彼 (*he*)); in French and in Italian, apart from distinct personal pronouns for males and females, there are two genders assigned to all nouns, i.e. masculine and feminine, and adjectives agree with nouns according to their gender; German is similar to French and Italian but it has three genders, i.e. masculine, feminine and neuter; and in the case of Russian, there are also three genders and the agreement involves pronouns (personal, possessive and relative), adjectives and predicates of the past, thus representing a complex gender system in both semantics and morphology[46].

In spite of the differences in gender systems all the six languages provide markers by which to indicate gender of the characters in the story. Yet apart from Chinese and Japanese where gender is not part of nominal morphology, formal problems of rendition do arise even in French and Italian: First, neither French nor Italian has neuter, which makes it difficult to recreate Carroll's switches between *it* and *he/she*. Second, what might at first sight look still more aggravating, the distribution of gender semantics is in different languages seldom the same, that is, whenever Carroll insists that the Mock Turtle be perceived as a male character, from the standpoint of nominal semantics in Italian, German, French and Russian it is impossible to follow the original directly, for their corresponding nouns are all feminine, cf. *la tartaruga* (It.), *die Schildkröte* (Ger.), *la tortue* (Fr.), čerepaha (Rus.) Hence, when confronted with the task of rendering

45 For more details concerning the use of these markers in Japanese, see, e.g. Janet S. Shibamoto Smith, "Gendered Structures in Japanese", in: Marlis Hellinger and Hadumod Bußmann, *Gender Across Languages, The linguistic representation of women and men*, Amsterdam/Philadelphia: John Benjamins Publishing Company 2003, Vol. 3, pp. 201–226 and Sachiko Ide, "Women's Language as a Group Identity Marker in Japanese", *ibid.*, pp. 227–238.

46 The best introduction into the comparative theory of linguistic gender offers Greville G. Corbett in his essays "Gender in Russian: An Account of Gender Specification and its Relationship to Declension", in: *Russian Linguistics*, Vol. 6, 1982, pp. 197–232; "Gender in Slavonic from the Standpoint of a General Typology of Gender Systems", in: *The Slavonic and East European Review*, Vol. 66, No. 1, 1988, pp. 1–20, and in the monograph *Gender*, Cambridge: Cambridge University Press 1991.

gender semantics in cases like this, translators have to demonstrate great creativity so as to make their readers at least to some extent familiar with the stylistic gender pattern of the original.

Of all the male characters in the book, as has been remarked, the masculinity of the Mock Turtle is made particularly prominent and for this reason a close examination of the way how he is introduced in different *Alice*-versions can serve as an apt approximation to the question as to how gender semantics is dealt with by translators. Of all the Chinese versions under discussion, the only one in which great attention is paid to the Mock Turtle's gender is ironically the very first, provided by Zhao Yuanren. He marks this figure as a male by a corresponding character *ta* 他 (*he/him*) in all the four perspectives, i.e. those of the Queen, Alice, the Gryphon and the author, exactly like in the original:

> p. 123: "'那么就跟我来，叫**他**来告诉你他的故事。'" (The Queen: "'Come on, then,' said the Queen, 'and he shall tell you his history.'"); p. 125: "'**他**为了什么事情那么苦啊？'" (Alice "'What is his sorrow?'") "'**他**自己在那儿做梦。'" (Gryphon: "'It's all his fancy'"); p. 133: "**他**瞧瞧阿丽思，想要说话似的" (The author: "He looked at Alice and tried to speak..")

In all the above instances, I have reproduced the masculine pronoun in bold. Now consider two later Chinese versions, one by Chen Fuan and one by Zhu Hongguo, both of whom do without any textual markers of masculinity in their rendering of the Mock Turtle and refer to him instead consistently by the neuter *ta* 它 (*it*):

> Chen Fuan (the Queen's introduction, p. 147): "ta de lishi 它的历史"; Alice, p. 149: "*ta wei shen me fa chou* 它为什么发愁"; the Gryphon, p. 149: "*ta jin zai na'ar xiaxiang* 它尽在那儿瞎想"; the author, p. 159: "*ta kan zhe Alisi xiang* 它看着阿丽思想"; Zhu Hongguo: The Queen, p. 97: "*ta* 它; Alice, p. 98: *ta* 它"; The Gryphon, p. 98: "*ta* 它"; the author, p. 105: "*ta* 它".

However, in spite of being close to gender semantics of the original, Zhao's pattern in some instances deviates from it, e.g. by making the Gryphon appear as a male even when in the original it is referred to as *it*, as in the following context (p. 133): *shuo zhe ta jiu ba Sujiayu de shenzi yaohuang yaohuang* 说着他就把素甲鱼的身子摇幌摇幌 (*said the Gryphon, and* ***it*** *set to work shaking him and punching him in the back.*)

Among the Japanese renditions under study, I could find none in which the gender of the Mock Turtle would have been marked by the masculine pronoun.

Consider the following renditions of the four perspectives that in the original make his masculinity explicit:

Seriu Hajime: p. 175: the Queen (his history) – "カメモドキに身の上話を申しつけよう" – (instead of using a pronoun, the translator repeats the noun to which it refers in the original, i.e. Kamemodoki = The Mock Turtle); Alice's perspective, p. 178: "Nani wo kanashindeiru no なにを悲しんでいるの" (Lit: "What is the sorrow?", i.e. the subject is not explicitly mentioned); the Gryphon's perspective, p. 178: "are wa minna, aitsu no kūsō na no sa あれはみんな、あいつの空想なのさ" (*Aitsu* may refer to either males or females); the author's perspective, p. 187: "Arisu no hō wo mite, hanashi wo shiyō to suru no desu ga, etc. アリスのほうを見て、話しをしようとするのですが…" (No pronoun is used here referring to the Mock Turtle. The subject is omitted altogether since its identity is clear enough to the reader from the context.)

Shōno Kōkichi: p. 139: (the Queen) "Nise umigame ni mi no uebanashi wo mōshitsukeyō ニセ海ガメに身の上話を申しつけよう" (Here the name of the Mock Turtle (Nise umigame) is used instead of a pronoun); p. 141: (Alice) "nani ga kanashii no deshō? 何が悲しいのでしょう?" ("What is sorrowful?", the subject is different from that in the original); p. 141: (the Gryphon) "Are wa minna, aitsu no kūsō na no sa あれはみんな、あいつの空想なのさ" (Here, again, *aitsu* is used to refer to the Mock Turtle); p. 149: (the author) "Umigame wa Arisu wo mitsume, etc. 海ガメはアリスを見つめ、" (The noun Umigame, lit.: *Sea Turtle* is used to refer to the subject.)

Tada Kōzō, p. 124: (the Queen) *are*, lit.: *that thing/that person* (not "kare" (*he*)), p. 126: (Alice) no pronoun is used; p. 126: (the Gryphon) again, *aitsu* is used; p. 133: (the author) "Game wa Arisu wo mite, etc. 亀はアリスを見て" lit., "Looking at Alice, the Turtle, etc.", the use of the noun *game*.)

As for the versions in the four languages under discussion that possess a well-developed category of gender, those in Italian, French and German are strikingly consistent: all of them have been guided by the conventional gender semantics of the corresponding nouns in their languages and have made the Mock Turtle appear as a female. Consider the following examples:

Fr. Berman, p. 207: "**la** Tortue–Façon–Tête de Veau"; p. 207: (the Queen) "**elle**…son histoire"; p. 209: (Alice) "son chagrin"; p. 209: (the Gryphon) "son imagination; p. 221: (the author) "**Elle** regarda Alice…"

Bué, pp. 140–143: "**la** Fausse-Tortue"; (Alice) "Que lest donc son chagrin?" (the Gryphon) "C'est une idée qu'**elle** se fait...", p. 151: "**Elle** regarda Alice..."

D'Amico, p. 90: (the Queen) "Porta questa signora a vedere **la** Finta Tartaruga e a sentire la sua storia"; p. 91: (Alice, no pronoun is used) "Perché è cosî triste?"; p. 91: (the Gryphon, no pronoun is used) "Ě tutta fantasia, sai: non ha nessun motivo di dolore"; p. 95. (the author's perspective) Guardò Alice e fece per parlare..."

Giglio, p. 223: (the Queen) "Vieni con me, ti farò raccontare la sua storia"; p. 237: (the author) "Poi dette un'occhiata ad Alice..."

Battistutta, p. 85: (The Queen) "Ti racconterà la sua storia"; p. 86: (Alice) "Cosa **la** fa soffrire cosî?"; p. 86: (the Gryphon) "Ě tutto nella sua fantasia, non ha nessun dolore, sai"; p. 91: "Guardò Alice e provò a parlare...

Oddera, p. 86: "Allora vieni con me e ti sarà narrata la sua storia."; p. 87: "Perché soffre?"; p. 87: "Ě soltanto una fantasticheria, la sua..."; p. 92: "Guardò Alice e cercò di parlare (Note that in this version none of the four perspectives indicates the character's gender.)

Pietrocòla-Rossetti, p. 135: "Vieni dunque, ed **essa** ti racconterà la sua storia."; p. 145: "Riguardò ad Alice e cercò di parlare." (Note that in rendering this fourth perspective, all the Italian versions reproduced here are similar to the above Japanese renditions and do not mention the subject at all,)

Zimmermann, p. 65: (the Queen) "**Sie** (die Falsche Schildkröte) soll dir ihre Geschichte erzählen."; p. 67: (Alice) "Was für einen Kummer hat **sie**?"; p. 67: (the Gryphon) "Es ist alles **ihre** Einbildung..."; p. 70.:(the author) "**Sie** sah Alice an und versuchte zu sprechen."

Enzensberger, p. 93: (the Queen) "**Sie** (die Falsche Suppenschildkröte) kann dir **ihre** Lebensgeschichte erzählen."; p. 95: (Alice) "Was hat **sie** denn für einen Kummer?; p. 95: (the Gryphon) "Das ist doch alles in **ihrer** Fantasie..."; p. 99: (the author) "**Sie** sah Alice an und mühte sich an zu sprechen..."

Teutsch, p. 100: (the Queen) "...dann soll **sie** (die Ochsenschwanzkröte) dir selbst erzählen..."; p. 102: (Alice) "Was hat **sie** nur für einen Kummer?"; p. 102: (the Gryphon) "Alles pure Einbildung bei **ihr**! **Sie** hat gar keinen, verstehst du?"; p. 108: (the author) "**Sie** sah Alice kummervoll an..."

Hansen, p. 81: "**Die** falsche Schildkröte"; p. 83: "Worüber grämt **sie** sich?"; p. 83: (the Gryphon) "**sie** bildet sich das alles nur ein"; p. 87: "**Sie** sah Alice an..."

Markers of the feminine – articles and personal pronouns – have been reproduced here in bold. Note that even in the instances that lack any explicit indication of gender, as in the French and Italian possessive forms *son/sua* that can refer to both masculine and feminine, or in numerous Italian versions where the initial personal pronoun is omitted the actual gender semantics remains perfectly clear: in all the above versions, it is the Queen's introduction which makes it explicit.

The high degree of consistency with which gender semantics is handled in all these versions that without any comment change the character's gender is all the more surprising if they are compared with Russian renditions. As we saw earlier, in this particular case Russian translators encounter exactly the same problem as their French, German, and Italian colleagues, for the respective Russian noun čerepaha *черепаха* (*turtle*) is also feminine. Nevertheless most Russian translators have chosen to reproduce here the original exactly rather than follow their own natural semantical conventions. Consider the following rendition by Demurova (p. 208):

– "А видела ты Черепаху Квази?"
– "Нет," – сказала Алиса. – "Я даже не знаю, кто **это такой**."
– "Как же," – сказала Королева. – "Это то, из чего делают квази-черепаший суп."
– "Никогда не видела и не слыхала," – сказала Алиса.
– "Тогда пошли," сказала Королева. – "**Он сам** тебе все расскажет."
Cf. p. 210: "Почему **он** так грустит?" p. 210: "Все это выдумки...Не о чем **ему** грустить." p. 220: "**Он** взглянул на Алису"

("Have you seen the Turtle Quasi?"
"No," said Alice; "I don't even know who it (lit.: *he*) is."
"How can it be?" said the Queen; "It's the thing Quasi Turtle soup is made from."
"I have never seen or heard of (it)," said Alice.
"Come on, then," said the Queen; "He himself will tell you everything."
(Cf. Alice's perspective, p. 210: "Why is he so sad?"; that of the Gryphon, p. 210: "It's all his fancy, ...he has no sorrow."; that of the author, p. 220: "He looked at Alice.")

All the pronouns in this rendition that make the masculine gender in all the four perspectives explicit have been, again, reproduced here in bold. The translator resorts to a fairly courageous strategy: by challenging the natural semantics of Russian, she expects her readers to accept masculinity of a feminine noun as easily as the Queen, Alice, etc. do in her text. Yet by transgressing conventions Demurova shows not only courage but also a subtle intuition of language since this feminine noun fits well into both masculine and feminine declensional patterns and sounds quite similar to nouns like *nerjaha* неряха ('sloven') which actually are both feminine and masculine. For this reason, Russian readers will be likely to follow here Demurova's story version without the slightest sense of uneasiness.

A similar strategy has been adopted by Olenič-Gnenenko and by Ščerbakov with one small difference: whereas Demurova provides her character with the personal name *Quasi* which has to reproduce the semantics of *Mock*, in Olenič-Gnenenko's text (p. 179) he is called *Мок-Тартль* (*Mok-Tartl'*), which is a transliteration of the *Mock Turtle* and Ščerbakov (p. 117) calls him *Čerepaha-Teljačji-Nozhki* (lit.: *the Turtle-(with)-Calf-Feet*) reminding the reader of one of Tenniel's illustration to the book. Yet nothing in these different proper names changes the Mock Turtle's masculinity and all of these translators expect their reading audience simply to forget the fact that the noun by which they have rendered *turtle* is in Russian a feminine. Somewhat different is the version by Zachoder (p. 92) who has introduced the character by an explicitly masculine noun and by an adjective agreeing with it in gender as *Rybnyj Delikates* "Рыбный Деликатес", lit.:a *Fish Delicacy*. Compared with these four Russian versions of the episode, Nabokov's rendition immediately strikes the eye as different, for he has chosen to invent a new word that sounds similar to *čerepaha* (*turtle*) and this new coinage could quite easily have been conceived as a male noun, yet his Čerupaha ("Чепупаха") turns out to be a feminine, thus he has chosen here the same way as German, French and Italian translators and considerably transformed the gender pattern of the original.

In what follows, the focus will be put on the question as to whether those versions in which the Mock Turtle is introduced as a male character systematically reflect the gender patterns in Carroll's text and thus constantly pay attention to gender as a stylistic quality, as a means by which linguistic form (pronouns, markers of male and female language, endings of adjectives and verbs) shows itself to be strongly interrelated with the conceptual level (psychology, aesthetics) or do it only occasionally. Since of all *Alice*-renditions that I could find the Mock Turtle's gender has been truly rendered only in Zhao Yuanren's Chinese and in four Russian versions, they deserve particular consideration. The analysis will concentrate on the material of Chapters II and III.

II.II

"Who in the world am I? Ah, that's the great puzzle!" This question which Alice has to ask herself in the course of Chapter II briefly summarizes its main subject, i.e. the identity problematics. Her body is no longer the same as a few hours before: one moment it suddenly opens out like a huge telescope so that she says "Good-bye" to her feet and then, quite unexpectedly, it shrinks rapidly away and she narrowly escapes the danger of disappearing completely. Her own self turns into something quite strange to her: she realizes that her knowledge of geography and arithmetic of which she was so proud in her normal life has now disappeared so that she believes to have turned into another girl; nor does she remember the poems she previously used to recite so easily from memory and, last but not least, the self-estrangement is increased by the fact that she nearly drowns in a pool of tears that she herself has shed a minute before. In Chapter III, this subject is continued, yet at a different level: here the focus is no longer put on her sudden changes but on her conversational skills as well as on all those qualities which she reveals in talking to others: her curiosity, readiness to help, patience, yieldingness, spontaneity, politeness, etc. As we saw earlier, these traits are shown contrastively: in Chapter III she is faced for the first time with a character that is openly conceived as her opponent, i.e. the Mouse whom she mentally addresses as a male at the end of the chapter. The textual switch from *it* to *he/his* is a sign suggesting a set of psychological qualities opposed to those of the heroine: pettiness, vulnerability, impatience, anger, etc. It is perhaps necessary to notice that similar contrasting signs are recurrent throughout the story: the pronoun group *he/him/his/himself* regularly signal the reappearance of these contrasting negative qualities that constitute a rather special semantical field of masculinity. Therefore they are not to be taken just as neutral and straightforward language material but rather as elements of style, i.e. they are suggestive and require interpretation.

A translator's attention to this sort of signals is of great importance, for unless the sense of contrasting images of masculine and feminine in the book is recognized, the reader has no possibility to learn about one of significant components of Carroll's aesthetics. In this connection, the following episodes from Chapters II and III deserve a detailed comparison with translation texts:

1. *Meeting the White Rabbit (Chapter II, cf. related episodes from Chapters I and IV)*

In Chapter II, the With Rabbit is introduced as a male by the author and is addressed by Alice as 'sir,' i.e. as a male who instantly proves to be full of fear:

> ...**he** came trotting along in a great hurry, muttering to **himself** as **he** came, "Oh! The Duchess, the Duchess! Oh! Wo'n't she be savage if I've kept her waiting!" Alice felt so desperate that she was ready to ask help of any one: so, when the Rabbit came near her, she began, in a low, timid voice, "If you please, **sir** –" The Rabbit started violently, dropped the white kid gloves and the fan, and scurried away into the darkness as hard as **he** could do.[47]

Consider the way the Rabbi is introduced at the beginning of Chapter I. The author employs here consistently *it/its*:

> ...when the Rabbit actually took a watch out of **its** waistcoat-pocket...she (Alice) ran across the field after **it**, and...was just in time to see it pop down a large rabbit-hole under the hedge.[48]

Whereas this character's psychology is not yet subject of the first Chapter, in Chapter II the multiple usage of masculine pronouns and Alice's form of addressing the Rabbit are signals which reinforce the prominence of the identity issue, i.e. it calls the reader's attention to the behavior of an explicitly male character. The male's fearfulness which is being described in this episode can therefore be considered quite an ironic approximation to the issue of gender and the same irony is perceivable later in Chapter IV where the Rabbit mistakes Alice for his housemaid and begins ordering her about. Here, the author refers to the Rabbit as *it*, whereas Alice uses a masculine pronoun:

> And Alice was so much frightened that she ran off at once in the direction it pointed to, without trying to explain the mistake that it had made. "He took me for his housemaid," she said to herself as she ran. "How surprised he'll be when he finds out who I am!"[49]

Masculinity shows itself first as fearful (Chapter II) and then as both authoritarian and short-sighted (Chapter IV.) It is thus marked by qualities which at first

47 *Alice*, pp. 21–22.

48 *Alice*, pp. 11–12.

49 *Alice*, p. 38.

might strike as contradictory, yet the author repeatedly lays great stress on exactly the same traits in the portraits of other males, e.g. the trembling, growling, angry Mouse; the King's "getting behind Alice" when speaking to the Cheshire-Cat[50], etc.

Among the translations under study, that by Zhao Yuanren comes particularly near to the pronominal pattern of the original: although in the above quotation from Chapter II (Zhao, p. 19) he employs *ta* 它 (*it*) to refer to the Rabbit from the author's perspective (*ta pao de hen jiji mang mang de* 它跑得很急急忙忙的), Alice (p. 19) addresses him as a male: Lao ninjia, mi si te 劳您驾，密斯忒 ("If you please, sir.") *Sir* is rendered here as "mi si te" which is a phonemic transposition of *mister*. In the related passage from Chapter I (Zhao, p. 5), the Rabbit is referred to as *ta* 它 (*it*), just as in the original, and in that from Chapter IV (p. 41), again following the original, Zhao uses *ta* 它 (*it*) to refer to the Rabbit from the author's perspective and makes Alice mentally address him as a male figure (*Ta na wo dang ta de yatou. Ta hui lai kan chu wo dao di shi shui, ta cai chayi ne!* 他拿我当他的丫头。他回来看出我到底是谁，那才诧异呢!)

Now consider as a comparison three Japanese versions which make use of no gender-specific markers in their rendition of the passage from Chapter II. Neither the author's perspective nor the words pronounced by Alice ("If you please, Sir") contain any information concerning the Rabbit's gender. Seriu Hajime (p. 32) has translated Alice's address as (p. 32) *anō, osoreirimasu ga* あのう、おそれいりますが (*excuse me, but…*), Tada Kōzō (p. 22) – as *anō, chotto* あのう、ちょっと (*Hm… Excuse me*) and Shōno Kōkichi (p. 29) – as *ano, shitsurei de gozaimasu ga* あの、失礼でございますが (*Hm, I'm sorry/Excuse me.*)

All the Russian versions under discussion follow here, by contrast, the natural semantics of "кролик" *krolik* (*rabbit*) which is a masculine noun and accordingly use masculine pronouns to refer to him as *on/ego* (*he/him*), etc. In the heroine's perspective, too, the character's masculinity is made explicit, e.g. in Demurova's (p. 92) "Простите, сэр" *prostite, ser* (*excuse me, sir*); (p. 122) "Он, верно, принял меня за горничную" (*He must have taken me for his housemaid.*) Similar or exactly the same versions have been provided by Olenič-Gnenenko (pp. 42, 74), Nabokov (pp. 14, 29), and Ščerbakov (pp. 40, 59.) On the one hand, this is a rare case in which semantics of a target-language is in complete accord with the gender pattern of the original in which the Rabbit is conceived as a male figure. On the other hand, however, these translations do not reproduce anything resembling the switches between *he* and *it*, which is among the work's important textual and stylistic qualities.

50 *Alice*, p. 91.

2. *Dinah vs. the terrier*

In her conversation with the Mouse (Chapter II), Alice is speaking nostalgically about her cat and a terrier of her neighbours. Both recollections provide the reader with a kind of scale against which to measure the emotional value in Alice's use of pronouns and to judge what pronouns she would use referring to animals she loves. As mentioned above, in contrast to what would seem to be the habitual use of pronouns in modern English, Alice prefers to use in these situations *she/it* groups rather than *she/he*, that is, in her language *it* does not suggest anything derogatory. Thus, in view of gender semantics, we can consider those versions of the book especially felicitous in which Dinah has been rendered as a female and the terrier – either as a neuter (as in the original) or, if the semantics of a given target-language does not allow that, as a female. A rendition of the dog by a masculine noun and, accordingly, the usage of masculine pronouns referring to it would, on the contrary, significantly impede the reader's perception of Carroll's style. And here, again, Zhao's Chinese version (pp. 25, 27) is the closest to the original: Dinah is introduced in it as a female by *ta* 她 (*she/her*) (*wo xiang ni kan jian le ta, ni ye yi ding jiu hui ai mao de* 我想你看见了她，你也一定就会爱猫的 "I think you'd take a fancy to cats if you could only see her") and the terrier – as a neuter by *ta* 它 (*it/its*.)

And again nominal gender semantics of Russian perfectly complies with translator's needs in this episode: Dinah can easily be rendered as *she* (*koška* (*female cat*)) and the terrier, too, as *she* (*sobaka/sobačka* (*dog, little dog*)) since no neuter noun exists for it in Russian. Whereas in all the versions discussed here Dinah has been rendered by a feminine noun, some translators have preferred masculine nouns for the terrier, e.g. Demurova (p. 104) *милый песик, маленький терьер* (*a sweet little dog, a terrier*) and Zachoder (p. 49) *чудный песик* (*a wonderful little dog*.) However, in versions with a feminine noun, this choice is occasionally accompanied by other masculine forms so that the gender pattern of the original gets completely obscured, e.g. in the rendition by Olenič-Gnenenko (p. 52) in which *замечательная собачка* (*zamečatel'naja sobačka* (*a nice little dog*, feminine)) is followed by *маленький терьер* (*malen'kij terrier* (*a small terrier*, masculine)) and all other nouns referring to the dog are also masculine, although it would have been quite simple to keep feminine forms throughout the passage.

3. *Fury*

The switch between *it* and *he* referring to the Mouse at the end of Chapter III is preceded by a short tale in which the Mouse appears as a victim of a cunning dog Fury. The masculinity of this dog is made explicit first by the author who refers to him as *he* ("Fury said to a mouse that he met in the house, etc.") and then by the Mouse who addresses him as 'Sir' ("'Such a trial, dear Sir, etc.'")[51]) A comparison of this episode with the two discussed above yields a somewhat different picture: whereas Zhao (p. 37) does not make the dog's gender explicit, some of the Russian versions render it as a male, e.g. Demurova (p. 116) provides it with a personal name *Tsap-tsarap* (*Цап-царап сказал Мышке*) which is a masculine and makes the Mouse address the dog as *sudar'* сударь ('sir') and Nabokov (p. 26) introduces the dog equally as a male using a masculine noun *pjos* пес ('dog.')

4. *The old Crab and her daughter*

A further relevant passage from Chapter III is a short dialogue between an old female Crab and her daughter in which both of the characters are referred to as females by the feminine pronoun *her* and by the noun *daughter*. The dialogue immediately follows the episode in which the offended Mouse leaves the scene and reads as follows:

> And an old Crab took the opportunity of saying to her daughter "Ah, my dear! Let this be a lesson to you never to lose *your* temper!" "Hold your tongue, Ma!" said the young Crab, a little snappishly. "You're enough to try the patience of an oyster!"[52]

This episode deserves attention as it contains the only instance of female personifications in the book. In itself, it can hardly serve as illustration of the gender-specific component peculiar to Carroll's style: it is neither opposed to all the ironical reversals of masculinity, nor does it represent any typically female stereotypes. Nevertheless it is marked by irony in opposing youth's impatience to the paternalism of the old age. Consider first Tada Kōzō's (p. 41) translation of it:

> すると年寄りの蟹がその機会をとらえて、自分の娘に言いました: "ねえおまえや、これを忘れないで、怒ったりするんじゃないよ." "黙っててよ、おっ母さん!… おっ母さんみたいじゃ牡蠣だって辛抱しきれないわ"

51 *Alice*, p. 33.
52 *Alice*, p. 36.

The daughter's phrase is concluded by the particle *wa* (わ) which is a typical marker of female language used for expressivity. In all the Japanese renditions available to me this particle also belongs among the most frequent words used by Alice. Though it is exactly the kind of perspective by which to make gender explicit which is entirely absent from the original (the first person never directly employs any formal linguistic means pointing to one's gender, it is rather indicated by the author and other figures in the text), yet in theory this perspective may be found to represent a perfect tool by which to reproduce gender patterns of the original: male figures could regularly mark their language as masculine employing corresponding linguistic markers and so appear as contrasting to figures whose language is marked by feminine forms; in cases when neuter is used in the original, for example, in switches from *he* to *it* (for the Mouse, the White Rabbit, the March Hare, the Dormouse, etc.) male language markers could be omitted, which would exactly reproduce the formal distribution of gender semantics in Carroll's text. However, I have not found any Japanese versions in which this strategy would have been consistently employed.

In Zhao's (p. 39) version, the gender of the characters is clear from the nouns he uses here, i.e. *nü'er* 女儿 (*daughter*) and *ma* 妈 (*mother*, in the daughter's answer), not from the pronouns, since he renders *her* by a neuter *ta* 它 (*it*.) As for the Russian renditions, the passage proves to be more challenging in this passage in respect to gender semantics than, e.g. for German translators who can simply rely on the natural semantics of *Krabbe* (*crab*, fem.) In Russian, by contrast, *krab* (*crab*) is a masculine noun and so, the translators had to display again much inventiveness in reproducing the original gender pattern: Demurova (p. 120) has substituted the Crab for a Jelly-Fish (*medusa*, fem.) and Ščerbakov (p. 56) has employed diminutive suffixation, so that his Old Crab is a feminine *Krabushka* (the dear old Lady Crab), but the daughter has turned into a masculine plural *Krabčatam* (*to the young baby Crabs*.) Both versions can be taken as good examples of a choice available to translators in a struggle against semantical conventions of their language. On the other hand, they also demonstrate how attentive translators occasionally prove to be to gender semantics of the original in contrast to other colleagues, e.g. to Olenič-Gnenenko (p. 69) who has used *staryj krab* (*the old Crab*, masc.), Battistutta (p. 28) – *un vecchio Granchio / il giovane Granchio* (*an old Crab*, masc. / *the young Crab*, masc.), and Bué (p. 39) – *un vieux crabe / le jeune crabe* (*an old Crab*, masc. / *the young Crab*, masc.)

5. The Mouse (the switch from it to he at the end of Chapter III)

The phrase containing this switch reads as follows:

> And here poor Alice began to cry again, for she felt lonely and low-spirited. In a little while, however, she again heard a little pattering of footsteps in the distance, and she looked up eagerly, half hoping that the Mouse had changed his mind, and was coming back to finish his story.[53]

To our frustration, if compared to all those numerous passages with the Mock Turtle in which Zhao and some Russian translators have been at great pains to remain as close as possible to the gender pattern of the original, neither Zhao nor any of the Russian fellow translators has attempted anything of the kind in this episode: whereas in Zhao's version (p. 39) the Mouse is referred to as *ta* 它 (*it*, *ta de lishi* 它的历史 *its history*), all the Russian renditions use the feminine noun *Myš Мышь* (*Mouse*):

> Olenič-Gnenenko (p. 71): "надеясь, что это Мышь переменила решение"; Nabokov (p. 28): "Надеясь, что Мышь решила все-таки вернуться"; Zachoder (p. 55): "А вдруг это Мышь передумала и все-таки вернулась"; Ščerbakov (p. 57): "А вдруг это Мышь передумала и решила вернуться"; Demurova (p. 120): "Может, это Мышь перестала сердиться и пришла, чтобы закончить свой рассказ?"

This consistency is all the more striking in view of the fact that both Zhao and the Russian translators could have quite easily kept the original pattern, e.g. by using *ta* 他 (*he/him*) in Chinese or by suffixation in Russian referring to the Mouse as *myšonok мышонок* (*a little mouse*, masc.) Surely, the latter method would have one great disadvantage of introducing a diminutive meaning which does not fit with the original. Yet it is worth pointing out in this connection that Zimmermann who was the first to translate *Alice* into German employed exactly this method in her rendition of the Mouse's speech and resorted to a shift between different gender forms in the following passage from Chapter III:

> "Ach", seufzte das **Mäuslein**, "ihr macht euch aus meinem Erzählen doch nichts;" Dabei sah **sie** Alice fragend an. ("Ach," said the Mouse, looking at Alice interrogatively, and sighing. "You don't care a bit about my history.")

53 *Alice*, p. 37.

Maus is a feminine noun in German and by building up the form *Mäuslein* (diminutive, neuter) as well as by using the feminine pronoun *sie* (*she*) referring to the Mouse later in the author's comment, the translator produces a shift in gender semantics which sounds quite natural, yet it does not have anything in common with Carroll's style, since Zimmermann's switch involves feminine and neuter rather than masculine and neuter.

That all the Russian renditions under discussion have also made use of a feminine noun suggests that none of them attempted a systematic reproduction of the original gender patterns. Demurova is the only one to my knowledge to have written a commentary on her translation principles and she reflects in it, among other things, on the issue of gender semantics[54]. According to her, the reason why the Cheshire-Cat, the Gryphon, the March Hare have been introduced by her as male figures is that male personifications exist in English poetry and folklore. On the other hand, the Caterpillar has been rendered in her text as a female character (as *gusenitsa*) because it is referred to by the author as *it*. Yet these grounds seem hardly sufficient in regard to the recurrent patterns in the distribution of gender semantics in *Alice*: though it is true that the Caterpillar is reflected by the author in neuter, Alice repeatedly addresses it as 'Sir' which in Demurova's version (p. 138) has been rendered by a rather confusing *sudarynja* сударыня (*madam*.)

In some other Russian versions, by the way of contrast, figures that – like the Caterpillar – are marked in the original by a switch between *it* and *he* have been rendered by masculine nouns, e.g. Ščerbakov (p. 68) makes the Caterpillar appear as *Šelkoprjad* (*silkworm*, masc.), Zachoder (p. 62) – as červjak (*worm*, masc.) and the Dormouse in Nabokov's *Alice* (pp. 59–60) is equally a male (*zverjok Sonja*, lit.: *the little animal Sonja*, masc.)

On the whole, all these examples produce quite a complex impression: even though Zhao's Chinese as well as Demurova's, Ščerbakov's and Zachoder's Russian renditions are sometimes fairly close to Carroll's gender patterns and, as we saw earlier, sometimes they had to overcome great difficulties in order to achieve this goal, it would appear that they did not capture the systematical way in the distribution of gender semantics in *Alice*. This is why none of them is really reminiscent of the stylistic qualities pertaining to it.

54 Demuurova, Nina M., "O perevode skazok Karrolla", in: *Ijulskij polden zolotoj: Statji ob anglijskoj detskoj knige*, Moskva: Izdatelstvo URAO 2000, pp. 87–123, here pp. 96–97.

Conclusion

By and large, the issue of gender has not remained neglected in Carroll studies. It is not without irony that one of them, written by Robert Phillips, lists a number of "good meanings" attributed by fellow researchers to *Alice*, e.g. taking the story to reflect an *unresolved Oedipal conflict*, the protagonist to represent *a symbolic equation for the phallus* and her adventures to be *a trip back into the mother's womb*.[55] On his part, Auden has made the following observation:

> As everybody knows, Dodgson's Muse was incarnated in a succession of girls between the ages of eight and eleven. Little boys he feared and disliked: they were grubby and noisy and broke things.[56]

In this chapter, I have tried to show that in *Alice* gender issue is by no means limited to Carroll's sympathy for girls and his dislike for grubby little boys. Alone his presentation of masculinity, with all the reversals of traditional sexist stereotypes and all the ironic contrasts highlighted between male figures and Alice, would seem to be enough to consider gender to be part of a carefully conceived and systematically implemented aesthetic plan. This might be not as spectacular as the "good meanings" discussed by Phillips. Still it deserves attentions, among other things, in light of the current critiques of sexist stereotypes in literature in general and in children's books in particular. The fact that translations, at least those available to me, have not yet thrown much light on this issue does not in any way result from deficits of target-languages in comparison with the language of the original but rather from a lack of attention that translators have directed to gender as a stylistic category in Carroll's work. Maybe some future versions of *Alice* will be more careful in this respect, and so, Carroll's upsetting traditional stereotypes would also become visible to the readers who cannot yet read the book in the original.

55 Robert Phillips, "Foreward" to Robert Phillips (ed.), *Aspects of Alice: Lewis Carroll's Dreamchild as Seen through the Critics' Looking-Glasses*, New York: Vintage Books 1971, pp. xvii–xxvi, here pp. xx–xxi.

56 Wystan Hugh Auden, "Today's 'Wonder-World' Needs Alice", in: Robert Phillips (ed.), Aspects of Alice: Lewis Carroll's Dreamchild as Seen through the Critics' Looking-Glasses, New York: Vintage Books 1971, pp. 3–12, here p. 11.

III. Nonsense and the Dialectic of Order

III.I

It may well strike as a paradox that two classical anthropological and philosophical studies probing into the meaning of order, Mary Douglas' *Purity and Danger: An Analysis of Concepts of Pollution and Taboo* (1966) and Elizabeth Sewell's *The Field of Nonsense* (1952) appeared shortly before the peak of a massive global wave of political protests, at a time, that is, when thinking and writing on order was not exactly fashionable. Many years after the first publication of her book, Mary Douglas remembered the circumstances responsible for its tardy success and termed it, half-jokingly, *a sleeper*, i.e. a book that "comes out of obscurity after lying dormant for some time."[57] Yet in spite of the fact that these studies may not have been in accord with the spirit of the time when first published both proved to be path-breaking for further research on the subject and hardly any work that has been written over the past seventy years on Nonsense leaves aside what once was so perceptively captured by Sewell's intuition, namely, that order, as strange as it would sound, is essential to literary Nonsense. Apart from the subject of order which connects the names of Douglas and Sewell, both adopt a similar approach to and both emphasize from the outset the importance of dialectics for our understanding of order, i.e. that any analysis of order necessarily throws up questions as to the meaning of disorder. As Douglas says of dirt and pollution which are among the key concepts in her study: "Reflection on dirt involves reflection of the relation of order to disorder, being to non-being, form to formlessness, life to death."[58]

Sewell's approach to the dialectics of order and disorder in her analysis of Nonsense might be judged more complex, for, contrary to expectation, she aligns Nonsense primarily with order rather than with disorder:

> Nonsense...takes the side of order and plays against disorder in the mind...Nonsense will presumably have to organize its language according to the principles of order, i.e. it will have to concentrate on the divisibility of its material into ones, units from which a universe can be built. This universe, however, must never be more than the sum of its parts, and must never fuse into some all-embracing whole which cannot be broken down again into the original ones. It must try to create with words a universe that consists of bits.[59]

57 Mary Douglas, *Purity and Danger*, Preface to the Routledge Classics Edition (2002.)

58 Mary Douglas, *op. cit.*, 1966, p. 5.

59 Elizabeth Sewell, *The Field of Nonsense* (1952), London: Dalkey Archive Press 2015, pp. 53–54.

In her investigation of Carroll's and Lear's literary productions, she thus does not identify Nonsense with illogicality, with reasons for constant misunderstandings between different figures or with confusing word meanings, since these would be but a few from a broad range of means on which the Nonsense game relies.

To Sewell, Nonsense is basically a principle of organization: it carefully weighs up what semantical groups of words can be used (concrete, simple and precise reference, no variability), what aesthetical categories to allow (e.g. ugliness rather than beauty), what kinds of relations may be established between its parts (disproportion, distinctness of separate elements), and so on. Therefore it is taken to mean a through and through rational business which is wholly controlled and directed by reason. In turn, disorder is understood by her rather as a means of contrast by which order may gain the maximum of visual sharpness:

> True Nonsense, as we have seen, is sane enough, for although it sides with order against disorder, it needs the latter for its antagonist and aims at keeping it engaged, not at suppressing it.[60]

One of the properties which is said to dominate the world of Nonsense is its absolute precision. This is directly associated by the author with the delight in number and logic which characterized the minds of Lear and Carroll.[61]

In regard to the *Alice*-books Nonsense is said to become a *consecutive narrative*[62], that is, the whole of the story is to be understood as Nonsense. This particular idea is illustrated by a rich variety of examples, e.g. Carroll's love for natural numbers, pseudo-series, rhymes, all of which are used to maintain "the principle of organization in Nonsense."[63] Speaking about linguistic manifestations of Nonsense, Sewell specifies the following:

> The syntax and grammar are not disordered...There is only one aspect of language which Nonsense can be said to disorder, and that is reference, the effect produced by a word or group of words in the mind. It is the sequence of references which is disordered by Nonsense, if the familiar sequence of events in everyday life is to be taken as the standard of order and sense.[64]

While it is undoubtedly true that Nonsense heavily relies on a mutual relation between order and disorder and that in its game reference, compared with oth-

60 Elizabeth Sewell, *The Field of Nonsense*, p. 163.
61 Elizabeth Sewell, *The Field of Nonsense*, p. 44.
62 Elizabeth Sewell, *The Field of Nonsense*, p. 7.
63 Elizabeth Sewell, *The Field of Nonsense*, p. 45.
64 Elizabeth Sewell, *The Field of Nonsense*, p. 38.

er linguistic levels, is given a predominant position, the term *reference* in Sewell's use deserves an exact specification, for in her theory it is not to be confused with objects of reality. It may be regarded as a particularly controversial point in her book that she holds a view of the world of Nonsense as well as of the order from which it is said to arise as one that is hermetically sealed up against reality, on which she constantly lays great stress. Since for most of the later studies on literary Nonsense its relation to reality has turned out to be quite a challenging issue it seems important to realize what Sewell seeks to achieve by rigorously separating Nonsense from reality.

As the first of the above quoted passages from her study suggests, Nonsense is a world made of words. According to Sewell, words are not to be mistaken for things from reality, since in this case Nonsense would stop being Nonsense and become magic[65]. Hence, reference that is disordered by Nonsense proves to have no connection with the world of things and, in short, is to be taken merely as a word meaning, so that the whole Nonsense-game comes to be reduced exclusively to meanings of words, i.e. as a rational activity under the mind's control. Since it carefully separates meanings from things in reality to which the words may refer in the speakers' minds, according to Sewell, once this has been understood, it does no longer matter how exactly we specify the relation of Nonsense to reality:

> In Nonsense all the world is paper and all the seas are ink. This may seem cramping, but it has one great advantage: one need not discuss the so-called unreality or reality of the Nonsense world.[66]

Sewell's attitude to this relation proves to be rather ambivalent: For one thing, it is said to be not as important as it would seem, yet at the same time in her theory it is required that Nonsense should be seen strictly as a world on its own, one that is separated from reality and the only purpose it serves is an intellectual amusement with which it provides its players, i.e. Carroll, Lear and their readers.

One might object that although Nonsense does not intend to change the world of things as magic does, its "disordered reference" is much more than a product of playing with word meanings. Again, psychology proves to be among the most crucial areas of the origin of Nonsense. On the one hand, Nonsense reveals specific traits that are characteristic of an excessively free treatment of reference (verbal arbitrariness, disbanding conventional codes, calculated deviations from logic, etc.) On the other, in *Alices*, Nonsense is not only a rational but also quite a provocative business: it openly challenges logic and in so doing

---

65 Elizabeth Sewell, *The Field of Nonsense*, p. 38.
66 Elizabeth Sewell, *The Field of Nonsense*, p. 17.

it constantly confuses the heroine, becoming one of the propelling forces of the plot. Alice's reactions to Nonsense that range from tacit puzzlements[67] to vigorous protests[68] are discussed by the author in acute detail, that is, Nonsense is not only being played, it is also subject to continuous reflections that accompany the story and the scale against which statements are measured as nonsensical is nothing but everyday life, that is, the world of things. The importance of reality is revealed by the fact that it constantly intervenes in the world of disordered reference through the heroine's mind. Therefore it seems rather problematic that Sewell insists on separating not only words and reality but Nonsense and the psychology of Carroll's characters, too, which she repeatedly stresses in her book. As an example, her view of Nonsense as a hermetically closed universe consisting of words is accompanied by the observation according to which it admits of no emotion.[69] And the protagonist herself who so often openly opposes the disorder of reference is regarded as part of Nonsense, which, among other things, is called to corroborate the idea that Nonsense requires precision:

> The demand for exactitude ... can also take the form of insistence on temporal order, or what is to come first, second and third: "No, no!" said the Queen. "Sentence first – verdict afterwards." "Stuff and nonsense!" said Alice loudly. "The idea of having the sentence first." (*Who Stole the Tarts?*)[70]

Ironically, in these words both the Queen and Alice are being equally approached as guardians of Nonsense, Alice may appear even more so than the Queen, since it is Alice who insists here on a *rational* sequence of events. It is most notably in this point, I believe, that the fundamental premise of Sewell's, i.e. her conviction that Nonsense arises from order rather than from disorder raises serious questions. The order (and the disorder) of numbers in Carroll's book may serve as another example. Even though it is perfectly correct that numbers play an important role in it, precision in dealing with them and careful attention to their sequence are in themselves by no means to be understood as pertaining to Nonsense. Whereas Alice defends rationality in number relations (as she does in the Trial-scene alluded to by Sewell in the above quote), the very opposite is the case with the Queen as with most of the inhabitants of Wonderland. In what follows, I would like to reproduce three episodes which follow a similar mathe-

67 *Alice*, p. 103.

68 *Alice*, p. 129.

69 Elizabeth Sewell, *The Field of Nonsense*, p. 129: "Nonsense can admit of no emotion...It is a game, to which emotion is alien."

70 Elizabeth Sewell, *The Field of Nonsense*, p. 88.

matical pattern and which can demonstrate differences in how characters of the story perceive order and disorder.

In Chapter VII, "A Mad Tea-Party", after the Hatter finishes his story about how he once offended Time so that time refused to move forward at his tea-party, Alice expresses an idea which triggers a new telling conversation in terms of Nonsense:

> A bright idea came into Alice's head. "Is that the reason so many tea-things are put out here?" she asked.
> "Yes, that's it," said the Hatter with a sigh: "it's always tea-time, and we've no time to wash the things between whiles."
> "Then you keep moving around, I suppose?" said Alice.
> "Exactly so," said the Hatter: "as the things get used up."
> "But what comes when you come to the beginning again?" Alice ventured to ask.
> "Suppose we change the subject," the March Hare interrupted, yawning. "I'm getting tired of this."[71]

Even if a great number of tea-things is put out on the table, this number as that of all possible seat changes is not unlimited. Hence, by asking what happens when the series of possible changes is completed Alice raises a fairly plausible and reasonable question which, however, remains unanswered since its obvious logic corners the Hatter completely. Now consider an episode from Chapter IX in which other inhabitants of Wonderland confront Alice with a free etymology of the noun *lessons*:

> "And how many hours a day did you do lessons?" said Alice, in a hurry to change the subject.
> "Ten hours the first day," said the Mock Turtle: "nine the next, and so on."
> "What a curious plan!" exclaimed Alice.
> "That's the reason they're called lessons," the Gryphon remarked: "because they lessen from day to day."...
> "Then the eleventh day must have been a holiday?"
> "Of course it was," said the Mock Turtle.
> "And how did you manage on the twelfth?" Alice went on eagerly.
> "That's enough about lessons," the Gryphon interrupted in a very decided tone.[72]

Since according to the rule which is freely invented by the Mock Turtle eleven is a number that concludes *any* series consisting of ten units it is entirely unclear,

71 *Alice*, p. 77.
72 *Alice*, p. 103.

e.g. how the series proceeds after the number *twelve*. Alice clearly sees that no other new series of numbers can be produced which would end with *eleven*. By her quite simple remark she again questions disorder in dealing with numbers, at which point the conversation gets promptly interrupted by Alice's opponents exactly like in Chapter VII. And, finally, consider a dialogue between Alice and the King during the trial (Chapter XII, "Alice's Evidence") in which the King invents a rule demanding that Alice should leave the court of justice:

> The King...read out from his book, "Rule Forty-two. All persons more than a mile high to leave the court."...
> "Well, I sha'n't go, at any rate," said Alice; "besides, that's not a regular rule: you invented it just now."
> "It's the oldest rule in the book," said the King.
> "Then it ought to be Number One," said Alice.
> The King turned pale, and shut his note-book hastily.[73]

Other than, e.g. in Chapter I in which Alice is guessing how many miles she has fallen down the Rabbit-hole (incidentally, this is also taken by Sewell as an instance of Nonsense[74]), in the above episodes she does not engage herself in guesses or assumptions concerning numbers but is rather reflecting on their exact mutual relations. Whereas the Mock Turtle and the King show an absolute arbitrariness in their dealing with numbers, Alice insists on their precise logical reference. In this point it would, again, be possible to draw a clear borderline in the psychological motivation of approaching words, numbers and their reference between Alice and the inhabitants of Wonderland, between order and disorder, sense and nonsense, rationality and arbitrariness, fixed rules of reason and the free flow of a nightmare.

Since Sewell considers all characters in the book to be equally representative of a rational order, this raises questions concerning obvious differences in their psychology. Though, on the whole, psychology is not among Sewell's chief concerns, there is one particular area of it to which she repeatedly turns in her discussion of Nonsense, being at the same time an area which – as in the case with the world of things – she actively seeks to separate from Nonsense, i.e. the dream. Sewell takes it to be a kind of disorder in which the distinctness of thought units is blurred and since dreams cannot be controlled and cannot be played with[75] she discards the idea of Nonsense-as-a-Dream and proposes instead one of Nonsense-as-a-Game:

73 *Alice*, p. 125.

74 Elizabeth Sewell, *The Field of Nonsense*, pp. 86–87.

75 Elizabeth Sewell, *The Field of Nonsense*, pp. 37–38.

> Nonsense is hostile to the dream. It is important to differentiate between this type of disorder, fluidity, the synthesis, the running together of pictures in the mind, and the type with which Nonsense works and which we have tentatively called a rearrangement in the series of word references.[76]

Among her arguments for opposing Nonsense to dreams, there is an observation concerning Carroll's mathematical orderly mind and a way of dealing with numbers which does not betray a dreaming disposition[77]. Yet, as I have tried to illustrate above, in the *Alice*-books, Carroll's way of operating with numbers is not the same with all figures and, for example, Alice's belief in logic and order makes her appear clearly different to the ways of handling numbers that are peculiar to the Hatter, the Mock Turtle and the King. In other words, I do not believe that the admittedly very important role with which order is invested in Carroll's work should be identified with an attempt to evoke disorder by means of rationality so as to appear visually sharp against its background, which is roughly the main assumption of Sewell's, but rather the other way around, i.e. with a quest for sense, an urgent need of clear reference and rules by which to secure success in interhuman communication.

By claiming that Nonsense is opposed to the dream, Sewell in effect tries to unsay the dream of Alice. Yet the story *is literally* about a dream and, what is more, the world of Wonderland, that is, the world of which Alice is dreaming might also be understood as a dream metaphorically, i.e. as one that is governed by irrationality and is opposed to the heroine's rational mind. When seen in this light Nonsense can hardly be reduced to mean a rational play intended for amusement. I believe that it rather arises from a deep concern about a possible loss of sense and meaning, confronting the protagonist and the reader with a situation in which all rules that make rational thought and speech possible are suddenly abandoned. This particular aspect of *Alice*, i.e. an acute awareness of unparalleled dangers of arriving at the very limits of language, when logic and conventions could no longer guarantee mutual understanding, may be interpreted as a most significant drama faced by the modern world. Yet, of course, its meaning gets obscured if Nonsense is regarded as a product of order.

Sewell's explicit refusal to consider that there is a clear psychological side to the issue of Nonsense, her claim that Alice's dream is in effect no dream at all but something that is inimical to dreams and defeats them[78], her laying great stress

76 Elizabeth Sewell, *The Field of Nonsense*, p. 40.

77 Elizabeth Sewell, *The Field of Nonsense*, p. 63: "The absolute reliability of the arithmetic in Carroll's Nonsense does not suggest the dreaming mind."

78 Elizabeth Sewell, *The Field of Nonsense*, p. 111: "one of the Nonsense ways of defeating dream is to pick up. the latter's principle elements, images, and use them for its own end."

on rationality as the only source of Carroll's Nonsense paradoxically result in Nonsense' losing its sense and aesthetical objective. I think, the crux of the problem in the view held by Sewell is that Nonsense is taken to mean solely a game and that the whole of the *Alice*-books is indiscriminately understood by her as Nonsense. In short, it is a refusal to recognize the limits that are set to Nonsense by Carroll and Sewell is by no means alone in taking this view. Anyone would, e.g. easily see parallels between Sewell's theory of Nonsense and that proposed later by Wim Tigges in his monograph on this subject, among other things, the following assumption: "Carroll makes use of nonsensical reasoning, reasoning which is nonsensical because it is logical."[79] Here, again, it may be objected that Carroll makes different characters follow different ways of reasoning, e.g. Alice's ways are opposed of those of the King who freely invents rules and numbers (Rule Forty-two) and who therefore can hardly be regarded as someone who is thinking logically. However, since Tigges is as little interested in the psychology of Carroll's characters as Sewell before him and, similarly to Sewell, states that one of the characteristics of Nonsense is a lack of emotional involvement[80], he is equally unaware of the limits posed to Nonsense in *Alices*. And in this respect it is also notable what he says of the relation between Nonsense and reality:

> Nonsense is not a priori meaningless. Neither does it merely suggest a topsy-turvy world. Nonsense does not describe an absurd world or absurd events, nor does it primarily demonstrate the absurdity or unreliability of language. In nonsense, language as such is dominant; it works on the assumption that the word is autonomous, and demonstrates this by creating a reality with language rather than either representing a reality, as in mimetic or naturalistic literature, or playing with language as in the curiosity. It is this creative use of language that makes nonsense effective and aesthetically pleasing.[81]

And, again, it is left out of consideration that in *Alices* Nonsense works effectively only owing to the fact that it is being reflected by the dreaming heroine's logical mind. Alice's rational thinking is that scale against which sense and nonsense are being measured and to her Nonsense is usually anything but pleasing. Hence, reality is here not simply newly created, e.g. by Carroll's introducing a Mouse that has to offer both a tale and a tail, but rather it is constantly present in the story providing those rules of order that are continually rejected by the inhabitants of Wonderland, which seems to be the principal source of Nonsense in the book.

79 Wim Tigges, *An Anatomy of Literary Nonsense*, Amsterdam: Rodopi 1988, p. 151.
80 Wim Tigges, *An Anatomy of Literary Nonsense*, p. 55.
81 Wim Tigges, *An Anatomy of Literary Nonsense*, pp. 256–257.

As in the case with Sewell, Tigges' views are, on the whole, representative of a widely maintained claim that every linguistic creation of the author's wit is to be interpreted as Nonsense. I don't believe that this view is accurate. Consider, for example, two puns, one from Chapter IX ("The Mock Turtle's Story") which is produced by the Mock Turtle ("'We called him Tortoise because he taught us'"[82]) and one based on the homophones *tail/tale* in Chapter III "A Caucus-Race and a Long Tale".[83] The former is, of course, an instance of Nonsense: it is based on an arbitrary confusion of reference, which is among the main aesthetical domains of Nonsense. Yet the latter is an actual enactment of both homophones, i.e. of both tale and tail in the plot: in Alice's imagination, the Mouse provides a *tale* in the form of a *tail*. Though it is true that this causes confusion and at some point Alice misunderstands the words in the Mouse's use, most readers of the story will easily recognize the reason of this confusion, exactly because it does not arise from verbal arbitrariness. Thus it is not quite plausible why all instances of Carroll's playing with words should be taken to be Nonsense.[84]

Among those rather rare scholars who have seen in Carroll's Nonsense more than an amusing intellectual play with language and who have also recognized the importance of both reality as a source of rational order and as a spiritual atmosphere of an epoch in which the *Alice*-books were created for our understanding of them, Donald Rackin and George Steiner should be particularly mentioned. The concepts of order and modernity are placed at the heart of critical enquiry in Chapter VI "Blessed Rage: The *Alices* and the Modern Quest for Order" of Rackin's monograph *Alice's Adventures in Wonderland and Through the Looking-Glass: Nonsense, Sense, and Meaning* (1991.) The general atmosphere of Wonderland is interpreted by Rackin as one of a God-less void imposed on Victorian intellectuals by Darwinian and post-Darwinian science. In his opinion, the inhabitants of Wonderland represent a model of nature which is entirely driven by laws of natural selection, the instinctual, endless round of adaptation and self-preserva-

82 *Alice*, p. 100.

83 *Alice*, p. 34.

84 Wim Tigges takes the wordplay *tale* vs. *tail* to be a typical example of Nonsense, *An Anatomy of Literary Nonsense*, p. 155. Cf. the essay by Zhang Qunxing, "Creation for Fidelity – Zhao Yuanren's Translation of Lexical Nonsense in *Alice's Adventures in Wonderland*", in: *International Journal of Comparative Literature and Translation Studies*, Vol. 5, No. 1 2017, pp. 71–79, in which all cases of word-play in the story are indiscriminately regarded as Nonsense. The purpose of this playing with words is usually described either as amusing and pleasing the audience or as didactic. Cf. the following opinion by Robert D. Sutherland, *Language and Lewis Carroll*, The Hague/Paris: Mouton 1970, p. 201: "In revealing the essential illogicality of some of the language's most common expressions, he (Carroll – V. V.) was, I have no doubt, trying to awaken his readers to the resources and limitations of English, encouraging them to pay attention to what they were saying, and warning them against carelessness in their linguistic habits."

tion[85], a nature without spirit and without any signposts of intelligible order. The confrontation between Alice and these creatures is said to symbolically suggest one between order and disorder, sense and nonsense:

> In the *Alices*, as in twentieth-century existential thought, human meaning is made in spite of the void, and, in making her order and meaning out of, essentially, nothing, the brave child Alice spitefully makes...what we may call sense out of nonsense, something out of nothing...Alice, in resisting her instinctive fears and the moral nothingness of her adventures, somehow makes of her spitefulness an affirmation of the human spirit.[86]

On his part, George Steiner takes the phenomenon of Victorian Nonsense to be closely bound up with the concept of 'the lacking word' which marks modern literature and which stands for a period in the history of Western culture between the seventies of the 19th century and the 'linguistic turn,' an epoch that is marked by losing the belief in the capacity of natural languages to capture the truth, by a breach between *word* and *world*, between meaning and reference, by dividing "a literature essentially housed in language from one for which language has become a prison."[87]

Both Rackin and Steiner, thus, take an entirely different approach to Nonsense compared with those theoreticians who interpret it as a purely amusing entertainment. To them, Nonsense reveals deep dramatic dimensions and the drama which is enacted in it is one of a lost order.[88]

Hence, Nonsense allows to be interpreted as a key category within an aesthetic program which continuously refers to sense and order. Its order is both a concep-

---

85 Donald Rackin, *Alice's Adventures in Wonderland and Through the Looking-Glass: Nonsense, Sense, and Meaning*, Twayne's masterwork studies, No. 81, New York: Twayne Publishers 1991, pp. 90–92. Cf. for the prominence of the motif of Nonsense in the spiritual life of a great number of Victorian intellectuals, see Daniel Brown's monograph *The Poetry of Victorian Scientists: Style, Science and Nonsense*, Cambridge: Cambridge University Press 2013.

86 Donald Rackin, *Alice's Adventures in Wonderland and Through the Looking-Glass*, p. 96.

87 George Steiner, *After Babel: Aspects of Language and Translation*, Oxford: Oxford Univ. Press 1975, esp. the Chapter "Word against Object," pp. 115–247, here pp. 184–185.

88 Cf. the study on Nonsense and its influence on other modern literary genres, among other things, on the metaphysical poetry of T. S. Eliot by James Rother, "Modernism and the Nonsense Style," in: *Contemporary Literature*, Vol. 15, No. 2, 1974, pp. 187–202. The author equally warns against regarding Nonsense as simply an amusing game, p. 187: "Certainly it is a rare occasion when Nonsense as literary discipline (not to be confused with 'nonsense,' indicating mere lack of sense) impresses us as simply amusing, without serious aspects or consequences... On the contrary, it is almost always a solemn business, maintaining the strictest of controls over both its inferences and its effects...Nor is Nonsense merely technique reserved for the portrayals of owls and pussycats, mad hatters and mock trials, since it has shown itself capable of creeping into more conventional forms of literature when least expected to do so."

tual background of the whole story and the material to which the author resorts in designing the confrontation between Alice and the inhabitants of Wonderland, i.e. linguistic and logical order. Since, when understood this way, Nonsense in itself cannot be part of order, it is invested with a purely dialectical role: in being opposed to sense, it perpetually refers to it, and so, it demarcates a borderline running between things that make sense and those that do not. Although philosophical readings of *Alice* will be in the focus of a separate chapter ("The Philosophers' *Alice*"), it is worth pointing out in this connection the debates about the concept of Nonsense in Wittgenstein's philosophy and the parallels that are often drawn between Wittgenstein and Carroll.

In Wittgenstein's writings, Nonsense is not always understood as absence of sense but sometimes also as a tool by which to refer to sense. In order to emphasize this particular aspect of Nonsense in Wittgenstein's thought, Danièle Moyal-Sharrock quotes the following passage from his *Philosophical Grammar*:

> ...when we hear the two propositions, "This rod has a length" and its negation "This rod has no length", we take sides and favour the first sentence, instead of declaring them both nonsense (Unsinn). But this partiality is based on a confusion: we regard the first proposition as verified (and the second as falsified) by the fact that "the rod has a length of four meters."[89]

That the first of the propositions is likely to be favored as verified is due to linguistic conventions within a language community whose members normally employ it in exactly the form indicated by Wittgenstein as part of defining sentences, i.e. whenever speaking about the length of objects. In a similar context, Denis McManus addresses the intelligibility of nonsense in Wittgenstein's philosophy and draws on his saying "Language sets everyone the same traps..."[90] It is important to notice both the affinity which he observes between this phrase and Carroll's aesthetics and the problematics which he ascribes to Wittgenstein's use of the words *same* and *everyone* in intercultural context:

> I have suggested that the philosophical confusions Wittgenstein examined can be seen as possessing a recognizable logic and that I am rendered vulnerable to them by virtue of speaking particular languages, a feature which is not a peculiarity of me as an individual... The *Tractatus* identifies some of "the same traps" that language "sets

89 Danièle Moyal-Sharrock, "The Good Sense of Nonsense: a reading of Wittgenstein's *Tractatus* as nonself-repudiating", in: *Philosophy*, Vol. 82, No. 319, Jan. 2007, pp. 147–177, here p. 160.

90 Ludwig Wittgenstein, *Culture and Value*, Ed. G.H. von Wright, Oxford: Blackwell 1998, p. 25: "Language sets everyone the same traps; it is an immense network of easily accessible wrong turnings..."

everyone" by tracing the confusing influence on our thinking of particular, multiple sources of items of pseudo-sense to which we speakers of that language are vulnerable. But, of course, in this sense, "the same traps" are precisely not set for *everyone*. Just as Carroll's humor cannot be translated into some languages, neither can the speakers of some languages succumb so some of the confusions that Wittgenstein targets…[91]

The basic idea behind this passage concerns the question of universal intelligibility of Nonsense: since its intelligibility is generally dependent on specific conventional codes within a given language community it would be plausible to assume that the *traps* addressed in the works of Wittenstein and Carroll would be different in kind to those found in languages that typologically and genetically are quite distinct from German and English. In what follows, I would like to focus attention on the translatability of Nonsense bearing in mind the above mentioned issue of the dialectic pertaining to Nonsense, i.e. Nonsense as a means of demarcating sense in both referring to order and being opposed to it.

It deserves being mentioned at this point that the translatability issue is closely connected to another problem which has also been addressed earlier in this chapter, i.e. the limits set to Nonsense in Carroll's work. When thinking which strategy is suited best for making Nonsense perform a similar task to that of the original the inter-lingual translator is confronted with a very specific kind of language traps in Carroll's work, i.e. with cases that in themselves do not imply anything nonsensical, yet tend to appear nonsensical when rendered literally. Most of these cases are purely semantic in nature, e.g. in an episode from Chapter XII "Alice's Evidence" where the King is referring to a mysterious poem, "'the most important piece of evidence'" in his eyes. One of its lines ("'But said I could not swim'") are taken by the King to be particularly suggestive of its author's identity so that he asks the Knave whether he can swim:

> "you ca'n't swim, can you?" he added, turning to the Knave. The Knave shook his head sadly. "Do I look like it?" (Which he certainly did *not*, being made entirely of cardboard.)[92]

While rendering this passage even in languages like Chinese and Japanese that are greatly dissimilar to English is not accompanied by any problems, it is different with Russian where the verb *plavat* (*to swim*) also covers the meaning of *to float on the surface of a liquid* and can refer to both animate and inanimate things (cardboard, wood, paper, etc.) A literal reproduction of the last phrase from the

91 Denis McManus, "Austerity, Psychology, and the Intelligibility of Nonsense", in: *Philosophical Topics*, Vol. 42, No. 2, 2014, pp. 161–199, here p. 188.

92 *Alice*, p. 128.

passage is therefore completely incomprehensible in Russian. This is, for example, the case with Demurova's (p. 258): "'Куда мне!' – сказал он. (Это было верно – ведь он был бумажный.") ("'How could I?' he said, which was true since he was made of paper.") Since the Knave admits being made of paper, any Russian reader will be likely to ask why in the world he cannot swim. A cautious translator will try to bypass this kind of semantic trap leading to an almost automatic production of Nonsense which is new to the original. Consider, e.g. the solution found by Nabokov (p. 111): "Этого, конечно, подумать нельзя было, так как он был склеен весь из картона и в воде расклеился бы." ("Which he certainly did *not*, since he was glued together of pieces of cardboard and would fall apart in water.") Hence, the translator provides his reader with information that is needed to understand why the Knave cannot swim: even though Nabokov is moving away from the original semantics, he neatly side-steps the problem of adding new Nonsense to it. Consider, as a comparison, another episode from Chapter IV in which Alice hears the White Rabbit say the following:

> "The Duchess! The Duchess! Oh my dear paws! Oh my fur and whiskers! She'll get me executed, as sure as ferrets are ferrets!"[93]

The Rabbit expresses his certainty about the punishment by referring to *ferrets*, that is, to an animal with which he is more than familiar in English culture. In Martin Gardner's commentary (p. 39) some cues are given as to this intimate relation between ferrets and rabbits: "Ferrets are a semidomesticated variety of the English polecat, used mainly for hunting rabbits and mice." To follow the logic of the Rabbit's words, the translator would need to refer to some appropriate object with which the rabbits are equally well familiar in a given target-language rather than reproduce the original literally, as, for example, Yamagata Hiro'o 山形浩生 does in his version (p. 49): "フェレットがフェレットであるくらい確実に、処刑されちゃうぞ!"[94]) Here, again, Nabokov's rendition reveals a better awareness of dangers to become unintelligible and to create Nonsense that is not part of the original. He does not translate the noun *ferrets*, since it refers to an animal which is entirely exotic to Russian readers but substitutes it for *cabbage* (p. 29): "Она меня казнит, это ясно, как капуста!" ("She'll get me executed, as sure as cabbage is cabbage!")

93 *Alice*, p. 39.

94 Yamagata Hiro'o 山形浩生 (Tr.), *Fushigi no kuni no Arisu* 不思議の国のアリス, Tokyo: Asahi shuppansha 2003.

Occasionally, new Nonsense comes about as a result of lacking attention to the negations. Chapter IX contains, for example, the following dialogue between Alice and the Duchess:

> "I dare say you're wondering why I don't put my arm around your waist," the Duchess said, after a pause: "the reason is, that I'm doubtful about the temper of your flamingo. Shall I try the experiment?"
> "He might bite," Alice cautiously replied, not feeling at all anxious to have the experiment tried.[95]

The Duchess does not put her arm around Alice's waist, since she is fearful of the flamingo; Alice, in turn, does not wish to be embraced, for the Duchess is extraordinarily ugly. Thus, neither of them produces Nonsense in this instance. Now consider the following Chinese rendition of the passage by Zhao Yuanren (p. 119):

> "我猜你一定在那儿想我为什么拿胳巴抱着你的腰。我是因为有点疑惑你那个红鹭鹚的脾气。让我来试验一下，好罢？" 阿丽思一点不在乎作这个试验。她小心地答道，"他许会咬疼你的。" ("I guess you're certainly wondering why I'm putting my arm around your waist. The reason is, that I'm a little doubtful about the temper of your flamingo. Let me try the experiment." Alice was absolutely indifferent about the experiment being tried. She answered cautiously: "He could bite you.")

What is left implicit and completely unclear by the translator is why the Duchess embraces Alice, why Alice is indifferent about the experiment alluded to by the Duchess and, after all, what is meant by the experiment which the Duchess desires to try. And so, Chinese readers will have every reason for recognizing an impressive amount of Nonsense in this passage, although no Nonsense is involved here in the original at all.

In the above examples produced by Demurova, Hiro'o and Zhao Yuanren, the reader faces a kind of Nonsense which is neither part of the original nor invested with any perceivable dialectical quality, since it does not demarcate sense, which seems among its most important aims in the *Alices*. The second section of this chapter will provide detailed illustrations of how translators render what in effect is Carroll's Nonsense in Chapters IV and V. Yet before doing so, let us consider briefly some of the key-areas of linguistic order on which Nonsense continually relies, i.e. the exact nature of those traps that language sets its users and translators. One particular group among these traps is purely semantic, consisting of puns and malapropisms that are generated by the arbitrary language use

95 *Alice*, p. 96.

of the inhabitants of Wonderland who constantly alienate words from their conventional reference. Since this group will be in the focus of two separate chapters (in "The Language of Violence" and, contrastively, in "Through the Eyes of a Child") they are not going to be addressed at this point. Here I would rather like to concentrate on three other instances of linguistic material which might help elucidate the issue of the translatability of Nonsense: first, rhymes and alliteration, i.e. cases in which Nonsense is a result of phonemic and semantic properties of words; second, cases in which it is produced by means of grammar (morphology) and, third, situations where Nonsense is determined by an intersection between semantics and syntax.

Contrary to the assumption that Nonsense does not admit of emotions and is rather alien to psychology I would like to illustrate the first of these groups by examining two examples where language use is quite obviously motivated by the heroine's state of mind. Even though Alice normally appears in the text as opposing Nonsense, her first experience of Wonderland, i.e. her falling asleep in the first chapter and her being suddenly confronted by a series of wonders make her lose control of her language and say the following:

> "...But do cats eat bats, I wonder?" And here Alice began to get rather sleepy, and went on saying to herself, in a dreamy sort of way, "Do cats eat bats? Do cats eat bats?" and sometimes "Do bats eat cats?" for, you see, as she couldn't answer either question, it didn't much matter which way she put it.[96]

In her dreaming mind, *cats* and *bats* merge, as do the borders separating all things that one perceives as distinct when being awake. This psychological disorder of dream manifests itself in connecting two rhyming nouns that differ only in the initial consonant. In terms of the translatability issue it would, perhaps, be natural to suppose that a literal rendition in languages that do not possess a pair of equally similar nouns would result in creation of quite a different kind of Nonsense than that of the original, i.e. in a mere absence of sense rather than in referring to order. Rather than doing so, the translator would be expected either to search for nouns that in a given language would rhyme with one of the two original nouns or develop some other strategies for making Nonsense appear in its dialectical function. Surprisingly few translators have chosen the first option, e.g.:

> Olenič-Gnenenko, p. 28: Ест ли кошка сороконожку? (Do cats eat myriapods?) Zimmermann, p. 4: Fressen Katzen gern Spatzen? (Do cats eat sparrows?) Demurova, p. 80: Едят ли кошки мошек? (Do cats eat blackflies?)

96 *Alice*, p. 14.

In these rhymes, the translators have found an easy and effective way to make Nonsense intelligible: *koška* (*cat*) rhymes with *sorokonozhka* (*myriapod*) in Russian and *Katzen* (*cats*) with *Spatzen* (*sparrows*) in German as naturally as *cats* and *bats* do in English, which reproduces the psychological pattern of Nonsense, the dreaming mind, precisely as it is designed here by Carroll. No less impressing are solutions found by Nabokov and Zhao Yuanren, both of whom keep the original pair of nouns although they do not rhyme in their target-languages. Let us consider Nabokov's version (p. 8):

> "Кошки на крыше, летучие мыши..." А потом слова путались и выходило что-то несуразное: летучие кошки, мыши на крыше. ("Cats on the roof and the bats..." And then the words got confused and seemed to mean something very odd: flying cats, mice on the roof....)

Although the nouns *koški* (*cats*) and *letučije myši* (*bats*) do not represent a pair of rhymes, by making cats sit *on the roof* (*na kryše*) the translator succeeds in finding a perfect rhyme for *bats*. In the second sentence, mice are sitting on the roof and cats are flying, which is rhythmically a felicitous phrasing and, again, the reader may feel why Nonsense comes about here, i.e. owing to the heroine's dream in which images are running together into a unity. Zhao's Chinese rendition (p. 9) which equally relies on combining nouns *mao* (*cats*) and *bianfu* (*bats*) that do not rhyme reads as follows:

> "猫子吃蝙蝠子吗？猫子吃蝙蝠子吗？" 有时候说说说乱了，变成"蝙子吃猫蝠子吗？吃子蝙猫蝠子吗？

It would be difficult to provide a good back-translation of this creation since the sense that is being demarcated here by Nonsense, most notably in the concluding phrase, is secured solely by the graphical design: first, the translator attaches the nominal suffix *-zi* to both of the nouns (*cats/bats*) and then he proceeds by changing the character combinations, and so *bianfu* (*bats*) turns into *bianfuzi* and *mao* – into *maozi*. Finally, in the last phrase, even the verb *chi* (*to eat*) is added the same suffix, thus turning into a *noun* (*chizi.*) In so doing, Zhao goes one step further than Carroll and makes three units – instead of the original two – merge in his calculated linguistic disorder. His solution is, therefore, based on suffixation as well as coinage of words, the latter method being, e.g. also represented in the German version by Teutsch (p. 16): "Fressen Katzen Fledermäuse? Flederkatzen fressen Mäuse oder fressen Lederfläuse Katzenmäuse?" Here, again, the conventional nominal semantics of *Katzen* (*cats*) and *Fledermäuse* (*bats*) fuse into one unity giving birth to hybrid dream creatures *Flederkatzen* (*flying cats*) and *Katzenmäuse* (*cat-mice*)

Another individual creation of an impressive linguistic disorder may be found in the following Japanese version prepared by Seriu Hajime (p. 19):

> ネコはコウモリを食べるかしら。ネコをコウモリは食べるかしら。

Though the nouns *neko* (*cats*) and *kōmori* (*bats*) do not rhyme, the translator makes the language follow the dream's nature by reversing the SOV (subject-object-verb) order which is normal in Japanese, changing the positions of *o* を / *wa* は particles and thus getting quite an unusual order of OSV (object ネコ (を) – subject コウモリ(は) – verb 食べる.)

In all these inventive translations, an absolute harmony is established between Alice's psychological experience of falling asleep and her linguistic adventure with *cats* and *bats*: the words get confused and the boundaries between imagined objects get blurred as she enters Wonderland. By contrast, literal renditions of the passage appear to be much less felicitous. Consider the following examples from some Chinese and Italian versions:

> Ma Teng (p. 12) 猫喜欢吃蝙蝠吗？ 蝙蝠喜欢吃猫吗？
> Zhu Hongguo (p. 9) 猫儿吃蝙蝠吗？ 蝙蝠吃猫儿吗？
> Oddera (p. 13): I gatti mangiano pipistrelli? I pipistrelli mangiano gatti? (the same in Battistutta p. 7)
> D'Amico (p. 21): I gatti mangiano i pipistrelli? I pipistrelli mangiano i gatti? (the same rendition in Giglio, p. 47)

No means has been found here by which to reproduce dream's disorder and this could not be explained by any deficits in the semantics of the two target-languages but should be rather ascribed to the strategy adopted here for translation, to the individual feeling and understanding of Nonsense in its relation to order.

As to the second group of linguistic manifestations of Nonsense at the morphology level I would, again, like to cite an example that may throw light on the psychology of Nonsense, more specifically, on how emotional Nonsense can occasionally be. It is in the very first phrase of Chapter II ("The Pool of Tears") in which Alice, being completely overwhelmed by her recent adventures, forgets the rule prescribing that polysyllabic words in English cannot be attached the comparative – *er* suffix and cries: "'Curiouser and curiouser!'"[97] In this case, again, the translators have to demonstrate great resourcefulness so as to match

97 *Alice*, p. 20.

the author's wit. Admittedly, this time the problem is not as complicated as in the afore-mentioned situation with rhymes and the task in hand is to find some fixed rule in a given target-language a violation of which would produce an effect comparable to that of the original. For example, in d'Amico's version (p. 26, "Stranissimissimo!") the siperlative suffix is used twice to serve this goal and Giglio (p. 61) attaches the adverb *molto* (*much*) to a superlative form: "Stranissimo, molto stranissimo!" Now consider some Russian renditions of the phrase:

> Nabokov (p.13): Чем дальнее, тем странше.
> Olenič-Gnenenko (p. 38): Все страньше и страньше." (The same rendition can be found in Demurova, p. 90)
> Zachoder (p. 45): Ой, все чудесится и чудесится!
> Ščerbakov (p. 39): Все необычайшей и необычайшей.

For the most part, the reproduced texts recreate a grammatical pattern of the original by building up inaccurate comparative forms (*страньше, странше, необычайшей.*) Zachoder is the only one to create a new verb: he takes a somewhat antiquated čudesit' (*to work wonders*, also: *to behave strange*) and turns it into a reflexive čudesitsja, which also is an obvious morphological disorder.

Of the Japanese and Chinese renditions, consider the following two in which it is not the grammar but rather the graphical design which results in Nonsense: Seriu Hajime (p. 29) renders the phrase by *tekohen da wa* てこへんだわ, which is a reversal of syllables in *henteko* へんてこ (変梃 *strange*, *weird*) and Zhao Yuanren (p. 17) translates it by *Yue bian yue xi han le, yue bian yue qie guai le!* 越变越希汉了，越变越切怪了! Here, it is a confusion of the characters in the words *xihan* 希罕 and *qiguai* 奇怪 which makes Alice's expression weird.

In short, even a cursory first examination reveals a vast potential for neatly recreating Nonsense by means of grammar in all the languages under discussion: to make its dialectical quality visible, it is usually enough to find some basic rule in a given target-language violating which Alice would as naturally express her emotions as in the original.

Finally, one of arguably the best Nonsense instances at the syntactic-lexical level may be found in a conversation between Alice and the Duchess in Chapter IX, shortly after the Duchess strikes both the protagonist and the reader by her verbal sleight-of-hand in paraphrasing the proverb "Take care of the pence and the pounds will take care of themselves" as "Take care of the sense, and the sounds will take care of themselves."[98] This is one of very rare cases where the dia-

98 *Alice*, p. 96.

lectics of Nonsense, i.e. its duty to refer to sense and order, is made explicit. The passage in question, known as the Duchess' sentence, runs as follows:

> "Be what you would seem to be" – or, if you'd like it put more simply – "Never imagine yourself not to be otherwise than what it might appear to others that what you were or might have been was not otherwise than what you had been would have appeared to them to be otherwise."[99]

When looking for the exact sources of logic and dis/order that produce a Nonsense effect in this case the following points seem to be most significant: First, the sentence is clearly embedded within the topic of the whole conversation, i.e. the relation of being to appearing, the question as to their mutual compatibility, which may be regarded as the key to the whole Nonsense scheme in the passage. Second, it is already at the level of form that the sentence contradicts the goal (the sense) which according to the Duchess it is going to serve: the Duchess announces it namely as *putting more simply* the initial dictum (*Be what you would seem to be.*) Finally, the dictum itself is understood as an explanation of or as a conclusion to what has been said before on the essence of mustard. Whatever Alice means to know about it (mustard is no bird, then, mustard is a mineral and, at last, it is a kind of vegetable[100]), the Duchess agrees with everything, which is equal to saying that to her mustard is anything what in this particular case it appears to be to Alice.

Both an exact understanding of the grammatical dis/order of the long sentence and an interpretation of it in the context of the mustard-definition as well as of the dictum seem to be necessary for discussing properties of its various translations. Since the Duchess' sentence belongs among the most complicated propositions made in the *Alice*-books an issue which it makes particularly prominent is one of freedom of interpretation. Among questions which have to be elucidated in this regard are the following: How much sense is being revealed by Nonsense? What kind of order is demarcated by its dialectics in this situation and what possibilities do Carroll's translators uncover for reproducing this highly challenging text passage?

Probably no other passage from Carroll's work has been so much subject to scholarly scrutiny as the Duchess' sentence. It has been interpreted as an amus-

99 *Alice*, pp. 96–97.

100 *Alice*, p. 96.

ing logical absurdity[101], derisive caricature[102], paralogism[103], an example of carnival aesthetics[104], of scholasticism[105], etc. Sometimes the sentence has been taken to reveal deep dimensions of meaning[106] yet, for the most part, scholars point out its extreme impermeability. I have devoted much effort to searching for studies which would not simply state its complexity but also explore what exactly figures among its challenges. Unfortunately, even in those works that are explicitly conceived as thorough investigations of Nonsense, I could find only some brief remarks concerning the impossibility of a linguistic analysis of this particular passage. For example, in his *Philosophy of Nonsense* (1994) Jean-Jacques Lecercle explicitly refuses to provide such an analysis in his following interpretation of the sentence:

> But here it is not a question of the readers' memory being inadequate to the length of the sentence, but rather of their powers of linguistic analysis failing them because a syntactic trick is being played for them, the exact nature or location of which they (this reader at least) cannot pinpoint. There may be a psychological explanation for this after all – I can take any amount of semantic incoherence in my stride, but syntactic chaos, because of the centrality of syntax, provokes the deepest unease. And, truly, the sentence is incomprehensible for syntactic, not semantic, reasons.[107]

101 Roger W. Holmes, "The Philosopher's 'Alice in Wonderland'", in: *Aspects of Alice*, p. 160. Cf. Salahuddin Choudhury, "Symbol as Boundary", in: *The Journal of Aesthetics and Art Criticism*, Vol. 37, 1979, pp. 433–443, here p. 439.

102 Jerry Farber, "Towards a Theoretical Framework for the Study of Humor in Literature and the Other Arts", in: *The Journal of Aesthetic Education*, Vol. 41, No. 4, 2007, pp. 67–86, here pp. 83–84.

103 Alwin N. Baum, "Carroll's 'Alices'": The Semiotics of Paradox", in: *American Imago*, Vol. 34, No. 1, 1977, pp. 86–108, here pp. 95–96.

104 Mark M. Hennelly, "Alice's Adventures at the Carnival", in: *Victorian Literature and Culture*, Vol. 37, No. 1, 2009, pp. 103–128, here p. 122.

105 E. Boyd Barrett, "Can There Be Tolerance without Understanding?", in: *The Journal of Religion*, Vol. 9, No. 1, 1929, pp. 20–37, here pp. 31–32.

106 Roger D. Abrahams, Barbara A. Babcock, "The Literary Use of Proverbs", in: The *Journal of American Folklore*, Vol. 90, No. 358, 1977, pp. 414–429, esp. pp. 427–428. Cf. Martin P. J. Edwardes, *The Origins of Self: An Anthropological Perspective*, London: UCL Press 2019, p. 29: "The Duchess' admonition to Alice is probably indecipherable (at least, I cannot find any unambiguous meaning in it, even when written down), but it does represent an important feature of selfness: the self seems to be defined through the interaction of different external viewpoints about the self. It is not simply an internal description…I am aware of myself because I am aware of you being aware of me."

107 Jean-Jacques Lecercle, *Philosophy of Nonsense: The intuitions of Victorian nonsense literature*, London: Routledge 1994, p. 57. Cf. Lecercle's comment to the passage from one of his later essays: "The Duchess's sentence in *Alice in Wonderland*, where multiple negation provides an image within *langue* of the limit that separates language from the silence of the ineffable." Jean-Jacques

In Robert D. Sutherland's comprehensive monograph *Language and Lewis Carroll*, the idea to look into the exact nature of the grammatical disorder in this sentence has equally been dismissed from the outset. Here, the question whether the sentence may be regarded as an explanation of the Duchess' dictum is cautiously entrusted to the symbolic logicians.[108] While I am also acutely aware of the complexities pertaining to the issue, it would be awkward to leave the question unanswered, for it is of paramount importance for examining translation versions, i.e. in order to see how free an interpretation actually is, at least some evidence is required of what exactly the translators set out to reproduce from the original phrase and, by contrast, what elements of its message they actively seek to avoid translating. Therefore, in what follows, I would like to present my tentative interpretation of the phrase.

I think that the moral of the dictum "Be what you would seem to be" is in full accord with the mustard-definition, yet in her explanation sentence the Duchess is moving away from this moral since the explanation suggests that it is impossible to be what one seems to be. This is at first clearly seen in the first section of the sentence: the words "Never imagine yourself not to be otherwise than what it might appear to others" may be paraphrased as "You are always different to what it might appear to others." Thereafter the argument gets complicated owing to a long series of negations and their relations to each other. The logical core of this second section of the phrase is, I believe, the following: "(appear to others)...not otherwise than....what ...would have appeared to them to be otherwise", or, still shorter, "not otherwise than...otherwise." Thus, it suggests a double reinforcement of the idea of "seeming being otherwise", i.e. what one seems to be is different from what one in effect is, which is quite in line with the first part saying that one is always unlike what might appear to others. And it is here that the problem arises: according to this proposition it would be impossible to be what one seems to be to others, that is, the sentence refutes the original claim of the very same moral which it is intended to confirm and to explain. I think that it is this point which serves as a source of Nonsense in the whole passage.

Lecercle, "'Bégayer la langue' – Stammering Language", in: *L'Esprit Créateur*, Vol. 38, No. 4, 1998, pp. 109–123, here p. 121.

108 Robert D. Sutherland, *Language and Lewis Carroll*, The Hague/Paris: Mouton 1970, pp. 188–189: "The Duchess' intended import for the expression *Be what you would seem to be* may or may not be accurately embodied in the alternative statement *Never imagine yourself not to be otherwise*...(I leave the final judgment to the symbolic logicians); but whether it is or it is not potentially, the latter utterance does not convey that meaning to Alice." Cf. the judgment about the reader's losing sight of the sense in the Duchess' sentence provided by Jacqueline Flescher: "Another way of deflecting the meaning is by complicating thought and syntax to such an extent that we lose sight of the meaning: 'Never imagine yourself etc.'" Jacqueline Flescher, "The Language of Nonsense in Alice", in: *Yale French Studies*, No. 43, 1969, pp. 128–144, here p. 140.

It is widely argued that Nonsense of the Duchess' sentence is rooted in syntax, yet the only problem with its syntax is its length. I believe that its semantics, first of all the mutual relations of its numerous negations, is far more intricate. First, it contains direct explicit negations (*never*, *not* (used three times).) Second, the adjective *otherwise* serves also as a negation meaning *being different to*, = *not being like something*[109]: it is also used three times throughout the sentence and two of these three instances are themselves directly negated: "*not* (*to be*) *otherwise*." Third, the semantics of *to appear* belongs here, too. Even though it is not a direct negation it serves as a means by which to question an affirmation of *being*. There are two direct combinations of negations in the sentence: one consisting of three units at the very beginning (*never ... not ... otherwise*) and a shorter one (*not otherwise*.) The first and the last words in the sentence are also negations: *never* and *otherwise*. Thus, in view of its form, the Nonsense effect produced by the sentence should principally be ascribed to the density of its negations and the complexity of modes in which these are related to one another.

With all this in the mind, I would like to turn now to the translatability issue and explore a number of inter-lingual versions of this highly challenging piece of Nonsense. First, it would probably be reasonable to focus on the overall subject of the sentence in translation texts. Since the relation of *being* to *seeming* appears to be the actual source of the disorder, which is as central to the sentence as to the dictum (the moral) and the discussion about the essence of mustard, it is crucial to ask whether this subject has been mirrored in the translations at all. Second, the form level shall receive sustained scrutiny, i.e. close attention has to be paid to the frequency of negations and to the question whether a given translation consists of one single period in which the relations between negations are as complex as in the original.

That contrasting *seeming* and *being* is by no means axiomatically part of every *Alice*-translation is easily seen from a comparison of the following two Russian versions by Demurova and Zachoder:

> А мораль отсюда такова: всякому овощу свое время. Или, хочешь, я это сформулирую попроще: никогда не думай, что ты иная, чем могла бы быть иначе, чем будучи иной в тех случаях, когда иначе нельзя не быть. (And the moral of that is: every vegetable has its season. Or, if you'd like it put more simply: never imagine yourself to be otherwise than you could be otherwise than being otherwise whenever it is impossible not to be otherwise.) (Demurova, p. 206)

109 This negative semantics of *otherwise* is probably most obvious when compared with its Russian and Chinese equivalents, cf. *ne takoj* не такой, *ne takaja* не такая, *bu tong* 不同, *bu ran* 不然, etc.

"Будь таким, каким хочешь казаться", или, если хочешь, еще проще, "Ни в коем случае не представляй себе, что ты можешь быть или представляться другим иным, чем как тебе представляется, ты являешься или можешь являться по их представлению, дабы в ином случае не стать или не представиться другим таким, каким ты ни в коем случае не желал бы ни являться, ни представляться." ("Be what you would like to seem to be", or, if you'd like it put more simply: "Never imagine yourself to be able to be or to appear to others otherwise than what you imagine or are or might appear to others, in order not to become or to appear to others the way you would neither like to be nor to seem to be.") (Zachoder, p. 91)

In Demurova's text, nothing whatever suggests a confrontation between being and seeming: her sentence deals only with the question how Alice should be and entirely omits the image of Alice in the eyes of the others. At the same time, the initial dictum does not allow any associations with the Duchess' sentence. The translator, thus, provides a piece of Nonsense yet it differs markedly from that of the original, for it represents merely an absence of sense and is not invested with any dialectical quality.

Zachoder's rendition is, by contrast, more complex: his dictum is much closer to the original and he also reproduces the problematics of being and seeming, yet their relation is again different to the original since the verb *byt'* (*to be*) is taken to correlate with *predstavljatsa* (*to appear*), i.e. as "to be or to appear", rather than to contrast with it. It is also notable that already the first section of the sentence which is quite easy to follow and reproduce (Never imagine yourself not to be otherwise than what it might appear to others) and which clearly suggests a contrast between being and appearing is absent here, although, on the whole, the translator seeks to provide a much more literal rendition than, for example, Demurova. And he is by no means alone in eliminating any cues suggesting order in the Duchess' words. Consider the following Chinese rendition of the passage by Chen Fuan (p. 143):

"别人觉得你是怎么个人，你就是怎么个人。" - 或者，如果你喜欢说得简单些，就是："不要想象你自己不是别人心目中认为你是的那种人，你过去是怎么个人或者可能是怎么个人也并非不是更早以前他们认为你不是的那种人。" ("You are what you appear to be to others." Or, if you'd like it put more simply: "Do not imagine yourself to be otherwise than what you appear to others to be; what you were in the past or might have been is not otherwise than what previously had appeared to others to be otherwise.")

Here, too, any trace of contrasting being and seeming has been eliminated and the sentence clearly corroborates the initial dictum which in itself is also a far cry from that of the original. The Duchess' sentence proves different from the original not only in terms of its subject but also at the formal level: its phrasing is much simpler and the number of negations has been significantly reduced, e.g. instead of the three unit negation at the beginning ("never … not otherwise") it provides a double negation ("Do not imagine yourself to be otherwise than what you appear to others.") A similar reduction of negations in the first section of the Duchess' sentence may be observed in a great number of *Alice*-renditions, e.g. in d'Amico's (p. 89: "Non immaginarti mai diverso da come potrebbe apparire agli altri….."), Zimmermann's (p. 63: "Bilde dir nie ein verschieden von dem zu sein was Anderen erscheint, etc."), Battistutta's (p. 83: "Non immaginare mai di essere diverso da come potrebbe sembrare agli altri…"), Olenič-Gnenko's (p. 167: "Никогда не воображай себя иным, чем это может показаться другим…")

By contrast, versions that reproduce here the exact pattern of the original are much less frequent than those that immediately adjust the Duchess' sentence to her original dictum. A correct rendition of the three unit negation may be found, e.g. in Berman's (p. 203: "Ne vous imaginez jamais ne pas être autrement que ce qu'il pourrait apparaître aux autres…") as well as in Hansen's (p. 80: "Bilde dir niemals ein, nicht anders zu sein, als es anderen scheinen könnte…") versions. In these two rare renditions Carroll's nonsense retains its dialectical function of revealing elements of order from which it continually desires to move away.

As already mentioned, the density of negations is not the only source of Nonsense in the original, one further being the textual sequence of the mustard-definitions, the dictum and the Duchess' sentence. Among those rare renditions which make the dictum immediately follow the mustard-definitions is that prepared by Ma Teng:

> "你觉得它看着像什么就是什么"；或者，你可以把话说得简单一些："永远要把自己想象成和别人心目中的你一模一样，因为你曾经或者有可能曾经在别人心目中是另外一个样子。" "It is just what it seems to you", or you can put it more simply: "You should always imagine yourself to be exactly like what you seem to others, for, in the past, you appeared or might have appeared different to them." (Ma Teng, p. 82)

Here, *mustard* has been made subject of the dictum and the explaining sentence is – contrary to the original – a clear corroboration of the dictum, i.e. since any object is precisely what it appears to others one need not try to be otherwise than what one seems to be. It is only in the concluding causal clause that Nonsense is allowed to show itself: it pretends to provide a cause for the main clause yet refrains from doing so. This is again an interesting solution to the issue of translatability. It minimizes Nonsense, the frequency of negations is reduced (e.g. the initial "Never …not otherwise" is substituted for a positive imperative in which the equality of *being* and *seeming* is being affirmed) and the original idea behind the sequence of the mustard-definitions, the dictum and the sentence (the dictum corroborates the definitions and is, in turn, negated by the sentence) is not reproduced.

From these examples, then, we can see that of all elements that are characteristic of Nonsense in the original translators tend to omit those that demarcate order. However, some renditions do furnish evidence of the translators' acute awareness of the actual role with which order and logic are invested in Carroll's Nonsense. Let us, for example, consider Nabokov's rendition:

> Мораль: Будь всегда сама собой. Или, проще: не будь такой, какой ты кажешься таким, которым кажется, что ты такая, какой ты кажешься, когда кажешься не такой, какой была бы, если бы была не такой.) The moral of this is: Be always yourself, or, to put it more simply: Never be what you seem to be to those to whom it seems that you are what you seem to be whenever you seem otherwise than what you might be if you were/had been otherwise. (Nabokov, p. 80)

Nabokov's passage is marked by quite comprehensible logical relations between *being* and *seeming*. Both the dictum and the Duchess' sentence express a call for action, i.e. you have to be different from what you may appear to a specific group of others. The Nonsense disorder comes about through restricting the range of this group (of others): be different from those (sic) who believe that you are what you seem to be. In other words, it is a call to being different from what one seems and, at first sight, this reading of the sentence may be regarded as corroborating the dictum (*Be always yourself*), yet this would be inaccurate since, according to the sentence, one cannot be oneself so long as one continues to appear at least to one different person to be what one is. Nabokov's Nonsense is, thus, accompanied by both humor and logic. Finally, a version of the Duchess' sentence prepared by Ščerbakov shall illustrate a similarly careful handling of Nonsense in its relation to order:

> "Будь, кем хочешь казаться". Или, проще говоря: "Никогда не считай себя не таким, каким тебя считают другие, и тогда другие не сочтут тебя не таким, каким ты хотел бы им казаться." "Be what you would like to seem," or, putting it more simply: "Never imagine yourself to be otherwise than what it ap-

pears to others, and then others will not take you to be otherwise than what you would like to appear to them." (Ščerbakov, p. 115)

Although this version of the sentence distinguishes between *yourself* and *others*, there is no confrontation between them, since, according to it, one automatically is what one appears to others. Therefore this sentence can be taken to mean an exact logical explanation of the initial dictum: Whilst it is possible to be what one pleases, one will never cease to seem what one is. The dismissal of a contrast between *being* and *seeming* does not result in minimizing Nonsense but, rather, increases its dialectical relation to order and makes it in the end appear as Sense, which represents quite a harmonic solution to the translation problem in question.

No matter whether the passage has been interpreted by the translators as marked by a mere absence of sense (which is by far the easiest option to take) or, the other way round, as invested with meaning (which represents a more complex reading), in none of the versions under discussion did the translatability issue turn out to be a problem of language in itself, laying bare its basic incapability to map the disorder of the original sentence onto its own surface expressions. In turning now to a long continuous text portion (Chapters IV and V), the question to consider is, what exact pitfalls are set here by the language and how the difficulties have been mastered in different translation acts.

III.II

One potent affinity shared by Chapters IV and V is that in both Alice's body appears as the main source of wonders and at the same time they are the last in which Alice is not yet able to exercise control over her own size. Nonsense – as the possibilities of language to keep up with the heroine's changes – is in both chapters closely related to this general subject. Consider, for example, the following passage from Chapter IV "The Rabbit Sends in a Little Bill":

> "It was much pleasanter at home," thought poor Alice, "when one wasn't always growing larger and smaller, and being ordered about by mice and rabbits. I almost wish I hadn't gone down that rabbit-hole...There ought to be a book written about me, that there ought! And when I grow up, I'll write one – but I'm grown up now," she added in a sorrowful tone: "at least there is no room to grow up any more *here*." "But then," thought Alice, "shall I *never* get older than I am now? That'll be a comfort, one

way – never to be an old woman – but then – always to have lessons to learn! Oh, I shouldn't like *that*!"[110]

Apart from the comparative form *pleasanter* which is reminiscent of the first phrase of Chapter II and underscores the emotional charge of the heroine's words, her agitation and nostalgia, in this passage, Nonsense rests primarily upon the semantics of *growing up*: its meaning suddenly appears relative to a given place and it is not the age but rather the bodily size which is taken as the basic criterion of judgement about being *grown up*. Thus, Alice is thinking of her age as secondary to her size and the logical conclusion that she is drawing from this consideration is the following: Since in this particular place (i.e. the Rabbit's house) there is no place for her to continue growing she would probably never get any older. This idea rests on interpreting *growing up* as *growing* and here the language suggests to her a development which in effect is beyond conventional reasoning, i.e. a new kind of relation between place and time (age) in which time appears to have got stuck, for the place in question does not permit any further growth and aging. And so Alice thinks that she would never get an old woman but instead she would have to learn lessons forever, that is, she weighs up advantages and disadvantages of the new logical relation she has just drawn which are completely comprehensible to the reader. Thereafter, the chain of logical conclusions which her interpretation of *growing up* suggests to her continues for some time till she becomes aware of some apparent flaws in it: "'Oh, you foolish Alice!' she answered herself. 'How can you learn lessons in here? Why, there's hardly room for you, and no room at all for any lesson-books!'"[111]

In order to achieve a similar Nonsense effect, the translator would need to search for a corresponding conventional pattern in the semantics of his/her language which could equally well be transgressed by the wonder of growing (up), that is, Nonsense should remain recognizable (as disorder) without getting entirely illogical. Consider the following French and Italian versions of the "...and when I grow up" vs. "but I'm grown up now":

Berman, p. 87: "quand je serai grande" vs. "mais je suis grande maintenant"; Sueur: "quand je serai grande" vs. "mais je suis une grande maintenent"; Bué, p. 46: "quand je serai grande" vs. "mais je suis déjà bien grande"; Petricòla-Rossetti, p. 46: "quando sarò grande" vs. "ma sono di già grande"; D'Amico, p. 42: "quando sarò grande" vs. "ma sono già grande"; Giglio, p. 105: "quando crescerò" vs. "ma io *sono* cresciuta"; Battistutta, p. 33: "quando crescerò" vs. "ma già adesso *sono* cresciuta"

110 *Alice*, p. 40.
111 *Alice*, pp. 40–41.

Apart from the last two versions, the translators have employed here an adjective (*grande*) which links up the meanings of *big* and *adult*. Since the reader clearly sees that in this episode Alice is confronted with a new wonder and has grown as big as a house the chain of conclusions triggered in her mind by this new experience is quite comprehensible. The same thing holds good for the verb *crescere* in the Italian versions of Giglio and Battistutta: it means both *to grow* and *to grow up* (e.g. "Sono cresciuto in Italia." ("I grew up in Italy.")) and thus it exactly reproduces the semantical pattern of the original. Now consider some Russian, Japanese and Chinese renditions of the phrases:

> Demurova, p. 124: "Вот вырасту и напишу …но ведь я уже выросла"; Nabokov, p. 31: "когда я буду большой…я уже и так большая"; Zachoder, p. 58: "когда я буду большая… да ведь я и так большая"; Ščerbakov, p. 60: "когда вырасту большая … Но ведь я уже выросла большая"; Seriu Hajime, p. 67: "大きくなったら、…　だって、いまだってもう大きいじゃないの"; Tada Kōzō, p. 46: "わたし、大きくなったら書くわ。" vs. "でも、今でも大きくなっているんだわ"; Shōno Kōkichi, p. 55: "大きくなったら" vs. "でもわたし今だってこんなに大きくなっているんだわ"; Ishii Mutsumi, p. 30: "大きくなったら" vs. "でも、今ももう大きくなってるのよね"; Zhao Yuanren, p. 45: "等我长大了"vs. "我现在可不是已经长大嘞吗？ "; Chen Fuan, p. 49: "等我长大了"vs. "不过现在我已经长大了": Ma Teng, p. 31: "等我长大了"vs. "可现在我已经长大了啊"; Zhu Hongguo, p. 37: "等我长大了"vs. "可是，眼下我不是已经长得够大了吗？ "

The consistency of all these versions is in fact baffling, which again reveals that Nonsense is by no means necessarily accompanied by insurmountable language traps. On the contrary, the above renditions demonstrate how transparent the chain of conclusions drawn by Alice in the original from the semantics of *growing (up)* proves to the translators and how easily they reproduce it in their languages by expressions that mean both *big* and *becoming an adult*: *vyrastu / budu bol'šaja* in Russian, *ōkiku nattara* in Japanese and *deng wo zhang da le* in Chinese. Consider, as another example, an episode from Chapter V in which, having nibbled a little of the right-hand bit of the mushroom, Alice's body begins shrinking rapidly and nearly disappears:

> Her chin was pressed so closely against her foot, that there was hardly room to open her mouth; but she did it at last, and managed to swallow a morsel of the left-hand bit.[112]

Similarly to the previous example, *room* is used here as a mass noun. However, the experience of her body is different to that in Chapter IV, for now it is not

112 *Alice*, p. 55.

changing proportionally but is rather shutting up like a telescope, i.e. it is the space between her head and her feet that is dwindling away. Here, again, the reader is faced with a game that involves both logic and linguistic conventions, yet this piece of Nonsense is not conceived as arising from Alice's linguistic imagination but as one that rests entirely on the author's ability to work wonders: relativity belongs among those numerous peculiar principles designed by Carroll which govern time and space in Wonderland. To translate this kind of wonder, the translator does not even need to search for expressions that link up various meanings and can naturally follow the semantics of the original, as, for example, Kurt Hansen, pp. 43–44:

> Ihr Kinn war so dicht auf ihren Fuß gedrückt, daß kaum so viel Platz da war, daß sie den Mund öffnen konnte, aber es gelang ihr schließlich, ein Stückchen von dem Bissen aus der linken Hand zu verschlucken.

Translation versions are, of course, not exactly the same in phrasing this passage, yet variations do not arise from a problem of understanding or one of an exhausting search for an adequate expression to map the idea of the original. They are rather due to different interpretations of some minor details, which can be seen in the following Russian renditions:

> Ščerbakov, p. 73: "Подбородок так прижало к туфлям, что рта было не раскрыть. Но наконец ей удалось откусить чуточку от левого куска." ("Her chin was pressed so closely against her shoes, that she couldn't open her mouth. But at last she managed to bite a bit off the left piece."); Nabokov, p. 45: "Подбородок ея был так твердо прижат к ноге, что не легко было открыть рот. Но, наконец, ей это удалось, и она стала грызть кусочек, отломанный с левого края." ("Her chin was pressed so closely against her foot, that it was not easy to open the mouth. But she did it at last and began nibbling the bit broken off the left side."); Demurova, p. 144: "Алиса взялась за другой кусок, но подбородок ее так прочно прижало к ногам, что она никак не могла открыть рот. Наконец, ей это удалось – и она откусила немного гриба из левой руки." ("Alice took up another bit but her chin was pressed so closely against her feet that she couldn't open her mouth. But she did it at last, and managed to bite off a little piece of the mushroom from her left hand.")

Textual variations involve the semantics of number (plural vs. singular), individual objects (*foot* vs. *shoe*, *left hand* vs. *the left side of the mushroom*), etc., yet in no way do they affect the meaning of what is happening, i.e. the disorder of Alice's shrinking away from the viewpoint of ordinary thinking, which seems to be the vital source of Nonsense in the episode. And, similarly, no significant challenges to the translation can be found in the further progress of wonders caused by the left-bit of the mushroom when Alice begins growing, again, not proportionally but strikingly asymmetrically: her neck comes to resemble a huge serpent and her head is diving in among the tops of high trees. [113]

While in Chapter V Alice's metamorphoses are entirely due to the specific laws that determine the order of growing large and small and that are quite different to the standards of everyday life, in the first example from Chapter IV ("And when I grow up" vs. "but I'm grown up now") it is the conventional semantics which does not keep up to the wonders and here Alice is not alone in bumping against language limits. Consider another dialogue from Chapter IV in which the Rabbit is discussing with his friends a big strange object hanging down from the window:

> "Now, tell me, Pat, what's that in the window?"
> "Sure, it's an arm, yer honour!"...
> "An arm, you goose! Who ever saw one that size? Why, it fills the whole window!"
> "Sure, it does, yer honour: but it's an arm for all that!"
> "Well, it's got no business there, at any rate: go and take it away!"[114]

As was the case with the first example from Chapter IV, the size of an object (*an arm*) is fundamental to the Rabbit's understanding of its semantics: since the strange object fills the whole window it cannot be an arm. By saying this, he actually repeats the language experience of Alice, for his language cannot keep up to the wonder which he is forced to witness. Yet by adding "at any rate" and thus granting the possibility for the object in question to actually be an arm he immediately levels the importance of its semantics: no matter whether it is an arm or not, the object has to be removed. This time, it is the semantics of parts and wholes which serves as a source of Nonsense. The *arm* is conceived of as a separate object whose essence is being reduced to its visible properties (*bulky, huge, obstructing*, etc.) rather than connected to a whole (a body), which would be suggested by the conventional semantics of this noun. Following this line of reasoning, the Rabbit anticipates one further episode of Nonsense from Chapter VIII "The Queen's Croquet-Ground" in which the King, the Queen and the executioner are discussing the possibility of beheading a Cat that has no body:

---

113 *Alice*, p. 56.

114 *Alice*, pp. 42–43.

> The King's argument was that anything that had a head could be beheaded, and that you weren't to talk nonsense.
> The Queen's argument was that, if something wasn't done about it in less than no time, she'd have everybody executed, all round.[115]

By ordering that the arm be removed from the window, the Rabbit uses similar argumentation and Nonsense principally results from his conviction that the obstacle should be removed even if it is an arm. Let us consider some renditions of this particular phrase:

> Shōno Kōkichi, p. 58: "まあいい、どう見ても、あの窓には無用の長物だよ。行ってとりはらってしまえ!" "Well, anyway, it has nothing to do in the window (lit.: for that window it is a useless bulky thing), go and take it away."
> Zhao Yuanren, p. 47: "那么，无论如何，它没有在那里的理，你去拿掉它！" ("Well, anyway, it has no reason to be there, go and take it away.")
> Pietrocòla-Rossetti, p. 49: "Bene, ma ei non ha niente da fare con la mia finestra, va, portalo via!" ("Well, but it has nothing to do in my window, go and take it away.")
> Hansen, p. 32: "Na ja, aber er hat hier jedenfalls nichts zu suchen; geh und nimm ihn weg!" ("Well, it has nothing to do here, go and take it away.")

As one can easily see, all the renditions follow more or less the same pattern and, again, apart from differences in minor detail the reproduction of Nonsense in this episode is not accompanied by any significant challenges. Thus, among all instances of Nonsense in the book, those that ironically prove to be the easiest to translate are ones that explicitly address the limits of linguistic conventions and situations in which language is falling short of the Wonderland experiences. The same thing also applies to the concluding episodes of Chapters IV and V: at the end of Chapter IV Alice encounters *an enormous puppy*[116] and in Chapter V she has to go to great lengths to convince the Pigeon that she is *a little girl*, which is heavily contradicted by her huge size and the serpent-like neck.[117] In both situations, language is again incapable of capturing the relations of sizes and their permanent confusing changes. The puppy is perceived by Alice as obviously dangerous and the Pigeon frantically tries to protect its nest from Alice as soon as it sees her face pop up high in the crowns of the trees. Thus, once again, the disorder produced by Nonsense involves limits of semantical conventions

115 *Alice*, p. 93.
116 *Alice*, p. 46.
117 *Alice*, p. 57.

and whenever translators have to deal with similar contexts, they do not encounter any notable difficulties.

One of the theories that have been discussed in the introductory part to this chapter holds the view, according to which Nonsense in Wittgenstein's and in Carroll's work has to be understood as resulting from conventional semantical properties of natural languages and the specific traps set by languages might represent unsurmountable obstacles for translation. Among the examples provided by Wittgenstein has been the phrase "the rod has a length": here Nonsense can be interpreted as a means to demarcate sense on the ground that it is customary to define the length of an object in English or German using precisely the same expression "an object x has a length of, etc." In Carroll's work, as I have pointed out, this dialectical property of Nonsense to demarcate sense by resorting to conventional semantical codes may also be clearly seen. However, in some of the book's episodes, language itself becomes a scene of action making its idiomatic expressions become part of the plot. Since such cases also involve conventional codes one would again expect them to confront translators with significant difficulties. Admittedly, this is quite a special kind of Nonsense, i.e. not one that contrasts with order and sense but, rather, one that in itself may perfectly be interpreted as revealing order. Consider, as an example, an episode from Chapter V "Advice from a Caterpillar" in which several expressions are employed to serve this goal and which is highly relevant to the discussion of the translatability issue. It is a passage from the conversation between Alice and the Caterpillar at the chapter's beginning:

> "Explain yourself!"
> "I ca'n't explain *myself*, I'm afraid, Sir," said Alice, "because I'm not myself, you see."
> "I don't see," said the Caterpillar.
> "I'm afraid I ca'n't put it more clearly," Alice replied, very politely, "for I ca'n't understand it myself, to begin with; and being so many different sizes in a day is very confusing."
> "It isn't," said the Caterpillar.[118]

In contrast to the earlier discussed examples where Nonsense mirrored the limits of linguistic conventions (*a (huge) arm, an enormous puppy, a little girl,* etc.), in this situation ordinary meanings of words are quite sufficient for capturing the reasons for confusion. Three particular expressions are involved here in Carroll's play with language: 1) *I can't explain myself, because I'm not myself* (Alice is in fact literally *not herself* after all the changes she has just gone through in Wonderland); 2) *you see* vs. *I don't see* (the Caterpillar literally cannot see what is wrong with Alice, since it encounters the heroine for the first time and can make no judge-

118 *Alice*, p. 49.

ment concerning her transformations); 3) *confusing* vs. *it isn't* (to a caterpillar, there is nothing confusing about changes of size and form and Alice should take it into account if she expects her conversation partner to sympathize with her.)

A comparison of different renditions again reveals a high degree of closeness to the original and this is not only the case with languages that are as closely related to English as, e.g. German, which can be demonstrated by the following examples: 1) Shōno Kōkichi, p. 67: "わたし自身ではないのですから" *(because I'm not myself)*, Chen Fuan, p. 63: "因为我现在不是我自己" *(because I'm not myself now)*, Zachoder, p. 63: "я – это не я" *(I'm not myself)*; 2) Shōno Kōkichi: "ごらんのように" *(as you see)* vs. "何もごらんにはなっておらん" *(I don't see anything)*; Chen Fuan: "你知道" *(you know, you see)* vs. "我不知道" *(I don't know, I don't see)*; Zachoder: Видите (you see) vs. Не вижу! *(I don't see)*; 3) Shōno Kōkichi: "まごつきはせん" *(I's not confusing)*; Chen Fuan: "不会的" *(It is not /It cannot be)*; Demurova: 138: "Нисколько" *(By no means.)*

All Nonsense episodes from Chapters IV and V, thus, represent cases that do not confront translators with any significant challenges and the main requirement for a felicitous rendition seems to reside in the translator's attention to what precisely constitutes the source of disorder in each individual episode and causes misunderstandings and confusions among the characters of the story. Quite a special case is represented by manifestations of Nonsense that arise from arbitrary linguistic behavior. Yet this will be the subject of two later chapters.

Conclusion

One of the central issues that have been raised in the theoretical part of this chapter was an understanding of Nonsense not as an all-encompassing element of the story but rather as one that is clearly delimited from order and that – thanks to its dialectical quality – regularly demarcates order and sense. Though the examples from Chapters IV and V discussed in the practical part do not yet evoke associations with the vast dramatic potential of Nonsense as it is revealed towards the end of Alice's journey through Wonderland, they still bear testimony to the fact that there is much more to Nonsense than a mere absence of sense exploited for intellectual amusement: even in the dialogue between Alice and the Caterpillar (Chapter V) in which Nonsense appears as a clear enactment of idiomatic meanings of words or in the mental soliloquy from Chapter IV in which Alice is weighing up the possible consequences of her new unnervingly huge size and has to assume that she would never get any older, Nonsense displays an inherent tension between order and disorder which is accompanied by confusion and reflects an exhaustive search for meaning and sense.

IV. Touching Cooks and Flying Cauldrons: What Is the Literal Meaning of a Word?

IV.I

In Book X of *The Odyssey*, Homer describes a transformation of Odysseus' men into pigs by Circe's charms. The episode refers to an act of magic: men are literally changed into pigs and thereafter – thanks to the intervention of Odysseus who himself narrowly escapes being transformed into a pig – they are turned back into men, once again quite literally. Both transformations are due to Circe's magical forces and have nothing whatever to do with any transfer of meaning: men are not called *pigs* metaphorically, i.e. owing to some apt image that would capture mutual affinities in their behavior, nor do pigs turn into men in a figurative sense for displaying similarities with humans. It is the very essence of magic in Homer's description that any transformation which is performed by it cannot be understood other than literally. And no metaphor was involved, when Odysseus used the word *swine* to refer to his comrades and pleaded with Circe for turning them back into men: "Circe, how can you ask me to show you gentleness? In this very house you have turned my comrades into swine…"[119] The miracle performed by Circe in response to Odysseus' pleads is described as follows:

> she (Circe) flung open the doors of the sty and set the men running out in the shape of fat and full-grown swine. Then they stood facing her, and she went to and fro among them, anointing them one by one with another charm. Their limbs began to shed the bristles that Circe's poison had planted on them, and they became men again, but younger than they had been before, and taller and handsomer to the eye.[120]

Although the word *swine* is used in this episode in its literal meaning, neither Circe nor Odysseus suggested that the swine might have lost their human essence, i.e. that they were not to be perceived as men under a spell. Nothing whatever evokes the idea that Odysseus may have forgotten this and addressed his comrades – literally – as *swine*. His whole concern was for them being freed from Circe's charms and given back their original form. Ironically, this particular episode has been taken as illustrating the fact that no difference exists between a literal and a metaphorical meaning, which was among the central insights of Don-

119 Homer, *The Odyssey*, Walter Shewring (Tr.), Oxford: Oxford Univ. Press 1980, p. 121.
120 Homer, *The Odyssey*, pp. 122–123.

ald Davidson, one of the most prominent representatives of analytic philosophy. The above passage inspired Davidson to the following interpretation:

> It can be an insult, and so be an assertion, to say to a man "You are a pig". But no metaphor was involved when (let us suppose) Odysseus addressed the same words to his companions in Circe's palace; a story, to be sure, and so no assertion – but the word, for once, was used literally of men.[121]

The suggestion to imagine that Odysseus once addressed his men by "You are pigs" in the literal sense rests on a firm conviction, that a metaphorical meaning of a word is completely reducible to a literal one. The only difference is said to be in the manner in which they are used, i.e. not in semantics, but rather in the intention which accompanies the word usage. According to Davidson, the art of communication is not concerned with the ability to differentiate between word meanings which one has learned as being firmly rooted in the conventions of one's language community and in each particular case to decide whether it is a literal meaning or a figurative (a transferred) one. Rather than being based on induction, assigning to a word that particular meaning which one expects most language users to assign to it in a given situation, communication is said to be crucially dependent on deduction, i.e. the ability to recognize the precise language intention of the speaker. Thus, it is the critique of the conventionality of semantics which is at the very heart of Davidson's language theory. The words "It can be an assault" from the above quotation may serve as a direct enactment of this critique: They imply that the phrase "You are pigs" – which, if applied to men, should conventionally be understood as an insult, as a transfer of qualities one associates with pigs to human beings, does not necessarily have to be interpreted pejoratively, since Odysseus does not intend any assault by addressing his comrades by it. Thus, the modality of "can be" proves to be of great importance for Davidson's communication theory, as it underscores the central idea of his essay which sets out as follows: "This paper is concerned with what metaphors mean, and its thesis is that metaphors mean what the words, in their most literal interpretation, mean, and nothing more."[122] While, in principle, it is said to be possible to imply by a metaphorical usage some meaning which reaches far beyond the literal as, e.g. in poetry, in Davidson's eyes, this has nothing whatever to do with semantics ("But intimation is not meaning."[123])

---

121 Donald Davidson, "What Metaphors Mean", in: Donald Davidson, *Inquiries into Truth and Interpretation*, Oxford: Clarendon Press 1984, pp. 245–264, here p. 259.

122 Donald Davidson, "What Metaphors Mean", p. 245.

123 Donald Davidson, "What Metaphors Mean", p. 256.

Whereas in the above mentioned essay it is the figurative meaning which forms the focus of Davidson's critique of semantics, in another article under the title "A Nice Derangement of Epitaphs" which equally makes a case for regarding semantics as exclusively pertaining to the field of pragmatics, his challenge to linguistic conventionality centers around the literal meaning. As the title suggests, malapropisms serve here as the main argumentation tool: *A Nice Derangement of Epitaphs* refers to the words of Mrs. Malaprop, i.e. the heroine from Sheridan's play *The Rivals* who displays a great passion for inappropriately using complicated rare expressions. For Davidson's argumentation against conventionality of semantics, it is crucial that, while being mistakenly used, these expressions hardly ever impede Mrs. Malaprop's mutual understanding with her interlocutors who in most cases interpret her words exactly as she intends them to be interpreted.

The theoretical value of malapropisms for Davidson's argumentation results from the fact that understanding them does not depend on a hearer's prior linguistic learning: "Someone who grasps the fact that Mrs. Malaprop means 'epithet' when she says 'epitaph' must give 'epithet' all the powers 'epitaph' has for many other people."[124] As in the above quoted essay, by saying "for many other people" Davidson provides a specification which lacks any theoretical justification, i.e. an explanation of how exactly one should estimate the quantity of people of whom this statement would be true. The idea which is implied in these words is that even if most speakers take an *epitaph* to mean something semantically quite distinct from *epithets*, in this particular situation – in Mrs. Malaprop's conversation – this difference is of no importance and *epitaphs* are actually understood as *epithets*. Davidson thus intends to provide a completely new interpretation of the literal meaning of an utterance, namely, one that is completely independent of one's prior learning or semantic competence and that is grasped by deduction, as something transitory, which exactly corresponds to the momentary intention of the speaker. This theory, labelled by Davidson *a passing theory*, is principally designed to strip the concept of litaral meaning off any associations with language conventions:

> ...the passing theory cannot in general correspond to an interpreter's linguistic competence... Every deviation from ordinary usage, as long as it is agreed on for the moment..., is in the passing theory as a feature of what the words mean on that occasion. Such meanings, transient though they may be, are literal; they are what I have called first meanings. A passing theory is not a theory of what anyone (except perhaps a philosopher) would call an actual natural language. 'Mastery' of such a language would

124 Donald Davidson, "A Nice Derangement of Epitaphs", in: Donald Davidson, *Truth, Language, and History*, Oxford: Clarendon Press 2005, pp. 89–108, here p. 104.

be useless, since knowing a passing theory is only knowing how to interpret a particular utterance on a particular occasion. Nor could such a language, if we want to call it that, be said to have been learned, or to be governed by conventions.[125]

Here, the literal is understood as transient, passing and deviant. It is agreed on for the moment. This theory clearly demonstrates how problematic the literal has come to be perceived in modernity. Apart from being understood as *passing*, its essence has become almost unfathomable. Since any simplicity and immediacy which one might be inclined to associate with it are discredited by the modern rationality as a myth, the literal has come to be seen in need of a complicated theoretical investigation trying to expose this deception for what it is. In Davidson's theory, this critical exposition demands it that the communication competence should be denied any connection with the mastery of semantics and rather be regarded as an ability to recognize passing intentions of language use. Making this proposal, he ignores that, e.g. in the case of Mrs. Malaprop it is not only her language intentions that count in her dialogues with other figures of the play, but also the intentions of the author who by no means accidentally gave her the name Malaprop, thus steering the language perception of the audience in a definite direction. In spite of all his theoretical expositions and specifications, what Davidson calls *the literal meaning* seems to be still firmly rooted in language conventions, because in order to understand that a word is used mistakenly for some other word, one has to be familiar with some prior knowledge of correct word usage, i.e. in this particular case, the readers (and not only the *dramatis personae*) are supposed to know the literal meaning of *derangement* and *epitaphs* as well as to recognize their similarity with *arrangement* and *epithets*, otherwise they would neither be able to recognize the malapropism or to know the reason for Mrs. Malaprop's extravagant name. Without knowing the ordinary or conventional meanings of the first two words, the meanings that are stored in one's mental lexicon, the communication between the dramatis personae would hardly be as successful as it is actually described. Maybe still more important, an aesthetical communication between the author and his public would hardly be possible in that case.

Yet it is striking how attractive Davidson's discarding of language conventions in his theoretical elaborations on the literal meaning proved to be for philosophers of language. For example, Catherine J. l. Talmage, while correcting Davidson by pointing out that it is not only the speaker's intention, but also her/his ability to be understood correctly, which is fundamental for language commu-

125 Donald Davidson, "A Nice Derangement of Epitaphs", p. 102.

nication[126], acknowledges the validity of his malapropism argument and the possibility to discuss the literal meaning as independent of semantical conventions:

> And, as we have seen, what his malapropism argument is designed to show is that what is essential in theory is simply that in interpreting the speaker's utterance the hearer use the theory of meaning the speaker intends him to use, something that can in principle occur without it being the case that either the speaker or the hearer has a knowledge of what words conventionally mean.[127]

Although, in one of her later works, she presents a complete revision of her previous skepticism of conventional usage by pointing out that Davidson's theory of meaning risks to be interpreted as absurdly individualistic and that it is primarily his criticism of language conventions which makes his theory appear very much like the language behavior of Humpty Dumpty[128], reproaches of this kind are easily refuted by analytic philosophers who defend Davidson. Christoph Demmerling, e.g. makes a case for a legitimate *condition of interpretability* (*Interpretierbarkeitsbedingung*) which is said to allow for an over-individualist understanding of Davidson's theory: "Beabsichtigt er (der Sprecher) nicht, so interpretiert zu werden, dann meint er es auch nicht.[129]" ("Unless he (the speaker) intends to be interpreted in this particular way, he does not mean it.") Even in cases of ambiguity, the speaker's intentions are said to be the only criterion by which to interpret her/his utterances. However, it is not made clear on what this *condition of interpretability* is objectively based and what exactly should be accepted as warranting a deduction of *the one* correct meaning intended by the speaker.

An emphatic support of Davidson's theory of language as well as new arguments against the conventionality of literal meaning were provided by Roger M. White in his essay "Literal Meaning and 'Figurative Meaning'" (2001.) Among other things, White engages himself in clarifying the exact import of the word *meaning* which he analyses alongside a number of different other terms such as *cause*, *reason*, *mind*, *knowledge*, *duty*, and *science*. In White's opinion, all of them represent complex conceptual units which change their exact meaning in the course of time. These semantical changes can also be observed synchronically within the use of different discourse subjects: Since these concepts correspond to vari-

126 Catherine J. L. Talmage, "Literal Meaning, Conventional Meaning and First meaning", in: *Erkenntnis*, Vol. 40, No. 2 (Mar., 1994), pp. 213–225, here p. 225.

127 *Ibid.*, p. 217.

128 Catherine J. L. Talmage, "Davidson and Humpty Dumpty", in: *Nous*, Vol. 30, No. 4 (Dec., 1996), pp. 537–544.

129 Demmerling, Christoph, *Sinn, Bedeutung, Verstehen: Untersuchungen zu Sprachphilosophie und Hermeneutik*, Paderborn: Mentis 2002, p. 52.

ous world-views and are connected with different metaphysical, religious, political, etc. ideas, different language users may have different perceptions in regard to their exact meaning. This particular characteristic, which he labels 'mobility in use', makes these concepts distinct from words like *asparagus* that display a high degree of semantic stability. Yet even in words like *asparagus*, the semantic stability is said to have nothing to do with language conventions:

> But the fact that the word "asparagus" has a highly stable use has nothing to do with the idea that it is regulated in its use by convention, whereas these words are not. It simply reflects the somewhat limited and highly predictable nature of our concern with edible plants.[130]

White thus distinguishes between semantical areas with either a high or low predictability nature. However, he does not provide comments as to where the borderline between these areas is supposed to be. This last question does not seem to be as important in his eyes as the Davidsonian insights into the utter uselessness of the term *convention* for discussing the meaning of *meaning*. The question, what in the first place can account for the fact that words with a high mobility in use have shared meanings and can be understood by different language users at all, is given the following explanation:

> They do not shift capriciously, nor, typically, in such a way that an audience is unable to adjust their understanding of the meaning to be given to a particular word. The need to preserve intelligibility will make for continuity between the present use of the word and previous uses, but the need for a speaker to articulate their own particular approach to a topic in hand will make for there also being discontinuities.[131]

Thus, the literal meaning is also understood here as a product of deduction: understanding is said to depend entirely on the reader's (hearer's) ability to adjust one's ear to those particular intentions which are expressed by the speaker and mistakes are avoided by a principle which is similar to the condition of interpretability in Demmerling's essay, – by the "need to preserve intelligibility". Yet it would seem that this principle can hardly replace the conventionality of the literal and, in cases of lexicalized metaphors, also that of the figurative meaning. Since not all acts of communication can testify to the speakers' awareness of the "need to preserve intelligibility", whenever it is not attested, there remains nothing to war-

130 White, Roger M., "Literal Meaning and 'Figurative Meaning'", in; *Teoria*, Vol. 67, No. 1, 2001, pp. 24–59, here p. 56.

131 White, Roger M., "Literal Meaning and 'Figurative Meaning'", p. 56.

rant intelligibility and protect from arbitrariness. This may be illustrated by a few readings of one of the central scenes in *Alice*, Chapter VI "Pig and Pepper". The topic in hand is the meaning of one particular word, which, similarly to the *asparagus* discussed in White's essay, displays a significant degree of semantic stability, in both its literal and (usually rather pejorative) figurative meanings, – *pig*.

In this scene, Alice witnesses how a baby suddenly changes into a pig. In spite of the apparent parallels with the above mentioned episode in Circe's palace from *The Odyssey*, the transformation in *Alice* differs from it in one significant point: other than in Homer's story, the miracle in Carroll's text follows a transformation in a word's meaning, i.e. from the figurative into the literal one. The Duchess is described as nursing a baby that is sneezing and howling continuously, which is why she addresses it with violence as "Pig!"[132] Not being able to calm the baby by this address, the Duchess considers giving it a beating, which she openly declares in her lullaby:

> "Speak roughly to your little boy,
> And beat him when he sneezes
> He only does it to annoy
> Because he knows it teases."[133]

After a series of energetic, yet fruitless educating attempts, the Duchess gets tired and finally flings the baby at Alice like a croquet ball, permitting her to nurse it a bit. As a nurse who is quite conscious of her responsibility for the baby's life, Alice decides to carry it away and, by doing so, to save it from the Duchess' custody. And while she is holding it, the baby that shortly before has been called "Pig!" by the Duchess turns into a real pig, no longer sneezing and howling, but snorting and grunting, as a literal pig would be expected to do. Having set the creature down and looking at it trotting away quietly into the wood, Alice continues to think about it sympathetically and reflects on the moral of the transformation which she has just witnessed in the following words:

> "If it had grown up", she said to herself, "it would have been a dreadfully ugly child; but it makes rather a handsome pig, I think." And she began thinking over other children she knew, who might do very well as pigs, and was just saying to herself, "if one only knew the right way to change them –"...[134]

132 *Alice*, p. 62.
133 *Alice*, p. 64.
134 *Alice*, p. 66.

The transformation act and the change from the figurative into the literal are accompanied by the expressions: "the baby *grunted* again", "it *grunted* again, so *violently*..." and "she...felt quite relieved to see it *trot away quietly* into the wood." The first verb *grunted* follows directly Alice's admonition: "'Don't grunt...that's not at all a proper way of expressing yourself.'"[135] Here, *grunt* is used in its figurative meaning: Alice is trying to teach the baby good manners and forbids that it behaves like a pig. Doing so, she follows the same logic of the figurative use as the Duchess ("Pig!"), albeit much more gentle. In the words that follow: "the baby *grunted* again", *grunted* is once again used figuratively, referring to the baby's unwillingness to learn good manners, but then, repeated again, it marks the baby's change into a literal pig, which is emphasized by the author's voice: "This time there could be *no* mistake about it: it was neither more nor less than a pig..."[136] Therefore, the transformation of the baby is accompanied by the same semantical change of the figurative into the literal of the verb *to grunt*, as is the case with the semantics of the noun *pig*. The last expression referring to the pig (*trot away quietly*) concludes the semantical series which, depending on the context, can be applied both to animals (literally) and to humans (figuratively). Yet the authorial comment ("there could be no mistake") makes it unequivocal that in this particular situation it has to be interpreted literally.

As most interpretations of this episode put the focus on the psychology of the figures, a discussion of them should be preceded by pointing out that the peaceful conclusion of the transformation scene (from the figurative *pig* into the literal *pig*; cf. *grunted violently* vs. *trot away quietly*) is in line with the dynamics of the whole plot development in Chapter VI. Whereas Alice is described as a rather timid participant in the conversation, which is underscored by the use of such attributes referring to Alice as "timid", "not...sure", "very politely", "glanced anxiously", the baby (before its transformation), the Duchess and the cook appear as her very opposites. Among the rich vocabulary which the author uses to characterize them, there are such expressions as "violent", "howling", "(saying) in a hoarse growl", "giving violent shakes", "tossing the baby violently", etc. Thus, Alice who is introduced into the conversation rather as a passive observer, whose only active action is trying to save the baby and to carry it away from the Duchess' house, is steadily contrasted by the author with the inexorable and wild behavior of the rest of the figures.

Consider the following interpretation of the episode provided by Donald Rackin in his "Alice's Long Journey to the End of Night" (1966):

135 *Alice*, p. 65.

136 *Alice*, p. 66.

The baby soon turns into an ugly, grunting pig – right in Alice's hands. Such a dramatized reversal of the conventional sentimental attitude towards children (the Duchess even shouts "Pig!" at the baby) is something besides a hit at above-ground morality – it is more like a denial of a customary emotional response. We may note here, that Carroll himself, usually so fearful of committing any social impropriety, could not in his letters and conversation always restrain his deep-seated disgust with all babies. But such information merely corroborates what any adult reader easily perceives: the baby-pig episode humorously portrays the arbitrary nature of conventional attitudes towards infants.[137]

In these words, the discontinuity between the figurative and the literal which is so crucial for the plot development in Carroll's text is completely levelled, very much like what happens in Davidson's theory of meaning. This does not only manifest itself in Rachin's interpretation of the baby's transformation as being in line with Duchess' addressing it as *pig*. More than that, by saying that the baby is changed into an ugly grunting pig, he departs from the original: as mentioned above, the verb *to grunt* is first used by Carroll figuratively in the description of the behavior of the baby and Alice refers the attribute *ugly* in her imagination to a boy into whom the baby might change one day, if it had not become a real pig, and not to this pig itself that, on the contrary, in Alice's eyes is quite *handsome*.

Although it is quite plausible that Rackin regards the Duchess' treatment of the baby as a reversal of the conventional sentimentality displayed by adults for their infants, he does not seem to take notice of the fact that being (or becoming) literal is one of the plot constituting qualities in Carroll's book. It is true that Alice observes the baby's transformation into a pig, yet she has absolutely no influence on it. Nor is it a product of her mistaken perception of a baby as a literal pig. By regarding literalness exclusively as a psychological quality peculiar to Alice and opposing her to an ambiguous world under-ground reigned by principles that cannot be comprehended by the conventional standards of logic and ethics, Rackin reaches the following psychological judgment:

(Alice) has reached the stage of development where the world appears explainable and unambiguous, that most narrow-minded, prejudicial period of life where, para-

137 Donald Rackin, "Alice's Long Journey to the End of Night", in: Donald Rackin (Ed.), *Alice's Adventures in Wonderland. A critical Handbook*, Belmont: Wordsworth Publishing Company 1969, pp. 339–361, here p. 350.

doxically, daring curiosity is wedded to uncompromising literalness and priggish, ignorant faith in the fundamental sanity of things.[138]

Here, literalness is taken to be a negative characteristic which is responsible for Alice's not being able to find her way in Wonderland and for eventually destroying it. A similar interpretation of the episode is provided by James R. Kincaid in an essay with the telling title "Alice's Invasion of Wonderland." In Kincaid's view, both the Duchess and the cook represent quite harmless beings: "she (the Duchess) and the cook only sneeze, miss each other with frying pans, and toss vigorously a thing which turns out to be a pig."[139] This short passage contains four textual mistakes. For the analysis at hand, the most relevant of them is the last one, i.e. saying "turns out to be a pig" instead of "turns into a pig *literally*". Carroll's artistic use of literalness is once again overlooked, which allows the critic to furnish the following characterization of the Duchess and Alice:

> The Duchess' version asserts a vigorous and confident life-force, quite at odds with Alice's pedantry and deathlike caution. In the end, this episode is climaxed not so much by the child's becoming a pig, but by Alice's reflection that she knew other children "who might do very well as pigs."[140]

Ironically, the idea according to which Alice is to be understood as a kind of Victorian Terminator, i.e. a violent and destructive actor, is once again due to disregarding the fact that it is not Alice but the author who insists on being literal and performs a metamorphosis of a human baby (that is addressed as a pig because of its behavior) into a real pig – from the figurative into the literal. Such instances of confusing subjects of action in the episode under study seem in most cases to arise from levelling the literal and the figurative meanings. The following example which is not significantly different to the first interpretations discussed above, might confirm this impression: "Alice is transformed into a kind of Circe, turning all those she controls into swine."[141] Here, again, Alice is assigned qualities and forces which she hardly displays in Carroll's text: possessing magical powers over others and the ability to transform men under her control into swine.

Similar acts of reading – usually brought forward in an emphatically earnest pathetic tone – do not display much interest in the language game in which Car-

138 Donald Rackin, "Alice's Long Journey to the End of Night", p. 341.

139 James R. Kincaid, "Alice's Invasion of Wonderland", in: *Publications of the Modern Language Association*, Vol. 88, No. 1, pp. 92–99, here p. 94.

140 James R. Kincaid, "Alice's Invasion of Wonderland", p. 94.

141 Roger Sale, *Fairy Tales and After: From Snow White to E. B. White*, Harvard: Harvard University Press 1978, p. 115.

roll engages himself with the reader. Even though Rackin lists *literalness* among negative qualities peculiar to Alice, the word does not imply any connection with linguistic mechanisms of the production of meaning. Rather than being opposed to the figurative, it is itself used figuratively, i.e. suggesting a lack of fantasy, spiritual inflexibility, and boredom. Viewed in this light, *literalness* (or *literal-mindedness*) is also ascribed to Alice in another pathetic piece of criticism produced by Terry Otten in which the following is said: "she (Alice) betrays the myopic vision of seven to ten years old, who psychologists tell us undergo an intense literal-mindedness."[142] One particular detail in Carroll's text which provokes Otten's righteous indignation is Alice's "thinking over other children she knew, who might do very well as pigs"[143]. Otten interprets this as a clear demonstration of a potential for tyranny which, in his eyes, completely neutralizes Alice's apparent naivety: "Though utterly naïve, she betrays a proclivity for violence, moral tyranny, and unswerving absolutism. Her vocabulary reflects her linear assumptions about truth."[144] Following this line of argumentation, the critic comes to put Alice on a par with the ferocious figures from William Golding's *Lord of the Flies* for equally representing "degeneration into adults"[145].

Looking back on the issue of the conventionality of the literal meaning, the fact that in the critical interpretations of the baby/pig episode which have been mentioned above, the semiotic relationship between the literal and the figurative in Carroll's text is completely left out of consideration is all the more peculiar as it concerns something quite common and easily discernable: it is no more and no less than semantic conventions that are ignored in these acts of reading, i.e. a discontinuity which most speakers, relying on their prior learning of semantics, would highly likely recognize between *pig/grunt* used pejoratively, meaning a reproach, an admonition, an insult of someone who does not behave properly, on the one hand, and the same words used literally, in neutral contexts no transfer of meaning is involved and the words refer directly to animals, on the other. In essence, these interpretations seem to be in line with the theoretical unease with which the literal meaning came to be approached within analytic philosophy, e.g. by Davidson and his followers: the search for correct authorial intentions (which would correspond to the speaker's intentions in Davidson's theory) is accompanied by adjusting the text to one's own speculative theory and by eventually alienating it from conventional semantic patterns to which Carroll systemat-

142 Terry Otten, "After Innocence: Alice in the Garden", in: Edward Guiliano (Ed.), *Lewis Carroll: A Celebration. Essays on the 150th Anniversary of the Birth of Charles Lutwidge Dodgson*, New York: Clarkson N. Potter 1982, pp. 50–61, here p. 50.

143 *Alice*, p. 66.

144 Terry Otten, "After Innocence: Alice in the Garden", p. 52.

145 Terry Otten, "After Innocence: Alice in the Garden", p. 52.

ically resorts in designing his plot, e.g. by making wonders of Wonderland follow the language, among other things, the changes from the figurative into the literal.

Quite a special case of approaching the issue of the literal and figurative meanings represents Celia Brown's monograph *Alice hinter den Mythen: Der Sinn in Carrolls Nonsens* (*Alice behind the Myths: The Sense behind Carroll's Nonsense* 2015). While she does not raise this issue directly, in her interpretation, she succeeds in discarding both the literal and the figurative, since all images in Carroll's text are taken to be allusions, i.e. figures that are invested with some special hidden symbolic meaning. Thus, the *sense* which the title of her monograph promises to bring to light from Carroll's nonsense is essentially a product of searching for intertextual cues which, once reconstructed, are expected to lay bare the exact intentions which the author of *Alice* decided to cover up from the reader's inquisitiveness. For example, she interprets Bill the Lizard as representing phallic potency, for the name *Bill* is a shortened form of William and therefore has to refer to William IV of the United Kingdom: "Da Bill zehn illegitime Kinder von seiner Maitresse, der Schauspielerin Dorothea Jordan, hatte, die 1817 starb, passten die phallischen Implikationen des Austritts der Eidechse durch den Kamin."[146] ("Since Bill had ten illegitimate children by the actress Dorothea Jordan, his beloved who died in 1817, it is fitting to interpret the Lizard's flight through the chimney as having phallic implications.") The monograph abounds in similarly spectacular insights. One of them refers to the *pig* from the baby/pig episode in Chapter VI and provides the following reconstruction of its symbolic meaning:

> Das Schwein im Titel „Pig and Pepper", verweist auf die Mysterien von Eleusis. Das Schwein wurde in der Antike verehrt und hatte eine besondere symbolische Bedeutung. Wie Alice trugen die Novizen bei der Initiation in die Mysterien jeweils ein Ferkel, das Demeter/Ceres heilig war und im Verlauf des Rituals gereinigt und geopfert wurde...Schmort da vielleicht ein Opferschwein im Topf der Wunderland-Köchin? Das Schwein in Carrolls Küche verwandelt sich in ein Schwein, als Alice ihn in den Arm nimmt. Dies erinnert an einen anderen Fall von Identitätsverwechslung, an *Die Acharner* von Aristophanes – auch das eine wichtige Quelle (sic) für Carrolls Plot.[147] (The pig in the title "Pig and Pepper" refers to the Eleusinian Mysteries. In antiquity, pig was a respected animal, invested with a special symbolic meaning. Similarly to Alice, at their initiation into these mysteries, each of the novices held a pig in their hands, a sacred animal associated with Demeter/Ceres which, in the course of the ceremony, was purified and sacrificed...Is it not a sacrificed pig that is being braised in the cook's cauldron? The pig from Carroll's kitchen

146 Cecilia Brown, *Alice hinter den Mythen: Der Sinn in Carrolls Nonsens*, Paderborn: Wilhelm Fink 2015, p. 124.

147 Cecilia Brown, *Alice hinter den Mythen: Der Sinn in Carrolls Nonsens*, p. 124.

turns into a pig that Alice takes into her arms. This is also reminiscent of another case of identity confusion, namely, of *The Acharnians* by Aristophanes, which is also (sic) one of important sources of Carroll's plot.)

By uncovering similarities between *Alice* and other works of world literature, Brown does not hesitate to call them – like in the reproduced quotation – important sources for Carroll and to ascribe to Carroll's figures symbolic meanings that can be illustrated by these works. E.g. the observation of the sacred meaning with which pigs were invested in antiquity is believed enough to support the conclusion that it is nothing else but a sacred animal that is being braised in the cook's cauldron in *Alice*. Yet the problem which arises in the light of this interpretation is that here, again, the literal meaning of words and images is completely disregarded: the literal turns into the symbolic and loses any interpretative value of its own. The same seems to be true of the figurative meanings which are assigned hardly any significance in Brown's attempt to unearth sense from Carroll's nonsense. As a result, it is not only the promised sense, but also a new variety of nonsense with which the reader of Brown's monograph is suddenly confronted, e.g. in trying to understand the meaning of the above "Das Schwein in Carrolls Küche verwandelt sich in ein Schwein, als Alice ihn in den Arm nimmt." ("The pig from Carroll's kitchen turns into a pig that Alice takes into her arms.")

Carroll's experimenting with language makes it appear as an integral part of the story, rather than as a mere medium of narration. Changes from the figurative into literal and vice versa are therefore significant turning points in the development of the story: in them, language itself turns out to be a way of wonderful transformations, adventures, and discoveries. Reading the story is thus comparable to re-discovering one's language and to perceiving all the semantical changes as parts of a coherent framework that at first sight might give the impression of something quite ordinary, familiar and conventional, yet, on the other hand, probably exactly due to this familiarity, it may also appear as too volatile and too transparent to be taken into account by some critics.

Following this journey of linguistic adventures, the reader perceives a discontinuity between the literal and figurative. As is described in Chapter VI, Alice begins to doubt about the human identity of the baby and ventures to look down into its face only after having carried it for some time away from the Duchess' house. Up to that moment and in spite of its having been called *pig* by the Duchess, the baby continues to be a human in Alice's eyes. Although quite a clear borderline separates the figurative and literal in the reader's (and Alice's) perception of the events, the moment in which the baby changes into a pig is also suggestive of other language dimensions, e.g. one of continuities between metaphorical and literal meanings. They suddenly appear as logically interrelated and this in turn accounts for a word's ability to have more than one meaning. Polysemy thus features as a vital source of wonders within the story. The transformation scene shows how both meanings merge and the transfer of meaning which in this episode is reversed from the figurative into the literal may be regarded as a most significant event within the language performance of the story. Such performance acts that are conceived as direct enactments of meaning transfer and represent an interplay of different meanings with which every language speaker is perfectly familiar (e.g. *pig* as an animal (the literal meaning) vs. *pig* as a human (the figurative meaning)) and to which Carroll repeatedly resorts in designing his plot.

In this connection it is worth recalling Wilhelm von Humboldt's idea concerning the paramount importance of imagination[148] to the constitution of any natural language. The act of meaning transfer in the episode from Chapter VI vividly reproduces those moments from the history of any natural language in which metaphors that at some point in the past had been newly created by the imagination of the respective language community suddenly became part of the lexicon. The birth of any lexicalized metaphor proves to be a fitting illustration of that particular play of collective imagination to which von Humboldt referred in his writings as a propelling force in language development and it is exactly this to which Carroll constantly directs his reader's attention by making transfers of meaning part of the story's plot. In so doing, he in effect creates a new paradigm of actions, that is, a motive which is repeatedly used in various episodes that are not necessarily conceptually connected to each other. On the other hand, many of such instances are mutually interrelated and thus may also be regarded as a particular kind of syntagmatic links within the work (consider, for example, Alice's "falling asleep" (fig.) vs. Alice's "falling through the earth" (lit.), or "upsetting the jurymen", i.e. putting them upside down (lit.) vs. Bill's "shock of being upset", i.e. both literal (*put upside down*) and figurative (*melancholic, sad*)). This sort of textual correlations which provides the work with a significant additional coherence and which nonetheless, as the above interpretations of the baby/pig episode reveal, is easily overlooked by the critics, deserves sustained scrutiny. In what follows, the baby/pig episode is taken as a starting point in the analysis of these intratextual links and is compared with other scenes from the book from the following three perspectives: 1) The use of figurative forms of address, e.g. "Serpent!" vs. "Pig!"; 2) The art of flying: who/what flies at different stages of the

148 In his French letter to Abel-Rémusat, Humboldt uses the term "la partie imaginative des langues" (Cf. Wilhelm von Humboldt, *Lettre à M. Abel-Rémusat, sur la nature des formes grammaticales en général, et sur le génie de la langue chinoise en particulier*, Paris: La Librairie Orientale de Dondey-Dupré 1827, pp. 11, 12.)

story, in what sense and for what reason? 3) The *world's moving faster*: the strategies of the figurative use and Alice's response to them.

1. *Serpent!*

If in Chapter VI the Duchess addresses her baby as "Pig!" ("'Pig!"'it was addressed to the baby...", p. 61), something similar happens also at the end of Chapter V, when the Pigeon sees Alice and says "Serpent!" to her ("'Serpent!' screamed the Pigeon.", p. 56.) The omission of the indefinite article suggests that the word is not used merely as referring to a danger which has been spotted by the Pigeon, but is rather a militant address to an opponent. Similarly to *pig*, in ordinary language, this word can be used either neutrally (referring directly to an animal, i.e. in the literal sense) or pejoratively (referring to a vicious person, i.e. figuratively.) Yet, in this particular scene, the relationship between the literal and the figurative is more complex than in the baby/pig episode, because, due to the context, the line dividing them is blurred: Shortly before being addressed as *serpent*, Alice is said to have undergone a new metamorphosis, upon which she has become extraordinarily long, with an immense neck, exactly like one of a huge serpent: "(Alice) was delighted to find that her neck would bend about easily in any direction, like a serpent" (p. 56.) Thus, Carroll explicitly uses the word *serpent* anticipating the Pigeon's first reaction at meeting Alice. In response to the Pigeon's address, Alice denies being a serpent ("'I'm *not* a serpent!' said Alice indignantly." p. 56) And during the dialogue that follows, she does not understand straightaway what exactly the Pigeon could have meant by this word. It is only after it tells her about sleepless nights it had to spend trying to protect its nest from serpents that Alice begins to see the reason of this address:

> "I'm very sorry you've been annoyed," said Alice, who was beginning to see its meaning. (p. 57)

Yet even after these soothing words the Pigeon is not appeased. Instead, it starts a long angry reply which, again, is concluded by the word *serpent* ("Ugh, Serpent!", p. 57.) Thus, for Alice, the whole conversation proves rather unsuccessful and it is especially after she honestly admits to have once tasted eggs that the Pigeon believes to have collected enough evidence of there being no essential difference between *little girls* and *serpents*.

Other than in Chapter VI, in which "Pig!" is used as a metaphor without any difficulties for the figures' understanding, it does not work here, since there is no consensus as to how exactly the literal meaning of *serpent* should be conceived of. The Pigeon's taking issue with the conventionality of the literal meaning allows a parallel between its attitude to semantics and Davidson's theory of meaning. In *Alice*, this obvious challenge to the literal meaning which once again results from the perception of language itself as a performance stage, is made possible by wonders which Alice goes through in Wonderland: it is namely that particular metamorphosis of her body shortly before the conversation which provides the Pigeon with sufficient logical means to deny a difference between two things (*serpents* vs. *little girls*) that have one common characteristic. Therefore, in this episode, Alice is alone to stick to the conventionality of the literary meaning, and as for its figurative use, which is signaled in the Pigeon's address and which – due to semantical conventions in English – would be comprehensible for any reader of the story, it is the literalness of the Pigeon which prevents any transfer of meaning and results in the pejorative use merging completely with the literal meaning.

The fact that Alice nonetheless displays a much better command of the literal than the Pigeon can be demonstrated by her ability to follow the Pigeon's argumentation. Even though she does not accept its reasons for calling her *serpent*, she understands its logic, or, as Carroll puts it, "she was beginning to see its meaning", as soon as she learned how it was worried about its offspring. And in this particular point, still another parallel can be drawn with Chapter VI, as the Duchess is introduced here as an exact reversal of a careful parent. On the other hand, in terms of her attitude to conventions and the literal, she represents the very opposite of Alice, which may be illustrated by her above mentioned lullaby:

"Speak roughly to your little boy,
And beat him when he sneezes:
He only does it to annoy,
Because he knows: it teases."

CHORUS
(in which the cook and the baby joined): –
"Wow! wow! wow!"
"I speak severely to my boy,
I beat him when he sneezes;
For he can thoroughly enjoy
The pepper when he pleases!"

CHORUS
"Wow! wow! wow!" (p. 64)

In contrast to other parodies in *Alice*, this song openly pursues a didactic aim: the Duchess explains how a child is to be treated when it does not behave itself and the funny thing is that domestic violence appears here as the only practicable means for achieving this aim. Thus, the message of the song is a threat rather than an appeasement that one might expect from a lullaby. Although, in trying to educate her baby, the Duchess demonstrates no less determination than the Pigeon does in defending its nest, in the end she shows no scruples about giving up her motherly concerns and flinging the intrepid grunting infant at Alice. Due to all this, the Duchess may be regarded as steadily moving away from the literal: the lullaby (Carroll calls it "a sort of lullaby", p. 64) turns into a declaration of war, but the war is lost as soon as it has been declared. The mother capitulates in the literal sense.

2. *The Art of Flying*

In Chapter V, Alice's encounter with the Pigeon is introduced by the image of its violent flight: "a large pigeon had flown into her face and was beating violently with its wings" (p. 56.) This is one of very few episodes in Carroll's text in which the verb *to fly* is used literally, i.e. referring to someone/something who/that is able to fly and does so on his/its own, without any external influence. It is one of the peculiarities of Carroll's plot that connotations of violence in the description of the Pigeon's flight systematically accompany those figures and things that are presented as flying also in the figurative sense, i.e. when forced to fly by an impact from without. Compared to the literal usage of the verb, instances of its figurative use are relatively frequent and these repeated occurrences of flying figures and things significantly underscore the tension between the literal and figurative in *Alice*. Consider the description of the conversation in the Duchess' kitchen shortly before the lullaby:

> While she (Alice) was trying to fix on one (subject of conversation), the cook took the cauldron of soup off the fire, and at once set to work throwing everything within her reach at the Duchess and the baby – the fire-irons came first; then followed a shower of saucepans, plates, and dishes. The Duchess took no notice of them, even when they hit her; and the baby was howling so much already, that it was quite impossible to say whether the blows hurt it or not.
>
> "Oh, *please* mind what you are doing!" cried Alice, jumping up and down in an agony of terror. "Oh, there goes his *precious* nose!" as an unusually large saucepan flew close by it, and very nearly carried it off. (p. 63)

The cook may be considered among the most mysterious figures in *Alice* and yet, during my research, I have not been able to find any detailed analysis of her position in the plot. Maybe the most thrilling thing about the cook is the motivation of her violent actions. Whereas the meditativeness of the Caterpillar smoking its hookah (Chapter V), the playful way in which the Cheshire-Cat suddenly appears – in parts – to the utter bewilderment of others (Chapter VI, Chapter VIII), the delight with which the huge puppy rushes at the stick held to it out by Alice (Chapter IV), are psychologically all quite comprehensible, it is a great enigma of the text that the cook should constantly appear in it as a sort of personified grenade launcher. One possibility to explain her behavior would be as one that is due to her environment, i.e. for being confronted with the incessant howling and sneezing of the baby and with the militant educational endeavors of the Duchess, both of whom drive the cook mad and make her work off her growing frustration in a series of violent fits. For the present analysis, it seems especially important that, owing to her boisterous disposition and impressive physical abilities, all objects within the cook's reach are set in motion, or to be more exact, all of them begin to fly through the kitchen.

The flight of the large saucepan in the above quotation nearly costs the baby its nose or even its life. Here, again, the image of a flying object is conceived as dangerous, to which Alice does not hesitate to draw the cook's attention. It is further remarkable what a dense net of associations is produced in the text by the cook's actions and by the flight of the kitchen utensils. The closest of them is that between the cook and the Duchess: the Duchess is said to be giving the baby a violent shake (p. 64), to be tossing the baby violently up and down (p. 64), to fling the baby at Alice (p. 64) upon which the cook throws a frying-pan after the Duchess (p. 64.) The actions produced by the Duchess constantly suggest that her way to nurse the infant is actually quite close to the cook's emotional treatment of the crockery. Although the image evoked by this parallel, i.e. the flight of the baby ("Pig!") which is tossed around without a moment's pause, is not made explicit by the use of the verb *to fly* in this particular episode, Carroll resorts to the transfer of meaning later, in Chapter IX, within the following conversation between Alice and the Duchess:

> "I've a right to think," said Alice sharply, for she was beginning to feel a little worried.
> "Just about as much right," said the Duchess, "as pigs have to fly..." (p. 97)

Connotations of danger that accompany the figurative *flight* of the saucepan caused by the cook are once again present here, although it is a completely different kind of danger than the one experienced by the baby in the kitchen: this time, it concerns rather the art of using words figuratively in order to neutralize one's interlocutor, to silence him/her by catching him/her off guard, even in the absence of any plausible motivation for doing so.

Associations with the flying saucepan also occur in the Hatter's song in Chapter VII:

> "Twinkle, twinkle, little bat!
> How I wonder what you're at!
> Up above the world you fly,
> Like a tea-tray in the sky."[149]

Note that here the source image for the flight comparison is not the twinkle, not the bat, but the tea-tray. Thus, considering the fact, that for singing this song the Hatter nearly gets executed by the Queen, it is once again the figurative use of the verb which causes trouble: Hearing the song, she takes it to be a grave offense of the time ("He's murdering the time! Off with his head!"(p. 77)), thus reacting to the transfer of meaning produced by the Hatter by still another metaphor which has serious consequences for the Hatter. Even though he stays alive, the *murder* of the time results for him in a tea-party in which the time *stands still*, i.e. once again the metaphorical turns into the literal in the great wonder performance of Carroll's language-plot.

Finally, Bill the Lizard should be mentioned here, a figure that may be regarded alongside the cook as one of the most dynamic characters of the book. Yet different to the cook, both the highest and the lowest points in Bill's dynamics are reached not on its own initiative but are caused by Alice. Both situations that are perceived by Bill as highly disagreeable and perilous once again involve a tension between the figurative and literal. In Chapter IV, Bill is first described as "a little animal scratching and scrambling about in the chimney" (p. 44). Being sent by the Rabbit through the chimney, Bill has to clarify the origins of the mysterious huge arm stretched out from the window of the Rabbit's house (the reader knows that this is Alice who, having stuck in the Rabbit's home, has suddenly become so large that there is no more place for her to grow other than through the window.) Hearing Bill approach her, Alice gives it a powerful kick by which Bill is forced to fly back through the chimney: "There goes Bill!" (p. 44). Upon a more or less happy landing (anyway, Bill stays alive), it tries to realize what exactly has happened to it and describes its flight experience in the following words:

149 *Alice*, p. 76.

"Well, I hardly know – No more, thank ye; I'm better now – but I'm a deal too flustered to tell you – all I know is, something comes at me like a Jack-in-the-box, and up I goes like a sky-rocket!" (p. 44)

The breathtaking velocity of the flight from the chimney makes Bill nearly speechless and it is only thanks to its friends' assistance that it is able to get on its feet again.

The other extreme point in Bill's dynamics is described in the last chapter of the book, shortly before Alice is asked to present her evidence at the King's and the Queen's trial. This time, Bill is unfortunate enough to be among the jurymen who are tipped over by the edge of Alice's skirt. Here, again, the plot involves a direct interaction of the literal and figurative: "(Alice) jumped up…upsetting all the jurymen on to the heads of the crowd below…" (p. 123) Of all the jurymen, the most minute description of *the state of being upset* is provided for Bill: "the poor little thing was waving its tail in a melancholy way, being quite unable to move." (p. 123) The *melancholy* that is expressed by its tail's movements fully corresponds to the semantics of the verb to *upset*, i.e. being put on one's head, and – by extension, figuratively – *feeling sad*. The same semantical play is continued in the scene in which the jurymen eventually recover from their sufferings:

As soon as the jury had a little recovered from the shock of being upset, and their slates and pencils had been found and handed back to them, they set to work very diligently to write out a history of the accident, all except the Lizard, who seemed too much overcome to do anything but sit with its mouth open, gazing up into the roof of the court. (p. 124)

Here, the word *upset* is again used literally and the whole episode may be regarded as a simultaneous enactment of both its literal and figurative meanings. And as is the case with figurative flights of figures and things that are accompanied by the idea of danger, this episode also involves similar connotations, underscored by the expression *the shock of being upset*. It is true that in this particular case it is only by means of associations that the figurative meaning is suggested and since all associations are more or less spontaneous, it could appear that expressions like "waving its tail in a melancholy way" and "too much overcome to do anything" are not necessarily connected with the repeated use of the verb *upset* in its literal meaning. Objections of this kind would be completely justified. Yet by drawing attention to these possible intratextual connections within the book, I did not intend to say that there are some compelling reasons for this kind of interpretation, but rather that these associations are by no means arbitrary and that their very possibility is largely due to the semantical conventions established in the course of the language development. Maybe no other book can clarify the philosophical debates about the literal and figurative better than Carroll's *Alice* exactly because here the tension between them never ceases. Being continuously enacted, this tension steadily addresses the reader's ability to re-discover mutual affinities in word meanings with which he/she is perfectly familiar due to the language conventions.

In order to illustrate this by still another examle, I would like to turn once again to the figure of the cook. She is introduced as as a person *stirring* the soup in a large cauldron. The verb *to stir* belongs into the same semantical series as *to touch*, *to move*, etc. She is stirring the soup, she is moving everything within her reach and makes the crockery fly through the kitchen. Therefore, due to the conventionality of English semantics, one option that is quite clearly left open for the reader is to refer to her as a – literally – *stirring*, *touching*, and *moving* character. Yet the psychological portrait with which Carroll provides the cook (as *boisterous*, *enraged*, *violent*, *dangerous*, etc.) does not allow for activating figurative meanings which represent a firm, i.e. a fully lexicalized, conventional part of the semantics of *moving* and *touching* in English. Nevertheless the option which the reader has at his/her disposal remains open and constitutes a significant element in the language performance of Carroll. The referential frame within which the option of a figurative reading of *touching* and *moving* arises is provided, like for any other lexicalized metaphor, by the conventionality of language use. As the second part of the present chapter will try to demonstrate, the impact of language conventions upon intratextual associations is especially visible in those translations that do not pursue the aim of being true to the semantics of the original but rather furnish a similar net of associations that arise from the semantics – and conventions of use – offered by one's own language, thus reproducing the story of Alice as a language performance.

3. The world's moving faster: *the strategies of the figurative use and Alice's response to them*

In Chapter VI, Alice encounters a figure that, due to her extreme changeableness, differs markedly from any other character in the story, – the Duchess. Whereas in this chapter she appears as a militant, angry and impatient nurse, in Chapter IX Alice is astonished at her sudden affection, placableness, and even tenderness. Yet there are two qualities which the Duchess never ceases to demonstrate: the ugliness and the love of the figurative use. This love of metaphors is a powerful instinct which dominates her perception of the world. One of her first expressions, i.e. the addressing of the howling infant by "'Pig!'" may serve as illustration of this instinct in action. As already mentioned, she repeats this word in chapter IX expressing doubts about Alice's right of independent thinking. According to her, Alice has as much right to think as *pigs have to fly*, an expression which is based on the authority of the proverb: "Pigs may fly, but it's not likely." The proverb provides her with a generalization and serves as a moral which she tries to find in any statement pronounced in this chapter. Yet the same inclination is displayed by her already in Chapter VI:

> (Alice): "Oh, *please* mind what you're doing!... Oh, there goes his *precious* nose!"...
> "If everybody minded their own business," the Duchess said, in a hoarse growl, "the world would go round a deal faster than it does."
> "Which would *not* be an advantage," said Alice, who felt very glad to get an opportunity of showing off a little of her knowledge. "Just think what work it would make with the day and night! You see the earth takes twenty-four hours to turn round on its axis –"
> "Talking of axes," said the Duchess, "chop off her head!" (p. 63)

In terms of the tension between the literal and figurative uses, this conversation displays an almost perfect symmetry: Alice is worried about the baby's nose which could suffer from the flying saucepan. *Nose* is used by her in no other but literal sense. In her reply, the Duchess suggests that everyone should be concerned rather with one's own business and *not poke one's nose into* other people's affairs, implying the figurative use of the same word, which is immediately followed by another metaphor, i.e. *the world's going round faster*. Alice's interpretation of this expression is again based on the literal meaning of *the earth's daily trajectory*, to which the Duchess reacts by playing with the homophony of *axis* vs. *axes*. Thus, the literal and metaphorical in this episode may well receive a psychological interpretation, as corresponding with some prominent features of the characters. The literal is both lifesaving (Alice's worries about the baby) and naïve. The figurative uses of words are completely lost on her: she does not realize that it is her, Alice, whom the Duchess actually means by her expression and that the Duchess is absolutely not concerned about *the Earth's turns abound its axis*. On her part, the Duchess displays as little ability or willingness to understand the literal meanings of the words suggested by Alice. In this, she appears as an indifferent nurse, an unfriendly interlocutor and, lastly, due to an increasing demonstration of this last quality in the course of the story, – as an aggressive imitator of the Queen who is obsessed with flying heads.

In a number of episodes, the literal proves extremely useful for Alice as a means of argumentation. At the end of Chapter VI, e.g. she faces the dilemma of choosing to whom of the two mad figures she had better go, to the Hatter or to the March Hare, and she decides to go to the latter for the following reason: "the March Hare will be the much more interesting, and perhaps, as this is May, it wo'n't be raving mad..." (p. 69) Her argument is based on the idiom "mad as a March hare" which is again turned by Alice into the literal. Another similar case is provided in Chapter VIII, in an episode in which Alice tries to defend the Cheshire-Cat whose manners and looks the King highly dislikes:

> "A cat may look at a king," said Alice. "I've read that in some book, but I don't remember where." (p. 91)

By turning the proverb into the literal, Alice provides an argument in favor of the Cat's behavior. And once again the literal appears as a means of help, of defending or saving another character whom Alice believes to face an imminent danger, of overcoming rudeness and aggression with which she is continuously confronted along the way through Wonderland. The literal may therefore be regarded as her proper domain, both linguistically, as an element of which she demonstrates a perfect command, and psychologically, as a way to perceive the world and to act accordingly. For this reason, it seems hardly justified to interpret Alice's use of the proverb "A cat may look at a king" as Lecercle does in the following passage from his *The Violence of Language* (1990):

> There is no denying Alice's skill when, a few lines later, she quotes a proverb: 'A cat may look at a king.' A proverb is a good instance of a case when one utters words, but does not aim at their literal meaning – a sort of extended dead metaphor, which shows that language itself denies the postulate of sincerity. Unless of course we adopt Davidson's analysis of dead metaphors, and decide that the only meaning of the sentence is the metaphorical, or proverbial one: there are things an inferior may do in the presence of his superior. But this occurrence is the case *par excellence* when it is impossible to hold such a view, for the said inferior and superior are, on this (highly unlikely) occasion, precisely a cat and a king. This is the *best* use of the proverb, for it is the only one in which the literal meaning coincides with the figurative; and it is also the worst, for this coincidence precludes the generalization on which the proverb is based...There is in this an implicit judgement on Grice's view of language – exact literalness, or saying what one means, is no solution.[150]

150 Jean-Jacques Lecercle, *The Violence of Language*, London: Routledge 1990, pp. 251–252.

The remarkable thing about this piece of criticism is that, while pointing out the possibilities to interpret Alice's use of the proverb as both the best and the worst ones, it promptly rules out the first option by specifying it in brackets as "highly unlikely". Since, according to the critic, a situation like that in Wonderland in which a cat is literally confronted with a king is not really probable, the only way that remains to judge about Alice's words is the negative one, i.e. as a reproach for resorting to the literal as a barrier that eventually prevents the generalization suggested by the proverb. The critic thus does not seem to recognize that generalizations are rather in line with the psychology of the Duchess, rather than of Alice, and that, by contrast, the manner in which the heroine uses words and proverbs, i.e. turning them into the literal, displays a clear pragmatic pattern (to help, to defend, to comprehend, to exert oneself for others' sakes, etc.) In Carroll's text, this pattern is diametrically opposed to the one characteristic of figures who display a love of generalizations.

For the present analysis, Leclerce's above quotation appears meaningful for the following reasons: First, it is illustrative of the predominant and sometimes rather confusing state of *Alice*-research in which the relationship between the literal and the figurative is at least marginally mentioned. Second, in his critical examination, Lecercle draws on representatives of analytic philosophy (e.g. Davidson and Grice) who, being directly affected by the post-modern crisis of meaning, make semantics and pragmatics go their separate ways and thus exemplify a rather strange set of theories for approaching *Alice*.

Another reason to regard Lecercle's study on *Alice* as a rare and noteworthy work is for his combining two areas of research, i.e. literary criticism *and* analytic philosophy, and for discussing *Alice* within the frame of the post-modern theoretical discourse. Yet it is characteristic of Lecercle's studies in general that he only seldom comes to reflect upon the issue of the literal and figurative meaning. This may be explained by the fact that, in his opinion, *Alice* displays a deficit of the figurative meaning, which is one of the central ideas of his further monograph *Philosophy of Nonsense: The intuitions of Victorian nonsense literature* (1994). In this work, Lecercle considers one of the predominant features of nonsense literature that it systematically avoids the figurative use: "Indeed, nonsense texts seem to deploy complex and ingenious strategies in order to avoid metaphors."[151] One of these strategies is said to be based on a hierarchy of levels in which everything, including semantics, is dominated by syntax:

151 Jean-Jacques Lecercle, *Philosophy of Nonsense: The intuitions of Victorian nonsense literature*, London: Routledge 1994, p. 63.

> Nonsense texts spontaneously treat language as a hierarchy of levels, the most important among them is syntax – take care of the syntax and the rest of language will take care of itself. Before Chomsky, practitioners of nonsense had an intuitive awareness of the centrality of syntax...the essence of the attitude of nonsense towards language lies in the fact that they play one level against the other, so that a law of compensation operates. Excess always counterbalances lack, and semantic incoherence is cancelled by either semantic series, or syntactic hypercorrectness, or both.[152]

Whereas the hierarchy of levels which Lecerlce observes in nonsense literature results in his opinion in a deficit of the metaphorical, in the eyes of his colleague Angelika Zirker it is, on the contrary, the literal which is said to be missing in *Alice*. Yet the fact that in her essay "'Alice was not surprised': (Un)surprises in Lewis Carroll's *Alice*-Books" she comes to speak about this subject at all does not reflect her interest in the relationship between the literal and the figurative meanings but is rather due to her critical reaction to an essay by Virginia Woolf on *Alice* in which the literal is said to constitute the main distinguishing feature of this work[153]. Contrary to Woolf, Zirker is rather skeptical about the value of literalness in Carroll's aesthetics for the following reason: "Alice is only literal at the end of *Wonderland*, when she exclaims 'You're nothing but a pack of cards!'"[154] By this remarkable observation of Carroll's sparsity of literal use in designing Alice's linguistic behavior and psychology, she produces an idea which, methodologically, perfectly correlates with Lecercle's critical productions on Carroll's aesthetics (e.g. on the deficit of the figurative use of words) and it seems to be no coincidence that Lecercle highly praised scholarly qualities of Zirker's study in his review of it[155].

A further illustration of how confusing the relationship between the literal and figurative can prove for a literary critic is provided by a work by a Soviet specialist of Carroll, Nina Demurova's essay "O perevode skazok Kerrolla" ("On translating Carroll's fairy-tales"). While she repeatedly mentions numerous cases of the author's making the figurative turn into the literal, which, according to Demurova, corresponds to a markedly childish perception of the world in *Alice*, the only example which she draws on for this is the following episode from *Through the Looking Glass*:

152 Jean-Jacques Lecercle, *Philosophy of Nonsense*, p. 68.

153 For more details concerning this piece of English literary criticism, see Chapter "On the language of a child".

154 Angelika Zirker, "'Alice was not surprised': (Un)Surprises in Lewis Carroll's Alice-Books", in: *Connotations*, Vol. 14.1–3, 2004–2005, pp. 19–37, here p. 27.

155 Jean-Jacques Lecercle, Response to Angelika Zirker, "Alice was not surprised", in: *Connotations*, Vol. 17, 2007/2008, pp. 281–286.

"Would you – be good enough – to stop a minute – just to get a breath again?' "I am good enough", the King said, "only I'm not strong enough. You see, a minute goes by so fearfully quick. You might as well try to stop a Bandersnatch!"[156]

It does not seem correct to interpret this as a turn from the figurative into the literal. The source of the language play is here rather the use of the verb *to stop* as an intransitive (in Alice's use of it, i.e. meaning *to wait a minute*) and as a transitive one (in the King's use, i.e. meaning *to stop smth.*, e.g. a *clock, a train, a conversation.*) In other words, "to stop a minute" is here as metaphoric an expression as "to wait a minute" or to "sit down a moment." Correcting such a small detail in the critic's discussion of Carroll's language seems meaningful as in Demurova's opinion the literal use of words is in no way characteristic of Alice alone, distinguishing her from other figures in the text, but of the whole book, i.e. of a childish view of the world peculiar to the author himself. For this reason, in her own Russian translation of this passage, she makes Alice use an expression (*sest na minutku*, lit.: to sit down for a minute) which is interpreted by the King as a metaphor (lit: as sitting down *on* a minute) and then turned into the literal by replying to Alice that it would be impolite to minutes if someone wanted to sit down on them.[157] By this intricate rendering, the translator actually reverses the psychological perspective which Carroll applies to the linguistic behavior of his figures.

Different to Demurova, who, even if marginally, examines the relationship between the literal and the figurative meanings and does not get an impression of deficits peculiar to either of them, Lecercle's and Zirkel's studies illustrate how *Alice* becomes part of an academic discourse that is not unsimilar to that of the analytic philosophy of language, e.g. in refusing to recognize (or to accept) either the figurative or the literal on their own terms[158]. In these readings of Carroll, the meaning is effectively subsumed by spectacular theories of use, which results in continuous attempts to deduce the author's intentions and to adjust

156 Nina M. Demurova, "O perevode skazok Karrolla", in: *Ijulskij polden zolotoj: Statji ob anglijskoj detskoj knige*, Moskva: Izdatelstvo URAO 2000, pp. 87–123, here p. 88.

157 Nina Demurova, "O perevode skazok Kerrolla", p. 88.

158 Among the most thorough critical discussions of analytic philosophers' approach to the issue of the literal meaning, there are the essays produced by Mark Gaipa and Robert Scholes "On the Very Idea of a Literal Meaning" (1993) as well as by Marcelo Dascal "Defending Literal Meaning" (1987.) Gaipa and Scholes challenge the view, according to which meaning is to be deduced from a speaker's intentions rather than being based on semantical conventions. This is one of the very few works known to me in which the conventionality is directly defended against theorists like Davidson. Dascal's essay is dedicated primarily to the psychological reality of the literal meaning, among other things, in a child's appropriation of language, and will be discussed in more detail in the chapter "Through the Eyes of a Child."

the use of the words from the original to one's interpretation. Thus, Alice comes to be invested with a variety of rather disquieting properties, e.g. as *Circe*, *a tyrant*, *a usurper*, *personified myopia*, *a symbolical figure referring to the Eleusinian Mysteries* etc. As these interpretations regularly leave out of consideration the author's systematic play with the literal and the figurative, any questions concerning (dis) continuities between them are automatically overlooked. Yet however spectacular these acts of reading may appear and however strongly the emphasis of analytic philosophy may be put on separating semantics and pragmatics, Carroll's text never ceases to reveal a significant unity of these areas of linguistics.

IV.II

One of the first language adventures experienced by Alice in Chapter VI happens during her conversation with the footman in front of the entrance into the house of the Duchess. To Alice's question "'How am I to get in?,' the footman replies by "'*Are* you to get in at all?'" (p. 62) The words by which Alice reacts to this undisguised lack of politeness anticipate one of the central motives in the events to follow, i.e. madness: "'It's really dreadful,' she muttered to herself, 'the way all the creatures argue. It's enough to drive one crazy!'" (p. 62) The footman's phrase which so dreadfully irritates Alice contains a pun based on the polysemy of the verb *to be*: while, in Alice's question, the verb has the meaning of possibility, in the footman's use it refers rather to necessity with connotations of permission. For rendering this pun in other languages, the translator, as usually, has three options: One of them would be a search for a perfect corresponding word by which both the form and the idea could be captured exactly as in the original and no comment would be necessary to help the reader understand the passage. Another option would be to render the pun by semantical means that significantly differ from the original. And, finally, the most puzzling third way to approach the problem would result in a refusal both to remain true to the semantics of the original and to reproduce the pun by some polysemantic word taken from one's own language. Of all translations of *Alice* that I have studied, the first solution was chosen only by a few translators into German and these renditions are the closest to the original, e.g. A. Zimmermann's, p. 37: "Wie soll ich denn hineinkommen?" ("How am I to get in?") "Sollst du überhaupt hineinkommen?" ("Are you to get in at all?") The German verb *sollen* displays a similar polysemantic pattern of *to be* in English: referring to the first person, it suggests possibility, and, when applied to the second or to the third person, it has rather the semantics of necessity. The same solution is provided in the translation by C. Enzensberger (p. 60): "Wie soll ich hineinkommen?" – "*Sollst* du denn hineinkommen?"

Among those translators of the text into German, who decided to follow the second way, are, e.g. Kurt Hansen (p. 50) with the following rendition of the passage: "Wie soll ich hineinkommen?" – "*Musst* du denn überhaupt hinein?" While the question of Alice is translated exactly like in the versions of Zimmermann and Enzensberger, the footman's answer may be re-translated into English as "Do you have to get in at all?" For some reason, the translator refuses to repeat the same modal verb (*sollen*) which is used by Alice and renders *are you* in the footman's phrase by another modal verb *müssen*. Thus, the pun of the original gets lost. A large number of translators chose a similar strategy of translating this passage, e.g. Pietrocòla-Rossetti (pp. 77–78) who refused to reproduce the pun and instead used two different modal verbs *potere* (*to be able to*) and *dovere* (*must, have to*): "'Come potrei fare per entrar dentro?' … 'Dovrà ella entrare?'" A similar rendition into French was provided by Henri Bué (p. 82): "'Comment faire pour entrer?' – 'Mais devriez-vous entrer?" While nothing in these renditions suggests anything like the word play of Carroll that is based on the polysemy of an English verb, the semantics of possibility and necessity is truly reproduced, which is also the case with the Japanese version of Shōno Kōkichi 生野幸吉 (p. 86): 「どうやってはいればいいの?」–「そもそもあんた、はいらにゃならんのかい」.

However, the vast majority of translations chose the third option, i.e. not only in refusing to reproduce Carroll's pun but also by creating new semantical patterns that at times have nothing in common with the original. In most of these translations, the first occurrence of *to be* is reproduced correctly by a corresponding verb, yet its repetition by the footman proved to be quite challenging or tempting to be understood completely different to the original. Many translators reproduced this second occurrence of *to be* by a verb that implies Alice's volition, wish, intention as, e.g. Zhao Yuanren 赵元任 (p. 71) who reads the passage as: "你到底想不想进去，这是第一个问题呀！你可知道。" ("You know, the first question is whether or not you would like to enter.") Similarly to Zhao Yuanren, who uses here the verb *xiang* 想 (*to intend*), is the Chinese rendition of the phrase by Chen Fuan 陈复庵 (p. 83) who prefers here the modal verb *yao* 要 (*to wish*): "你到底要不要进去？" ("Do you want to enter or not?") By using the form *tai* たい which expresses the modality of volition, a similar rendition was produced by Tada Kōzō 多田幸蔵 in Japanese: "「「おまえさん、いったい、はいりたいのかね」" On his part, Seriu Hajime 芹生一 (p. 106) chose here a synonymous word *tsumori* つもり, referring again to the intention of Alice, rather than to a necessity suggested by Carroll's pun: "「あんたはいったい、はいるつもりかい」" ("Are you going to enter at all // Do you intend to enter?")

Of all the translations, the most distant from the original are those provided by V. Nabokov and N. Demurova. In Nabokov's version (pp. 50–51), Alice hears the following reply to her question: "Удастся ли вообще Вам войти?" ("Will you manage to get in at all?"), whereas Demurova (p. 158) makes the footman pronounce: "А стоит ли в него попадать?" ("Is it worthwhile getting in?") These choices are all the more peculiar, as distancing oneself from the original is by no means motivated by the linguistic picture of the world which would impede a correct reproduction of Carroll's pun in Russian, as, for example, is the case with the title of Walter Benjamin's essay "Die Aufgabe des Übersetzers" which poses an unsettling challenge for translators who, wishing to save the pun, would have to search for a rare word that, like in German, would mean both *task* and *surrender*. In spite of this challenge, Carroll's pun could be rendered in Russian quite simply, e.g. by playing with the category of aspect peculiar to Russian verbs: "Как мне войти?" – "А входить ли тебе туда вообще?" The aspect of the verb (perfective – suggesting possibility, imperfective – necessity) would provide a more or less exact equivalent for the word play in the original. Quite simple possibilities for rendering the pun can also be found in Chinese, e.g. by playing with different meanings of *ke* 可 in *ke(shi)* 可是 (*but, yet, however*) and *keyi* 可以 (*can/may/might*) in: "我可怎么进去？" "你可不可以进去？" The equivalence with the original would not be here as exact as in the use of Russian aspects, yet the play with words would be based like in *Alice* on a word's having more than one meaning. Zhu Haoyi's 朱浩一 (p. 78) version is actually quite close to this kind of solution and reads as follows: " '我要怎么样才能进去？' – '你应该先问，你可不可以进去？' " ("'How am I to get in?' – 'First, you should ask if you are allowed // if you may enter.'") Yet, though the footman's answer contains the *keyi* (*may/might*), no pun is produced here, as Alice does not use any word beginning with *ke*, which would secure a play of different meanings in the dialogue. Summing up, the question, why it was the third of the above mentioned options which proved so attractive to a large number of *Alice*-translators, cannot be answered by references to the impact imposed upon their thinking by their language structures. Distancing themselves from the original in rendering this particular episode may be rather due to a flight of fantasy to which they felt inspired by Carroll's language, which once again resulted in significant extensions of the *Alice*-plot in their versions.

Trying to judge about the quality of a translation and saying that some of them are closer to the original than some others, may appear presumptuous. Yet the present study departs from the conviction that *Alice* is not an *opera aperta* and that for its interpreters it should be possible to share at least a rough consensus concerning the regularity with which Carroll designed the development of his plot as well as the psychology of the figures. For example, in the above mentioned conversation between Alice and the footman, this regularity is expressed in a figure's desire to use polysemy in order to confuse Alice. This belongs among the psychological paradigm of snubbing which is shared by numerous characters in the book, e.g. by the King referring to his inability to stop a minute. Yet as soon as the episode is rendered by semantical patterns that differ from that of the original, e.g. in Zhao Yuanren's "Do you want to get in?" or in Demurova's "Is it worthwhile getting in?", the episode ceases to represent this paradigm: the footman's words do not characterize him as a dismissive, confusing, or indifferent interlocutor, but, on the contrary, as a figure that is sympathetically listening to Alice and is concerned about what steps she is going to make next. Thus, differences in semantics result in immediate changes of psychological portraits.

Nowhere does the translators' attention to the psychology in the plot development appear visually as sharp as in the art to reproduce the chains of associations which traverse the text. The interplay of the figurative and the literal which was discussed in the first part of this chapter may be regarded as one of the most significant elements by which these associations are shaped. Therefore an examination of whether or not a translation suggests at least some of these intratextual links of the original seems to be one of the criteria to judge about its quality. For example, one of the central events in Chapter VI is the transformation of a baby into a pig. In languages which allow that a person who does not behave (the motif of sneezing and howling) can be addressed as a *pig* (the form used by the Duchess), it is much easier to reproduce associations between this figurative use of the word and a literal *pig* into which the baby eventually transforms in Alice's arms, than in languages displaying different conventions of using the word. Thus, in German, Russian, Italian, and French reproducing the corresponding associations is much easier, than, e.g. in Chinese and Japanese. In this particular aspect, the impact of the linguistic picture of the world is much more prominent than in rendering two distinct meanings of *to be* in the conversation between Alice and the footman. However, even in German or Russian versions of *Alice*, it is by no means always the case that the figurative meaning of "Pig!" is reproduced or that any importance of this form of address for the development of the plot is made visible for the reader. Among the German translations which I know, there are only two versions that provide an explicit motivation of this figurative address of the baby by the Duchess in the lullaby, – the translations of Barbara Teutsch (1989) and of Charlotte Strech-Ballot (1949). Barbara Teutsch (pp. 65–66) renders the lullaby as follows:

"Schlafe, mein Prinzchen, schlaf ein,
Sonst haue ich dir eine rein!

Du weißt genau, wenn du niest,
Wie das die Mutter verdrießt!
Schlafe, mein Ferkel, schlaf ein!"
(die Köchin, das Baby im Chor: "Rabäh! Rabäh! Rabäh!")

"Schlaf jetzt, du Niesferkel mein,
Sonst haue ich dir eine rein!
Stets hast du Pfeffer vertragen,
Aus Trotz nur willst du mich plagen!
Schlaf endlich, Ferkel, schlaf ein!"

In this version of the song, the word *pig* is repeatedly used by the Duchess in a figurative meaning (*mein Ferkel – my pig(gy)*, *du Niesferkel mein – you, my sneezing pig(gy)*), which emphasizes the address form used in the original and which considerably facilitates the readers' construction of corresponding chains of associations that accompany the baby's later transformation into a real pig. In her rendition, Charlotte Strech-Ballot (p. 42) proceeded similarly, making the Duchess compare the baby with a pig in her lullaby: "Schlaf, Kindchen, fein! Siehst aus wie'n kleines Schwein! Wenn du nicht hörst zu niesen auf, Schlag ich dir feste hinten drauf!" ("Sleep my baby, sleep fine! You look just like a little pig! If you don't finish sneezing, I'll give you a good beating on your back!") Both of these translations represent clear cases of transforming the original story, as in Carroll's text the lullaby does not contain any references to the image of a pig. The rest of the German translations which I consulted do not have any additions of this kind and their readers, like the readers of most French, Italian and Russian versions of *Alice*, are provided with no supplementary cues emphasizing the association between the Duchess' address of the baby and its eventual metamorphosis. Yet to recognize this intratextual connection should not be a difficult task for them, since all of these languages are quite familiar with the semantical convention of using the word *pig* both literally and in the figurative (pejorative) meaning. Quite different are the semantical conventions of using the corresponding words in Chinese (*zhu* 猪, *zhuluo* 猪猡) and Japanese (*buta* 豚[159]). In these languages, it is hardly conceivable that a baby be called *a pig* for sneezing and howling. Although in Chinese, the word *zhuluo* can be used pejoratively, it can refer

159 The pejorative use of *buta* when referring to corpulent people (cf. *fatty* in English) is not relevant here, since nothing in *Alice* suggests this meaning.

in this meaning only to adults as a reproach for their lack of cultivation or for having committed a serious offense. Nevertheless in most Chinese and Japanese versions the address of the Duchess ("Pig!", e.g. by Zhao Yuanren, p. 73: *ni zhe zhu* 你这猪, Zhu Haoyi, p. 79: *zhu* 猪, Ma Teng, p. 52: *zhu* 猪, Chen Fuan, p. 85: *zhu* 猪, Seriu Hajime, p. 109: *kono buta* このブタ, Tada Kōzō, p. 74: *buta* 豚!) is not supplied with any commentary, which makes it difficult for their readers to recognize any logical connection between the episodes referring to pigs in Chapter VI, i.e. to see the sense of the transformation from the figurative into the literal in Carroll's text[160].

One of the theses discussed in the theoretical part of this chapter was related to the psychological motivation of the figurative and literal meanings which, among other things, may be observed in the way of acting and speaking peculiar to Alice whose element is that of the literal, or in that characteristic of the Duchess, who, by contrast, shows quite a weakness for the figurative, e.g. in the following dialogue: "'Oh, there goes his *precious* nose!'" – "'If everybody minded their own business, the world would go round a deal faster than it does!'" – "Which would not be an advantage…Just think what work it would make with the day and night!"[161] The words of the Duchess mean that it is not correct to poke one's nose into other people's affairs: while she does not use the word *nose* directly, it is suggested by the semantical pattern of the English expression *to mind one's own business* and, as a figurative use, it matches perfectly the literal use of the same word (*nose*) by Alice. The award which, according to the Duchess, would be warranted if everybody minded their own business is also expressed metaphorically, i.e. "the world would go round a deal faster." Thus, the figurative uses of words by the Duchess are framed by two literary uses of the same words by Alice: the baby's nose and the rotations of the Earth. A true rendition of the psychological motivation of these linguistic happenings confronts the translators with difficulties which are similar to reproducing associations that accompany the noun *pig*: two images are needed that would correspond to the idea of a nose which should not be too long as well as for the world which goes round smoothly. In this case, again, the rendition proved especially challenging

160 A detailed examination of the abusive language in the history of Chinese culture is provided by Liu Fugen 刘福根 in his *Hanyu lici yanjiu* 汉语詈词研究 (*A Study of the Abusive Language in Chinese*, 2008.) One of the central groups of words analyzed in this monograph represents figurative expressions in which humans are referred to as animals, among other things, as *pigs*, for lacking cultivation, e.g. in *zhu gou bu ru* 猪狗不如 (*worse than pigs and dogs*) and *fengshi* 封豕 (*a thick boar, a covetous person*). Similarly to calling someone a *barbar*, these expressions can only be applied to adults, i.e. people, who are expected to display civilized behavior, rather than to babies, see Liu Fugen, esp. pp. 144 ff.

161 *Alice*, p. 63.

for translators into Chinese and Japanese. In Chinese, the figurative use of *a long nose* (*dabizi*大鼻子) is, e.g. common when depreciatingly referring to the Westerners (and, by contrast, *a short nose* (*xiaobizi*小鼻子) – when referring to the Japanese), yet when it is needed to say that someone should not interfere, it is not the image of a *nose*, but rather that of a *hand* (*shou* 手) which comes to mind of a speaker of Chinese in the corresponding idiom 插手 *chashou* (lit.: *to poke one's hand*), and for a Japanese speaker it is a *head* (*kubi* 首) which is used figuratively in the *kubi wo tsukkomu* 首を突っ込む (lit.: *to poke one's head into smth.*) The easiest option is, as always, to provide a literal translation of the passage without encumbering oneself with a search for a fitting image, which is, e.g. the case with Ma Teng's version (p. 57): "如果世界上的每一个人都关心自己的事" (lit.: "If everybody in the world minded their own business") and with that provided by Chen Fuan (p. 87): "要是人人留神自己的事" (lit.: "If everybody took care of their own business.") Both translators provide a rendering which is close to the original, yet in neither of them could the reader perceive anything reminiscent of those regular semantic moves from the literal to the figurative that mark the language of the original.

Translators into languages that offer direct semantical equivalents for the English *to poke// to stick one's nose into smth.*, choose different strategies in rendering the dialogue. Since using such direct expressions is not at all necessary to evoke corresponding associations in the readers' minds (in the original, this expression is not used either), most renditions refrain from any additional means to emphasize these associations, e.g. in the version by Zimmermann (p. 40): "Wenn jeder nur vor der eigenen Tür fegen wollte..." ("If everybody swept the floor at their own doors") and that by Enzensberger (p. 62): "Wenn jeder in seinen eigenen Suppentopf schauen wollte" ("If everybody were looking into the soup in their own pots.") Neither of these renditions contains any direct correspondence to the *nose* which is literally used by Alice and then figuratively suggested by the words of the Duchess. Yet while applying German expressions which – in contrast to the above mentioned Chinese renditions of the phrase – are markedly different to the one used in the original, the associations which are evoked by them in the consciousness of German readers are exactly like those in the English original: the Duchess is thus reproduced as obstinately sticking to the figurative, which is among her major characteristics in Carroll's design.

Another strategy is represented by Nabokov (p. 52) and Demurova (p. 160) who put additional emphasis on the association by making the Duchess pronounce a verb that, in Russian, is commonly used as a figurative expression for someone's poking one's nose into other people's affairs: *соваться* (*to poke / to stick*) cf. *совать свой нос* (*to poke one's nose*). And still another strategy was chosen by Zachoder (p. 72) whose rendition is the only one that I could find in which the association is directly reconstructed: "Если бы никто не совал носа в чужие дела, мир завертелся бы куда быстрей, чем сейчас." ("If nobody poked the nose into other people's affairs, the world would go round much faster than now.") In this version, the translator does not only follow the logic of Carroll's language design, but goes one step further and lets the Duchess counter Alice's literal use of an expression by a direct repetition of it in the figurative meaning. Finally, quite an opposite way of rendering the relationship between the literal and figurative meanings (and, by doing so, the psychology of the characters participating in the dialogue), may be illustrated by the Russian version produced by Ščerbakov (p.81): "Если бы каждый начал думать, что делает.., – все вокруг завертелось бы только держись!" ("If everyone were thinking what they are doing, the world would go round a good deal faster!") In this interpretation, the words of the Duchess refer to the violent behavior of the cook rather than to Alice. By this sudden shift of attention to the cook whose actions, by the way, are being completely ignored by the Duchess in the original ("The Duchess took no notice of them..."[162]), the translator openly refuses to provide even the slightest correspondence to the semantical shifts between the literal and figurative in Carroll's story.

There is probably no other passage in the book in which translators display so much unanimity as in rendering the flight of the saucepan that nearly costs the baby its nose: "an unusually large saucepan flew close by it." (p. 63) Versions in which, for some reason, the semantics of *flying* is not reproduced directly, like those by Zimmermann (p. 39) and Enzensberger (p. 62) who respectively used the verbs *vorbeifuhr* (*passed by*) and *flitzte* (*dashed*), represent rather rare cases. In contrast, most translators provided exact equivalents of the verb *to fly*, e.g. Tada Kōzō (p. 75): *tonde* 飛んで, Seriyu Hajime (p. 110): *tonde kite* とんできて, Zhao Yuanren (p. 75): *fei guo* 飞过, Zhu Haoyi (p. 80): *fei* 飞, Chen Fuan (p. 87): *fei guo* 飞过, Kurt Hansen (p. 53): *vorüberflog*, Henri Bué (p. 86): *venait de voler*, T. Pietrocòla-Rossetti (p. 81): *volò vicino*, Demurova (p. 160): *proletelo* пролетело. From the point of view of intratextual associations which persist between all flying objects and figures in Carroll's text, special attention deserve the rather numerous cases in which the translators proceeded like Zachoder in his above mentioned rendition of the dialogue between Alice and the Duchess, i.e. not only following the original, but going one step further and densifying the *flight* semantics by using it more frequently than in the original. For example, in the original, the flight of the saucepan is anticipated by a number of other equally flying kitchen utensils, yet Carroll did not use the same verb (*to fly*) to refer to them: "the fire-irons

162 *Alice*, p. 63.

came first; then followed a shower (sic) of saucepans, plates, and dishes" (p. 63.) In many translations, the verbs from this passage have been rendered by semantic equivalents of *to fly*, e.g. in the versions of Solovjova (p. 93): "сначала полетел ухват" ("the fire-irons flew first"), bei Tada Kōzō (p. 75): まっさきに火箸がとんできました。("the fire-irons flew first"), T. Pietrocòla-Rossetti (p. 81): "pria volarono le molle" ("the fire-irons flew first.") A back translation of the phrase from languages that are as dissimilar as these ones yields the same wording in English, which may be interpreted as a sign of a deep congeniality shared by the translators and of a close attention to the logic of Carroll's language.

In a number of translations, semantics of *flying* was also significantly densified in other episodes that were discussed in the theoretical part of this chapter, e.g. in the kitchen scene in which the Duchess takes leave of her baby as follows: "'Here! You may nurse it a bit, if you like!' the Duchess said to Alice, flinging the baby at her as she spoke."[163] In his version, Ščerbakov (p. 81) makes the baby that is entrusted to Alice *fly* to her: "'На! Хочешь – понянчи!' – И младенец полетел на руки к Алисе." ("'Here, nurse it, if you like!' – and the baby flew into Alice's arms.") The baby's movement thus exactly repeats the flight of the saucepan launched by the cook's hand, which emphasizes the affinities in the psychology of the Duchess and the cook: both of them are violent and, as Alice immediately recognizes it, both represent serious dangers for the baby that she finally decides to save by carrying it away.

As already mentioned, Carroll creates regular connections between the semantics of *flying* and actions that various figures are forced to perform by others, i.e. in *Alice*, *a flight* is as a rule conceived in the figurative sense and represents an image which refers both to someone who actively participates in the plot and to a figure that immediately suffers from these actions. Thus, any flight is primarily understood as dangerous and, by densifying the figurative use of the corresponding semantics of *flying* in their renditions, the translators laid additional emphasis on this regular linguo-psychological characteristic of the *Alice*-books, e.g. in Ščerbakov's version, the flight of the baby underscores its inability to resist the actions of its violent nurse.

In this rendition, the impact of the language on the development of the plot perfectly complies with the logic of the original, although the translator consciously makes use of an expression which is different to Carroll's text. Similar examples can be provided also for the episode in which Bill the Lizard is catapulted by Alice from the chimney in the Rabbit's house. In his description of this scene, Carroll refers to the reaction of Bill's comrades, who observe what is happening, by the exclamation: "There goes Bill!" (p. 44) He does not use here any

163 *Alice*, p. 64.

words from the semantical field of *flying* and in the whole episode there is only one expression directly referring to this field, namely, "like a sky-rocket". In Zachoder's translation (p. 60), the exclamation made by Bill's comrades is rendered by a repeated use of the verb *to fly*: "Эй, Билль летит! Летит!" ("Look, Bill is flying! Flying!") This Russian version expresses a profound admiration for Bill's capacity to fly. Other renditions, in which Bill is explicitly referred to as flying, have been provided by Ma Teng (p. 33): "快看，比尔飞出来了！" ("Look, Bill has flown out!"), by Zhu Haoyi (p. 54), who rendered the phrase exactly as Ma Teng; by Enzensberger (p. 43): "Da fliegt Egon!" ("Look there, Egon is flying!") As for Bill's report about what has just happened to it in the episode, many translators also preferred here an explicit use of the semantics of *flying*, as, e.g. Zhao Yuanren (p. 49): "我就像个旗花似的飞上去嘞！" ("I flew upwards like a sky-rocket!") as well as Ma Teng (p. 33): "我就被撞得像火箭一样飞了出来！" ("I was kicked out and flew like a sky-rocket!")

In Zachoder's version, the semantics of *flying* is further extended in Chapter XII, in the trial-episode in which Carroll's play with mutual transformations of the figurative and the literal meanings represents an important event in the development of the plot. The phrase "Alice jumped up,…upsetting all the jurymen on to the heads of the crowd below…"[164] is rendered by Zachoder (p. 109) as follows: "Все присяжные полетели вверх тормашками на головы публики." ("All the jurymen flew upside down on to the heads of the crowd.") The verb *poleteli* (*flew*) (again, used figuratively with the usual unpleasant connotations characteristic of the language psychology throughout the story) corresponds here to the English *upsetting*, a word, which in this phrase is used literally and shortly later turns into the figurative. As already mentioned, this particular instance of turning a literal meaning onto a figurative one is suggested by the following description of Bill the Lizard, who is among the jurymen upset by Alice's shirt: "(Bill) was waving its tail about in a melancholy way"[165]; "too overcome to do anything but sit with its mouth open."[166]

Translators who pay careful attention to the relationship between the literal and figurative search for semantical means in one's own language by which it could be recreated and made comprehensible to the reader. For example, Solovjova (p. 174) found the following solution for the complicated task of rendering the interplay between the literal and metaphoric in the trial-episode: In her translation, "Одна только Ящерица была слишком потрясена, чтобы что-нибудь делать…" ("except for the Lizard, who was too overcome to do anything…"), the

164 *Alice*, p. 123.
165 *Alice*, p. 123.
166 *Alice*, p. 124.

word *overcome* is rendered by the Russian *potrjasena*, which has both the literal meaning *shaken* and the figurative *shaken=overwhelmed* and therefore fits precisely into the semantical pattern of the English *upset* as well as into its realization in Carroll's plot design. The translator's choice of the word completely relies on the conventionality of its semantics in Russian. Nevertheless, due to the perfect closeness to both the literal and figurative meanings in the language of the original, it represents an individual linguistic discovery, i.e. an unforeseen happy result of an intensive search within an immense quantity of material in the target-language semantics. In Nabolov's (p. 107) as well as in Ščerbakov's (p. 145) versions that were published at a later date, the passage reads exactly like in the text by Solovjova. On the other hand, Demurova refrains from reproducing Carroll's semantical play and provides a verbal portrayal of Bill, e.g. in the phrase "сидел неподвижно" (p. 252) ("was sitting without moving"), which does not remotely suggest any similarity with the interplay of the literal and the figurative in Carroll's use of the participle *overcome*. Among other versions which display a refusal to reproduce this interplay, there it the Italian one provided by Pietrocòla-Rossetti (p. 174: "la Lucertola che non s'era riavuta" ("the Lizard that had not come to itself yet")). Yet this apparent act of a translator's capitulation before the original cannot be explained in terms of insurmountable obstacles imposed upon him by his language: as is the case with the above discussed Russian renditions of the passage, Italian also offers happy findings for those who share Carroll's delight at playing with literal and figurative meanings, which may be illustrated by the version by Oddera (p. 110): "il Lucertolino, che sembrava... troppo scosso" ("the little Lizard that seemed too overcome"). Like *potrjasena* in Russian, *scosso* in Italian combines the literal (*shaken*) and the figurative (*shaken=overwhelmed*) meanings which are quite close to *overcome* in the original. Here, again, the linguistic discovery of the translator is a product of both his personal sharp intuition and of the semantical conventions shared by him with his language community: he does not invent anything new, nor does the Italian reader have to deduce anything from his intentions in order to recognize the perfectly clear semantical pattern of the participle *scosso*. Thus, a search for a correct expression in the translation act may be regarded as successful, when it not only reproduces the semantics of separate words from the original but also the association chains that these words set off in the reader's mind. The Russian and the Italian renditions of *overcome* provided by Velingerova and by Oddera seem to be especially felicious exactly for this reason, as they do not make these associations disappear.

Finally, one particular scene from Chapter VI should once again be mentioned here in order to make the power of the linguistic picture of the world appear with visual sharpness. It is a scene from the kitchen in the house of the Duchess in which the cook's eccentric behavior is introduced by quite an unspectacular reference to her "stirring a large cauldron which seemed to be full of soup[167]". Due to the semantical conventions in English, the cook might be thought of as *stirring* not only literally, as introduced here by Carroll, but also in the figurative meaning (as close to *moving*, *exciting*, *inspiring*, etc.) Although the attribute *stirring* does not suit the psychological portrait of the cook and for this reason would be more or less automatically discarded by the interpreter, this act of discarding the figurative meaning is a reaction to an option with which the language inevitably confronts the readers, i.e. in carefully observing all the numerous metamorphoses of the literal and figurative meanings as one of the major sources of wonders in Carroll's text, in this particular case, they would also have to decide whether or not the figurative meaning fits the character as much as the literal does. And again, there is nothing deductive, subjectivistic or fantastic about this option which arises from semantical conventions in English as naturally as the participle *rührend* does in German or *roerend* – in Dutch, both revealing a similar semantical pattern of literal (*stirring (the soup)*) and figurative (*stirring=exciting*, *moving*) meanings.

However, a corresponding way to reproduce this option is not in every language as easily to find as in German and Dutch. For example, in Japanese, there are various expressions for the figurative meaning of *stirring* in English, such as *kandouteki* (感動的), *kangaibukai* (感慨深い), *namidagumashii* (涙ぐましい), *isamashii* (勇ましい), *horotto* (ほろっと), etc. Yet none of these words has anything in common with the literal meaning of *to stir*. Consider the following rendition of the passage by Shōno Kōkichi (p. 87): "Ryorionna wa ōkina nabe wo kakimazeteimashita." "料理女は大きななべをかきまぜていました。" ("The cook was stirring a large cauldron.") No Japanese reader would ever consider the (im) possibility of associating the verb *kakimazeru* by which the verb *to stir* is translated in this version with qualities suggested by the figurative meaning of *stirring* in English or by any of its various Japanese equivalents. Somewhat different is the situation with the Russian *trogatel'nyj* (*трогательный* = the figurative meaning of *touching* by the transfer of *trogat трогать* (*to touch*) to psychological semantics): this word cannot be regarded as a perfect correspondence to *touching* (or *stirring*, *moving* in English), because it is an adjective, and not a participle. A formally corresponding word would rather be *trogajushij* (*трогающий*, lit.: *touching*), yet this is only a formal correspondence, since this participle is never used in Russian to refer to qualities suggested by the figurative use of *stirring* in English. This is a telling example of the power pertaining to the linguistic vision of the world: although, in the English original, the cook is introduced as literal-

167 *Alice*, p. 62.

ly *moving*, *touching* and *stirring* everything within her reach, it is only the literal meaning of these words in English that the reader would be likely to accept as fitting the cook's way to behave, i.e. as directly referring to actions she performs. Since her character is rather diametrically opposed to qualities associated with someone who is "moving, touching and stirring", the figurative meaning of these expressions would promptly be discarded by the reader. Yet a direct reproduction of this interplay of the literal and figurative can only be found in those versions of *Alice* that strictly follow the semantical patterns of the original, e.g. in Zimmermann's (p. 37): "(die Köchin) rührte in einer großen Kasserolle", in Hansen's (p. 50) "(die Köchin) rührte in einem großen Kessel" or in Enzensberger's (p. 61): "(die Köchin) rührte in einem großen Kessel", all of them meaning: "The cook was stirring a large cauldron."

What appears particularly remarkable about these last illustrations is a perfect correspondence of the translated text to the language of the original and to the association chains which are reproduced almost automatically. In fact, no time-consuming search was needed in order to provide an adequate expression for *stirring*. By contrast, in languages that do not offer such direct parallels, not even a most exhausting search could guarantee a felicitous rendition: translators are either forced to give up the task of reproducing the associations altogether, or must come up with images and associations which are new to the original. Yet even by making the reader follow a train of associations which are new to Carroll's text, they occasionally provide unexpected new correspondencies to the language and the psychology of the story, as, e.g. Zachoder (p. 71, *помешивала*) and Ščerbakov (p. 80, *помешивая*) did, in rendering *stirring* by a semantically close Russian verb *pomešivat* (*помешивать*, lit.: *to stir slowly*) that can easily evoke in the reader's consciousness the association with *being mad*, a quite common figurative meaning of the participle *помешанная* of this verb (*pomeshannaja = crazy, mad*). This may also count as an individual discovery, fitting both the regularity in Carroll's switches between the literal and figurative and the psychology of the respective character (the cook). Yet, again, the discovery does not represent a creation of some new word meaning which the readers should be able to deduce from the translators' intentions and rests entirely on semantical conventions that the translators share with the rest of their language community.

Conclusion

Ironically, it was Carroll, a classic of nonsense literature who demonstrated maybe better than any other author to the world what a significant role language conventions play for ordinary and aesthetic communication. If, for example, in Chapter III, the Mouse tries to convince everybody that, after swimming in the pool of tears, its story would make all of them dry, by saying this, it actually anticipates one of the key theses of the language philosophy of Donald Davidson. Both the Mouse and Davidson, namely, share the idea that there is no significant distinction between metaphorical and literal meanings. And, again similarly to Davidson, the Mouse attempts to neutralize the discontinuity between the literal and the figurative in the language perception of its listeners. That it does not succeed in achieving this goal is clearly demonstrated by Alice's frank response to the question as to how she feels after hearing its story: "As wet as ever, it doesn't seem to dry me at all."[168] Alice's feeling *as wet as ever* is in turn a personal direct experience of the discontinuity between the literal and figurative meanings, i.e. of a linguistic phenomenon that is a most vital ingredient within Carroll's plot. A similar enactment of the tension between the figurative and literal which, however, results in a completely different direct experience of a word's meanings, happens in Chapter VI, when Alice witnesses how a baby that is addressed by the Duchess – figuratively – as "Pig!" eventually turns into a pig in the literal sense. This particular wonder also closely follows language conventions associated with both the figurative and literal meanings. Hence, the journey through Wonderland is designed as a way following which even the most familiar aspects of one's mother tongue suddenly turn into a set of adventures.

Translators who seek to be congenial with Carroll and follow his use of language have to perform the same magical act: their versions of *Alice* testify to a re-discovery of one's own language and to an experience of what might at first sight appear as trite and unspectacular as a sudden miracle. Every time, these miracles refer the reader back to things within one's reach, every discovery is based on what he/she is completely familiar with and for this reason the whole story as well as all the felicitous renditions of it may be compared with the pivotal event in another classic of world literature, i.e. Maurice Maeterlinck's *L'oiseau bleu*: the awareness of real wonders being close at hand.

168 *Alice*, p. 31.

V. The Philosophers' *Alice*

V.I

Among the strangest and most disagreeable situations experienced by Alice in Wonderland are the moments in which she suddenly becomes unable to recite correctly the poems that in her normal life she knew perfectly well, e.g. in Chapter II "The Pool of Tears" when she has to admit to herself that the words do not come "the same way as they used to do"[169] and refer to a strange lazy crocodile and not, as they would be expected, to the busy bee from one of the poems she once learned. Unable to explain, what is happening to her, Alice's first idea is that she may have changed into somebody else, since being herself she could never have *meant* anything similar to what she has just *said*. The conceptual relationship between *meaning* and *saying* belongs to the recurrent motives of Carroll's book and one of the related episodes from Chapter VII contains a passage which has proven especially attractive for philosophers. Before turning to discuss the reasons why this particular passage has inspired a great number of scholars to the compilation of philosophical commentaries, it should be remembered that the above mentioned situation in which Alice is going through a kind of self-estrangement is anything but usual for her. Although this experience confronts her with one of the most fundamental questions of philosophy – "Who am I?" – and the strange unexplainable words she has just produced may be interpreted as originating from a source of profound wisdom, she usually feels completely at home in her language. This is demonstrated by her even in those rare cases in which she intentionally tries to conceal what she means, for example, in an episode from Chapter VIII when she evades giving an honest answer to the Cat's question how she likes the Queen and says: "'Not at all,' said Alice: 'she's so extremely –' Just then she noticed that the Queen was close behind her, listening: so, she went on 'likely to win, that it's hardly worth while finishing the game.'"[170] As in situations in which Alice instinctively relies on her language to help other figures, e.g. the baby in Chapter VI ("Oh, *please* mind what you're doing!"[171]) or the Cat in Chapter VIII ("A cat may look at a king."[172]), here, the language again appears as a means of protection: having quickly changed her mind and decided not to say what she actually thinks about the Queen, Alice

169 *Alice*, p. 23.
170 *Alice*, p. 90.
171 *Alice*, p. 63.
172 *Alice*, p. 91.

escapes the danger of offending the Queen who is standing behind and listening to the conversation. Yet there can be no doubt that in spite of her cautious reply nothing has changed about her real attitude to the Queen, i.e. about the way to *think* about her which this time Alice decides not to unveil by her words. This is an example of rather rare situations in which Alice has to say something different to what she really means. By contrast, much more often are the cases in which she appears too rash with her words, as, e.g. in an episode from Chapter V in which she does not hesitate to openly admit to the Pigeon that like any other little girl she has already tasted eggs: "'I *have* tasted eggs certainly,' said Alice who was a very truthful child..."[173] Even though in this case it may have been not particularly clever to make this confession which causes the communication to fail, the most prominent feature emphasized here by the author is Alice's truthfulness. This predicate explicitly refers to Alice's language behavior and it seems to be one of the general ideas of the *Alice*-books that in itself language is never reflected in them as something misleading, repellent, deceptive, or illogical. Similar qualities are never presented as pertaining to language itself, but rather to the language behavior of the respective figures, e.g. the hysterical language of the Queen, the twisted language of the Duchess, the verbal arbitrariness of the Mock Turtle, the arrogant way to speak characteristic of the Caterpillar, etc. That language does not appear as an abstract subject either of a criticism or of a defense may also be demonstrated on the example of the above mentioned passage from Chapter VII:

> "Do you mean that you think you can find out the answer to it?" said the March Hare.
> "Exactly so," said Alice.
> "Then you should say what you mean," the March Hare went on.
> "I do," Alice hastily replied; "at least – at least I mean what I say – that's the same thing, you know."
> "Not the same thing a bit!" said the Hatter. "Why, you might just as well say that 'I see what I eat' is the same thing as 'I eat what I see'!"
> "You might just as well say," added the March Hare, "that 'I like what I get' is the same thing as 'I get what I like'!"
> "You might just as well say," added the Dormouse, which seemed to be talking in its sleep, "that 'I breathe when I sleep' is the same thing as 'I sleep when I breathe'!"
> "It *is* the same thing with you," said the Hatter, and here the conversation dropped...[174]

173 *Alice*, p. 57.
174 *Alice*, pp. 73–74.

The interpretation which I would like to propose for this conversation is based on the pragmatics of the figurative and the literal as well as on the psychology of the related figures. I believe that Alice's statement does not contain any logical mistake. Except for the rare cases like the one mentioned above in which she is not the master of her own words or whenever she resorts to language as a means of self-protection, she normally says what she means and means what she says. As is remarked by the author, truthfulness is one of characteristic features of Alice's language, and the above conversation at the Mad Tea party is but a new demonstration of this particular quality: the words "I mean what I say" express the same idea as "I say what I mean" when taken literally to mean no more or no less than "I am honest." By contrast, the Hatter and the March Hare confront her with two statements that may be interpreted as figurative ones, i.e. as forms of expression with which Alice shows the greatest difficulties of understanding throughout the story. The phrase "I eat what I see" can by all means express the same idea as "I see what I eat", when it is understood metaphorically as referring to someone who is voracious (ravenous, greedy, insatiable.) Similarly, the phrase produced by the March Hare may also be understood in the figurative sense: referring to a possessive person, "I get what I like" would mean roughly the same as "I like what I get." On the contrary, the concluding proposition produced by the Dormouse does not contain any transfer of meaning and its validity is not accepted by the Hatter exactly for this reason, i.e. for being literal: referring to the Dormouse, "breathing when sleeping" does literally mean the same as "sleeping when breathing." Although the story does not provide details concerning the Hatter's voraciousness and the March Hare's possessiveness[175], the propositions made by them in order to confound Alice are argumentatively not strong enough to prove that her own statement is logically incorrect. They only attest to a discontinuity between the literal and the figurative which is used as an effective rhetorical means. Thus, in terms of the relation between the literal and the metaphorical, the conversation may be regarded as perfectly symmetrical and as fitting the formula A (the literal) is to B (the figurative) as D (the literal) is to C (the figurative.)

175 A fitting illustration of the possibility to read the utterance of the Hatter as a metaphorical one is provided by Francis Huxley in his *The Raven and the Writing Desk*, London: Thames and Hudson (1976) in which this reading becomes part of a minute reconstruction of a possible answer to the riddle posed by the Hatter ("Why is a raven like a writing-desk?", p. 73.) Huxley, *op. cit.*, p. 41: "...as the Trial scene has to do with Who Stole the Tarts, we shall permit ourselves to extend the meaning of *raven* into *ravenous*, which the Hatter must have been if tea was his only meal. Having done so, the meaning of 'I eat what I see' must be looked for on the writing-desk, where it might well appear as the old adage that to study is to read, mark, learn and inwardly digest."

The only problematic thing about Alice's words which is quickly recognized by her interlocutors as an opportunity to confound her is the conclusion of her thought: "that's the same thing you know." By saying this, she does not seem to take into account that truthfulness which she herself so often displays throughout the story does not belong among universal human qualities. Neither truthfulness nor greed nor possessiveness is universal and for this reason the conclusion (and only the conclusion) at which she arrives in the end may be seen as deserving criticism. However, not even this point of critique would completely be justified, for it is not at all clear that by these words Alice intends a generalizing statement. And if she did, her attitude should not necessarily be met with criticism, since learning that honesty and humanity cannot be expected of everyone usually results from some of the most dramatic experiences in man's life[176] and it is only towards the end of her journey through Wonderland that Alice becomes fully conscious of this as well. However, as already mentioned, it is not evident that Alice intends to produce a statement which would have universal validity. I believe, her words refer rather personally to herself and, if this is the case, they deserve neither critique nor justification.

Yet this is exactly the point which inspired a number of philosophically minded readers to comment on Alice's faultiness and to seek remedies by which her errors could be corrected. Consider the following reflections on the passage produced by Roger W. Holmes in his essay "The Philosopher's *Alice in Wonderland*" (1959): "Sometimes Carroll finds an unforgettable illustration of a major principle. We know that if all apples are red, it does not follow that all red things are apples: the logician's technical description of this is the non-convertibility *simpliciter* of universal proportions."[177] The major principle introduced here by Holmes does not really seem to be a fitting interpretation of the above conversation, at least as far as Alice's words are concerned, since it reduces them to an equation

176 With great mastery, this idea is centrally displayed in one of the most dramatic stories by Anton Chekhov *Quite an Everyday Trifle* (*Житейская мелочь*, 1886), in which an eight-year-old boy Aljosha confesses in secret to an old friend of his divorced mother that he occasionally meets his father without his mother knowing. The adult friend swears not to tell a word about it to the boy's mother and breaks his word without any remorse – as if it were quite an everyday trifle – as soon as he sees her again. The boy's reaction to this first encounter with treachery is rendered as follows: "Aljosha sat down in a corner and, filled with terror, reported to his sister how he had just been cheated. He was trembling, stuttering, weeping; for the first time in his life, he was brutally confronted with a lie. He had not known before that apart from sweet pears, delicious cakes and expensive watches, there were also many other things in this world for which no names existed in the language of a child." (Anton Checkov, *Sobranije sočinenij*, Vol. IV, Moskva: Hud. Literature 1962, p. 356.)

177 Roger W. Holmes, "The Philosopher's *Alice in Wonderland*" (1959), in: Phillips, Robert (Ed.), *Aspects of Alice*, New York: Vintage Books 1971, pp. 159–174, here p. 161.

between "all that is said is meant" and "all that is meant is said" and thus leaves aside what would seem to be the crucial element in her proposition, i.e. the self and the psychological motivation of what is being said. Another philosophical commentary to the above passage has been produced by Peter Heath in *The Philosopher's Alice* (1974.) It reads as follows:

> In recommending Alice to say what she means, the Hare allies himself with conceptualists, for whom meaning something is one thing, and saying it another. The Hatter, who insists that meaning what you say is distinct from this, implies that it is words that mean, and thereby sides with nominalism (Jourdain, p. 24.) Alice, who amalgamates the two, has a supporter in Wittgenstein, who objected to internal meanings ([49], pp. 34 ff., 145), though it is not likely that he would have approved of her defense of this point of view (cf. Pitcher [in Fann], p. 329, and Shibles, pp. 24–25.) (Holmes, pp. 134–135; Carney and Scheer [11], p. 155; Manicas and Kruger [27], p. 275.)[178]

It is rather doubtful that the statement "you should say what you mean" should be seen as suggesting conceptualism, nor do the words produced by the Hatter let him automatically appear as a nominalist. Yet the most curious thing about this translation of Carroll's passage into the language of philosophy seems the opinion, according to which Alice is interpreted as an amalgamation of the two. Among the names to which Heath refers his readers, that of Ludwig Wittgenstein (1889–1951) is the most prominent one. Wittgenstein's philosophy represents also an important point of reference for Pitcher's and Shilbles' readings of Carroll, mentioned by Heath in the above quote. By saying that Alice's words would be likely to find a supporter in Wittgenstein for objecting to internal meanings, Heath may have thought of the following element of Wittgenstein's philosophy of language: Since, according to Wittgenstein, men are "entangled in a net of language, not being conscious of this" ("im Netz der Sprache verstrickt und wissen es nicht."[179]), it should be recognized as the primary aim of philosophy to help men's minds awaken and break free from the traps posed by language. Already in his *Tractatus Logico-Philosophicus* (1921) it is said that philosophy is to be understood as *a critique of language* (*Sprachkritik*) (T 4.0031)[180].

Similarly, in later years, he would speak about philosophy as a *battle*, e.g. in the *Philosophical Investigations* (1953): "Philosophy is a battle against the bewitch-

178 P. Heath, *The Philosopher's Alice*, New York: St. Martin's Press 1974, pp. 67–68.

179 L. Wittgenstein, *Philosophische Grammatik*, in: Ludwig Wittgenstein, *Schriften*, Vol. 4, Rush Rhees (Ed.), Frankfurt am Main: Suhrkamp. 1969, p. 462.

180 L. Wittgenstein, *Tractatus Logico-Philosophicus*, London: Routledge 1955, 62.

ment of our intelligence by means of language."[181] A philosopher is understood as a liberation fighter or as a doctor, since he examines his questions as if they were *diseases* ("wie eine Krankheit."[182]) One of these philosophical diseases investigated by Wittgenstein was the idea according to which meaning and saying could represent two different things. *The Blue Book* (his lecture notes from 1933–1934) contains the following reflections on this subject:

> the forms of expression: "to say something" //"'to mean something" which seem to refer to two parallel processes. A process accompanying our words which one might call the "process of meaning them" is the modulation of the voice in which we speak the words; or one of the processes similar to this, like the play of facial expression. These accompany the spoken words not in the way a German sentence might accompany an English sentence, or writing a sentence accompany speaking a sentence; but in the sense in which the tune of a song accompanies its words. This tune corresponds to the "feeling" with which we say the sentence. And I wish to point out that this feeling is the expression with which this sentence is said, or something similar to this expression.[183]

In this quotation, Wittgenstein focuses on the linear course of mental processes which cannot be manifested other than in words. Among inevitable philosophical implications of this is the conviction that no mental process (like thinking, hoping, believing) can proceed independently from the verbal medium[184]. By pointing this out, Wittgenstein wishes to expose the fallacy of the idea that it is possible to say something, simultaneously meaning it in a different way. The word "meaning" belongs for him to the particularly resistant diseases that should be cured by philosophers: "'Meaning' is one of the words of which one may say that they have odd jobs in our language. It is these words which cause most philosophical troubles."[185] Yet even though it would indeed be difficult to

---

181 L. Wittgenstein, *Philosophical Investigations*, Tr. by G. E. M. Anscombe, Oxford: Basil Blackwell 1953, p. 47e. Cf. *The Blue Book*: "Philosophy, as we use the word, is a fight against the fascination which forms of expression exert upon us." (Ludwig Wittgenstein, *Preliminary Studies for the "Philosophical Investigations" Generally Known as The Blue and Brown Books*, Oxford: Basil Blackwell 1969, p. 27.)

182 L. Wittgenstein, *Philosophical Investigations*, p. 92e.

183 L. Wittgenstein, *The Blue Book*, p. 35.

184 L. Wittgenstein, *The Blue Book*, p. 41.

185 L. Wittgenstein, *The Blue Book*, pp. 43–44. The word "meaning" is addressed here primarily as internal meaning, i.e. it corresponds to the verb "to mean" (to be earnest about what one says, to intend smth. by one's words). Much more prominent in Wittgenstein's philosophy is the criticism of semantic meaning in general which he tries to substitute by the notion of *use*, thus reducing semantics to pragmatics, as, for example, in *Philosophical Investigations* 120, p. 49e: "You say: the point isn't the word, but its meaning, and you think of the meaning as a thing of the same kind as the word, though also different from the word. Here the word, there the mean-

think of a mental process designated by the verb *to mean* other than as one consisting of words, Wittgenstein's criticism could hardly question all the semantical properties pertaining to this verb, as, e.g. *to intend to say*, *to signify*, *to convey*, etc. Whenever emphasis is laid on the fact that one means what one says, it directly conveys the speaker's intention, i.e. his/her assurance that he/she does not conceal anything by his/her words and wishes them to be taken seriously. And this seems also to be the case with the above episode from Chapter VII. Carroll, as has been remarked, suggests a variety of different ways to approach the conceptual relation of *saying* to *meaning* and all of them are psychologically motivated, as, for example, in situations in which Alice recites poems without understanding their meaning (and therefore obviously not meaning the words produced by her) or, vice versa, whenever she does not dare to say something the way she means it, since she knows that otherwise she would appear impolite, as, e.g. in Chapter IX, reflecting about the Duchess' permission to regard everything she says as a kind of present: "'A cheap sort of present!' thought Alice. 'I'm glad people don't give birthday-presents like that!' But she did not venture to say it out loud."[186] This is a kind of internal meaning which, as Carroll explicitly states, remains unpronounced. Yet all psychological facets of meaning would appear redundant if Alice's assertion, according to which she says what she means (and vice versa), were interpreted à la Wittgenstein, i.e. as "it is impossible to say something without simultaneously meaning it."

The question which arises in light of studies that – similarly to *The Philosopher's Alice* – are explicitly conceived as philosophical approaches to Carroll's book is why they so persistently steer clear of psychology. Hypothetically, this attitude could be interpreted as due to the conviction that psychology bars the way to philosophical abstractions. A philosophical reading may be understood as one which would make the mathematician and logician Carroll reconcile with his original field of interests from which, as it would seem, he distances himself in his *Alice*-books. Thus, the principal aim of a philosophical approach to his literary work would be to make it as accessible to philosophers as his studies on mathematics are to mathematicians. Peter Heath's above quoted monograph

ing. The money, and the cow that you can buy with it. (By contrast: money, and its use..)" I agree with Marcelo Dascal that the notion of "use" does not make much sense when it is applied to substitute meaning and to make the context dominate linguistic expressions entirely: "On this view, communication becomes a guessing game, where the context not only provides the clues to disambiguate or otherwise interpret the expression uttered, but must also provide, regardless of *which* expression is uttered, the initial (as well as final) clue as to what it means." (Marcelo Dascal, "The Language of Thought and the Games of Language", in: Michael Astroh, D. Gerhardus, and G. Heinzma (Eds.), *Dialogisches Handeln: Eine Festschrift für Kuno Lorenz*. Heildeberg: Spektrum Akademischer Verlag, pp. 183–191, here p. 186.)

186 *Alice*, p. 97.

contains only short personal commentaries to Carroll's work and seeks to provide an accurate collection of thoughts concerning Carroll that have previously been produced by other philosophers. By contrast, studies by George Pitcher, Warren Shibles and Jean-Jacques Lecercle are much more detailed and may serve as better illustrations of how exactly *Alice* is approached by philosophers and how profitable this reading proves for them in the end.

In George Pitcher's essay "Wittgenstein, Nonsense, and Lewis Carroll" (1965), Wittgenstein and Carroll are said to represent not merely two congenial authors, but ones who are "truly spiritual twins."[187] According to him, it is only to the superficial eye that they might appear as worlds apart[188], since the primary task pursued by both of them is a fierce and uncompromising exposition of nonsense, i.e. of logically erroneous statements that have to be exorcized from philosophy once and for all:

> ...the respect in which Wittgenstein and Carroll are most deeply "at one", in which they become true spiritual twins. If any thesis can be said to lie at the heart of Wittgenstein's later philosophy, one of the plausible candidates would certainly be the doctrine that much of the nonsense and puzzlement to be found in philosophy is the direct result of one fundamental kind of mistake – namely, that of wrongly treating a word or phrase as having exactly the same kind of function as another word or phrase, solely on the basis of the fact that they exhibit superficial grammatical similarities.[189]

One of the key-words in this characterization is "mistake": both philosophers are believed to be equally engaged in correcting mistakes, either in the language and thought of their colleagues or, in Carroll's case, in the language of his figures. To back up this idea, Pitcher draws a parallel between Wittgenstein's observation that a transition from some to all is not always meaningful (PI 344, 345) and a scene from *Alice* (Chapter V) in which the Caterpillar asks Alice to recite the poem "You're old, Father William" in order to ascertain what exactly is the trouble with her memory. This poem by Robert Southey with the full title *The Old Man's Comforts and how he gained them* is a highly didactic piece of Victorian literature and represents a dialogue in which an old gentleman instructs a young man how to become virtuous without wasting time. Yet in the version of the poem recited by Alice, there is no trace of the virtues which are praised in the original. Instead of referring to a wise old gentleman, her words sudden-

187 G.Pitcher, "Wittgenstein, Nonsense, and Lewis Carroll", in: The Massachusetts Review 1965, pp. 591–611, here pp. 606–607.

188 *Ibid.*, p. 611.

189 *Ibid.*, pp. 606–607.

ly introduce an eccentric, brainless and gluttonous old misfit who, standing on his head, promises his young interlocutor to kick him downstairs for his annoying questions.[190] Alice's poem is thus a parody which is completely stripped off any didacticism and represents an exact opposite of the original. Yet the parody would not make much sense if it did not contain some clearly recognizable allusions to the original. In order to realize that this is a parody, the reader should be provided with connections between both texts and therefore it is by no means strange that Alice's version of the poem retains some of the central motives of the original, e.g. young man's addressing the old one by "You're old, Father William." By producing this parody, Alice proves to the Caterpillar exactly what she wishes to prove, i.e. that her memory is playing tricks on her in Wonderland and the words won't come the way they used to in her normal life. Even though some words in her recitation truly reproduce passages from Southey's poem, the parody may be regarded as a complete reversal of the original, which is pointed out by the Caterpillar immediately after hearing the poem:

> "That's not said right," said the Caterpillar.
> "Not quite right, I'm afraid," said Alice timidly; "some of the words have got altered."
> "It's wrong from beginning to end," said Caterpillar decidedly...[191]

It seems rather doubtful that in the above passage Carroll intended to expose logical mistakes, either of Alice or of the Caterpillar. Both judgments rest on logical reasoning, only that, as it so often happens throughout the story, the difference between them is psychologically motivated, which is suggested by the use of the respective adverbs "timidly" and "decidedly." Whereas Alice is too much confused to admit that the old man of whom she has just been talking is completely unfamiliar to her and tries to hide her embarrassment behind the fact that some of her words have reproduced the original exactly, the Caterpillar sticks to its direct ways to confront Alice with facts and insists that her poem was completely different to the original, in spite of some words shared by both texts. Pitcher refers to this controversial point, taking the Caterpillar to task for the following logical error:

> ...the charge was much too harsh to be intelligible: for although it is quite possible to recite a poem and get some of the words wrong, it is not possible to recite a given poem and get *all* of the words wrong – for then one is not reciting *that poem* at all.[192]

190 *Alice*, p. 54.
191 *Alice*, p. 54.
192 G. Pitcher, *op. cit.*, p. 600.

Following Pitcher's argumentation, any poem sharing at least one or a few words (pronouns, conjunctions, particles, etc.) with any other poem should then be understood as a copy (a recitation) of this poem, which does not seem really convincing. I believe that a parallel between the above episode from *Alice* and Wittgenstein's dictum concerning occasional conceptual discontinuities between parts and wholes would rather make sense if the parody pronounced by Alice is understood as completely different to Southey's didactic poem. However, this kind of interpretation would make the Caterpillar appear as logically superior to Alice, which, in turn, would imply yet another psychological contradiction, since the author's sympathy is with Alice rather than with the Caterpillar. The problem with Pitcher's critique of the Caterpillar (as with his various further corrections of Alice and other figures in Carroll's text) is that, in order to underpin his claims concerning spiritual affinities between Wittgenstein and Carroll, he is searching for instances of nonsense even in cases where Carroll would have hardly intended it to be found. In the above episode from Chapter V, it is rather the parody itself, i.e. Alice's sudden and totally unexplainable anti-didacticism which causes a nonsensical effect, and not her or the Caterpillar's reaction to this parody. On the other hand, it would seem to be the most significant difference to Wittgenstein that in his book Carroll never tries to be didactic: he does not aim at instructing, healing and correcting the illogicality of his heroine but sympathetically observes her, as she is going through all the metamorphoses in Wonderland, even if in some grotesque situations, as in the above recitation scene, he cannot help but smile at Alice's embarrassment. Yet the comic effect pertaining to this scene was hardly intended by him as a means of correction or as a critique against nonsense produced by his figures.

The comic element in the *Alice*-books does not escape Pitcher's attention, yet, since he approaches Carroll as Wittgenstein's "true spiritual twin", it defies easy categorization, e.g. in his following commentary to a conversation from Chapter VII ("'I mean what I say, etc.'") in which a new parallel is drawn between Carroll and Wittgenstein's above mentioned theory of internal meanings:

> Wittgenstein regards the picture with suspicion, since it is dangerously apt to mislead the philosopher; Carroll, on the other hand, simply has fun with it. We sometimes – and mothers of young children, quite often – speak of saying something and meaning it ("I told you to put on your overshoes and I *meant* it!"). This form of expression inevitably gives rise to the idea that the *saying* is one thing and the *meaning* it another – a mental act or private feeling or whatever, that accompanies the saying. Wittgenstein

argues against this idea: in doing so, he is defending Alice – at least up to a point – against the March Hare and the Mad Hatter...[193]

Unsurprisingly, the word "fun" refers here to a situation which is anything but funny for Alice herself and the only plausible explanation of this word usage would be the perception of Alice as one of whom other figures make fun. Pitcher does not display much interest in the reasons why no understanding is reached between the figures in this episode (a failure of communication like in Alice's conversation with the Pigeon in Chapter V) and adjusts the conversation between Alice, the Hatter and the March Hare to Wittgenstein's theory. In doing so, he proceeds similarly to Heath and leaves aside the subject, i.e. the "I" in "I mean what I say." Consequently, the phrase again appears as a generalizing statement which aims at articulating an exact relationship between saying and meaning and Alice comes to be seen as a true spiritual twin of the Duchess, i.e. a through and through didactic person who is passionately searching for a moral in everything she sees and who is the accomplished master of generalizations.

In spite of his overall approach to the spiritual affinities between Carroll and Wittgenstein, he observes one following essential difference between them: "it (nonsense – V. V.) tortured Wittgenstein and delighted Carroll. Carroll turned his back on reality and let us happily into his (wonderful) world of myth and fantasy. Wittgenstein, being a philosopher, exerted all his efforts to drag us back to reality from the (horrible) world of myth and fantasy."[194] To sum up, Pitcher's philosophical essay approaches Carroll as an author who, delightedly playing a game of nonsense and turning his back on reality, is fully committed to the same task as Wittgenstein, i.e. to expose and to correct errors and cofusions in his figures' language. Didacticism is thus perceived as the key idea of the *Alice*-books and it is thanks to this particular quality that they would be likely to stir the interest of philosophers.

A further philosophical abstraction of Alice has been produced by Warren Shibles in the chapter "A Philosophical Commentary on *Alice's Adventures in Wonderland*" of his monograph *Wittgenstein, Language and Philosophy* (1970.) His general approach to the book is similar to that of Pitcher, yet he arrives at far more radical conclusions than his predecessor. Shibles also regards the book as a sum of linguistic errors and the whole journey through Wonderland is seen as one through endless violations of logic: "when ordinary language goes on holiday people get misled. It is seen that this is exactly what happens to Alice in *Alice in Wonderland* and it happens as she continually bumps her head against the limits

193 G. Pitcher, *op. cit.*, p. 605.
194 G. Pitcher, *op. cit.*, p. 611.

of language."[195] His commentary to the book is preceded by some of the major ideas of Wittgenstein's philosophy, e.g. that a meaning of a word is its use, and that metaphors should generally be viewed by philosophers with particular skepticism[196]. In essence, being quite similar to Pitcher's essay, the work produced by Shibles is intended to help its readers penetrate into the very depth of Wittgenstein's philosophy of language and internalize his great aversion towards metaphysical speculations. The following passage from his commentary to the beginning of Chapter VI "Pig and Pepper" may illustrate Shilbles' congeniality with Wittgenstein concerning metaphysics:

> Alice's question "How am I to get in (the door)?""assumes that she is to get in at all. This reminds us of such questions we ask as "Who created the world?" which assumes that somebody did create it. But possibly no one created the world and we don't know what it would be like for a person to create it.[197]

In Shibles' work, the space of Wonderland is being transformed into a kind of Purgatory in which mental confusions as reflected in questions like who created the world have to be effectively eliminated. Among other things, he considers *Alice* to be a practicable manual against literalness. The same Chapter VI in which Alice expresses her hope that the March Hare will not be raving mad, as this is May, "at least not so mad as it was in March"[198] inspires Shibles to the following idea:

> But certainly, "mad as a March hare" and "mad as a Hatter" are loose expressions not to be taken too literally. Do not ask if a hare is literally mad in March but not in May. One is reminded of Brueghel's painting of Netherland proverbs which renders various sayings literally.[199]

In these reflections, he seems to overlook that literalness represents one of the most fundamental plot constituting categories in the book. In general, not being really interested in its textual organization, he rather seeks to figure out what can be gained from reading *Alice* in order to conjure up the spirit of Wittgenstein

195 Warren A. Shibles *Wittgenstein, Language and Philosophy*, Dubuque: Kendall Hunt 1970, p. v.

196 W. Shibles, *op. cit.*, p. 5. The actually highly ambivalent attitude of Wittgenstein towards metaphor has attracted lots of scholarly attention. See, for example, Jerry H. Gill (Ed.), *Wittgenstein and Metaphor*, Washington D. C.: Univ. Pr. of America (1981) as well as Ulrich Arnswald, Jens Kertscher, Matthias Kroß (Eds.), *Wittgenstein und die Metapher*, Berlin: Parerga (2004).

197 W. Shibles, *op. cit.*, p. 22.

198 *Alice*, p. 69.

199 W. Shibles, *op. cit.*, p. 23.

and one of his remarkable findings referring again to the episode from Chapter VII ("I mean what I say", etc.) and linking it, as was the case with the readings by Heath and Pitcher, with Wittgenstein's critique of internal meanings[200], interprets it as a confirmation of Carroll's extremely cautious attitude to literalness:

> Less theoretically we do differentiate between "I mean what I say" and "I say what I mean." That is, we use them in different contexts. They only cause problems if we begin to look into them or try to take them literally and ask, for instance, "How do I mean what I say or say what I mean?"[201]

The interpretation that I proposed above for the conversation from Chapter VII in which the statements produced by Alice and the Dormouse were understood as literal ones and therefore conceptually different to those of the Hatter and the March Hare, can certainly not be corroborated by Shibles' analysis, since he dismisses literalness in general as a confusing category. And again similarly to Pitcher, by justifying Alice's statement as being quite in line with Wittgenstein's critique of internal meanings, he neutralizes any subjectivity pertaining to her words and makes them appear as a general judgment about language. The final result of his philosophical abstraction is also highly didactic, more specifically it is again a critique of language in which language is stripped off any connections with the psychology of the related figures and appears as an abstraction used as a measure of correct thinking. Thus, the primary practical task of Shibles is to point out and to correct the manifold errors in the language and thought of Carroll's figures and in this compulsion to correct he proves absolutely merciless, so that among all the inhabitants of Wonderland there is hardly anyone who is permitted to continue speaking the way designed for them by Carroll. For example, while reflecting upon the conversation between Alice and the Cheshire-Cat from Chapter VI in which Alice asks the Cat which way she ought to go and is assured that she will get somewhere if only she walks long enough[202], Shibles kills two birds with one stone by correcting both Alice's question and the Cat's answer, for: "Of couse, walking "long enough" has nothing to do with get-

200 Among further investigations on Lewis Carroll in the context of Wittgenstein's philosophy of language, the most detailed are the essays by David Wagner "The uses of nonsense: Ludwig Wittgenstein reads Lewis Carroll", in: *Wittgenstein-Studien*, Vol. 3, No.1, pp. 202–216 (2012) and by Leila S. May, "Wittgenstein's Reflection in Lewis Carroll's *Looking Glass*", in: *Philosophy and Literature*, Vol 31, pp. 79–94 (2007), both focusing on the issue of nonsense and the concept of language games.

201 W. Shibles, *op. cit.*, p. 25.

202 *Alice*, p. 67.

ting "somewhere"[203]. It is not quite clear to what authority the "of course" is supposed to refer here, since in the given context, the meaning of *somewhere* is close to *everywhere* and, at least retrospectively, after having arrived *somewhere*, Alice is sure to see that she has been walking *long enough* to reach this point. Or, to give one more example of the language critique by Shibles, in his comment to the question of the Dormouse if Alice has ever seen such a thing as a drawing of a muchness[204], he elaborates on what would seem to be among the greatest blunders of humans in general:

> Muchness is obviously incorrectly regarded here as a thing instead of a modifier... Not being a thing 'much' cannot be drawn (much less drawn from a well). Neither can we draw memory. To this we may add that neither our internal states nor objects such as invisible ghosts or God can be drawn. But why would one want to draw them? ...Carroll seems to suggest that what thought is and, if it is anything, how it relates to language is not at all clear. The problem may be so deep because we are misled into looking for entities where there are none, and asking improper or meaningless questions.[205]

It can hardly be conclusively answered if the philosopher seriously intended to determine in this passage what exactly has driven, e. g. Dürer to produce his *Melancholie* or Michelangelo to paint the *Creazione di Adamo*. Shibles may have meant it rather as a rhetorical figure which would provide his analysis with more persuasive power. However that may be, it is remarkable how much is negated by these words: not merely the visual arts which are automatically made inexistent, but at the same time also the actual source of arts, the spirit (the invisible), the imagination as well as the possibilities of a medium in which the spiritual can manifest itself, – the language. This kind of philosophy of language does not only attest to a deep aversion towards metaphysics as well as to serious doubts about spiritual matters: these doubts primarily concern the language itself, its capacity, not merely to provide means to refer to the visible reality, but also to extend this reality and to make man get access to what is invisible.

The episode from the *Alice*-book which has given rise to so much criticism in Shibles' essay might primarily be seen as an act of fantasy and as an appeal to Alice's and the reader's ability to imagine the picture of the "much of a muchness", i.e. of an expression that people normally use without noticing the peculiarity of its form and idea. The same holds good for a great number of further episodes in the book in which Carroll appeals to the readers' linguistic fanta-

203 W. Shibles, *op. cit.*, p. 23.
204 *Alice*, p. 80.
205 W. Shibles, *op. cit.*, pp. 30–31.

sy and tries to make them rediscover images even behind idioms that normally might appear quite inconspicuous as, e.g. *falling asleep*, *killing the time*, *mad as a March hare*, etc. Expressions like these may equally be reproached for referring to entities "where there are none", yet, stirring the associative thinking, they enable man to recognize connections between phenomena that are seemingly unrelated. Following this way of thinking, sooner or later, one is probably likely to get back to metaphysics which is so severely negated by Shibles. Yet the point here is not to correct Shibles, i.e. not a negation of another negation, but rather the question concerning possibilities to interpret what in the philosophers' criticism appears as a source of errors and as in need of correction, on the contrary, as a promising chance for cognition and communication.

The keen interest with which Carroll's work is usually met among philosophers has already been discussed in various studies. In his monograph *Philosophy of Nonsense: The Intuitions of Victorian Nonsense Literature* (1994), Jean-Jacques Lecercle makes the following enthusiastic observation concerning this particular fascination: "we understand why Carroll is the philosopher's favourite teller of tales, why he provides an inexhaustible fund of quotations and episodes for illustration and analysis..."[206] According to Lecercle, it is all too easy to understand the philosophers' fascination with the *Alice*-books, since nonsense alone implies a good deal of language philosophy[207]. Joining the philosophical discussions of *Alice*, he provides in his book his personal theory of nonsense as well as of its significance for Carroll's aesthetics. The following passage from his interpretation of the conversation from Chapter VII ("at least I mean what I say, etc.") may illustrate that he also regards the book primarily as one that needs to be thoroughly checked for mistakes and Carroll – as an author who virtually insists that the mistakes of his figures should be carefully collected and corrected by logicians:

> Alice has become seriously muddled. She has made a gross mistake. Linguistic inversion does not preserve meaning, as the Hatter, soon followed by the March Hare and the Dormouse, tells her in no uncertain terms...In spite of our natural antipathy for the Hatter, we must confess he is right. 'I say what I mean' is not the same thing as "I mean what I say". But on the other hand, we may also understand Alice. She is speaking a natural, not a logical, language, where the situation is not clear cut...In fact, in a natural language, rather than a straightforward logical opposition we will have a gra-

206 J.-J. Lecercle, *op. cit.*, p. 115.
207 *Ibid.*, p. 115.

dation of semantic differences. "I eat what I see" is clearly different from "I see what I eat." What about "I eat what I chew" and "I chew what I eat"?[208]

In my above interpretation of the conversation, I suggested that linguistic inversion is not necessarily accompanied by changes in semantics, neither in literal statements (Alice; the Dormouse) nor in the figurative ones (the Hatter; the March Hare.) Therefore I do not think that it is mandatory to discuss the episode as one that is marked by logical errors. In essence, Lecercle follows his philosophical predecessors, even though he does not explicitly mention Wittgenstein. What is striking is that while discussing the changes caused by the linguistic inversion, he mentions the words produced by the Dormouse alongside those of the Hatter and the March Hare, although the proposition made by the Dormouse reproduces the same semantical pattern as that of Alice, which is why it is turned down by the Hatter and the matter is dropped in the end.

On the other hand, it is also remarkable how uneven Lecercle's critical judgment is pronounced: he begins it by discussing "a gross mistake" committed by Alice and some lines later produces a much more moderate correction, full with sympathy with Alice's language which is said to be not logical but natural. Defending this approach, Lecercle provides a list of further examples of "natural" statements that are intended to illustrate "a gradation of semantic differences" rather than "a logical opposition." The above comparison of "I eat what I chew" and "I chew what I eat" is followed by "I breathe when I'm alive" vs. "I'm alive when I breathe"[209] and "I espy what I catch sight of" vs. "I catch sight of what I espy."[210] The conclusion at which Lecerlce arrives in the end is quite optimistic: "we must admit that inversion does preserve meaning, unless we deny the possibility of synonyms."[211] Yet however abundant the examples of semantical gradations in natural languages may be, the whole list might appear redundant considering

208 *Ibid.*, p. 121. Cf. another critical interpretation of the passage provided by Robert D. Sutherland, *Language and Lewis Carroll*, The Hague/Paris – Mouton 1970, p. 193: "But she (Alice) makes the error of assuming that the converse, 'I mean what I say,' has the same import as her original statement, 'I say what I mean.' The Hatter and Hare are quick to point out that technical converses do not necessarily have the same meaning: 'I see what I eat' is not equivalent in import to 'I eat what I see.' A further complexity is introduced by Carroll when the Hatter declares that the Dormouse's pair of converses, 'I breathe when I sleep' and 'I sleep. when I breathe,' are, when predicated of the Dormouse, "the same thing." Both statements may indeed be true when predicated of the Dormouse; but their being able to be applied to him with equal validity does not signify that the meanings of the two expressions are the same. Each has its own logical import."

209 *Ibid.*, p. 122.

210 *Ibid.*, p. 122.

211 *Ibid.*, p. 122.

the fact that Carroll's text in itself is clear enough to interpret the statements of the parties to the dispute (e.g. "I see what I eat" and "I eat what I see") as synonymous and not necessarily as mutually contradicting in terms of logic.

What in Lecercle's opinion may be opposed to Alice's language is a "careful" language of philosophers[212]. By "careful" he might have meant a well-considered, cautious, moderate way of using words, which would seem certainly correct, since all the above mentioned authors of philosophical commentaries to Carroll display a detached, cautious and markedly didactic style of writing. Even though not all of their points and corrections may appear convincing, the way of their argumentation can definitely be opposed to the "natural" language of Alice, which, so far my impression, is one of the main reasons for the great irritations produced by the language of Carroll's figures on philosophical critics, for writing the *Alice*-books, Carroll essentially performs an act of self-estrangement, distancing himself from logic as the necessary measure of correct language and thought. When, for example, he makes the Caterpillar advise that Alice should break off two pieces from different sides of a perfectly round mushroom, eating which she would become able to control her growing taller and smaller, there is no way to determine at which point each of these different sides begins. From the purely mathematical (and logical) perspective, the situation is extremely dangerous for Alice since one of the two theoretically possible mistakes would make her disappear completely, i.e. reduce her size to zero. Yet neither the Caterpillar nor Alice wastes any time thinking about mathematics and the possibilities to master the puzzle, e.g. by drawing a straight line through the middle of the circle, which does not appear as a logical error, since in the end it proves enough for Alice simply to stretch her arms round it "as far as they would go"[213] in order to get hold of two different pieces. This is not to say that the episode would not be interesting for logicians. Yet logic does not play in it the role of the only dependable criterion of judgement and for this reason it would seem that in all the philosophical essays mentioned above it is not only the language of various figures in the *Alice*-books which is exposed to criticism and corrections, but also one of the fundamental features of Carroll, i.e. the ability to take a step back and to reflect upon himself with irony, not performing the role of a logician who is neutrally observing and commenting on what is happening in his story, but making logic, mathematics and language appear as major sources of wit and humor.

---

212 *Ibid.*, p. 120.

213 *Alice*, p. 55.

V.II

A significant difference in the approach to Carroll's text between philosophical critics and translators is, of course, that the translators have to accept all the linguistic and logical challenges which – in spite of the great fascination the *Alice*-books exert on the philosophers – are met with criticism and exposed to corrections in the above mentioned philosophical commentaries. I have never come across any translations in which the language of Carroll's figures would be polished according to the laws of logic and the probably most felicitous renditions are exactly those whose authors seek to be congenial with Carroll and employ their language imagination even in the most desperate situations in which language, at first sight, does not provide any solutions for an adequate rendition, as, e.g. in the story told by the Dormouse about three sisters who were living at the bottom of a well:

> "and they drew all manner of things – everything that begins with an M –" "Why with an M?" said Alice. "Why not?" said the March Hare…(The Dormouse went on:) "– that begins with an M, such as mouse-traps, and the moon, and memory, and muchness – you know they say things are 'much of a muchness' – did you ever see such a thing as a drawing of a muchness!" "Really, now you ask me," said Alice very much confused, "I don't think–" "Then you shouldn't talk," said the Hatter.[214]

Consider the following version of this passage provided by Zhao Yuanren (p. 97):

> "她们吸许多样东西——样样东西只要是 '呣' 字声音的——" 阿丽思道， "为什么要 '呣' 字声音呢？" 那三月兔道， "为什么不要？" … "样样东西只要是呣字声音的，譬如猫儿，明 月，梦，满满儿——你不是常说满满儿的吗——你可曾看见过满满儿的儿子是什么样子？" 阿丽思更被它说糊涂了，她道， "老实话，你问起我来，我倒没想到——" 那帽匠插嘴道， "既然没想到，就不该说话。"
> ("They drew all kinds of things, everything that begins with the sound of the character 呣 (m)." Alice said: "Why with the sound of the character 呣 (m)?" The March Hare said: "Why not?" … (The Dormouse continued:) "All kinds of things that begin with the sound of the character 呣 (m), such as a cat (mao'er), the moon (yueliang), dreams (meng), plentifulness (manmanerde). Don't you often say that 'things are plentiful.' Have you ever seen what the 'ful' of plentiful looks like?" Alice was still more confused and said: "To be honest, as you ask me now, I would never have thought –" The Hatter interrupted her and said: "In this case you should not talk.")

214 *Alice*, p. 80.

A careful back-translation of the passage also requires much linguistic imagination since the wonderful invention of the Chinese translator for "a drawing of muchness" has the literal meaning of "What does the son of plentifulness look like?" The word "plentiful" (*manmanerde*) contains in the Beijing dialect the suffix "儿er", just like the suffix "ful" is part of the word "plentiful" in English. Zhao separates this suffix from the stem of the Chinese word and puts it together with a new suffix "子zi". This new combination means "son" (*erzi* 儿子) and simultaneously sounds similar to the "*character er*" (*erzi* 儿字.) Thus, an English rendition of Zhao's word-play which sounds so natural and witty in Chinese would hardly be possible without a long commentary. Among other possibilities of translating it would be, e.g. "What do the knees of muchness look like?" (However, the obvious problem with this last version is that the noun "knees" ends with a voiced consonant, whereas the [s] in "muchness" is voiceless.) Both of the non-literal renditions would aim at paying tribute to Zhao's inventiveness, just as his version does to Carroll's wit. Of course, Zhao's linguistic finding has been produced by his imagination and does not aim at a literal rendition of the original. All the other translators who chose the same strategy of rendering this passage have provided their own individual inventions for "a drawing of muchness", e.g. Zhu Jie 朱洁 (p. 102) makes the sisters in the well draw objects that begin with a [č] *changge* 唱歌 (*singing*), 差不多 *chabuduo* (*quite similar*); in Ma Teng's (p. 67) rendition the corresponding objects begin – graphically – with the character *lao* 老 (*old*) and the last unit in his series is *laoduo*老多 (*a great many*.) The arguably most mysterious Chinese translation of this passage has been provided by Chen Fuan (p. 117): here, it is impossible to understand, in what way things begin with an "M" – as Chen translates it – since the series of things which are enumerated by the Dormouse does not contain any single one with an [m] as its initial sound. His series is: *haozijia* (*mouse-trap*), *yueliang* (*moon*), *jiyi* (*memory*), *duobanxiangtong* (*much of a muchness.*) It is only by means of a back-translation that the reader can guess the idea behind Chen's strategy: he translates Carroll's series directly and does not bother to seek for a series of objects which would correspond to Carroll's idea, thus providing a completely incomprehensible Chinese version of this passage.

By comparing all these back-translations of the passage, one is confronted with a vast variety of quite different readings, which is similar to the situation with Warren Weaver who, being impressed by great differences between some Japanese versions of Carroll's work, reached the conclusion that Japanese suffered from being substantially different from English.[215] However, as the above Chi-

215 Warren Weaver, *Alice in Many Tongues: The Translations of Alice in Wonderland*, Madison: The Univ. of Wisconsin Press 1964, p. 108: "(Japanese) seems to suffer from the fact that this language communicates in a way which is really substantially different from English."

nese versions reveal, the problem in similar cases does not arise from the structure and the semantics of languages into which Carroll (or anyone else) is translated, but rather from the translation strategy. The most infelicitous among the four Chinese versions quoted above is, in my view, the one produced by a translator who did not feel free to let his imagination work and confronted the Chinese readers with a totally incomprehensible set of words. By contrast, the other three versions display much more freedom: their authors followed Carroll's technique and, having found suiting semantical equivalents for the word-play, produced texts that are perfectly understandable for any reader of Chinese.

Among the translations of the passage into other languages, the closest to the original are the French ones produced by Jean-Pierre Berman and Laurent Paul Sueur, as both of them have found the way to reproduce both the initial sound of the series in the original and the semantics of its units, cf. Berman (p. 169): "machines-attrape souris, et morceau de lune, et mémoire, et du 'même'" ("mousetraps, and a piece of the moon, and memory, and muchness") and Suer (a freer rendition of semantics): "maison, Mars, mémoire ou multitude" ("a house, Mars, memory or muchness.")

The original passage is peculiar insofar as – similarly to the episode with the Mouse's tail in Chapter III – its meaning relies on the graphical design of the text and, because of this, translating it requires an exact interpretation of the capital "M" with which "all manner of things" begins in the story told by the Dormouse, i.e. whether it is to be understood as a sound, a letter, a letter name or (for Chinese) as a character. In the original, as in most renditions of the *Alice*, the "M" stands for a letter, but not for a letter name. Even though some translators chose a different letter by which to begin their respective series, e.g. the "S" in the German version by Enzensberger which refers to the *Schnapphase*, i.e. the March Hare, most of them are not concerned with the name of this letter. The only exception which I have been able to find in European languages is the Russian version prepared by Ščerbakov (p. 98) in which the series is rendered as follows: "эмблемы, эмали, эмиров, эмоции".[216] Here, the initial sound is an open [ɛ] and not an [m] and the translation rests on interpreting the "M" as the name of a letter which in Russian is called "em", exactly like in English. All the examples taken by Ščerbakov are semantic loans from Latin, so that by retranslating the whole sequence from Russian we get a perfectly neat set of English correspondences: *emblems*, *email*, *emirs*, and *emotions*. This rendition also results from the

216 Bold italics are mine.

translator's imagination and represents an individual and original way of reading and reproducing the story[217].

The question which the Dormouse asks Alice (whether she has ever seen something like a drawing of a muchness) puzzles her, so that she, as so often within this chapter, does not know how to react to it. Similar puzzlements resulting from language surprises are in every particular case intended rather than incidental and every time they pose significant difficulties for translators since their task is not merely to show that Alice is puzzled and that words fail her but to make it comprehensible for the reader why exactly she is confused, which again requires much creative imagination. One of the probably simplest cases of this kind is the riddle posed by the Hatter: "Why is a raven like a writing-desk?"[218]

The Chinese and Japanese renditions of this phrase do not show significant variations of meaning. For example, Tada Kōzō's version (p. 88) 黒鴉が書きもの机に似てるのはなぜだい?, being a literal rendition of the riddle, contains the particle *dai* which makes it sound somewhat less direct than Seriu Hajime's (p. 128) カラスとつくえと似ているの、なあぜだ。 In the versions produced by Zhao Yuanren (p. 85, 为什么一个老鸦象一张书桌子?) and by Ma Teng (p. 60, 一只乌鸦为什么会像一张写字台呢?), the singular semantics of the *raven* and the *writing-desk* is made explicit, whereas Chen Fuan (p. 103) does not use any indications of number semantics and his version (为什么乌鸦象书桌？) may equally well be back-translated either in singular or in plural ("Why are ravens like writing-desks?")

By contrast, the renditions into Western languages that I have consulted display more differences and in every particular case it is crucial, how exactly the translators conceive of the possible solution to the riddle. Wherever the solution is seen in the initial consonant of both nouns, the translators search for some fitting combinations of words, e.g. A. Zimmermann (p. 46): "Warum ist ein Rabe wie ein Reitersmann?" ("Why is a raven like a horseman?") and Henry Bué (p. 100): "Pourquoi une pie ressemble-t-elle à un pupitre?" ("Why is a magpie like a writing-desk?") Quite a special case is represented, on the other hand, by the versions which make the riddle refer to differences between two objects, as, e.g. in C. Enzensberger's (p. 70): "Was ist der Unterschied zwischen einem Raben und einem Schreibtisch?" ("What is the difference between a raven and a

217 By contrast, quite a natural approach to the "M" as a letter name is displayed by the translators into Japanese in which a syllabic writing system is used, so that the respective linguistic objects in the Japanese versions automatically begin with a name of a letter, e.g. in Shōno Kōkichi (p. 113): *ne de hajimaru mono* ネではじまるもの "things that begin with the letter *ne*", Seriu Hajime (p. 143, the same rendition), Waki Akiko (p. 103): *sa de hajimaru mono* さではじまるもの "things that begin with the letter *sa*", etc.

218 *Alice*, p. 73.

writing-desk?") as well as in B. Zachoder's (p. 77): "Какая разница между пуганой вороной и письменным столом?" ("What is the difference between a scared crow and a writing-desk?") Finally, in extremely rare cases, the objects referred to in the original have been substituted by the translators for completely different ones, as, e.g. in Ščerbakov's (p. 89): "Что общего между скамейкой и торговым заведением?" ("Why is a bench like a commercial institution?")

The conversation that has been in the focus of the first part of this chapter also belongs to the puzzling situations in which Alice is completely confused by the statements produced by her new acquaintances, among other things, by the Hatter's and the March Hare's attempts to convince her that saying "I mean what I say" is different to "I say what I mean." Although, this particular passage does not confront translators with great challenges, some of them have produced versions which have little in common with the original, e.g. Zachoder (p. 77) makes the Hare pronounce the following correction: "You might just as well say that 'I learn what I do not know' is the same thing as 'I do not know what I do not learn.'" ("Я учу то, чего не знаю." // "Я не знаю того, чего не учу.") This would seem to be one of the frequently recurring cases in which Zachoder seeks to adapt the text to children's understanding, as, for example, he also does in another episode from Chapter VII in which the March Hare encourages Alice to "have some wine."[219] In Zachoder's text (p. 76) *wine* has been replaced with *a piece of cake*. Similarly, much freedom in the reproduction of the conversation is displayed by Nabokov who simply cuts out the March Hare's statement ("You might just as well say that 'I like what I get' is the same thing as 'I get what I like.'") The issue of the relationship between *saying* and *meaning* is given by Nabokov (p. 60) also a completely new rendition, which is not motivated linguistically, i.e. by the power of the Russian picture of the world, but rather by his individual interpretation of the passage:

> "А Вы знаете, что говорите?" спросил Мартовский заяц.
> "Конечно", поспешно ответила Аня. "По крайней мере, я говорю, что знаю. Ведь это то же самое."
> "И совсем не то же самое", воскликнул Шляпник. "Разве можно сказать 'Я вижу, что ем' вместо 'я ем, что вижу'?"
> "Разве можно сказать", пробормотал Соня, словно разговаривая во сне, "'Я дышу, пока сплю' вместо 'я сплю, пока дышу'?"
> ("And do you know what you are talking about?"– said the March Hare.
> "I do," Ann hastily replied. "At least I say what I know. It's the same thing, isn't it?"

219 *Alice*, p. 72.

"Not the same thing a bit!" said the Hatter. "Would it be possible to say 'I see what I eat' for 'I eat what I see'?")

"Would it be possible to say," muttered the Dormouse, which seemed to be talking in its sleep, 'I breathe when I sleep' for 'I sleep when I breathe'?")

Nabokov not merely cuts one of the statements of the March Hare, but also changes the semantics of the verb in its first question: instead of "to mean" (думать), Nabokov takes here the verb "to know" (знать), which underscores Alice's perseverance and self-assurance, that is, qualities that are quite different to the honesty suggested by her words in the original. The symmetry of the form, peculiar to the whole conversation, i.e. the possibility to interpret it as a parallel sequence of literal and figurative statements, as has been discussed in the introductory part, has also been abandoned in this Russian version. It cannot conclusively be answered what exactly caused Nabokov to come up with such an unusual reading, yet whatever it may have been, it was certainly not the influence of semantic im/possibilities of Russian or the complexity of the original. By contrast, the following episode from Chapter VII generally proves as a real challenge for translators due to its complexity:

"What a funny watch!" she remarked. "It tells the day of the month and doesn't tell what o'clock it is!" "Why should it?" muttered the Hatter. "Does *your* watch tell you what year it is?" "Of course not," Alice replied very readily: "but that's because it stays the same year for such a long time together." "Which is just the case with *mine*," said the Hatter. Alice felt dreadfully puzzled. The Hatter's remark seemed to her to have no sort of meaning in it, and yet it was certainly English.[220]

The above episode shortly precedes the Hatter's story about a court concert two months before: at the concert, he was singing a song (*Twinkle, twinkle, little bat, etc.*) that was met with great dissatisfaction by the Queen and interpreted by her – literally – as a gross insult of time. Following the Queen's judgment ("He's murdering the time!"[221]), time becomes personified, i.e. it turns into one of the most important figures of the story who has actually been insulted and reacts to it accordingly: *he*[222] won't move on any longer, so that it is always six o'clock at the Mad Tea party. Whereas in Alice's perception of the world, time is an objective category, moving at an equal pace for everybody, the Hatter's personal expe-

220 *Alice*, p. 73.

221 *Alice*, p. 77.

222 *Alice*, p. 75: "'If you knew Time as well as I do,'" said the Hatter, 'you wouldn't talk about wasting it. It's *him*.'"

rience with it is completely different. However, in the above quote, Alice has more than one reason for being puzzled: first, she has not yet learned anything about the concert given by the Queen or about its consequences, and, second, due to the author's play with pronominal semantics – the possibility to interpret the respective pronouns either as referential or as expletive ("dummy pronouns") ones – the formulation of the Hatter's speech is anything but unambiguous. "Your" in his question to Alice is referential, yet "it" is expletive; in Alice's reply ("it stays the same year for such a long time"), "it" is also used expletively, i.e. it is taken to fulfil syntactical requirements only. However this pronoun is the subject in Alice's phrase and the problem in Hatter's reply to it ("Which is just the case with *mine*.") is that *mine* – which is never expletive – cannot be definitely related either to the "it" or to the nouns "year" // "time" in Alice's sentence. The equivocal use of the pronoun *mine* by the Hatter can be associated either with his watch, or with time, but in both of these instances the relation is not a definite one, which fully accounts for Alice's confusion.

Rendering this episode, translators are therefore required to reproduce a dialogue that is obviously marked by ambiguity and to make it plausible for readers why Alice cannot follow the words produced by the Hatter. In effect, this time, Alice's confusion has proved to be quite an uphill task for a number of translators. Consider the following Chinese rendition of the passage by Zhao Yuanren (p.89):

> "你的表会告诉你什么年吗？" 阿丽思很容易地答道，"自然不会，那可是因为我们能够许许多多时候在同一个年里不换年的缘故。" 那帽匠道，"就跟我的情形简直一样。" 阿丽思觉得这话很不明白。她觉得那帽匠那句话一点什么意思都没有，可是听又象好好的一句话。
>
> ("Can your watch tell you what year it is?" Alice replied promptly: "Of course not, because we can stay within the same year for a very long time." The Hatter said: "That's exactly the case with me." Alice could not understand these words. To her, the Hatter's phrase did not have any sense at all, and yet it sounded quite correct.)

In Zhao's version, there is nothing ambiguous about the Hatter's words: he actually agrees with Alice's statement and admits that his situation is exactly the same as with everyone else. Since the pronoun *wo* 我 (*me*) in the Hatter's reply is perfectly in accord with Alice's *women* 我们 (*we*, referring to all people, people in general), Alice does not have any reason to be puzzled. Another Chinese rendition, prepared by Chen Fuan (p. 105) reads as follows:

"当然不，"阿丽思立即回答道，"可这是因为一年的时间是那么长呀。""我的表也正是这样，"帽匠说。阿丽思觉得非常不明白。她觉得帽匠的这句话似乎没有什么意思，可又确实是英国话。

("Of course not," Alice replied hastily, "but it's because a year lasts for such a long time." The Hatter said: "That's exactly the case with my watch." Alice could not understand it at all. To her, there was no sense in the Hatter's words and yet it was certainly English.)

In this rendition, Alice again should not be irritated by the Hatter, since he makes it quite explicit that his watch is no exception to what she has just said: as any other watch, his is one for which a year lasts too long to be told extra, in addition to hours and minutes. By contrast, Alice's confusion seems plausible enough in the following translation by Ma Teng (p. 61–63):

"你的表告诉你今年是哪一年吗？""当然不会阿，"爱丽丝马上回答道，"可是很长一段时间里，年份是同一个年份呢。""这个情况和我的表不报时间是同一个原因。"帽匠说。爱丽丝被帽匠的话弄得莫名其妙，这句话听起来很难和之前的话联系起来，然而这句话是地地道道的英语。

("Does your watch tell you what year it is now?" "Of course not," Alice replied promptly. "It stays the same year for a very long time." "That's exactly the reason why my watch does not tell what o'clock it is," said the Hatter. Alice was very puzzled by this, as it was absolutely difficult to link it to what he had previously said, and yet it was obviously English.)

The logical inconsistency which has intentionally been added by the translator to the Hatter's statement is the following: his watch is said not to tell the time for exactly the same reason why, in the eyes of Alice, watches usually do not tell what year it is. The fact that, by saying this, the Hatter is only seemingly inconsistent is explained by him to Alice shortly afterwards in his story about the concert given by the Queen. In Ma's rendition, close attention is paid to Alice's reactions to the language and logic of other figures: it is made quite comprehensible what exactly Alice cannot understand, and for this reason Ma's version of this particular passage may be regarded as by far more reader-friendly than the ones by Zhao and Chen. Yet different to the original, the confusing effect is achieved in Ma's text not by the use of pronouns and thus represents a purely individual creation. Actually, it would seem that in this particular episode Chinese and Japanese are better suited for reproducing the original confusion of pronominal semantics than, say, Italian, French or Russian since in Chinese and Japanese the gender of objects to which possessive pronouns refer is not indicated. However, as illustrated above by some examples in Chinese, translators prove not always conscious of this formal affinity with English. The easiness with which they may come really very near to the demands of the original can be demonstrated by Tada Kōzō's (p. 90) Japanese rendition:

> 「だけど、それは長いこと年が変わらないからよ」「わしのがちょうどそんな具合さ」と帽子屋が言いました。アリスはおそろしくまごついてしまいました。帽子屋のことばはなんの意味もないように思われたけれど、たしかに英語ではあるのです。
> ("But this is because years do not change for such a long time!" "That's exactly the case with mine," said the Hatter. Alice was terribly confused. There seemed to be absolutely no meaning in the words of the Hatter, and yet it was certainly English.)

Here, the pronoun *washi no* わしの produces the same effect as *mine* in the original, so that the translator does not need any additional inventions in order to reproduce an exact copy of the original. By contrast, in languages in which the gender of objects is automatically formally marked in the pronominal inflections, it is much more complicated to achieve a similar closeness. Consider the following French version by Laurent Paul Sueur:

> "Est-ce que ta montre à toi t'indique l'année?" "Bien sûr que non", répondit Alice sans hésiter; "mais c'est parce qu'elle reste dans la même année pendant très longtemps."
> "Ce qui est exactement le cas de ma montre," affirma le chapelier.
> ("Does your watch tell you the year?" "Of course not," Alice replied without hesitation. "But that's because it (=the watch-V. V.) remains in (sic) the same year for so long".
> "That's exactly the case with my watch," maintained the Hatter.)

It may easily be seen, that in this version nothing is reminiscent of the original play with pronominal semantics, since it is quite clear to what objects all the pronouns refer: in the phrase pronounced by Alice, *elle* (*it*) refers to *the watch* (*montre*), and in the Hatter's words, *ma* (*my*) refers also as clearly to his *watch*. Thus, the idea of the original gets lost and the one who would surely have all the reasons to be confused by the dialogue's progress is not Alice but rather the French reader, being unable to understand what has caused Alice's irritation about the Hatter's remark. It would be redundant to produce further illustrations of formal categories that in languages like French impede a true reproduction of the ambiguity in this passage. Yet it should be pointed out that in spite of all the existing formal difficulties, it is still possible to find a logical solution to the problem, as is shown in the following translation by Nabokov (p. 61) into Russian where the gender of objects in singular to which possessive pronouns refer is also always made explicit in the pronominal inflexions:

"Ну и что же," пробормотал Шляпник. "Или по Вашим часам можно узнать время года?" "Разумеется, нет," бойко ответила Аня. "Ведь один и тот же год держится так долго." "В том–то и штука," проговорил Шляпник. Аня была ужасно озадачена. Объяснение Шляпника не имело, казалось, никакого смысла, а вместе с тем слова были самые простые.

("Now what?" muttered the Hatter. "Does your watch tell you what season it is?" "Of course, not," Anja replied promptly, "It's because one year lasts for a very long time." – "And that's exactly where the trouble begins," – said the Hatter. Anja was terribly puzzled. The explanation given by the Hatter did not make any sense, and yet the words in it sounded quite simple.)

Nabokov resorts here to an unexpected twist the idea of which has little to do with the pronominal forms: by making the Hatter complain about the course of time before Alice learns how he once "murdered the time" at the Queen's concert, he creates a context in which Alice's confusion would appear quite conceivable.

The insult of Time is an episode which provides particularly ample food for linguistic imagination. On the one hand, it refers to the complex semantic field of "time" and requires an intensive search for metaphors which would match the ones used in the original; on the other hand, it is the issue of the male gender attributed by the Hatter to the time/Time in his story that makes it difficult to maintain closeness to the original. The episode reads as follows:

"I think you might do something better with the time," she said, "than wasting it in asking riddles that have no answers."

"If you knew Time as well as I do," said the Hatter, "you wouldn't talk about wasting *it*. It's *him*."

"I don't know what you mean," said Alice.

"Of course you don't!" the Hatter said, tossing his head contemptuously. "I dare say you never spoke to Time!"

"Perhaps not," Alice cautiously replied: "But I know how to beat time when I learn music."

"Ah that accounts for it," said the Hatter. "He wo'n't stand beating."[223]

Shortly afterwards, the Hatter tells about his bad luck at the Queen's concert and about the Queen having blamed him for murdering the time[224]. Thus, on the whole, the episode contains three expressions that suggest a rather unfriendly management of time: *wasting time*, *beating time*, and *murdering* (or *killing*) *the time*. Of course, the second expression (*beating time*) does not have any negative

223 *Alice*, p. 75.
224 *Alice*, p. 77.

connotations in the normal usage, yet the Hatter is playing with the polysemy of the verb *to beat*. He takes it to mean *to hit* (instead of *to mark the rhythm*) and insists that Time – Father Time – is a living being which would surely not like being beaten.

Every language possesses a set number of semantic possibilities to express unkindness towards time: e.g. in Japanese, *time* can be *squandered* (*tsubusu* 潰す), it can be *lost* (*ushinau* 失う), but it cannot be *killed* like a person (*korosu* 殺す.) The verb *tsubusu*, in turn, can be associated with smashing potatoes, with slaughtering livestock, with squandering talents or whiling away the time, but not with killing or murdering a person. In Tada Kōzō's version, the play with polysemy of the verb *to beat* is entirely levelled by means of an explicit indication that *time* in *to beat time* is to be understood as *musical time* (拍子を打つ *hyōshi wo utsu*, p. 94) and not as *toki* 時 or as *jikan* 時間 which are the general names for time in Japanese. For *wasting time*, he takes the quite conventional verb *tsubusu* 潰す(p. 91), yet *murdering the time* is rendered by him – contrary to all semantical conventions in Japanese – by *korosu* (p. 94): あれは時を殺しているぞよ!("He is murdering the time!") This last choice may have been motivated by the Hatter's logic according to which time is *him* (this is rendered by Tada Kōzō (p. 91) as 時ってあの人だよ ("By the way, Time is a person.")) By contrast, a much more cautious Japanese version of the passage has been provided by Shōno Kōkichi who uses *tsubusu* for both *wasting* (p. 106) and *murdering* (p. 109) the time and makes Time appear not as *a man* (*him*) but as *a living being* (いきもの *ikimono*, p. 106), without any further specification. The semantics of *beating time* is in this version (p. 107), similarly to that by Tada Kōzō, rendered by a conventional expression which is free of any ambiguity as *toki wo hakaru* 時を計る (*to measure time*.) An equally cautious management of time is represented in the Chinese translations by Zhuao Yuanren (pp. 89, 91) and Ma Teng (pp. 63, 64) who do not allow (the) time to be murdered: whereas they use the same verb *zaota* 糟蹋 (lit.: *to squander*) for both *to waist* and *to murder*, *beating time* is rendered by them by a term that literally refers to music *dapaizi* 打拍子.[225]

The insults to which Time/time is being exposed in the above mentioned Japanese and Chinese renditions would seem quite harmless if compared with some of the Western versions of *Alice*. For example, to Pietrocòla-Rossetti (p. 102) the verb *uccidere* (*to murder, to kill*) must have appeared not strong enough, which is why in his text, the time is (lit.) *being assassinated* ("Egli sta assassinando il tem-

225 Ma Teng, p. 63; Zhao Yuanren pp. 89–91: In his translation, Zhao chooses first the expression *da shihou* 打时候 (lit. *beat time*), but fearing that his readers might not understand the expression, it is explained in a foot-note as "beating musical time" (*dapaizi*), p. 91.

po!"), and Nabokov's imagination was inspired to produce the following interpretation of the passage (Nabokov, p. 62):

> Аня устало вздохнула:
> – Как скучно так проводить время!
> – Если бы вы знали Время так, как я его знаю, – заметил Шляпник, – вы бы не посмели сказать, что его провожать скучно. Оно самолюбиво.
> – Я вас не понимаю, – сказала Аня.
> – Конечно, нет! – воскликнул Шляпник, презрительно мотнув головой. – Иначе вы бы так не расселись.
> – Я только села на время, – коротко ответила Аня.
> – То-то и есть, – продолжал Шляпник. – Время не любит, чтобы на него садились.
> (Anya sighed in exhaustion:
> – It's so boring to pass the time like that!
> – If you knew Time as well as I do – remarked the Hatter, – you wouldn't dare say that it's boring to pass it. It has a high self-esteem.
> – I don't understand, – said Anja.
> – Of course, you don't, – the Hatter said, tossing his head contemptuously. – Otherwise you wouldn't sit here for so long.
> – I only sat down a minute, – Anja replied timidly.
> – That's it, – said the Hatter. – Time doesn't like that (lit.: doesn't like people to sit on it.)

The first word-play created here by Nabokov rests on the polysemy of the verb проводить (*to pass*): whereas in Alice's use, it has the meaning of *to spend* (*time*), the Hatter takes it to mean *taking leave of* (*time.*) In the second case, the translator introduces the set expression "сесть на время" (*to sit down for a short while, for a minute*) in which "на время" (literally: *on the time*) means "for a while", but can and is interpreted by the Hatter as "sitting down on the time", thus heavily offending its self-esteem. A. Ščerbakov (p. 91) uses the same word as V. Nabokov for *wasting time*: проводить, but with a completely different meaning: "Кому понравится, что его хотят провести? Он вас и сторонится." ("Nobody likes being cheated. That's the reason why he avoids you.") And in Z. Solovjova's version (p. 109), time highly dislikes people who try *to get to grips with it* (справляться со временем), which is also quite an original way of rendering the English idea of *wasting time*. Of all Russian versions that I have studied, the arguably most dramatic variety of time-management has been discovered by the imagination of Nina Demurova (p. 176) who rendered the episode as follows:

– Если вам нечего делать, – сказала она с досадой, – придумали бы что-нибудь получше загадок без ответа. А так только попусту теряете время!
– Если бы ты знала Время так же хорошо, как я, – сказал Болванщик, – ты бы этого не сказала. Его не потеряешь! Не на такого напали!
– Не понимаю, – сказала Алиса.
– Еще бы! – презрительно встряхнул головой Болванщик. – Ты с ним небось никогда и не разговаривала!
– Может, и не разговаривала, – осторожно отвечала Алиса. – Зато не раз думала о том, как бы убить время!
– А-а! тогда все понятно, – сказал Болванщик. – Убить Время! Разве такое ему может понравиться!
("If you don't have anything to do," Alice said indignantly, "you should have thought of something better than asking riddles without answers. Doing this, you are simply wasting (losing) time!"
"If you knew time as well as I do," said the Hatter, "you would not be talking like that. It cannot be lost. It's not of that kind of things!"
"I don't understand," said Alice.
"Of course not," the Hatter tossed his head contemptuously. "I bet you've never talked to it!"
"Perhaps not," Alice answered cautiously, "but I often thought of how to kill time."
"I see, now everything is clear," said the Hatter: "To kill time! It would not like such an idea for sure!")

Although in Russian there is an expression which corresponds exactly to *beating time* ("отстукивать/отбивать время"), for some reason, Demurova – like Nebokov before her – did not use it and preferred to render it rather by *убить время* (*to kill/to murder the time*.) Moreover, the same verb was used by her several times in the rendition of the episode in which the Queen accuses the Hatter of murdering the time:

"Well, I'd hardly finished the first verse," said the Hatter, "when the Queen bawled out, "He's murdering the time! Off with his head!"[226]

Consider the following rendition of the passage by Demurova (p. 178):

"– Только я кончил первый куплет, как кто-то сказал: "Конечно, лучше б он помолчал, но надо же как-то убить время"! Королева как закричит: "Убить Время! Он хочет убить Время! Рубите ему голову!"

226 *Alice*, p. 77.

("As soon as I finished the first verse, somebody said: 'Sure, he'd better keep silent, but time should be killed anyway.' The Queen, (hearing this), bawled out: 'To kill Time! He wants to kill Time! Off with his head!'")

Thus, murdering of the time appears in this text with a much higher frequency than in the original, which again does not result from some semantic peculiarities of Russian but rests entirely on the strategy of the translator who feels free to reorganize the text according to her vision of the story. One more thing that is striking about Demurova's version is that, although she makes time appear as an actually or potentially insulted being, the personification of the time ("you wouldn't talk about wasting *it*. It's *him*."[227]) remains untranslated. Since this phrase, pronounced by the Hatter, is particularly challenging in terms of the language picture of the world, i.e. from both the point of view of semantics and that of formal grammatical categories, it is worth demonstrating what felicitous solutions some translators have found for its rendition.

Of course, the biggest challenge lies in the category of gender (*it's him.*) For languages that have grammatical gender, translators have to choose between two basic options: whereas in languages in which time is a masculine noun (like in Italian and in French), translators are required to resort to other categories in order to recreate the personification of the time, in languages in which time is a feminine (like in German) or a neuter (like in Russian) noun, the personification act is automatically accompanied by a change of gender, which, in turn, requires a plausible interpretation. Consider the following example of the first of these options which has been provided in Italian by Pietrocòla-Rossetti (p. 99):

> "Ma credo che sarebbe bene di passar meglio il tempo, che perderne, proponendo indovinelli che non hanno senso." "Se lei conoscesse il Tempo come lo conosco io," rispose il Cappellaio, "non direbbe che noi ne perdiamo. Non si tratta di me, ma di lui."
> ("I believe, it would be much better to do something else than wasting time and asking riddles without meaning." "If you knew Time as I do," said the Hatter, "you would not say that *we* are wasting it. It's not about me, it's about him.")

Other than in the original, the emphasis is first laid here not on the pronoun *ne* referring to *time* but on the verb *perdiamo* (*lose*) and its implied subject (*we.*) In the concluding words, the Hatter sets himself in opposition to time putting stress on two pronouns, *me* (*me*) and *lui* (*him.*) A different solution has been found by Bruno Oddera (p. 66) whose version reads as follows:

227 *Alice*, p. 75.

"Se tu conoscessi il Tempo bene quanto me" – disse il Cappellaio – "non parleresti di sprecarlo come se fosse una cosa. È una persona."
("If you knew Time as well ass I do," said the Hatter, "you would not talk about wasting it, as if it were a thing. It is a person.)

Here, the translator resorts to the semantics of the verb *sprecare* which usually refers to things and not to people (except when it is used reflexively as *sprecarsi*, i.e. *to waste oneself*.) Oddera makes the Hatter correct what, in his eyes, is an obvious mistake, since Alice's use of words suggests that time is inanimate.

As for the second option, the following original interpretation of the phrase has been provided by Barbara Teutsch (pp. 76–77):

"Wenn du so vernünftig wärst, dann würdest du nicht von 'die' Zeit, sondern von 'der' Zeit sprechen!" sagte der Hutmacher.
"Ich verstehe nicht, was Sie meinen", sagte Alice.
"Du natürlich nicht!" meinte der Hutmacher verächtlich. "Ich nehme an, du hast noch nie mit 'der' Zeit gesprochen!""
"Kann sein", sagte Alice vorsichtig. "Aber ich weiß, was das ist, wenn man Zeit totschlägt!"
"Na, das erklärt alles!" rief der Hutmacher. "So etwas behagt der Zeit ganz und gar nicht – merkst du den feinen Unterschied – 'der' Zeit! Du mußt ihn freundlich behandeln…"
("If you were reasonable enough, you would not be talking about Time in the accusative, but in the dative case!" said the Hatter.
"I don't understand what you mean," said Alice.
"Of course not!" the hatter said contemptuously. "I suppose, you have never talked with Time in the dative case!"
"Maybe not," Alice said cautiously. "But I know what it means to kill time!"
"Well, that explains a lot," the Hatter exclaimed. "Time greatly dislikes such treatment, note – time in the dative case – this makes quite a difference! You have to treat him kindly.")

It is only in the last phrase that the pronoun *ihn* (*him*) is used here. Throughout the episode, Alice is being encouraged by the Hatter to think that *time* which in German is a feminine noun (*die Zeit*) is a masculine being. This is suggested grammatically by pointing out that it is a mistake to use the feminine article 'die' when speaking about time (*von der Zeit*) since the preposition *von* requires the use of the dative case which formally coincides with the masculine article in the nominative case. This is the only German rendition among all that I have studied in which the personification of the time and the change of its gender semantics has been achieved purely by means of grammar, which again demonstrates the impressive power of language imagination in overcoming the limits of its fixed grammatical patterns in order to come as near as possible to the demands of the original.

Conclusion

Philosophical critiques of Carroll have often aimed at making him reconcile with logic, i.e. with a field from which he would seem to move away in his *Alice*-books. For the careful correction of logical errors that have been collected in these readings, they may be regarded as peculiar manifestos of language critique imbued with didacticism and antimetaphysical vigour. By contrast, the most felicitous renditions of *Alice* display a completely different approach to the language of its figures: instead of correcting what might appear as logically incorrect, they attempt to reproduce the original language patterns as exactly as possible. Even though by doing so translators often reach the limits of their languages, in the end they provide their readers with texts that are by no means less inspiring the thought than the corrections to which Carroll has been exposed by philosophers.

VI. Behind Dandelion Trees: The Language of Numbers, Measures, and Sizes

VI.I

The experience of numbers, measures, and sizes belongs to the most exciting adventures of Alice along her journey through Wonderland. If, in the normal world, nothing about her counting and measuring skills would appear strange, insufficient or illogical, numbers and measures in Wonderland turn out to be quite a big mystery to her. In Chapter V, after having grown taller and shorter repeatedly in the course of her journey, which always happened all of a sudden and in the long run proved to be rather tiring, she learns from the Caterpillar that the way to control her size would be by eating from two sides of the mushroom on which it was sitting: one side would make her grow taller, the other – shorter. Yet the Caterpillar's advice poses for Alice the following puzzle: since the mushroom is perfectly round, there is no way to figure out where the one side ends and the other begins. In another episode from Chapter XII, she hears that the life of the accused Knave is made dependent entirely on the interpretation of a highly enigmatic poem which is the only available piece of evidence at the King's trial. The poem has to be read by the White Rabbit who performs the role of a court usher. Not sure, where to begin with reading, the Rabbit receives from the King the following instruction: "'Begin at the beginning,' the King said, very gravely, 'and go on till you come to the end: then stop.'"[228] In his commentary to this passage, Peter Heath takes the King's words to be a kind of algorithm, quite comparable with programming languages used for computers today: "Since the wits of these machines, though speedy, are approximately those of a rabbit, it will be seen that there is nothing at all odd about the use of such an instruction in the present case."[229] Contrary to this position and in defense of the White Rabbit, it could be objected that, although the poem itself – as a text – has a beginning and an end, the same cannot be said about the story which it tells: it has no development, no inner movement from a start to a conclusion. Being quite similar to determining different sides of a round mushroom in Chapter V, a reading of the poem could begin at any point, without any loss of sense.

Constant changes which measures and sizes go through in Wonderland make occasionally the language itself reach its limits: e.g. it cannot keep up with Alice's rapid growing at the end of Chapter V, so that in her dialogue with the

228 *Alice*, pp. 126–127.

229 Peter Heath, *The Philosopher's Alice*, New York: St. Martin's Press 1974, p. 116.

Pigeon that is confronted with her enormous serpent-like neck winding above high trees, Alice is at great pains to convince the Pigeon that she is only *a little girl*, and in the concluding episode of Chapter IV, after having grown extremely small and seeing a huge *puppy*, much bigger than herself, she, on the contrary, begins to doubt about the aptness of the word *puppy* to refer to it. These doubts explain the great caution with which she addresses it: "'Poor little thing!' Alice said, in a coaxing tone…"[230]

Naturally, the tension pertaining to the relationship between language and number in the original gets significantly enhanced in its translations since in addition to the necessary attention that should be paid to the events which directly concern numbers and measures in Carroll's text, translators have to be careful about possibilities and dangers in the corresponding relationship which they observe in their own languages and which often markedly differs from that of the original. For example, translators into French, Russian and Italian have to decide, what grammatical number to use in the Caterpillar's addressing Alice by: "Who are you?" By taking a plural form, Henri Bué (p. 61, "Qui êtes-vous?") and Petricòla-Rossetti (p. 59, "Chi siete voi") make the address form sound pointedly formal and distanced. For the episode, in which Alice receives the Caterpillar's advice to break off pieces from different sides of the mushroom, Zhao Yuanren (p. 61) offers the following rendition: "一只手擘了一块下来。" ("Alice broke off a piece with one of her hands.") Although one of the possible interpretations of this phrase in Chinese would be that Alice actually used both hands (an idea suggested by the semantics of *mei* 每 (*each*) which may be implied by *yi zhi shou* 一只手 (*one hand*)), the first available option of reading suggests rather the idea of singular: "with one of her hands", i.e. in the eyes of Chinese readers, the passage can be understood as ambiguous, whereas there is nothing ambiguous about this phrase in the original. Consider still another example from the dialogue between Alice and the Pigeon in which Alice tries to contradict her interlocutor's assertion that she is a serpent and not a little girl. Alice's words "little girls eat eggs quite as much as serpents do"[231] were translated by C. Enzensberger (p. 57) as follows: "kleine Mädchen essen genauso oft Eier wie Schlangen" ("Little girls eat eggs as often as snakes (do).") This is also quite an ambivalent rendition and displays a double meaning which is new to the original: it can be understood either as "little girls eat eggs as often as snakes" or as "the point in which little girls are similar to snakes is that both of them eat eggs".

The present chapter probes into the language of numbers, measures, and sizes in translation texts from two different perspectives: First, the focus will be put

230 *Alice*, p. 46.
231 *Alice*, p. 57.

on cases in which translators, when rendering some passages of *Alice*, spontaneously follow the same semantical and grammatical patterns. In these cases, it will be, using the famous dictum Martin Heidegger's, quite clearly *language* itself that *speaks* (*die Sprache spricht*) and makes translators more or less automatically move in a particular direction which is natural to their linguistic habits. From the theoretical point of view, the following issues will have to be shed light upon: First, the chapter will analyze the category of indefiniteness and its rendition in different languages, primarily those without articles, i.e. without grammatical means that are used exclusively as markers of this category (Chinese, Russian, and Japanese.) Second, the distinction of count and mass nouns will be examined, which especially for Chinese, though by no means for it alone, proves to be a highly problematic area in linguistics and anthropology. Third, being closely connected with the first two theoretical issues, a special form of indefiniteness, the so-called *generic indefiniteness* will be discussed within a comparative frame of analyzing counting in different languages. After probing into these theoretical questions, all of which will primarily concern *language that speaks*, i.e. natural and automatic linguistic processes (and, by contrast, also cases that illustrate translators' struggling for an adequate expression in languages that do not provide them with corresponding natural ways of speaking), a completely different situation of dealing with numbers, measures, and sizes will be studied, in which it will not be the language, but rather a creative individual who speaks and distances him/herself consciously from the original by insisting on a free rendition of the text even if his/her language offers quite obvious direct means of an exact adequate translation.

In linguistics, the category of in/definiteness in languages that lack articles has received lots of scholarly attention. It would be impossible and unnecessary to provide here an exhaustive review of the discussions on this subject. Instead, I would like to focus on studies that have played an especially prominent role in theoretical approaches to the in/definiteness in languages like Chincse and Russian. When reading relevant studies on Chinese, it is striking that most of them are chiefly concerned with classifiers and discuss them as markers of in/definiteness, e.g. L. Cheng and R. Sybesma who make the following statement: "Neither Cantonese nor Mandarin has a definite article. However, both languages have the equivalent of a definite article, namely, classifiers."[232] On the contrary, L. Julie Jiang makes the case for the role of classifiers as markers of indefiniteness in the so-called "bare classifier phrases [Cl-NP], (i.e. phrases consisting of only a classi-

232 Cheng, Lisa Lai-Shen, Rint Sybesma, "Bare and not so Bare Nouns and the Structure of NP", in: *Linguistic Inquiry*, Vol. 30, No. 4, 1999, pp. 509–542, here p. 522.

fier and a noun without numerals.)"[233] The same view is held by Walter Bisang and Yicheng Wu: "In Mandarin Chinese, the [CL-N] construction is limited to the postverbal position and is interpreted as indefinite: 'laoban mai-le liang che' ('The boss bought a car.')"[234] Both positions are highly contestable: against the former, it could be objected that, in Mandarin Chinese, definiteness is expressed, when a classifier is preceded by a demonstrative pronoun, e.g. in *zhe ben shu* 这本书 (*this book*), *na liang che* 那辆车 (*that car*). Definiteness results rather from the use of the demonstrative pronouns, and not from the classifiers. On the other hand, as far as the indefiniteness of bare phrases is concerned, in most cases it is suggested by the numeral *yi* 一 (*one*) which is implied by these phrases and which is often omitted in informal speech, except when being put at the beginning of a sentence. Therefore, again, the category of indefiniteness does not result from using a classifier, but – in this particular case – by the numeral *yi* (*one*). From the comparative perspective, this numeral deserves much attention, both in languages like English, German, French, in which articles are used, and in languages with no articles, like Chinese and Russian, in which this same numeral – losing in part or completely its typical numeric semantics – is regularly used to mark indefiniteness.

As early as 1924, the grammaticalization of the numeral *one* in a number of languages was discussed by Otto Jespersen in his *The Philosophy of Grammar*[235]. In 1970, David M. Perlmutter published an influential article which focused on the direct historical development of the indefinite article *a/n* in English from the numeral *one*[236]. Since then, numerous further studies have been issued to discuss the universality of similar processes in natural languages and to propose different schemas of a genealogy which numerals that correspond to *one* in English went through during their grammaticalization. Talmy Givón proposed a theory, suggesting a development from an early stage, at which the numerals with the semantics of *one* were used as markers of referential-indefinite nouns (for example, *ein/e* in German: "eine Freundin, die sie dort traf" or *odin/odna* in Russian "одна подруга, которую она там встретила,..."), to a stage when they could mark both referential and non-referential indefinite nouns, as in English: "A horse is

233 L. Julie Jiang, "Marking (In)definiteness in Classifier Languages", in: *Bulletin of Chinese Linguistics*, Vol. 8, 2015, pp. 319–343, here p. 323.

234 Walter Bisang, Yicheng Wu, "Numeral classifiers in East Asia", In: *Linguistics* 2017, Vol. 55 (2), pp. 257–264, here p. 258.

235 Otto Jespersen, *The Philosophy of Grammar*, Chicago: The University of Chicago Press 1992, pp. 113–114.

236 David M. Perlmutter, "On the Article in English", in: Manfred Bierwisch and Karl Erich Heidolph (eds.), *Progress in Linguistics: A Collection of Papers*, The Hague/Paris: Mouton 1970, pp. 233–248. This essay was a revised and expanded version of a paper presented at a seminar in syntax at Harvard University in February, 1967.

a four-legged animal" (non-ref.)[237] In another study, produced by Bernd Heine, the grammaticalization process of these numerals encompasses the following five historical stages: Stage I: The Numeral (one car.); Stage II: The presentative marker (Russian: Zhyl-byl *odin* starik. (Once upon a time, there lived *one* old man...)); Stage III: The specific marker (German: Es war *ein* Mann, der gestern vorbeikam, keine Frau. (A man came here yesterday, not a woman.)); Stage IV: The nonspecific marker (Russian: Kupi mne *odnu* gazetu. (Will you buy a newspaper for me, please?)) Stage V: The generalized article (Spanish: Un día venían *unos* hombres. (One day there came some men.))[238] In the course of similar studies, some researchers focused on the examination of development stages of the numerals with the semantics of *one* within different individual languages, as, for example, Willy Birkenmaier[239] in his essay on the grammatical functions of *odin* (*one*) in Russian and Elena Gorishneva in her doctoral dissertation *The Variety of Functions of the Numeral and Indefinite Marker 'one' in Bulgarian and Russian*[240]. Both of these works discuss the possibilities of an exact differentiation of the grammatical function of *один* (*one*) as a numeral from other functions, primarily that of the indefiniteness marker.

In what follows, the same question will be investigated on the material of some Chinese and Russian renditions of Carroll's text. Yet before doing so, one fundamental speculative problem should be mentioned which reaches beyond the purely formal aspects of the development of the numeral *one* to the marker of referential indefiniteness and concerns its particular conceptual suitability for performing this function. To the best of my knowledge, no other work has analyzed this problem as thoroughly as Talmy Givón's above mentioned essay, and since this issue proves to be illuminating not only from the point of view of the category of in/definiteness, but also from that of other questions which have to be clarified in the present chapter (e.g. the mass/count distinction as well as the relationship between individuals and kinds in the process of counting), Givón's opinion deserves being quoted here at length:

237 Talmy Givón, "On the Development of the Numeral 'One' as an Indefinite Marker", in: *Folia Linguistica Historica* II/1 1981, pp. 35–53, here p. 48.

238 "Indefinite Articles", in: Bernd Heine, *Cognitive Foundations of Grammar*, Oxford: Oxford University Press 1997, pp. 66–82, here pp. 72–73.

239 Willy Birkenmaier, "Die Funktion von *odin* im Russischen", in: *Zeitschrift für slavische Philologie*, Vol. 39, No. 1, 1976, pp. 43–59.

240 Gorishneva, Elena, *The Variety of Functions of the Numeral and Indefinite Marker 'one' in Bulgarian and Russian*, Herne: Gabriele Schäfer Verlag 2016. Many thanks to Elena Gorishneva for her friendly correspondence and for sharing her research with me.

When a new referential argument is introduced for the first time into discourse, the speaker obviously *does not* expect the hearer to identify it by its unique reference. Rather the speaker first identifies it to the hearer by its *generic/connotative properties*, as *one member out of the many within the type*. This is a peculiar situation, where the speaker wishes to perform two seemingly conflicting tasks:
(i) Introduce a new argument as *referential/existing*; but
(ii) Identify it by its *generic/type properties*.
The numeral "one" – rather than other numerals – is uniquely fitting to perform such a complex, contradictory task. First, like all qualifiers it implies existence/referentiality. But further, in *contrastive* use it implies also "one *out of many*", "one *out of the group*" or "one *out of the type*"[241]

In other words, this very early stage of the grammaticalization of the numeral *one* into a marker of indefiniteness is regarded by Givón as reflecting a dialectical relationship between the singularity of a discrete member of a discourse (an individual) and a plural continuum in which this individual is simultaneously related to a particular group of beings (a kind.) Thus, the conceptual characteristics which will be in the focus of predication at later stages of the grammaticalization of the numeral *one*, e.g. as a marker of nonreferential ("John is a teacher") or of generic ("A horse is a four-legged animal") indefiniteness, are also observed at this early stage of the grammaticalization. In order to verify the universality of this assertion, in what follows, the focus will be put on some renditions of *Alice* into three languages that do not use any articles: Chinese, Japanese, and Russian.

Towards the end of Chapter IV, Alice encounters a huge puppy that frightens her out of her wits and makes her dodge behind a great thistle: "Alice dodged behind a great thistle, to keep herself from being run over..."[242] Zhao Yuanren (p. 51) provides a following translation of this phrase: "阿丽思就连忙躲在一大株蒲公英后头" ("At once, Alice dodged behind a huge dandelion (tree).") Compared with the original, in the formal structure of the sentence in Chinese (disregarding the difference in the semantics of *thistle* (Chin. *ji* 蓟) and *dandelion* (*pugongying* 蒲公英) as being of no relevance here), the indefinite article is rendered by means of the numeral *yi* 一 (*one*); and a classifier (*zhu* 株) as well as an adjective (*da* 大 *great*) are inserted between this numeral and the object to which it refers (*pugongying*). The classifier *zhu* determines to what general class of things this particular object is related, i.e. in this case a class of trees and plants. Both the choice of the numeral *yi* (*one*) and that of the classifier *zhu* are motivated by the norms of Chinese syntax, and it is only the choice of the classifier which in

241 Talmy Givón, "On the Development of the Numeral 'One' as an Indefinite Marker", p. 52.
242 *Alice*, pp. 46–47.

this particular case could vary, e.g. by introducing the object as related to the class of grasses and trees (*yi ke pugongying* 一棵蒲公英) or as that of flowers (*yi duo pugongying* 一朵蒲公英).

Consider some other Chinese renditions of the phrase:

Chen Fuan (p. 59): 阿丽思躲到一棵大蓟后面 ("Alice dodged behind a (lit.: *one*) great thistle(tree).")

Ma Teng (p. 36): 爱丽丝急忙躲进一排树丛后面 ("Alice hastily dodged behind a (lit.: *one*) grove of bushes.")

Guan Shaochun, Zhao Mingfei (p. 35): 爱丽丝急忙躲进一排蓟树丛后面 ("Alice hastily dodged behind a (lit.: *one*) grove of thistle bushes.")

Zhu Haoyi (p. 57): 爱丽丝赶忙躲到一株巨大的蓟草后面 ("Alice hastily dodged behind a (lit.: *one*) huge thistle blade.")

An anonymous translation from Taiwan (p. 53): 爱丽丝赶快躲到一大丛的蓟花后面 ("Alice hastily dodged behind a (lit.: *one*) large thistle thicket.")

Zhu Hongguo (p. 42): 艾丽丝闪到蓟树丛后面 ("Alice dodged hastily behind (a) thistle bush(es).")

The versions agree structurally in one particular point, namely, that with the exception of the last one produced by Zhu Hongguo who refrains from making the number of the object explicit, all other renditions contain the formal marker *yi* (*one*). The grammatical function of this word is, however, more than just an indication of number and displays the same features of grammaticalization as the English indefinite article in its evolution from the numeral *one*: neither in the Chinese nor in the original English text can *yi/a(n)* be modified by such further quantifications as, e.g. *zhi* 只 (*only one thistle*) or 正好 *zhenghao* (*exactly one thistle*) or be semantically opposed to other numbers. Apart from referring to the singularity of the object, *yi* in the Chinese renditions functions as a marker of referential indefiniteness precisely as it does in the original. As such it marks the individuality (*a thistle*, *a bush*, *a thistle-blade*) and the existence of an object which is initially introduced into discourse as well as its relation to a definite class of things with which the reader is supposed to be familiar (retranslated by me as *a tree*, *a thicket*, *a grove*.) The fact that, except for Zhu Honguo's rendition, all others follow exactly the same grammatical pattern allows for the assumption that the choice of the marker *yi* does not arise from the linguistic originality or artistic creativity on the part of the translators, but that it is rather the language itself that prescribes an almost automatic usage of this device in similar contexts. Comparing the Chinese versions with some translations of the phrase into Japanese which also represents a classifier language one may get an impression of equally automatic choices made by Japanese translators, yet on the basis of completely contrary evidence: none of the versions to which I was able to get access uses, e.g. *ichi* 一 (*one*) or any other device to mark either singularity or referential indefiniteness:

Tada Kōzō (p. 54): 大きな薊のうしろに身をかわしました。("(Alice) dodged behind a great thistle // behind great thistles.")
Shōno Kōkichi (p. 64): 大きなアザミのうしろにひらりと身をかわしました ("(Alice) dodged swiftly behind a great thistle // behind great thistles.")
Seriu Hajime (p. 80): 大きなアザミのかげにかくれました ("(Alice) hid away in the shadow // shadows of a great thistle // of great thistles.")
Ishii Mutsumi (p. 33): 大きなアザミのかげに隠れた。("(Alice) hid away in the shadow // shadows of a great thistle // of great thistles.")
Waki Akiko (p. 57): 大きなアザミのかげにさっと隠れました。("(Alice) hid quickly away in the shadow // shadows of a great thistle // of great thistles.")

The absence of any markers of referential indefiniteness in the reproduced Japanese versions causes ambiguity in terms of number semantics: the object may equally correctly be interpreted either in singular or in plural. This grammatical pattern which is as characteristic of Japanese as the use of *yi* (*one*) in similar cases is of Chinese allows for the conclusion that the grammaticalization of the numeral *one* into a marker of referential indefiniteness is not a universal development, although it can be observed in a variety of languages that are typologically wide apart. On the other hand, the comparison of Chinese and Japanese versions may illustrate what differences some of the languages which usually are addressed as structurally close (e.g. in being equally referred to as *classifier languages*) may actually display.

Now, consider some translations of the phrase into Russian, a language, in which – as discussed in great detail in the above mentioned studies by Elena Gorishneva and Willy Birkenmaier – the numeral *odin* (*one*) displays a highly advanced degree of grammaticalization:

Zachoder: "Алиса тем временем юркнула за большой куст чертополоха..." ("Meanwhile, Alice dodged behind a big thistle bush.")[243]
Nabokov: "Тогда Аня ... юркнула под защиту огромного чертополоха..." ("Then Anya dodged away and found protection under a great thistle.")[244]

243 Zachoder, *Prikljućenija Alisy v strane čudes*, p. 61.
244 Nabokov, *Anja v strane čudes*, p. 37.

Demurova: "Алиса увернулась и спряталась за куст чертополоха..." ("Alice dodged behind a thistle bush.")[245]

Ščerbakov: "Алиса укрылась за куст чертополоха " ("Alice hid behind a thistle bush.")[246]

While it would be quite natural to use in this case *odin* (*one*) as a marker of referential indefiniteness (e.g. as "за один большой куст" (lit.: *behind one great bush*)), the translators refused to do so. Yet in contrast to the Japanese renditions of the phrase, the absence of this marker does not result in any ambiguity concerning number semantics: the singularity of the object is made explicit by the noun inflections (*куст, чертополоха*). Thus, in terms of the grammaticalization of the numeral *odin* (*one*), the potential possibility to use this number as a marker of referential indefiniteness allows to regard Russian as positioned somewhere in the middle between Chinese and Japanese.

On the other hand, compared with Russian and Japanese renditions of Carroll's text, it is striking how far the grammaticalization process of *yi* has progressed in Chinese. Consider the following examples which may serve as further illustrations of its use as a marker of referential indefiniteness: (*Alice*, Chapter I, p. 11) The Rabbit took *a watch* out of its waistcoat-pocket – Zhao Yuanren (p. 5): 兔子当真在它背心袋里摸出一只代表 (*yi zhi daibiao – one watch*); (*Alice*, Chapter I, p. 13) She took down *a jar* from one of the shelves as she passed – Zhao Yuanren (p. 7): 她经过一个架子的时候就伸手把一个小瓶子拿了出来 (*yi ge xiao pingzi – one small bottle*); (*Alice*, Chapter II, p. 24) I'll stay down here till I'm *sombody else* – Zhao Yuanren (p. 21): 我就还在这儿底下呆着，等我是了一个别人再看 (*yi ge bie ren – one different person*), bei Ma Teng (p. 17): 除非我再变成另外一个人 (*lingwai yi ge ren – another // one different person*); (*Alice*, Chapter IV, p. 39) to be going messages for *a rabbit* – Zhu Haoyi (p. 48): 在帮一只兔子跑腿 (*yi zhi tuzi – one rabbit*), etc.

As is the case with Russian, the use of *yi* as a marker of referential indefiniteness is not obligatory in modern Chinese. In spoken colloquial speech it is often omitted, except when it is put at the beginning of a sentence. Yet even in cases of its omission, Chinese and Russian semantics remains quite sensitive to the category of referential indefiniteness. In such situations, *yi* is always implicitly present (e.g. by saying "wo mai le liang che" 我买了辆车 ("I bought a car") one can only mean *one* car, never two or three, etc); and in Russian, the number semantics of *one* is in most cases clearly rendered by the noun inflections. Thus, both languages steadily reflect the dialectical relation between individuals and kinds which was so perceptively observed as characteristic of referential indefiniteness

245 Demurova, *Alisa v strane čudes*, p. 134.

246 Ščerbakov, *Prikljućenija Alisy v strane čudes*, p. 66.

by Givón and this has important consequences for discussing the issue of the count/mass distinction. For example, considering once again the above translation of Zhao Yuanren in which the referential indefinite object is translated as *yi da zhu pugongying* 一大株蒲公英 (*one/a great dandelion*), in order to understand this phrase, one has to relate this individual object first to a large class of things associated with the classifier *zhu* (*trees, plants, flowers*) and then, narrowing the conceptual focus, to relate the same object to a particular group of plants known as *pugongying* (*dandelions.*) Close attention to this relationship between individuals and kinds is especially important in examining Chinese syntax and semantics, for there is probably no other academic area in which studies on differentiating count and mass nouns are as confusing as in Sinology. Yet before discussing this matter in detail, it should be pointed out that the function of *yi* as a marker of referential indefiniteness in singular is the result of a long historical process. As such, it is thus similar to the use of individual classifiers which became normative circa during the Yuan dynasty (13th–14th centuries) and was by no means obligatory in the classical era. Since this is usually neglected in discussions on the count/mass distinction in Chinese, in what fallows, there are some illustrations of the function of *yi* as well as of the use of individual classifiers in classical Chinese.

The classifier *zhu* 株 in Zhao Yuanren's translation which, due to the particular situation to which it is applied in Chapter IV of *Alice* (Alice has namely changed in size and become much smaller than a flower) could be retranslated into English as *a (dandelion) tree*, can be traced back in exactly the same meaning to classical Chinese sources as well. As an example, Chen Shou's 陳壽 (233–297) *San guo zhi* 三國志 (*Records of the Three Kingdoms*), "Zhuge Liang zhuan《諸葛亮傳》("The Biography of Zhuge Liang") contains the following detail concerning the years Zhuge Liang (181–234) spent in Chengdu: "成都有桑八百株，薄田十五頃，子弟衣食，自有餘饒。[247]" ("In Chengdu, we had eight hundred mulberry trees and fifteen *qing* land. That's why our children surely had plenty to wear and eat.") In this phrase, *zhu* is a classifier which is used for counting trees. As for the use of *yi* (*one*) to refer to indefinite objects, it can also be traced in classical Chinese texts. Yet it is important to bear in mind some substantial differences between such instances and the above discussed use of *yi* as a marker of referential indefiniteness in modern Chinese: First, in classical Chinese, no classifier is needed to link *yi* with a noun and, second, it is the original purely numeric meaning which dominates its semantics in classical Chinese. The following examples from the *Mengzi* 孟子 (*The Book of Mencius*) may serve as illus-

247 Chen Shou 陳壽, *San guo zhi* 三國志 (*Records of the Three Kingdoms*), Beijing: Zhonghua shuju 1973, p. 927.

trating this point: *er bu zu yi ju yi yu* 而不足以舉一羽[248] ("not enough strength to lift (even) one (single) feather"), *zhong ri er bu huo yi qin* 終日而不獲一禽[249] ("During the whole day (they) did not get (even) one (single) bird."), *yue rang yi ji* 月攘一雞[250] ("taking (only) one fowl a month", note that no *yi* is used here before *yue* ("month")), *li bu neng sheng yi pi chu* 力不能胜一匹雏[251] ("not strong enough to lift a duckling"), *ji qi wen yi shan yan, jian yi shan xing* 及其聞一善言，見一善行[252] ("Whenever he heard a (= one single; any) good word or saw a (=one single; any) good action.") In all the given phrases, *yi* serves to emphasize the quantity of an object to which it refers, and even though in every single case it can be translated into English by the indefinite article, it is only in the last example in which the numeric semantics may be interpreted as merging with that of indefiniteness (i.e. as *any/whatever good word, any/whatever good action*.) In all other examples, indefiniteness is not relevant to the discussed subject: *yi* (*one*) in (*only*) *one* (*single*) *feather*, (*only*) *a duckling*, (*only*) *one fowl* refers exclusively to the quantity of objects which are being described.

From the point of view of indefiniteness, one particular episode from Chapter I "Liang Hui wang zhang ju shang" 梁惠王章句上 ("King Hui of Liang" I/7)[253] may be regarded as especially illuminating: King Xuan宣of Qi 齊 sees **an ox**[254] being lead along the hall (*you qian* ***niu*** *er guo tang xia zhe* 有牽牛而過堂下者.) As soon as the King learns that the ox is to be sacrificed, he orders that it be freed and exchanged for **a sheep** (*yi* ***yang*** *yi zhi* 以羊易之.) In a dialogue with Mencius, the King explains that it would not be correct to interpret this action as an expression of greed and emphasizes it by the question: *Wu he ai* ***yi niu****?* 吾何愛一牛？ ("How should I begrudge **an ox**?") The real motive is said to be rather the King's inability to bear the looks of an ox that is stricken with fear. That's why he orders that it be exchanged for a sheep (*gu yi* ***yang*** *yi zhi ye* 故以羊易之也). Of all the cases that refer to indefinite objects and that can be translated into English by nouns linked with the indefinite article *a*/*an* (*an ox*, *a sheep*), there is only one phrase in which the numeral *yi* (*one*) is used and in this case, again, it may be interpreted as a means of emphasizing numeric semantics. James Legge might have had similar considerations in mind, when he decided to render this particular occurrence of *yi* in his English translation not by the indefinite article,

248 Zhu Xi 朱熹 (Ed.), *Si shu zhang ju ji zhu* 四書章句集注, Beijing: Zhonghua shuju 2008, p. 206.
249 Zhu Xi 朱熹 (Ed.), *op. cit.*, p. 264.
250 Zhu Xi 朱熹 (Ed.), *op. cit.*, p. 270.
251 Zhu Xi 朱熹 (Ed.), *op. cit.*, p. 339.
252 Zhu Xi 朱熹 (Ed.), *op. cit.*, p. 353.
253 Zhu Xi 朱熹 (Ed.), *op. cit.*, pp. 207–208.
254 Bold italics are mine, V. V.

but by the numeral *one*: "How should I grudge one ox?"[255] A similar rendition was also provided by Edwin G. Pulleyblank who translated it as "Why should I begrudge one ox?"[256] In the rest of the passages referring to indefinite objects, the Chinese text does not contain any explicit marker either of the number or of the indefiniteness. It is also important to bear in mind that in previously reproduced examples of the use of the numeral *yi* in the *Mengzi*, no classifier is inserted between it and the nouns to which it refers: *yi yu* 一羽 (*one feather*), *yi qin* 一禽 (*one bird*), *yi pichu*[257] 一匹雏 (*one duckling*), *yi shan yan* 一善言 (*one good word*), *yi niu* 一牛 (*one ox*.)

When similar expressions are translated from classical into modern Chinese, it is required that a classifier should be put between a numeral and a noun. The last case, *yi niu* (*one ox*), would be, e.g. rendered as *yi tou niu* 一頭牛 (*one head of ox = one ox*), a group of oxen would be formally quite close to English *yi qun niu* 一群牛 (*one = a group of oxen*), exactly like a race of oxen *yi zhong niu* 一種牛 (a/one species of ox), etc. In every of these modern Chinese renditions, *yi* constantly relates an individual to a particular kind of beings.

Yet much more often than not this instance of individuation in Chinese is overlooked and, as a result, not only the process of counting in Chinese is regarded as exotic and as completely at odds with counting in article languages, but even the most basic semantical properties of Chinese nouns come to be perceived as most exotic and not directly translatable into languages like English without a special commentary on their quantificational nature. This is, e.g. the case with Richard Sharvy's influential essay "Maybe English Has No Count Nouns: Notes on Chinese Semantics. An Essay in Metaphysics and Linguistics" (1978) in which it is considered necessary to distinguish the nominal semantics in Chinese from that in English for the following reasons: "dictionaries that translate niu as 'ox,' or 'tiao' as 'ticket' are misleading, since the words 'ox' and 'ticket' in English seem to carry 'a principle of individuation,' i.e. a measure, as part of their meaning. But niu, piao, and all Mandarin nouns lack such a built-in measure."[258] This idea suggests that any noun in Chinese has to be regarded as a mass noun and any instance of its quantification should be understood as a portion of this mass. In order to illustrate this, Sharvy draws on the Chinese expression *yi ke pingguo* 一颗苹果 (*one apple*) which, according to him, should be correctly translated into English not as *an/one apple* but rather as "a ball of apple"[259]. Among some nec-

255 James Legge, *The Works of Mencius*, Hong Kong: Hong Kong University Press 1960, p. 140.

256 Edwin G. Pulleyblank, *Outline of Classical Chinese Grammar*, Vancouver: UBC Press 1995, p. 59.

257 *Pichu* is a not to be understood as a [Cl-N], but rather as a determining-determined construction, meaning *duckling* (lit.: *a duck nestling*.)

258 Richard Sharvy, *op. cit.*, in: *Studies in Language*, 1978, Vol. 2, No. 3, pp. 345–365, here p. 355.

259 Richard Sharvy, *ibid.*, p. 362.

essary consequences of this theory is a conviction that Chinese represents a radically different way of conceiving individuals and kinds than, say, English, Russian, and French, because in Chinese the reality cannot be reflected other than as a sum of portions: *an apple* as *a ball/a piece/a portion of apple*, *two people* as *two portions of man*, *three languages* as *three portions of language*, etc. And this, in turn, means that the language is not able to introduce individuality or plurality into discourse, since expressions like *two portions of a language* cannot capture the existence of two different languages as two distinct individuals. However spectacular this theory might appear, it cannot be interpreted other than as a misconception. Yet browsing through the works dedicated to counting in Chinese, one will easily see that ideas like those proposed by Sharvy are shared by a large number of linguists: Since nouns in modern Chinese can be used with numerals only if accompanied by classifiers, this is generally taken as enough evidence of there being no count nouns in this language at all[260]. The conviction, according to which all nouns in Chinese are mass nouns[261], triggers speculations about a specifically Chinese perception of the relationship between nouns and kinds which sometimes is automatically projected upon all classifier languages. L. Julie Jiang' following statement may serve as illustration: "Nouns in classifier languages are not properties but kinds, so they cannot satisfy the semantic requirements of the numerals..."[262] Whereas in characterizing semantic properties of Chinese nouns L. Julie Jiang operates with a somewhat enigmatic opposition of properties and kinds, Gennaro Chierchia, writing on the same subject, makes use of a no less striking opposition between kinds and predicates. According to him, all nouns in classifier languages which he calls "Languages without Count Nouns"[263] are mass nouns or names of kinds that resist being used as predicates:

> The noun zhuozi "table" is a name for the table-kind. We can turn it into a predicate n(zhuozi). However, liang cannot apply directly to it, because n(zhuozi) is mass. Liang(n(zhuozi)) is ungrammatical for the same reason that three furnitures is. A clissi-

260 Niina Ning Zhang, *Classifier Structures in Mandarin Chinese*, Berlin: Walter de Gruyter 2013, p. 29; p. 52.

261 "Some languages, such as Chinese, have only nouns that behave as mass expressions." (Susan Rothstein, "Counting and the Mass/Count Distinction", in: *Journal of Semantics*, Vol. 27, 2010, pp. 343–397, here p. 348.) "In Mandarin Chinese, all nouns show the grammatical properties of mass nouns, and none can be directly counted." (Susan Rothstein, *Semantics for Counting and Measuring*, Cambridge: Cambridge University Press 2017, p. 89.)

262 L. Julie Jiang, "Marking (In)definiteness in Classifier Languages", in: *Bulletin of Chinese Linguistics*, Vol. 8, 2015, pp. 319–343, here p. 331.

263 Gennaro Chierchia, "Plurality of Mass Nouns and the Notion of "Semantic Parameter", in: Susan Rothstein (Ed.), *Events and Grammar*, Dorderecht: Kluwer Academic Publishers 1998, pp. 53–103, Section 5: "Languages without Count Nouns", pp. 90–99.

fier, in the case at hand zhang, is needed to individuate a level suitable to counting… Common nouns are in a way assimilated to proper names in Chinese type languages. They are names of kinds.[264]

It is all the more remarkable that in spite of the clearly perceivable radical nature of his theory, Chierchia explicitly denies any difference between Chinese and English in terms of how the reality is structured[265]. Yet his words suggest no more and no less the same as Sharvy's statements concerning the semantics of Chinese nouns: the noun *table* (*zhuozi*) is to be understood as a name of kind which allows quantification only as one of portions: *one table* as *one portion of table*, *two tables* as *two portions of table*, etc. And as the above quotation from Chierchia's essay demonstrates, one of the distinctive features of his theory is to regard terms like *table* and *furniture* in Chinese at the same conceptual level without raising the question under what generic term the noun *zhuozi* (*table*) would actually fall. By doing so, he completely obscures the conceptual relationship between a distinct countable object (*zhuozi*) and the Chinese mass noun for *furniture* (*jiaju* 家具). One of the natural logical consequences of this theory is that, in Chinese, the expression corresponding to *a table* in English is not only structured as *a portion of table* (which might strike some speakers of English as extraordinarily odd), but simultaneously as *a portion of furniture* (which, in turn, would sound much more familiar to the English ear.)

Somewhat less radical is a theory proposed by Manfred Krifka who arrives at the following conclusion in his comparative study on Chisese and English nominal semantics:

> Mass nouns and mass noun constructions in English can be treated exactly like nouns in Chinese. Count nouns, however, are different. They do not need a classifier, but rather combine directly with a numeral. This difference can be captured in two ways – by assuming that either English numerals or English count nouns have a "built-in" classifier. So, a Chinese NP like *san zhi xiong* and an English NP like *three bears* actually can mean the same – they rely on different semantic means to arrive at the same semantic end (see also Sharvey 1978). However, there is at least one difference: whereas *san zhi xiong* can only apply to collections of three individual bears, three bears can also apply to bear species, as in *san zhong xiong*. That is, the measure function in numerals or count nouns is underspecified, it can be either OU or KU, object unit or kind unit.[266]

264 Gennaro Chierchia, *ibid.*, p. 93.

265 Gennaro Chierchia, *ibid.*, p. 97.

266 Manfred Krifka, "Common Nouns: A Contrastive Analysis of Chinese and English", in: Gregory N. Carlson, Francis Jeffry Pelletier (eds.), *The Generic Book*, Chicago: The University of Chicago Press 1995, pp. 398–411, here: p. 406.

In Krifka's theory, it seems to be ignored that in spite of the quite obvious meaning of *zhong* as *kind*, there is no simple semantical continuum between *zhi* (used for separate discrete objects) and *zhong* (as a collective term for all individual objects within the kind) and that the expression *san zhong xiong* may be understood exactly like *san zhi xiong* as referring to *object units*, i.e. to individuals (*races/species*) within a class (*all known specimens/races/species of bears.*) Therefore, a correct translation of *san zhong xiong* into English would be "three species of bears". In other words, among possible quantifications of the kind *xiong* (*bear*) as object unit, there is not only one referring to a number of individual specimens as in *yi zhi xiong* (*one (individual) bear*), but also a variety of expressions indicating larger quantities of the kind (e.g. *a group of bears, a heard, a race, a species of bears*, etc.), all of them referring to object units exactly like the words *a group, a heard, a race* do in English. And the difference between *san zhi xiong* and *san zhong xiong* in Chinese is exactly like that between *three (individual) bears* and *three species of bears* in English, i.e. not an opposition of individuals and masses, but rather one between different object units within a kind (*bear*). It is noteworthy that the confusing point in Krifka's theory is the conceptual volume of the term *kind*: it does not refer to the whole of *bears* (an abstraction of all individuals and species within a corresponding taxonomy), but rather to a *sub-kind* (*a species*) which in itself is – in English as in Chinese – a reference to an object unit. Although it is perfectly true that, when counting objects in Chinese (in contrast to English), one has to decide between classifiers corresponding to individual specimens and those referring to other object units (a race/a species), it seems important that in both cases the objects display the equal quality of being discrete units rather than different portions of mass.

As illustrated in the above Chinese translations of the phrase "Alice dodged behind a great thistle" as well as in other examples in Chinese in which *yi* (*one*) is as regularly applied to mark the indefiniteness of an object as the indefinite articles are in English, apart from the usage of classifiers in Chinese, the actual conceptual difference in terms of counting between English and Chinese is not as big as it would seem. Recalling once again Givón's observation concerning the conceptual suitability of the word *one* to mark the category of referential indefiniteness, i.e. the dialectical relationship between an individual object and a kind of things to which it is conceptually related, when used in this function, *one* in English and *yi* in Chinese make the unity of individuals and kinds appear as their prominent characteristic. It should also be noted that all the above examples of the usage of *yi* as a marker of referential indefiniteness of objects in singular represent exactly the same cases as those which Bloomfield regarded as the key criterion for determining count nouns in English in contrast to mass nouns, i.e. their ability to be used with an indefinite article and have a plural[267]. Ironically, one of the main reasons why a number of linguists deny the countability of all nouns in Chinese is the fact that Chinese has no indefinite articles. This argument, combined with the observation that a classifier has to be placed between a numeral and a noun in the process of counting, is usually regarded as enough evidence of an exclusive mass nominal semantics in Chinese. Yet considering the regularity with which *yi* (*one*) is used in modern Chinese as a marker of referential indefiniteness, this purely formalistic view of Chinese semantics appears little convincing, or even openly misleading.

In their essay on the semantics of count and non-count nouns in classifier languages, Alan Bale and Jessica Coon make the case for a critical revaluation of the utility of differentiating mass and count nouns[268]. Advocating such a negative approach, the authors seem not to consider the fact that the conceptualization of mass and count nouns is as fundamental a principle of categorization in Chinese as it is in the semantics of Dutch, English, or Russian. Studying this principle is extremely important for understanding the relationship between language and reality. By refusing to examine the related questions, e.g. how exactly the process of counting is linguistically organized, what objects in reality and what abstractions are conceived as countable and what others – as masses, one automatically gives up the large area of Chinese linguistics which is highly illuminating from the anthropological and philosophical perspective. Among the most prominent questions pertaining to this area of knowledge belongs the linguistic segmentation of human experience and of reality, as it is collectively perceived in a language community: If, for example, *snow* in Russian has both a singular and a plural forms (*снег* vs. *снегá*), but only a singular in German (*Schnee*), if *advice* in English functions as a mass noun and is quantified in portions (*a piece of advice*), but the corresponding noun in Italian means a discrete unit which can be directly counted (*consigli*), if *tanpopo* タンポポ (*dandelion*) in Japanese – like in German or in English – stands for a countable object, yet the corresponding German noun (*Löwenzahn*, lit: *the lion-tooth*) can refer in its plural form only to the teeth of a lion, and never to dandelion flowers (these can be counted like in Japanese by means of classifiers: *zwei, drei Stück Löwenzahn* (*two, three pieces of dandelion*), the same phenomenon of linguistic segmentation of reality can be observed in Chinese and there seems to be absolutely no reason for neglecting it.

267 "Mass nouns never take *a* and have no plural." (Leonard Bloomfield, *Language*, New York: Holt, Rinehart and Winston 1933, p. 205.)

268 Alan Bale, Jessica Coon, "Classifiers Are for Numerals, Not for Nouns: Consequences for the Mass/Count Distinction", in: *Linguistic Inquiry*, 2014, Vol. 45, No. 4, pp. 695–707, here p. 705.

Both Otto Jespersen and Anna Wierzbicka have pointed out that the conceptualization of objects as mass or count nouns within a language does not correspond to a stable pattern of grammatical behavior which would eternally remain unchanged and in this fixed form be preserved in dictionaries. Jespersen illustrates this by the following example: "It is curious that while Southern English and Standard Danish looks upon *porridge* and *grød* as singulars, the same words are in Scotland and Jutland treated as plurals...With immaterial mass-words it is the same: much knowledge must be rendered in German *viele Kenntnisse*, in Danish *mange kundskaber*."[269] On her part, Wierzbicka has examined a number of cases in which one and the same noun can be interpreted either as a count or as a mass one according to the situation in which it is used. In the following sentence, presented in her study as an example, the noun *table*, which is a classical example of a count noun in English, takes on the semantics of masshood: "There was not enough table for everybody to sit at.[270]" Both Wierzbicka and Jespersen define mass nouns as ones that do not display any particular fixed outline:

> In the case of things conceived of as individual objects (such as bottles or chairs) we could not move or remove the parts without destroying the qualitative identification of the object. In other words, if we move or remove some parts of a bottle or a chair, the object in question may well cease to be a bottle or a chair. This is why they are seen as objects with a definite (fixed) outline. The meat or the butter on a dish will also have a definite outline, but this outline is not fixed, i.e. it can be changed (by moving or removing some of the parts), and the meat will remain meat, and the butter, butter.[271]

Wierzbicka's attempt to draw a clear border-line between mass and count nouns illustrates how complicated the definition of both groups proves to be even when they refer to simple physical objects rather than to abstractions. Against the argument, the countability of objects which she draws on in the above quotation results from the integrity of their physical form or from the fixed outline of their bodies, it could be objected that a broken bottle or a chair lacking a leg do by no means automatically cease to be a bottle and a chair. Unless they are smashed to pieces and made lose their original form completely, both continue to be individual countable objects. Still another objection would be the following: in German, English, Italian, Russian, etc., there are lots of countable objects

269 Otto Jespersen, *The Philosophy of Grammar* (1924), Chicago: The University of Chicago Press 1992, p. 199.

270 Anna Wierzbicka, "'Oats' and 'Wheat': The Fallacy of Arbitrariness", in: John Hayman (Ed.), *Iconicity in Syntax: Proceedings on a Symposium on Iconicity in Syntax*, Amsterdam/Philadelphia: John Benjamins, 1985, pp. 311–342, here p. 316.

271 Anna Wierzbicka, *ibid.*, p. 317. Cf. O. Jespersen, *op. cit.*, p. 198.

which do not display any fixed outline: a *forest* in English (cf. *un bosco* in Italian, *ein Wald* in German, *лес* in Russian, etc.) continue to be a forest, even when some of its trees are removed, a sea remains a sea, even after one of the rivers flowing into it has completely dried out; *a plain*, *a fire*, *a sentence* which has not yet been finished, – examples like these are past all counting. Nevertheless the borderline which separates all these objects from the rest of reality, the outline (even if not necessarily as fixed as in Wierzbicka's theory), or the form peculiar to them would seem to be among the actual primary definitional elements of countable objects.

In what follows, some of mass and count nouns from *Alice* (Chapter I) will be compared with corresponding nouns in translations, among other things, those into Chinese which, as mentioned above, is among the most controversial languages in terms of the count/mass distinction. The comparison is intended to clarify, how exactly the conceptualization of individual objects and masses manifests itself in different languages and what role is given in this conceptualization to the presence or absence of a particular borderline (outline or form).

At the beginning of Chapter I, Alice is falling down through a deep rabbit-hole which is said to have gone on straight *for some way*[272]. Since her fall lasts surprisingly long, Alice has *plenty of time*[273] to look about her and to examine all the objects on her way. In both expressions which I have italicized (*for some way* and *plenty of time*), the nouns behave exactly like the *table* in Wierzbicka's example: *way* and *time* display the semantics of masshood, although in English they are also frequently used as count nouns (e.g. *one way or another*; *another time*, etc.)

By comparing translations of these phrases, one can easily see one common rendition pattern even in versions produced in languages which are structurally and genetically wide apart: Except for the quite frequent cases in which translators chose to render *for some way* by an adverb (cf., Ma Teng, p. 10: *zui kaishi* 最开始 – *first*, Seriu Hajime, p. 15: *shibaraku* しばらく – *first* (*for a while*), Zimmermann, p. 3: lief *erst* geradeaus – *first* went straight on, Nabokov, p. 6: *сперва* шла прямо – *first* went straight on, etc.), in most versions, the rendition is based on using a noun which – in all languages under study – can quite clearly be interpreted either as a count or as a mass noun. In cases when a count noun is used, most translators make the numeral *one* precede it, as, e.g. B. Oddera, p. 10: *per un certo tratto* – *for a certain while* (cf. the plural *ai tratti* – *at times*), C. Enzensberger, p. 10, K. Hansen, p. 8, B. Teutsch, p. 14 all render it by *ein Stück weit* – *a (short) way*. The same is the case in most Chinese renditions, e.g. by Chen Fuan, p. 7: *you yi duan lu* 有一段路 – *for a while* (lit.: had *one* stretch of road), cf. Zhao Yuanren, p. 5: *xian yi duan* 先一段 – *on the first stretch* (lit.: *one* stretch), Zhu Hong-

272 *Alice*, p. 12.
273 *Alice*, p. 12.

guo, p. 6: *kaitou yi duan* 开头一段 – *on the beginning stretch* (lit.: on the beginning *one* stretch), etc. I believe that there is absolutely no difference between the expressions *yi duan*, *un tratto*, *ein Stück* in terms of their countability. It refers to the first stage of Alice's journey through Wonderland, to her first experience of its space, the first step that in all versions which make the numeral *one* or the indefinite article accompany the noun in question appears as a self-contained unit. Practically all the translations of the second expression (*plenty of time*) are, by contrast, similar inasmuch as they make use of a mass noun and thus systematically refuse to draw any borderline in constructing the denotation of *time*, as, e.g. Seriu Hajime, p. 15: *jikan ga jūbun atta* 時間がじゅうぶんあった – *had enough time*, Zhu Hongguo, p. 7: *you chongyu de shijian* 有充裕的时间 – *had plenty of time*, , B. Oddera, p. 10: *ebbe tutto il tempo per* – *had all the time to*, K. Hansen, p. 8: *hatte genug Zeit* – *had enough time*, Ščerbakov, p. 30: *есть время* – *there is (enough) time*, etc. It is therefore not a discrete element of experience, conceived of as a countable finite unit (as in *ein Stück*, *un tratto*, *yi duan*, etc.), which is concerned here, but rather one that is measured purely in terms of its approximate quantity, as sufficiently (or more than sufficiently) available: The idea of time is that of a mass which by itself neither possesses any distinct outline nor represents any individual finite unit.

Further examples of count/mass semantics may be taken from another episode of Alice's journey through the earth in which she tries to calculate how many miles she has covered during her fall. The author's comment to this mathematical endeavor reads as follows: "though it was not a *very* good opportunity for showing off her knowledge, as there was no one to listen to her, still it was good practice to say it over"[274]. Of the two syntactically equivalent expressions "a very good opportunity" and "good practice", it is only in the first one that the noun (*opportunity*) is preceded by an indefinite article, whereas *practice* – being a mass noun – does not require any article in this instance at all. *Knowledge* is equally a mass noun: it can neither take a plural nor be directly counted. Consider the following translations of this passage into Japanese, Chinese and Russian, i.e. languages in which no articles are used to mark either definiteness or indefiniteness:

> Seriu Hajime, p. 17: ここではきいている人がないから、知ったかぶりのしがいがないけれど、それでも、くりかえし口にだしてみれば復習にはなると、アリスはそう思ったのでした。(As nobody was present to listen to her, it was not worthwhile showing off her knowledge (lit.: to pretend to know), but still Alice thought it would make (good) practice to repeat (it).)

274 *Alice*, p 13

Chen Fuan, p. 5: 虽然旁边没人听着，不算是一个很好的机会来显示她的知识，可是她说一遍也总是一次很好的练习。 Although there was no one listening to her, and it was not really a (lit.: *one*) good opportunity to show (off) her knowledge, but still it was a (lit.: *one*) good exercise to say it over.")

Ščerbakov, p. 32: И хотя случай проявить свои познания был не очень удачный, – ведь слушателей-то не было, – поупражняться заранее, как произносить такие вещи, тоже не мешало. (And although it was not really a good opportunity to display her knowledge, as there was nobody to listen to her, it was not useless to do a timely exercise in pronouncing such things.)

Out of the three versions, in terms of formal marking of contability, the Japanese one displays the maximum distance from the original: Since the passage does not contain any numerals or other quantifiers that could have served as indicators of countability, countable nouns (like *hito* 人 – *person*) are formally not recognizable as such. As was mentioned in the above analysis of the episode, in which Alice dodged behind a great thistle, due to the absence of any explicit markers of countability in Japanese, any back translation from it might be accompanied by ambiguity concerning the number of nouns in question. By comparing the translation version by Seriu Hajime with other renditions into Japanese, one can easily see how consistent Japanese translators are in following the same semantic pattern, e.g. in Tada Kōzō's (p. 12): *yoi kikai* よい機会 (*a good opportunity*) and in Shōno Kōkichi's (p. 15): *ii kikai* いい機会 (*a good opportunity*) versions, the count noun *kikai* (*opportunity*) is formally in no way different to the mass noun *chishiki* 知識 (*knowledge*).

By contrast, in Chinese and Russian, the translators automatically use the formal means of marking count and mass nouns provided in their languages: In the above version by Chen Fuan, the count nouns *jihui* 机会 (*opportunity*) and *lianxi* 练习 (*practice*) are directly preceded by the numeral *yi* (*one*) and a corresponding classifier (*ge* // *ci*) as markers of indefiniteness for singular count nouns. As some other Chinese renditions may demonstrate, the use of these markers in Chinese is not mandatory: In their text, Guan and Zhao (p. 7) do not use *yi ge* construction for rendering *a good opportunity*, yet in translating the expression *was good practice* they use the classifier *ge* before the noun, thus automatically suggesting *yi* (one), i.e. idea of singularity. In doing so, they make one major difference explicit in what regards the conceptualization of countability and masshood in Chinese and English: whereas *practice* is a mass noun in the original, it appears as a count noun in Chinese. Although countability is generally much more present at the formal level in Chinese than in Japanese, yet at times Chinese renditions may be interpreted equally as ambiguous in terms of the semantics of number, as, e.g. the beginning of the phrase in Chen Fuan's version which is inasmuch similar to that of Seriu Hajime as he does not provide any explicit markers of number and his version *suiran pangbian mei ren ting zhe* 虽然旁边没人听着 may be understood either as *Although there was no one to listen to her* or as *Although there were no people to listen to her*. By contrast, Guan / Zhao (p. 7) and Zhu Hongguo (p. 8) prevent this ambiguity by using the explicit marker of number (*yi*) accompanied by the classifier ge in: *mei you yi ge ren zai ting ta* 没有一个人在听她 (lit.: *there was not one person to listen to her*.) As for the formal marking of countability in the reproduced Russian translation, it is limited to the mandatory use of plural inflections of count nouns (*познания*, *слушателей*, *вещи*). Other than in the last Chinese example, the sentence provided by Ščerbakov could be modified by the use a corresponding numeral *odin* (*one*) only referring to the people listening to Alice (e.g. in *не было ни одного слушателя – there was not one person to listen to her*), not to the nouns *opportunity* and *practice*. And since Russian noun in singular, when lacking any quantifiers, are not formally marked as count or mass ones, the category of countability in Russian may be regarded as formally organized in a way that is similar to Chinese.

In spite of the differences which the three languages without articles display in terms of marking the countability, the conceptualization of nouns as count and mass ones as well as the awareness of whether in a given context one has to do with individual, discrete and countable objects or with masses and portions are as distinct as in article languages. *Zhishi* 知识 (*knowledge*) in Chinese and *chishiki* 知識 (*knowledge*) in Japanese, both being mass nouns, are conceptually as clearly opposed to the count noun *ren* 人 (*man/person*) in Chinese and *hito* 人 (*man/person*) in Japanese as *knowledge* is to *a person* in English: *knowledge*, *zhishi*, *chishiki* convey the idea of a collective unit which is quantified in portions and, in contrast to the count nouns *ren*, *hito*, *person*, cannot be counted by numbers.

The fact that one and the same phenomenon of reality can be captured only by a mass noun in one language, by a count noun in another and in still another language – both by a mass and a count nouns belongs among the most prominent features of the various pictures of the world reflected in natural languages. As in the above quotation from Jespersen, an English expression like *much knowledge* (a singular form) would have to be translated into German by a plural: *viele Kenntnisse*. Yet the noun *Kenntnis* is also quite frequently used in singular, e.g. in the expression "eine profunde Kenntnis", whereas *das Wissen* which is another German noun for *knowledge* is a mass noun and is used in singular only. Both *Wissen* and *knowledge* are quantifiable only in portions (e.g. much/enough/little knowledge vs. viel/genig/wenig Wissen). By contrast, *Kenntnis* – similarly to another German noun *Erkenntnis* (*realization/recognition*) – stands for an individual unit, as, e.g. within a series: *viele Kenntnisse, eine Reihe von Erkenntnissen*. On the other hand, it would not make much sense to put the nominal expression *der Baum der Erkenntnis* (*The Tree of Knowledge of Good and Evil*) in plural, as it refers to one individual tree at the beginning of human history and the word Erkenntnis stands for a process (*learning*) rather than for a discrete unit. A similar case may be found in Russian semantics: *древо познания* is composed of two count nouns, but their combination is used in singular only. The fact that in a number of Russian translations, the words *to show off her knowledge* from the above quoted passage were translated in plural (*познания=knowledge, Erkenntnisse*)[275], illustrates how sensitive the semantics of natural languages is to the ideal input of one and the same word used either in plural, i.e. as a count noun emphasizing a great plurality of information items stored up in one's memory, or as a singular mass noun focusing on the idea of *knowledge/Erkenntnis* as a result of learning process. Here, once again, the conceptualization of a mass noun is accompanied by a rejection to draw any boundary lines or to provide the denotation of the word with any – not even very vague – outline, whereas in the cases of its countable counterparts the boundary dividing individual units is ever present, as, e.g. in German: *diverse, vielfältige, unterschiedliche Erkenntnisse*.

Still another telling example of the impact upon the linguistic vision of the world exerted by a distinct conceptualization of nouns either as count or as mass ones can be found at the end of Chapter I: As soon as Alice recognizes the own inability to get the key by which to open the door into the garden of Wonderland, she begins to cry and immediately advises herself she'd better stop crying. The author's comment to this piece of advice reads as follows: "She generally gave herself very good advice, (though she very seldom followed it.)"[276] Like any other mass noun, *advice* is used in singular (therefore it is referred to by the corresponding pronoun *it* at the end of the phrase) and there is no indefinite article preceding this noun. In French and in Italian, most translators chose not the singular, but the plural which sounds quite natural for the corresponding noun semantics in these languages, as, e.g. Bué, p. 12: "se donner de très-bon**s** conseil**s** (bien qu'elle **les** suivît rarement)"; Oddera, p. 17: In genere, dava a se stessa otti**mi** consigl**i** (sebbene **li** seguisse molto di rado); and Battistutta, p. 10: Generalmente dava a se stessa consigl**i** molto sagg**i** (anche se di rado **li** seguiva.) The plural indicators – the inflections of nouns and adjectives (*très-bons, ottimi, saggi*) as well as the pronoun forms that accompany them (*les, li*) – are marked in bold. German translators had the options to render the mass noun *advice* either by a

275 Cf. Zachoder, p. 41: *своими познаниями*; Demurova, p. 80: *свои познания*.
276 *Alice*, p. 18.

somewhat antiquated, yet from the point of view of the grammatical behavior quite similar noun *Rat(h) w*hich, in this particular meaning, is used in singular only, or by a corresponding count noun *Ratschlag*. Zimmermann (p. 6: "Sie gab sich oft sehr guten Rath…") chose the first option, whereas Teutsch (p. 20), Hansen (p. 13), and Enzensberger (p. 16) followed the second way and put the noun in plural (*die Ratschläge*.) Most Russian versions also contain a corresponding count noun in plural, as, e.g. Nabokov, p. 11; Ščerbakov, p. 37; Zachoder, p. 44, all of whom rendered it by *советы*.

In terms of the count/mass distinction, Chinese translations proved particularly diverse in choosing either a count or a mass noun as being an apt equivalent for *advice*. Guan / Zhao (p. 11) provide the following rendition: "她经常爱给自己下个命令（虽然她很少听从这种命令）。"("She usually loved giving orders to herself, although she only seldom followed such orders.") At the first position (*ai…xia ge mingling*, lit.: "loved to give an order"), the noun *mingling* is preceded by the classifier *ge* which explicitly indicates it as a count noun: the *ge* stands for singular and marks the object as referential indefinite. The second occurrence of *mingling* (*order*) is accompanied by the classifier *zhong* which relates the object to a particular kind of objects (*such orders* or *orders of this kind*.) Most Chinese versions to which I had access rendered the noun by a count equivalent, e.g. Zhu Haoyi (p. 22) *jianyi* 建议 (*proposal*), Ma Teng (p. 14) *mingling* 命令 (*order*), Chen Fuan (p. 13) *quangao* 劝告 (*recommendation*), etc.

Quite a special case represents Zhao Yuanren's version (p. 13): "她平常自己常劝自己很好的劝话（可是很少听她自己的劝。）" ("She usually found for herself very good words of persuasion, but she seldom listened to her own persuasions.") The expression *quanhua* 劝话 which, compared with other above mentioned Chinese renditions of *advice*, is a rather rare occurrence and which should best be back translated by a plural form (*words of persuasion*) does not really refer to a typical count noun, since *hua* (*words*, *language*, *saying*) either evoques the image of language as a whole system (e.g. *baihua* 白话 – *colloquial language*) or that of composed verbal segments, rather than one of a single lexical word that is clearly distinct from any other equally separate lexicon entries. In the process of counting, it therefore usually appears with plural or collective semantics, as, e.g. in *yi xi hua* 一席话 – (*everything that is said*, *the sum of a speech*) or as in *yi ju hua* 一句话 (*a phrase*, *a saying*). Compared with the opposition of two plural forms of the noun *Wort* in German, i.e. with *Worte* (meaning *a cohesive speech unit*) and *Wörter* (meaning *separate unrelated words*, e.g. lemmas within a dictionary), the Chinese *hua* seems to correspond better to the first of these forms: *Worte*. In terms of the count/mass distinction, another remarkable case is the choice of this particular word for the noun *English* from the beginning of *Alice*, Chapter II:

"'Curiouser and curiouser!' cried Alice (she was so much surprised, that for the moment she quite forgot how to speak good English.)"[277]

Zhao Yuanren, p. 17: 连话都说不好了("she could not even produce the right words…")
Chen Fuan, p. 17: 连正经的英国话都说不好了("she could not even produce correct English words.")
Guan / Zhao, p. 12: 竟说不成话了 ("suddenly she could not speak.")
Zhu Haoyi, p. 25: 她连话都没办法好好说 ("She could not even manage to speak correctly.", lit.: *to produce words correctly*.)

In the reproduced renditions, it is not only striking how close the semantics of the Chinese noun *hua* (collective semantics) comes to the semantics of *English* (which actually can be interpreted as a mass noun), but also the fact, that out of the four versions, three explicitly refused to translate *English* by an exact Chinese equivalent which would be either *yingyu* 英语 or *yingwen* 英文. Here, it is certainly not language that speaks, but rather the translators themselves who explicitly refuse to apply linguistic means which are naturally provided by their languages for an absolutely correct rendition of a foreign idiom and thus make the course of the narration follow their own personal will. By highlighting this detail, I actually anticipate a subject which will be centrally discussed at the end of the chapter, i.e. the translators' decision to distance themselves from the original which is motivated by a particular strategy of adaptation rather than by actual differences between languages. In this particular case, it is not only the translators into Chinese who refused to render *English* by a corresponding equivalent: a similar approach has been adopted by Seriu Hajime (p. 29) who made Alice all of a sudden forget *how to produce words correctly* (*chanto shita kotoba* ちゃんとしたことば) or by Teutsch (p. 21) who rendered the phrase by a short comment that *Alice had no better idea than that* ("…fiel ihr nichts Besseres ein.!") Hansen (p. 15) makes Alice forget *her good German* ("ihr gutes Deutsch"), D'Amico's (p. 26) Alice forgets *the rules of grammar* (*le regole della grammatica*), a solution which is somewhat moderated by the adverb *perfino* (*almost*) in Giglio's version (p. 61) in which it is said that Alice *almost forgot the grammar* (*dimenticò perfino la grammatica*). Among the Russian versions, the arguably most curious ones are those by Zachoder (p. 45), according to whom *Alice suddenly lacked common expressions so that she began to come up with words of her own* (ей уже не хватало обыкновенных слов, и она начала придумывать свои) and by Demurova (p. 90) whose Alice simply *forgets how to speak* (забыла, как нужно говорить.) Compared with all these innovative ways to interpret what exactly Alice actually forgot in this episode,

277 *Alice*, p. 20.

quite a big exception represents the text by Luigina Battistutta (p. 15) who makes Alice forget nothing but English: "era così sorpresa, che s'era perfino dimenticata di parlare in buon inglese" ("she was so surprised that she almost forgot how to speak good English.")

However surprising it may appear that such a large number of translators refused to translate the simple word *English* by a corresponding noun, it is still comprehensible that by doing this they tried to provide a compromise solution for a tricky problem: In their translated versions, Alice does not speak English and it might strike the Chinese, Italian or Russian readers if they were informed that the translated Alice suddenly forgot English rather than their own native idiom. At this point, venturing a last look back on the problematics of the count/noun distinction and trying to draw a conclusion to it, it seems particularly important that in all the examples provided above, both for count nouns (*consigli*, советы, *mingling*, *quangao*) and for the mass ones (*advice*, *English*, *hua* 话, *ihr gutes Deutsch, etc.*), their conceptualization is totally dependent on the possibility to draw a border-line between a corresponding object that possesses its characteristic individuality/form/outline and the rest of reality (count nouns) or on the absence of such a possibility (mass nouns.) At least in this particular point, for all languages discussed in this book it is language itself that speaks in making count nouns follow the principle of individuation, i.e. distinguishing discrete objects from both other individuals and masses.

The last theoretical aspect to which I would like to turn in this chapter concerns a particular kind of propositions which are known as *generic* or *characterizing* sentences. They refer to the properties of objects with which these are automatically associated, i.e. to their typical qualities. In a large number of episodes, Carroll demonstrates how enigmatic this kind of propositions which at first glance might appear quite trivial can actually prove to be, as, e.g. in the scene in which Alice for the first time encounters the grinning Cheshire Cat and admits that she did not know cats could grin at all. Thereupon, she gets to hear from the Duchess the following illuminating statement: "'They all can,' said the Duchess. 'And most of 'em do.'"[278] The fact that not all cats do something which all of them are supposed to be able to do touches the very core of the logical peculiarity of generic sentences, namely, that they allow exceptions. In the following words, Nicholas Asher and Michael Morreau have expressed their amazement about this property:

> But this is the puzzling thing about generics: their truth conditions connect them at best only very loosely with particular facts about the world. Potatoes contain vitamin C even though large numbers of them are boiled for so long that it is lost. Pota-

278 *Alice*, p. 63.

> toes would contain vitamin C even if *all* of them were to be boiled for so long that it is lost...This tolerance of exceptions has for a decade or more frustrated efforts in linguistics, philosophy, and artificial intelligence to provide a rigorous account of generic meaning, and of modes of argument to which generic sentences give rise.[279]

Truth conditions would be better complied with, if those premises were mentioned on which a respective generic quality of an object would hypothetically highly likely be neutralized, just as in the just quoted example with potatoes containing vitamin C. However, even in this case the problem is not really solved, since the sheer infinite number of such hypothetical premises still impedes any generic statement to perfectly meet truth conditions: as in the given example, boiling would by no means be the only conceivable factor causing potatoes to lose vitamin C. Therefore, the statement produced by the Duchess might well be interpreted as showing much perspicacity: she is namely not in the least interested in informing Alice about any possible circumstances which would cause a Cheshire Cat to stop grinning. The present chapter does not pursue the aim of a detailed examination of the relationship between generic statements and truth; the focus shall be put rather on formal differences which accompany the linguistic composition of these sentences, i.e. on the question how exactly thinking generics is manifested in words. Here, again, the use of the numeral *one* (or the impossibility to apply it) will be taken as evidence of *language that speaks*, i.e. of a power which no thinking and speaking individual is able to resist.

As I have remarked earlier, both Talmy Givón and Bernd Heine considered the use of *one* in non-referential or generic statements among last stages of its grammaticalization process and displaying the maximum distance from its original predominantly numeric semantics (opposed to other numerals like *two*, *three*, etc.) In studies on Chinese, too, a similar function of the numeral *yi* (*one*) has received much scholarly scrutiny. For example, the following example is examined in both the essay presented by Wu Yicheng and Adams Bodomo "Classifiers ≠ Determiners" and in the monograph by Niina Ning Zhang *Classifier Structures in Mandarin Chinese*:

> "Yi jia feiji de sudu bi yi sou lunchuan de sudu kuai." 一架飞机的速度比一艘轮船的速度快 ("An airplane's speed is faster than a ship's.")[280]

279 Nicholas Asher, Michael Morreau, "What Some Generic Sentences Mean", in: Gregory N. Carlson, Francis Jeffry Pelletier (eds.), *The Generic Book*, Chicago: The University of Chicago Press 1995, pp. 300–338, here p. 300.

280 Wu Yicheng, Adams Bodomo, "Classifiers ≠ Determiners", in: *Linguistic Inquiry*, Vol. 40, No. 3, 2009, pp. 487–503, here p. 492. Niina Ning Zhang, *Classifier Structures in Mandarin Chinese*, Berlin: Walter de Gruyter 2013, p. 93.

Both studies focus on the neutralization of numeral semantics of *yi* in statements of this kind, i.e. in which it has rather to be interpreted as a marker of generic indefiniteness. Yet, in the given sentence, it is not without reservation the case that the numeric semantics is suppressed completely: Since both 'yi jia feiji' (*an airplane*) and 'yi sou lunchuan' (*a ship*) are being compared according to some purely quantitative characteristics (i.e. measuring their speed or efficacy in numbers), the mutual relation of both instances of *yi* is nothing but numeric. The fact that numeric semantics in sentences of this kind can quite naturally be supplemented by generic semantics and refer to qualities that are supposed to be typical of a given object, can be illustrated by the following Chinese idiom: "Yi ge heshang you shui chi, liang ge heshang tiao shui chi, san ge heshang mei you shui chi." 一个和尚有水吃，两个和尚挑水吃，三个和尚没有水吃 ("One monk has water to drink, two monks carry water to drink, three monks have no water to drink.") Variations of this saying, with all possible number combinations, may be found in other languages, too, as, e.g. *sieben Köche verderben den Brei* (German: Seven cooks spoil the porridge), *у семи нянек дитя без глазу* (Russian: A child who has seven nurses loses one eye), all of them roughly matching the meaning of *too many cooks spoil the broth* in English. Turning back to the generic meaning of *yi* in the first example above, it can be safely suggested that, in terms of their efficacy (velocity), the conjunction of *an airplane* with *a ship* is just like that of *one monk* (efficacy) and *three monks* (inefficacy): both cases refer to a stable relation of numbers (*one vs. one // one vs. three*) as a generic quality of the respective objects. Setting up this kind of proportion may attest to the fact that in the example sentence discussed by Wu/Bodomo and N. N. Zhang the numeric semantics of *yi* is by no means suppressed. Consider some further examples which both studies use to illustrate the generic function of *yi* in modern Mandarin Chinese:

"Yi ge zhanshi yao suishi zhunbei wei guo xisheng ziji." 一个战士要随时准备为国牺牲自己。('A soldier should prepare to sacrifice himself anytime for his country.')[281]
"Yi wei hao laoshi bu jinjin jiao xuesheng zenme xuexi." 一位好老师不仅仅教学生怎么学习 ("A good teacher doesn't just teach students how to study.")[282]
"Yi ge ren yao you liangxin." 一个人要有良心 ("A person should have moralities.")[283]
"Yi zhong zongjiao zong you qi wenhua genyuan." 一种宗教总有其文化根源 ("A religion always has its cultural origin.")[284]

281 Wu/Bodomo, *op.cit.*, p. 492.
282 Wu/Bodomo, *op.cit.*, p. 492.
283 Niina Ning Zhang, *op. cit.*, p. 93.
284 Niina Ning Zhang, op. cit., p. 93.

Strictly speaking, since all of the reproduced occurrences of *yi* express an opinion about something, i.e. prescribe rather than describe (*a* has to be this; *b* has to be that), none of them can serve as a typical illustration of a generic statement. Consider, by contrast, some Chinese renditions of the short phrase by which the Cheshire Cat tries to convince Alice that it is mad exactly like any other inhabitant of Wonderland: "A dog is not mad."[285]

> Zhao Yuanren, p. 81. 一个狗是不疯的 A dog is not mad.
> Zhu Haoyi, p. 88: 狗儿不疯，对吧？ Dogs are not mad.
> Ma Teng, p. 58: 狗是不疯的，你同意吗？ – Dogs are not mad.
> Chen Fuan, p. 95: 一条狗是不疯的… A dog is not mad.
> Zhu Hongguo, p. 66: 狗是不会疯的 Dogs are not mad // Dogs cannot go mad.
> Guan / Zhao, p. 56: 狗是不疯的 Dogs are not mad.

The formal consistency of these renditions is actually baffling. In cases in which *yi* is obviously used as a generic marker, I translated it into English by the indefinite article, whereas the phrases which omitted *yi* were rendered in plural, since both in Chinese and in English a plural form is the closest alternative for expressing genericity. Now consider the following translations of the phrase into Russian:

> Zachoder, p. 75: "Начнем с собаки. Возьмем нормальную собаку, не бешеную. Согласна?" ("Let's begin with a dog. Let's take a normal dog as an example, not a mad one. Do you agree?")
> Nabokov, p. 56: "Начнем с того, что собака, например, не сумасшедшая. Вы с этим согласны?" ("Let's begin with the fact that the dog, for example, is not mad. Do you agree with that?")
> Demurova, p. 164: "Начнем с того, что пес в своем уме. Согласна?" ("Let's begin with the fact that the dog is not mad. Do you agree?")
> Ščerbakov, p. 86: "Будем исходить из того, что собака нормальна." ("Suppose, the dog is normal.")

In none of the reproduced versions, the generic idea suggested by the indefinite article in the original is made recognizable. It would not be at all as problematic as it would seem to reproduce this idea in Russian, yet by different means than using a corresponding numeral *odin* (*one*), as, e.g. by adding an adverb or an adjective with generic semantics "обычно собаки не бешены" ("usually dogs are not mad") vs. "обычная собака не бешеная" ("(a) usual/normal dog is not mad"), by using a typical Russian generic construction relating an object to a particular

285 *Alice*, p. 68.

kind of beings "собака не бешеное животное" ("(A) dog is not (a) mad animal"), etc. In his version, Zachoder displays the maximum distance from the original by drawing on a particular kind of dogs (those that are not mad) as an example, not a quality peculiar to all dogs in general. In the rest of the examples, the translators completely suppressed the category of indefiniteness which is quite clear in the English sentence: Since in the Russian versions by Nabokov, Demurova, and Ščerbakov the noun *dog* is rather understood as a definite one and since there was no mentioning of any dog prior to the conversation, Russian readers of these renditions should have every reason to wonder what on earth the Cheshire Cat is talking about. Once again, it would be quite easy to render the indefiniteness here, e.g. by adding some supplementary pronouns or adverbs that clearly suggest its idea (какую-нибудь собаку (some/any dog), собаки как правило...(as a rule, dogs), etc. No conclusive answer could be provided for this general refusal of Russian translators to reproduce the idea of genericity, yet the more important point is that the numeral *odin* (*one*) does not figure among the abundant means by which this lack could be corrected. As Elena Gorishneva rightly concluded in her dissertation on the semantics of *odin* (*one*) in Russian and Bulgarian, "*odin* does not extend beyond the stage of the specificity marker.[286]" Now consider some translations of the phrase into German:

Zimmermann, p. 43: Ein Hund ist nicht toll.
Hansen, p. 57: Ein Hund ist nicht verrückt.
Enzensberger, p. 67: Ein Hund ist doch nicht verrückt.
Teutsch, p. 70: Ein Hund ist nicht verrückt.
Sester, p. 45: Ein Hund ist nicht verrückt.

The almost complete likeness of these translations as well as their absolute closeness to the original can once again demonstrate the power which the language exerts upon its speakers in terms of numbers and masses: whereas in the Chinese versions of the phrase the reader may easily discern one and the same visually sharp syntactical pattern of using either the generic *yi* or a plural form, and in the Russian texts, on the contrary, due to the impossibility to render the English indefinite article directly by the numeral *odin* (*one*), it can equally easily be observed that only an intensive search for an adequate expression may save translators from capitulation, the German renditions illustrate a complete consistency which is achieved quite naturally, without any effort on the part of the translator. In the second section of this chapter, some further examples of generic statements will be examined in detail. Yet to conclude the present theoretical

286 Elena Gorishneva, *The Variety of Functions*, p. 48.

part, I would like to turn to a principally different kind of language use by a translator that is manifested not in a natural force which the language exerts upon its speakers, naturally steering them in a particular direction in the translation act, but vice versa in the translator's freedom from any external force and in his/her ability to make the language as well as the narration development smoothly follow his/her own individual intention.

In a large number of instances, the obvious original motivation of a free rendition of numbers, measures, and sizes is a desire to domesticate the original, i.e. to adapt it to the norms of one's own language. Yet, on the other hand, there are cases (Vladimir Nabokov's *Alice* is maybe the most exemplary of them), in which this freedom reaches far beyond domestication needs and results in the creation of textual association chains that are completely new to the original. Consider the following example of how Nabokov treats numbers and measures in his translation of a passage from Chapter I:

> I must be getting somewhere near the center of the Earth. Let me see: that would be four thousand miles down, I think...[287] (Nabokov, p. 7: Должно быть, я уже приближаюсь к центру земли. Это, значит, будет приблизительно шесть тысяч верст... (I must be getting near the center of the Earth. That would be approximately six thousand *verst* down...))

Similarly to another passage in which Nabokov (p. 6) substituted *orange marmalade* for *strawberry-jam*, a specialty with which a Russian – at least during Nabokov's lifetime – was supposed to be far more familiar, the distance covered by Alice during her fall through the Earth is calculated here in Russian miles (*versty*). Nevertheless Nabokov provides a number which comes very close to the figure in the original: Since one versta is 1066 meters long and an English mile measures 1609 meters, the figure of 6000 verst in Nabokov's version approximately corresponds to the 4000 miles in the original. In a similar manner, the figures are adapted by Nabokov in an episode from Chapter XII in which Alice is requested to leave the court of justice because she is *more than a mile high*[288]: here, too, the *mile* is rendered by *a versta* (Nabokov, p. 108.) Concerning the measures which might have appeared especially exotic in the eyes of a Russian reader, as, e.g. *mile* and *foot*, by adapting them to the norms of Russian Nabokov prevents serious complexities in the text reception. Yet, as is demonstrated in the following example from Chapter I, his domestication strategy is not all-encompassing and, e.g. *inches* have not been substituted for any other measure:

287 *Alice*, p. 13.

288 *Alice*, p. 125.

And so it was indeed: she was now only ten inches high, and her face brightened up at the thought that she was now the right size for going through the little door into that lovely garden.[289] Cf. Nabokov, p. 10:"Действительно, она теперь была не выше десяти дюймов росту и вся она просияла при мысли, что при такой величине ей легко можно пройти в дверцу, ведущую в дивный сад. (Indeed, she was now no more than ten inches high, and she brightened at the thought that this size made it easy for her to enter the wonderful garden.)

In his translation, *inch* has been rendered by *дюйм* (Dutch: *duim*), a Russian borrowing from Dutch, a measure word that alongside a great number of other loan expressions became part of the Russian lexicon under Peter the Great. Although the measure unit to which this word refers is completely obsolete in modern Russian, any Russian reader is familiar with this word since his/her childhood, for the Russian name of the heroine in Hans Christian Andersen's famous *Thumbelina* is Дюймовочка (lit.: *a girl who is one inch high*.)

Nabokov also makes use of this word that corresponds exactly to the original in his rendition of the following dialogue between Alice and the Caterpillar from Chapter V:

(Alice said), "Three inches is such a wretched height to be." "It is a very good height indeed!" said the Caterpillar angrily, rearing itself upright as it spoke (it was exactly three inches high.)[290] Cf. Nabokov, p. 44: "Три дюйма – это такой глупый рост!" "Это чрезвычайно достойный рост!" гневно воскликнула Гусеница, взвиваясь на дыбы (она была как раз вышиной в три дюйма. ("Three inches is such a wretched height!" "It is a very honorable height!" said the Caterpillar angrily, rearing itself upright (it was exactly three inches high.))

On the contrary, in the episodes in which the measurement unit is *foot*, Nabokov systematically avoids any exact specifications, as, e.g. in his (pp. 14 and 16) omission of Carroll's comments from Chapter II according to which Alice was *rather more than nine feet high*[291], yet shortly afterwards, having grown small after using the Rabbit's magical fan, she suddenly became only *about two feet high*[292]. Both figures are missing in Nabokov's text. It would be superfluous to provide further numerous examples of such a free handling of numbers. In most cases, they may be interpreted as an attempt of domestication, yet not in Chapters XI and

289 *Alice*, p. 17.
290 *Alice*, p. 54.
291 *Alice*, pp. 20–21.
292 *Alice*, p. 24.

XII in which his rearrangement of Carroll's figures seems to follow a completely different strategy: In Chapter XI, during the questioning of the first group of witnesses, the court of justice receives three different statements concerning the exact date on which the tea party began: on March 14th (according to the Hatter), an March 15th (according to the March-Hare), and on March 16th (according to the Dormouse.) Thereafter, the jurymen did not limit themselves to record the statements, as requested by the judge, but accompanied this by what would seem a completely irrational act: "the jury eagerly wrote down all three dates on their slates, and then added them up, and reduced the answer to shillings and pence"[293] Nabokov (pp. 100–101) slightly rearranges the figures: instead of 14, 15, and 16, he indicates 14, 14 and 16, and significantly changes the mathematical act done by the jury: "и те с радостью записали все три ответа один под другим, потом сложили их и вышло: 44 копейки." ("They eagerly wrote down all the three answers one below the other, then added them up and the result was: 44 kopecks.") Although Nabokov's substitution of *shillings* and *pence* for *kopecks* can be interpreted as an obvious domestication act, this cannot be said about the result figure 44, a complete innovation on his part which reappears in Chapter XII in the King's order that anyone who is more than a mile high leave the court immediately: while in the original this order is introduced as "Rule Forty-two"[294], in Nabokov's (p. 108) version it is addressed as "Закон сорок четвертый" ("Rule Forty-four.") The figure 44 quite clearly connects two passages of the text which in the original are only thematically related to each other, namely, by furnishing further testimony to the unprecedented absurdity and arbitrariness reigning at the court. Apart from the arithmetical correctness of the added figures (14+14+16=44), the behavior of the jury may be interpreted as absurd as the King's order from Chapter XII. The translator's imagination that manifests itself in the introduction of the figure 44 in Chapter XI as well as in replacing 42 with 44 in Chapter XII might therefore be interpreted as being fully in accord with the spirit of the original and as providing a fitting accompaniment to the way the characters behave. Introducing these innovations into the *Alice*-story, Nabokov quite openly shows his own presence in the text and this demonstration of freedom has nothing whatever to do with domestication.

Nabokov's free intervention into the language of numbers and measures in *Alice* has not passed without leaving a strong impression on his critics. According to one of them, Nabokov acts as a *usurper* whose *assault on Wonderland* had the consequence that the whole story was subjugated by the translator's unre-

293 *Alice*, p. 117.
294 *Alice*, p. 125.

strained imagination[295]. This is not the place to discuss the tenability of similar criticisms. Suffice it to say that Nabokov is by no means alone to allow himself obviously free adjustments of the original to his translated version. Most changes in the language of numbers and measures in the texts produced by his colleagues seem to be psychologically motivated: either as attempts to highlight some character traits of the figures, which could make the development of the story logically more comprehensible, or out of caution about their readers who might feel embarrassed if confronted with measurement units with which they are not familiar. Consider A. Zimmermann's translation as exemplary of the first of these groups. In the dialogue between Alice and the Caterpillar in Chapter V, Alice complains about her height being only three inches and thus offends the Caterpillar that is said to be *exactly three inches high*[296]. In Zimmermann's version (p. 31) Alice's complaint is rendered as follows: "drei und einen halben Zoll ist gar zu winzig" ("three and a half inches is such a tiny height"), i.e. Alice is depicted as half an inch taller than the Caterpillar, thus furnishing it with all the more reason for feeling angry.

On the other hand, domesticating the language of numbers and measures for the readers' convenience may also be illustrated by various renditions, such as those provided by Zhao Yuanren, Barbara Teutsch, Christian Enzensberger, etc. Teutsch's *Alice* may be regarded in this respect as a particularly noteworthy case. In order to achieve the highest mathematical precision, she accurately transposed the figures that in the original refer to inches and feet into centimeters: in her rendition of the dialogue between Alice and the Caterpillar, both are said to be *seven and a half centimeters high* (*siebeneinhalb Zentimeter*, p. 55), in another episode from Chapter V, the indication of *nine inches* turns into *twenty-five centimeters* (*fünfundzwanzig Zentimeter*), and at the end of Chapter VII in which Alice is depicted as being *one foot high*, Teutsch (p. 83) translated the figure into *approximately* (sic) *twenty-eight centimeters* (*ungefähr achtundzwanzig Zentimeter* groß.) In view of the overall accuracy in her translation of figures that at times, like in the last example, appear as unusually bulky, the word *approximately* (*ungefähr*) may strike as stylistically odd. In still another episode from Chapter XII, in which Alice is requested to leave the court for being one or even two miles high, Teutsch (p. 129) translated these figures by "fünfzig Meter" (*fifty meters*) and "ein hundert" (*one hundred meters*) respectively, thus producing an act of domestication which is quite obviously imprecise. This last example demonstrates that the domesti-

295 Beverly Lyon Clark, "Nabokov's Assault on Wonderland", in: J. E. Rivers and Charles Nicol (Eds.), *Nabokov's Fifth Arc: Nabokov and Others on His Life's Work*, Austin: University of Texas Press 1982, pp. 63–74.

296 *Alice*, p. 54.

cation of measures for readers' convenience may follow not only the principle of precision, but also that of probability. Similarly to Nabokov's and to a large number of other renditions of *Alice*, this approach to the original is not a necessary result of a distance separating different languages or of different pictures of the world imposed by languages on their speakers, but rather one of the translator's free will to actively co-organize the language as well as the plot development of the story.

VI.II

One of the specific traits of Chapter VIII "The Queen's Croquet Ground" is that, apart from abundant numbers featuring in it, numbers also constitute its narrative frame: it sets out with the depiction of *three* anxious gardeners, all of them representing a playing card (a Two, a Five, and a Seven), who are busy at work painting *a* (*one*) white rose-tree red, and it is concluded by a puzzle concerning the exact relation between a whole and its parts, i.e. the question whether it is possible to decapitate a cat, if except for the head of this cat nothing is present. Thus, numbers and quantifiers symbolically connect the whole of the narration development in this chapter and it belongs among the most difficult tasks of the translator to recreate the language of numbers as naturally and comprehensibly as it has been designed in the work by the mathematician Carroll. Consider the very first phrase of the chapter:

> A large rose-tree stood near the entrance of the garden: the roses growing on it were white, but there were three gardeners at it, busily painting them red.[297]

That a correct rendition even of such a phrase which at first might appear absolutely simple may in reality be accompanied by massive difficulties can be illustrated by the following two Japanese translations:

> Waki Akiko, p. 106: "庭の入り口には、大きなバラの木が植わっていました。その木には白いバラが咲いていましたが、おりしも園丁が３人がかりで、せっせとそれを赤くぬっているところでした。" – ("Large/a large rose tree/s were/was planted at the entrance of the garden. White roses /a white rose were /was blooming on this/these tree/s and just at that moment three gardeners were busily painting them / it red.")

297 *Alice*, p. 83.

Cf. Seriu Hajime, p. 146: "大きなバラの木が、庭の入り口の近くに立っていました。バラの木は白い花をつけているのに、庭師が三人がかりで、せわしげに赤くぬっています。" ("Large/ a largre rose tree/s stood close to the entrance of the garden. The flower/s growing on it was/were white, but three gardeners were busily painting them/it red.")

Both translators do without any specification of the fact that there is only one rose-tree in this scene. The only figure that is made explicit in these renditions is *three*, i.e. the number of the gardeners involved. Formally quite close to these renditions are also those provided by Shōno Kōkichi (p. 117) and Tada Kōzō (p. 102) who equally make only the number of the gardeners explicit, not that of the tree(s) or flower(s). In the discussion of referential indefiniteness in the introductory part of this chapter, it has already been mentioned that omissions of this particular kind result in ambiguity concerning the number semantics and that, furthermore, they testify to the limits of a seemingly universal grammaticalization of the numeral *one*. In Japanese, the corresponding numeral has not been grammaticalized to function as the indefinite article in English. Now consider the rendition of numerals and quantifiers referring to the nouns *tree* and *roses* in some Chinese versions:

Zhao Yuanren, p. 101: *yi da ke meigui* 一大棵玫瑰 (*one* large rose-tree) // *shangtou de meiguihua dou shi bai de* 上头的玫瑰花都是白的 (*all* the roses on it were white)
Chen Fuan, p. 121: *yi ke hen da de meiguishu* 一棵很大的玫瑰树 (*one* large rose-tree) // *meiguihua dou shi bai de* 玫瑰花都是白的 (*all* the roses were white)
Ma Teng, p. 69: *yi ke hen da de meiguishu* 一棵很大的玫瑰树 (*one* large rose-tree) // hua quandou shi baise de 花全都是白色的 (*all* the roses were white)
Zhu Hongguo, p. 81: *yi ke gao da de meiguishu* 一棵高大的玫瑰树 (one large rose-tree) // *shangmian kaizhe bai meiguihua* 上面开着白玫瑰花 (white rose(s) were blooming on it)
Guan / Zhao, p. 68: *yi ke da meiguishu* 一棵大玫瑰树 (*one* large rose-tree) // hua shi bai se de 花是白色的 (its flower(s) were (was) white)

Only the last two versions display a certain similarity with the Japanese renditions in the following point: unless the number semantics of the object *flower(s)* (*hua shi bai se de*) is explicitly indicated, the most probable interpretation of it would be the plural. As for the first three versions, all of them provide the object with a clear indication of number semantics by using the quantifiers *dou* 都 and *quan dou* 全都 (*all*).

From the grammatical point of view, compared with any other numbers in the text, *one* proves to be especially flexible and able to perform various logical and, as will be demonstrated in what follows, psychological functions. No other number confronts the translator with similar difficulties as this particular one. Consider, e.g. a further episode from Chapter VIII in which Alice is anxious to catch sight of the Queen. Carroll depicts the royal procession as a long and complex one, composed of several units, each of them containing ten guests: "First came ten soldiers, next the ten courtiers... After these came the royal children; there were ten of them...Next came the guests, mostly Kings and Queens...last of all this grand procession, came THE KING AND QUEEN OF HEARTS."[298] It may strike as strange that the key figures of the procession should appear after everybody else. Yet apart from such a complex composition, there is nothing particularly challenging to a translator either about its arrangement or about the number *ten* which figures so prominently in the passage. Consider, on the contrary, a further scene from the same chapter in which the enraged Queen orders that the servants, prostrated at her feet, be turned over and show their faces: "The Queen... said to the Knave: 'Turn them over!' The Knave did so, very carefully, with one foot."[299] The rendition of this passage proved to be problematic for those translators who perceived a certain contradiction in the parallel use of *carefully* and *with one foot* referring to the actions of the Knave. The Russian renditions display the utmost sensibility in this respect: Ščerbakov (p. 105) makes the Knave demonstrate extreme carefulness by turning the servants over *gently with the tip of his shoe* (*осторожно, кончиком башмака*); Zachoder (p. 85) makes him *gently* employ *the tip of his foot* (*осторожно, носком ноги*), which is also the solution found in Nabokov's rendition (p. 71, *осторожно, носком одной ноги.*) In the eyes of these translators, *one foot* was definitely too much to guarantee a careful treatment of the servant, for which reason all of them decided to mitigate the number semantics of the expression. Enzensberger's (p. 82) version represents a similar case in German: the Knave employs *gently the tip of his foot* ("sorgfältig, mit einer Fußspitze".) Yet a large number of other translators by no means interpreted *one foot* as something standing in the way of a careful behavior, so that it was rendered by them exactly like in the original, e.g. by Zimmermann (p. 55, *mit einem Fuße*), by Zhu Honguo (p. 85: *yong yi zhi jiao* 用一只脚), and by Chen Fuan (p. 127: *yong yi zhi jiao* 用一只脚.) Somewhat different are the renditions provided by Zhao Yuanren (p. 105: *na jiao*拿脚) and that by Guan/Zhao (p. 71: *yong jiao* 用脚): as the number semantics has not been made explicit here at all, it is quite possible to interpret both versions not only in singular, but also in plural (*with his feet*). And one particular rendition which is diametrally opposed to the interpretations of Ščerbakov, Zachoder and Enzensberger is found in the German *Alice* by Barbara Teutsch (p. 88): "Der Bube machte das geschickt (sic)

298 *Alice*, p. 85.
299 *Alice*, p. 86.

mit dem linken Fuß." ("The Knave did it skillfully (sic) with his left foot.") In German, "links" (*left*) suggests an especial lightness or skill in performing a task (cf. *etwas mit links erledigen – to do blindfold.*) Used in this episode, *the left foot* appears as a most natural means to discipline one's servants. Thus, the translator does not only perceive any contradiction between the semantics of *carefully* and *with one foot*, but interprets both as fitting a required skill of which the Knave displays a perfect command.

A particular case is represented by quantifications of count and mass nouns. Chapter VIII contains numerous instrances in which one and the same noun appears as both a mass and a count one, e.g. *pity* (cf. *take pity on smb. // what a pity*). One of the relevant passages refers to a misunderstanding in a dialogue between Alice and the Rabbit in which Alice learns about the dangerous situation faced by the Duchess:

> "She's under sentence of execution." "What for?" said Alice. "Did you say 'What a pity!'?" the Rabbit asked. "No, I didn't," said Alice: "I don't think it's at all a pity. I said 'What for?'"[300]

The misunderstanding results from the alliteration of the question "What for?" and Alice's exclamation "What a pity!", and the task confronted by the translator of the passage is to find two alliterating expressions in his/her own language by which to reproduce the misunderstanding. In terms of the translation technique, the case is inasmuch particular as there are numerous renditions of *Alice* whose authors go much further in their alliterations than Carroll. In the original, the short pronoun *what* is enough to provoke the confusion. Similarly short are, e.g. the alliterating words in Tada Kōzō's (p. 109) *naze na no* なぜなの？ (*why?*) vs. *nante okinodoku na* なんてお気の毒な (*Ooh, what a pity!*) as well as in Jean-Pierre Berman's (p. 183): *Pour quelle raison?* (*Why?*) vs. *quel dommage* (*what a pity*). In contrast, much more linguistic imagination has been at play in those versions in which the alliteration is triggered not by the interrogative but by the object it refers to, as, e.g. in Nabokov's (p. 72): *За какую шалость?* (*Why?*, lit.: *for what mischief?*) vs. *какая жалость* (*what a pity*), with the alliterating nouns *šalost* (*mischief*) and *zhalost* (*pity*) as well as in a similar solution found by Oddera (p. 76): *Per quale reato?* (*for what crime*) vs. *Che peccato!* (*What a pity*!)

If in the last example it was only the phonemic quality of two interrogatives or of two alliterating nouns that posed problems for the translators, consider a still more troublesome case in which the difficulty arises from the conceptualization of a noun as either a count or a mass one:

300 *Alice*, p. 88.

"How are you getting on?" said the Cat, as soon as there was mouth enough for it to speak with. Alice waited till the eyes appeared and then nodded. "It's no use speaking to it," she thought, "till its ears have come, or at least one of them."[301]

Whereas the ears of the Cheshire-Cat that is slowly becoming visible in this passage are conceptualized as count nouns, its mouth is not, which is strongly suggested by the quantifier following it: *mouth enough*. Alice's judgement concerning the identity of the Cat as well as the suitable moment in which to address it follows the same logic as in an episode from Chapter I in which she is reflecting about her own identity:

"But it's no use now," thought poor Alice, "to pretend to be two people! Why, there's hardly enough of me left to make *one* respectable person."[302]

By using the noun *mouth* as a mass in Chapter VIII, she thus reproduces the same act of thinking in which she previously imagined her own self (*me*). The languages that are examined in this study provided translators with various means by which to recreate this act of thought. In a number of cases in which translators refused to reproduce the author's play with the semantics of count/mass distinction, their decision might be explained by a lack of attention to the language of the original, as, e.g. in Barbara Teutsch's German version (p. 91) in which the relevant phrase is rendered by a count noun: "sagte die Katze, sobald ihr Schnäuzchen sichtbar war" – "the Cat said, as soon as its little mouth was visible". Cf. two other German versions in which the conceptualization of *mouth* as a mass is captured as naturally as in the original: in Zimmermann's (p. 58): *sobald Mund genug da war* (*as soon as there was mouth enough*) and in Enzensberger's (p. 86): *sobald Mund genug zum Sprechen erschienen war* (*as soon as there was mouth enough to speak.*) By the use of the same means, the maximum closeness to the original was also achieved in the Italian and French translations by D'Amico (p. 83): *non appena ebbe abbastanza bocca per parlare*; Battistutta (p. 76): *appena ebbe abbastanza bocca*; Giglio (pp. 203, 205): *non appena apparve di lui quell tanto di bocca che bastava per parlare*; and Sueur (without page numbers): *assez de bouche pour parler.*

Although it would also be quite possible to reproduce the play with mass semantics in Russian (e.g. by using the partitive singular *появилось достаточно рта*), the passage actually proved to be quite a challenge to the Russian translators. Considers the following two renditions of it:

301 *Alice*, p. 90.

302 *Alice*, p. 18.

Ščerbakov (p. 108) "– Как дела?" спросил Кот, едва только рот его явился достаточно для того, чтобы разговаривать. Алиса подождала, пока появятся глаза, и кивнула Коту. "Пока хоть одно ухо не появится, – подумала она, – отвечать бесполезно." "How are you getting on?" said the Cat, as soon as his mouth appeared sufficiently for him to talk. Alice waited till the eyes appeared and then nodded at the Cat. "It's no use speaking to it," she thought, "till at least one of its ears has come."

Zachoder (p. 88) "Ну, как успехи?" спросил Чеширский Кот, как только рот его достаточно проявился, чтобы говорить. Алиса обождала, пока появятся глаза, и тогда молча кивнула. "Говорить с ним еще рано, – думала она, – надо подождать ушей. Или хоть одного уха." ("Well, how are you?" said the Cheshire Cat, as soon as his mouth appeared sufficiently for him to talk. Alice waited till the eyes appeared and then nodded silently. It's too early to speak to him," she thought, "I'll have to wait till its ears have come, or at least one (of them.)")

Whereas the rendition of *ears/ear* was not accompanied by any perceivable difficulties, the same cannot be said about that of the mass use of *mouth*: In both versions, it is reproduced as a count noun and the only medium by which the semantics of mass is suggested is the adverb достаточно (*sufficiently*) added to the verb. A similar version has been provided by Nabokov (p. 74): "'Как ваши дела?' спросил Кот, как только рот его окончательно наметился." ("'How are you getting on?' said the Cat, as soon as its mouth appeared completely.") He also makes use of an additional adverb *окончательно* (*completely*.) Since the addition of the adverbs *sufficiently/completely* could as easily accompany a plural form (e.g. in появилось достаточно ртов *enough mouths appeared* / рты наметились окончательно *the mouths appeared completely*), as a singular, in all the three Russian versions the mass noun semantics gets lost. As for the rendition provided by Demurova (p. 196), she does not even use an adverb to suggest any mass connotations in the passage and by her как только рот его обозначился в воздухе (*as soon as its mouth became discernable in the air*), she moves further away from the original than the rest of her Russian colleagues.

By venturing a look back on the controversy over the count/mass distinction in Chinese as well as on the wide-spread assumption, according to which Chinese operates only with mass noun semantics, an examination of some Chinese renditions of the passage may once again reveal how far from reality this view actually is. I have not found any single one in which *mouth* would have been rendered as a mass noun. By contrast, most of them follow the same pattern as in the Russian versions. Consider the following examples:

Zhao Yuanren, p. 109: 那猫一到它的嘴现够了 (As soon as the mouth of the Cat appeared sufficiently…)

Chen Fuan, p. 133: 猫的嘴巴现够了 (The mouth of the Cat appeared sufficiently…)

Ma Teng, p. 76: 猫的嘴刚一出现就急忙问道 (The cat asked, as soon as its mouth appeared…)

Guan / Zhao, p. 73: 猫刚出现了能说话的嘴就问。(As soon as the mouth appeared for speaking, the Cat asked…)

Zhu Haoyi, p. 114: 在嘴巴大到可以讲话以后 (When the mouth was big enough for speaking…)

In all of the above Chinese versions, *zui* (*mouth*) could hypothetically quite naturally be substituted for a noun in plural (e.g. *liang zhi yanjing xiangou le* 两只眼睛现够了 *both eyes appeared sufficiently*, etc.) The fact that in both Russian and Chinese examples *mouth* has been conceptualized as a count noun is also corroborated by the semantics of verbs that refer to it, such as проявиться, наметиться (*to appear*, *to show one's form clearly, to become quite discernable*), 大到 *da dao* (*became big enough*), etc. All of them suggest a possibility of drawing a border-line between the object (mouth) and the rest of reality: as soon as this border-line is clear enough, the Cheshire-Cat becomes able to talk. However, in the original as well as in the renditions that are close to it, the corresponding noun is formally introduced as a mass: *mouth enough*, *abbastanza bocca*, *Mund genug*, etc.

The great mystery of the Cheshire-Cat in the eyes of other characters in the story is that in most cases it appears in parts. In the following words (Chapter VI), Alice expressed her sincere wonder about this ability: "Well! I've often seen a cat without a grin,…but a grin without a cat! It's the most curious thing I ever saw in all my life!"[303]

In Chapter VIII, this peculiarity of the Cat causes a heated dispute between the executioner, the King, and the Queen: Whereas the King insists on the possibility to decapitate anything possessing a head, and the Queen's argument is that all those who are present will be decapitated unless the head of the Cat be immediately cut off, the executioner is the only one to come up with a logical argumentation: "The executioner's argument was, that you couldn't cut off a head unless there was a body to cut it off from: that he had never had to do such a thing before, and he wasn't going to begin at his time of life."[304]

In regard to the count/mass distinction, special attention deserves the parallel use of two count nouns preceded by an indefinite article: *a head* and *a body*. Both stand for nonreferential indefinite objects and exemplify a rule, according

303 *Alice*, p. 69.

304 *Alice*, p. 93.

to which a decapitation – in whatever context – is possible only if both of these objects co-exist. Thus, it is a situation, in which languages that in spite of having no articles demonstrate a high degree of grammaticalization of the numeral, corresponding to *one* in English, would be most likely to use it. Consider the following renditions of this passage into Chinese:

> Zhao Yuanren, p. 113: 要是没有个身子可以把头从它上杀下来的，那就无头可杀 (Unless there is a body from which to cut off a head, there is no head which could be cut off.)
> Chen Fuan, p. 137: 除非有一个身子，才能把一个脑袋从身上砍下来，要不然你就没法砍头 (Only if there is a body, it is possiblle to cut off a head from it, otherwise there is no way to cut it off.)
> Zhu Hongguo, p. 91: 除非有个身子，才能砍下脑袋来，否则是不可能的。(Only if there is a body, it is possible to cut off a head, otherwise it is not possible.)
> Guan/Zhao, p. 86: 除非有身子，才能从身上砍头，光是一个头是没法砍掉头的 (Only if there is a body, it is possible to cut off a head from it. If a head is all you have, there is no way to cut it off.)
> Ma Teng, p. 80: 有身子，才能从身上把头砍掉，仅仅是一个头是没有办法砍掉的 (You need a body to cut a head off from it. If a head is all you have, there is no way to cut it off.)

As was the case with referential indefiniteness discussed in the theoretical part of this chapter, it is striking how consistent the Chinese translators are in using either the classifier 个 *ge* which implies the semantics of *yi (one)* or directly the numeral *yi*. In the first three versions, the classifier precedes the noun *body*, in the last two *yi* is used before the noun *head*. Although the numeric semantics of *yi* is significantly suppressed (it does not function in opposition to other numbers and is used rather as a marker of indefiniteness), the noun to which it refers perfectly meets the conditions for being considered a count noun. The same is true of the noun accompanied by the classifier *ge*.

Finally, an episode from Chapter VIII deserves to be mentioned in which the indefinite article is used to mark genericity. Witnessing how irritated the King is over the Cat's presence, Alice recalls the following saying from some book she has read: "A cat may look at a king.[305]" The particularity in using the saying in this episode is that any figurative meaning that normally is suggested by it is absent here and it is deliberately chosen to excuse a cat that *is* literally looking at a king. German and Italian translators of the text had the option to employ here a saying which closely fits the English idiom, i.e. *Sieht doch die Katze den*

305 *Alice*, p. 91.

Kaiser an[306] (used by Sester, p. 84) and *Un gatto può guardare un Re*[307] (used by Pietrocòla-Rossetti, p. 123 as well as by Giglio, p. 207.) Surprisingly, only few translators chose this particular option, while the most common solution proved to be in paraphrasing the saying, as, e.g. in Enzensberger, p. 87: *Eine Katze braucht den König nicht zu fürchten* (*A cat should not be afraid of a king*)) or in translating the phrase directly, as, e.g. in Hansen, p. 76: *Eine Katze darf einen König ansehen* (*A cat may look at a king.*) As for the French renditions, many of them (Henri Bué, p. 128; Berman, p. 189, Sueur) make use of a set phrase which is adapted to the context of *Alice*. Thus, the proverb *Un chien regarde bien un évêque* (*A dog may look at a bishop*) received the following variation: *Un chat peut bien regarder un roi* (*A cat may look at a king.*)

On the contrary, in Japanese, Chinese, and Russian, i.e. languages that, as far as I know, do not provide translators with any fitting set expression, no option exists to directly recreate the original play with the figurative and literal meanings. Noteworthy is here the choice of the formal means for rendering the generic indefinite article. Recalling the theories concerning the use of the generic *yi* in Chinese, discussed in the theoretical part, it appears striking that none of the Chinese renditions examined by me made use of it. Consider the following versions:

> Zhao Yuanren, p. 111: 猫也能看皇帝 (A cat / cats can look at a king/kings.)
> Chen Fuan, p. 135: 猫可以望着国王。(A cat/cats may look at a king/kings.)
> Ma Teng, p. 77: 猫是可以看国王的。(A cat/ cats may look at a king/kings.)
> Guan / Zhao, p. 74: 猫是可以看国王的。(A cat/cats may look at a king/kings.)
> Zhu Haoyi, p. 116: 猫也有仰望国王的权利。(A cat/cats has/have the right to look up at/to a king/kings.)

Unlike the previously discussed translations of the phrase "A dog is not mad", for which there were at least two versions that contained the generic *yi*, none uses it in the present example, which may be interpreted as a signal of only a relative grammaticalization degree of the numeral *yi* in modern Chinese. At the formal level, in this particular situation, the Chinese translators proceeded similarly to their Japanese colleagues, cf. Tada Kōzō, p. 114: 猫にも王さまを見る権利はある (A cat/ cats has/ have also the right to look at a king) and Shono Kokichi, p. 129: ネコも王さまを見てかまわないって (It's no problem when (a)cat(s) look/s at a king.) The honorific sama さま after ō 王 (おう) *king* in Japanese may be inter-

306 Cf. Ida von Düringsfeld, *Sprichwörter der germanischen und romanischen Sprachen, vergleichend zusammengestellt*, Leipzig: Herman Fries 1872, p. 867.

307 Cf. Teodor Flonta, *A Dictionary of English and Romance Languages Equivalent Proverbs*, Bucureşti: Teopa 1992, p. 378.

preted as suggesting rather the idea of a singular, for which reason the noun is preceded by the indefinite article in the back-translations. Yet this is in no way indicative of any grammaticalization of the numeral *ichi* (*one*) in Japanese which is not used here at all.

Apart from the version provided by Nabokov (p. 75) who renders the phrase freely as "Смотреть всякий может" ("Anyone may look") and makes the Cat itself (and not Alice) pronounce it, Russian translators also demonstrated a striking consistency in this passage. Zachoder (p. 88), Ščerbakov (pp. 109–110), and Demurova (p. 198) put both nouns in plural, e.g. Zachoder: "А кошкам разрешается смотреть на королей." ("And cats are allowed to look at kings.") Interpreting this rendition, a Russian reader would be highly likely to take it for a generic statement. Since the numeral *odin* (*one*) has not achieved the grammaticalization level at which it could function as a marker of genericity, the plural form represents the simplest as well as the most comprehensible way to render genericity. Unlike the above discussed Russian translations of the phrase "A dog is not mad" in which the same form of expression could have naturally been used for rendering generic semantics, here, the formal consistency of the renditions once again demonstrates the power of language to steer the movement of thought in a particular direction: *Language speaks.*

Conclusion

In this chapter, I have taken various numeric operations by which the mathematician Lewis Carroll accompanied the language of the *Alice*-story as an opportunity to reflect upon the grammatical and semantical behavior of numbers in the original as well as in its translations. Even those formal elements which might appear trivial to the readers of the original, such as the use of indefinite articles in some quite common situations or the count/mass noun distinction, provided a fruitful ground for an analysis of some fundamental questions concerning language as a whole, as an individual organ of thinking. Of course, the chapter was not intended as an all-embracing examination of the language of numbers. Many aspects addressed in it deserve further separate in-depth studies, as, e.g. the use of the generic *yi* in Chinese (to what extent it involves the usage of normative or proscriptive semantics and how exactly normative statements are logically related to genericity); a critical reassessment of such general terms as *classifier languages* referring to languages – like Chinese and Japanese – that in effect display fundamental structural differences to one another; the conceptualization of the partitive in languages from different families (as the Slavic, the Romance, and the

Germanic ones.) For the sake of brevity, some important questions could not be regarded at all, as, e.g. a comparative study of the cardinal and ordinal numbers. Further readings of *Alice* could in all probability be highly fruitful for discussing issues pertaining to this field, e.g. the theory according to which it belongs among universal characteristics of natural languages, even such structurally different as English and Japanese, that their cardinal numbers are purely syntactic, whereas the ordinal ones are, *by contrast* (sic), semantic[308], etc. The diversity of questions arising here for a linguist is actually overwhelming and there can be no doubt that, more than once, they will make readings of *Alice* turn into new sets of adventures in the future.

308 Thomas Crump, *The Anthropology of Numbers*, Cambridge: Cambridge Univ. Press 1992, p. 39.

VII. Through the Eyes of a Child

VII.I

As was in the focus of my investigation in Chapter IV, one of the central qualities peculiar to the psychology and the language behavior of Alice is her attitude to the literal meaning. That the literal is generally considered to play quite a special role in the development of children's psychology and language acquisition has already been borne out by numerous studies in psycholinguistics, e.g. by Marcelo Dascal who in an essay in defense of the literal meaning focused on the language of children and their gradual necessary learning of fundamental differences between the literal and figurative:

> It may be true that...the child, when acquiring language, understands in the same way the metaphoric and the literal. But it is no less true that the child learns, at some moment in its linguistic career, to distinguish between them, and from that moment onwards the two are interpreted in ways that are essentially distinct.[309]

In other words, language acquisition presupposes both the ability to make use of the literal and of the figurative (metaphorical) and one to distinguish between them. The literal meaning is among other things understood as a bridge crossing which the child gradually achieves the mastery of the metaphorical. That this particular function does not disappear even in adulthood is illustrated by Dascal on the example of a Freudian joke: "The first Jew asks: Have you taken a bath? The second replies asking the other in return: Why? Is there one missing?"[310] As Dascal points out, "the "primary" meaning of the expression must be available, even though its "secondary" meaning has become conventionalized into an idiom."[311]

Yet how exactly do children proceed to develop the mastery of the figurative in their consciousness? Psychologists who have studied this question arrived at the conclusion that at the age of six-seven years children often display a certain resistance against the use of dead metaphors, i.e. fixed analogies and similes with which they are permanently confronted when hearing adults speak. Kornej Chukovsky's *From Two to Five* (1933) contains an episode in which a young boy is watching the sunset at the beach and asks: "The sun sets in the sea. Why is there

309 Marcelo Dascal, "Defending Literal Meaning", in: *Cognitive Science*, Vol. 11, 1987, pp. 259–281.
310 Marcelo Dascal, *op. cit.*, p. 270.
311 *Ibid.*

no vapor?"[312] In a great number of languages, words like *sunset* and *sunrise* constitute set expressions of the lexicon, yet an adult speaker would not be likely to be confused by their obviously unscientific nature and geocentrism, arising from the Ptolemaic belief that the Sun orbits the Earth. A probable reason for this adult insensitivity might be the loss of the pictorial quality originally associated with these expressions: adult consciousness no longer perceives connections between word components (e.g. *sun* and *set*) as reflecting real relations between natural objects, such as the Sun, the Earth, a sea, etc. Maybe only those who possess an extraordinarily acute creative imagination can get over this loss and come up with new vivid intuitions of an intimate relation between language and reality, as is documented, e.g. in one of Anton Chekhov's short stories in which the author describes how at dawn "the Sun is kissing the Earth on the horizon."[313] A child may be regarded as similar to an artist in this particular point, since its fantasy re-connects language to the world and actively reproduces the relations between observed natural objects which at some point in the past resulted in the emergence of corresponding linguistic analogies, such as *sunset* and *sunrise.*

What in the eyes of a normal adult would appear to be a set and self-evident part of the vocabulary is experienced by a child as an actual happening. And as is the case with the perception of an artist, this action which since times immemorial has been reflected in the language in a fixed unmoving form is suddenly accompanied by new associations. Yet in contrast to artists who are fully aware of the figurativeness pertaining to expressions like *the sun kissing the earth*, no transfer of meaning is involved in similar observations made by a child: the vapor which the young boy misses above the sea in Chukovsky's depiction is understood as literally as his interpretation of the scene in which he observes how the sun touches the sea while setting.

On the other hand, children's imagination may also produce analogies that are new to the semantics of their mother tongue, yet constitute set expressions within the lexicon of other languages. In the classical study on child psychology *Die Seele des Kindes* (*The Child's Soul* 1882), William Th. Preyer expressed great surprise about a boy who was complaining of "Zahnhimmel-Weh" (lit. "tooth-heaven-ache") because he did not know the noun *Gaumen* (*palate*.)[314] Preyer found remarkable the analogy created by the boy between *palate* and *heaven*. He might have been still more surprised if he had learned that this analogy, though

312 Kornej Chukovsky, *From Two to Five*, translated by Miriam Morton, Berkeley: Univ. of California Press 1971, p. 21.

313 Anton Chekhov, *Rano!* (*Early!* 1887), in: *Sobranije sochinenij*, Moskva: Hud. Literatura 1962, Vol. V, p.120: "Солнце на горизонте уже целуется с землей..."

314 Willian Th. Preyer, *Die Seele des Kindes: Beobachtungen über die geistige Entwicklung des Menschen in den ersten Lebensjahren*, Leipzig: Grieben 1890, p. 279.

not existent in German, is present, e.g. in the semantics of Russian and Dutch, cf. Russ. *небо* (*heaven*) vs. *нёбо* (*palate*) and Dutch *hemel* (*heaven*) vs. *gehemelte* (*palate.*) Of course, one could not go into the matter by asking why the analogy is missing in German. What really matters is something quite different, namely, that the imagination of a child has produced a picture which potentially is perfectly suitable to enter the lexicon of any language. To put it another way, at least from the point of view of Russian and Dutch semantics, the example provided by Preyer may serve as illustrating a vivid reproduction of one of the past stages in the language evolution. And in this case, again, it would be misleading to interpret the analogy as a metaphor. Much more appropriate seems the view expressed by Clara and William Stern in their *Die Kindersprache* (*The Children's Language* 1975), according to which similar analogical expressions are better understood as reflecting an organic unity of word and object which results in a word coinage on the basis of language material with which the child is familiar[315].

Both cases introduced above – that of a child's perceiving a natural event that at some stage in the past caused in the imagination of its language community the emergence of a pictorial set expression and actively reproducing it in its language (*sunset/vapor above the sea*), on the one hand, and that of making an analogy which exactly corresponds to certain set expressions in other languages (*palate / heaven*), on the other, – confirm Michael Halliday's critical revision of some conventional views concerning children's language acquisition as well as the parallels which he draws between this process and language evolution:

> For a long time children's language development, or "language acquisition" as it came to be rather misleadingly called, was thought of as a kind of progressive approximation to a goal, a goal that was extrinsically fixed and defined, so that each new step was seen as an imperfect attempt to attain it. Although the child's efforts are no longer dismissed as irrelevant "mistakes", but rather are seen as strategies and tactics for learning, there is still the view that the mother tongue is what the child is striving to "acquire" right from the start. In my view this conception is wide of the mark. What small children are doing is learning how to mean; and the guiding principle is neither approximative (imitating what is around) nor performative (guided by an innate grammar) but epigenetic. The child is building up a potential; and in doing so is essentially tracking the processes whereby language first evolved.[316]

315 Clara and William Stern, *Die Kindersprache*, Darmstadt: Wissenschaftliche Buchgesellschaft 1975, pp. 390–391.

316 Michael A. K. Halliday, "Representing the Child as a Semiotic Being (One Who Means)" (1998), in: M. A. K. Halliday, *The Language of Early Childhood*, London/New York: Continuum 2004, pp. 6–27, here p. 26. Steven Pinker discusses several instances which could serve as further illustrations of children's tracking the processes of language evolution. One of the language

The stage at which children are "learning how to mean" may be interpreted as not yet accomplished, immature or even wild and primitive. Yet there is also a completely different approach to it as one from which men gradually move away when becoming adults and lose all the qualities peculiar to it: freedom, sincerity, immediateness, frankness. Children's freedom as it manifests itself in their language behavior may strike adults as obviously defective. However, this does not alter the fact that the imagination revealed in children's language is by no means arbitrary or illogical. Consider the following dialogue between two children recorded by Kornej Chukovsky:

> "My daddy himself told me this..."
> "My mommy herself told me that..."
> "But my daddy is himselfer than your mommy – my daddy is much more himselfer..."[317]

This English rendition could not have cost its translator much trouble: it reproduces exactly the Russian original and illustrates the freedom with which children approach their language, i.e. in this particular case it is an obvious violation of the rule that there is no comparative form of the pronoun *himself* in English (as is the case with the Russian pronoun *sam сам*.) And in all the other languages discussed in this study, it is also possible to find a rendition which would exactly reproduce the original and be perfectly comprehensible, e.g. by creating a comparative degree of the corresponding pronouns in Italian (*stesso – più stesso*), Chinese (*ziji* 自己– *ziji de duo* 自己得多) or German (*selbst – selbster*.) During my *Alice*-courses in Heidelberg and Kyoto, whenever we had a session on the language of childhood, I asked my students to try and think of some way to translate the above short dialogue into the language of adults. Surprisingly, it usually took rather long till someone came up with a more or less comprehensible adult version, roughly meaning: "The authority of my father greatly surpasses that of your mother!" The perfect translatability of the dialogue both into other "natural" languages (those of Italian, Chinese, German children) and into that of adults testifies to a flawless logic peculiar to its language.

overgeneralizations by children which he describes in *Words and Rules* (1999) is the discovery of a series of new nouns by the omission of the final *s*, for example 'downstair' (for 'downstairs'), 'mik' (for 'mix'), 'len' (for 'lens'), etc. As Pinker observes: "We laugh, but adults do the same thing, or at least our ancestors did. *Cherry* is a back-formation from *cerise*, and *pea* is the invented singular of the mass noun *pease*, as in the nursery rhyme 'Pease porridge hot, pease porridge cold.' Many people have to be reminded that there is no such thing as a *kudo*: The noun *kudos* is singular, from the Greek word for glory." (Steven Pinker, *Words and Rules*, New York: Basic Books 1999, pp. 192–193.)

317 Kornej Chukovsky, *From Two to Five*, translated by Miriam Morton, Berkeley: Univ. of California Press 1971, p. 1.

Yet this kind of logic, with all its immediateness and openness in perceiving the world, can at times be extremely difficult to access. It is not coincidental that in their study on the children's language Clara and William Stern address it among other things as *a language of primitive peoples* (*die Sprache der Naturvölker.*)[318] One of the probably deepest stories by Anton Chekhov, entitled *Doma* (*At Home* 1887), is dedicated to capturing immeasurable complexities which may actually be hidden behind this primitiveness. The story is about a widowed prosecutor who having come back home one evening learns from the governess that his seven year old son Seryozha secretly takes tobacco from his father's table and smokes. The governess complains that all her attempts to appeal to Seryozha's conscience have been in vain and the boy won't listen to anything she says. What follows is a long conversation in which the father tries all possible means of persuasion in order to make Seryozha give up smoking. Yet neither his enumeration of various harms that tobacco causes to health nor the exposition on the inviolability of others' private property does seem to produce on the boy any impression. Again and again, the father gets the feeling of lacking the right words. In a mental struggle for a fitting rhetorical means, his intuition tells him that the only practicable method would be to think in the way his son does. However, having a glance at the drawings made by Seryozha during their talk, the prosecutor becomes more than ever convinced that this is exactly the thing to which he has absolutely no access:

> From daily observation of his son, the Prosecutor was convinced that children, like savages, have their own distinctive artistic views and demands which are beyond the comprehension of adults. Upon careful observation, Seryozha might seem abnormal to an adult. He found it admissible and reasonable to draw people taller than houses, and to convey with a pencil, besides objects, his sensations too. Thus the sounds of an orchestra he depicted in the form of spherical, smoky spots, and whistling – in the form of a spiral thread…In his conception, sound was closely contiguous to shape and color, so that every time he was coloring in letters, he invariably colored the sound L yellow, M red, A black, etc.[319]

Seryozha defends one of his drawings in which a soldier is shown as big as a house by saying that the soldier's eyes would have been invisible if he had been drawn smaller. The boy's sympathy with the drawn figures that he perceives not as produced by imagination but rather as real feeling and thinking ones, sud-

318 Clara and William Stern, *Die Kindersprache*, p. 324.

319 Tr. by Hugh Aplin, in: *Anton Chekhov's Selected Stories*, ed. by Cathy Popkin, New York: W. W. Norton & Company 2014, p. 35.

denly suggests to the father a solution to his problem: He improvises a fairy tale about an old rich tsar living in a huge crystal palace. His only companion is his son who takes up smoking, gets ill and dies. The grief-stricken father is left all alone. One day, the palace is attacked and robbed by bandits. They kill the tsar and destroy the palace garden. By this short and simple tale the prosecutor addresses the very way of thinking that only a short while before appeared to him wild and inaccessible, i.e. the ability to take the imaginary for the real and to sympathize with one's figures.

The effect produced by the fairy-tale is immediate: overwhelmed by it, Seryozha does not wait for any further explanations and expositions to come and swears not to smoke ever again. The lesson the father has gained from this conversation primarily concerns the conceptual reversal of the predicate *wild*: what he originally tended to associate with wildness and primitiveness, has now appeared to him completely comprehensible. It was the logic of what is probable which in the end made the communication successful. This kind of logic allows no violence or arbitrariness and is based on the ability to imagine things as they could happen in real life. All the episodes of the fairy-tale – the son's illness, the tsar's death, the destroyed garden, etc. – are persuasive exactly due to this particular quality, following the logic of probability and making Seryozha sympathize not only with the tsar, but also with his own father[320].

At Home testifies to the author's thorough attention to children's language and psychology as well as to the complexities in the communication between adults and children. Although childhood may be regarded as its main theme, it was written definitely not for children's reading. It is well-known that Chekhov only seldom wrote for children, which he once explained in one of his letters:

> То, что у меня, по-видимому, подходит для детей, – две сказки из собачьей жизни…А больше у меня, кажется, нет ничего в этом роде. Писать для детей вообще не умею, пишу для них раз в десять лет и так называемой детской литературы не люблю и не признаю. Детям надо давать только то, что годится и для взрослых. Андерсон, «Фрегат Паллада», Гоголь читаются охотно детьми, взрослыми также. Надо не писать для детей, а уметь выбирать из того, что уже написано для взрослых, т.е. из настоящих художественных произведений; уметь выбирать лекарство и уметь дозировать его – это целесообразнее и прямее, чем стараться выдумать для больного какое-то особенное лекарство только потому, что он ребенок. (From everything I have written, there are only two tales about dogs which, I think, would be suitable for children's reading…I don't have anything else of this sort. I cannot write for children at all, I write for them

320 Cf. Jean Piaget's observation about the child's conceiveing the world as "more logical than it really is." (Jean Piaget, *The Language and Thought of the Child*, London: Routledge 1926, p. 212.)

once in ten years only. Besides I don't like and don't accept the so called children's literature. You should give to children only things that suit grown-ups as well. Children love reading Anderson, *Frigate Pallada*, Gogol. Grown-ups like reading them too. One should not write for children, but rather be able to choose from what has already been written for grown-ups, i.e. from real pieces of fine literature. To be able to choose a medicine and to give the correct portion of it is much more reasonable and honest than trying to invent some special medicine for a patient only because he is a child.)[321]

In this piece, Chekhov addresses reason and honesty as basic requirements for children's aesthetic and mental development as well as for a successful communication between adults and children. It is true that childhood represents quite a special stage of life, yet, in Chekhov's words, it does not imply the necessity for "some special medicine" or for regarding a child as underdeveloped only because it has not reached adulthood. As suggested in *At Home*, a child may on the contrary turn out to be in possession of a particular kind of wisdom, to be a teacher for the adult, which illustrates a principal continuity between the languages of child – and adulthood rather than an unbridgeable gulf dividing them.

Understood this way, i.e. as an ideal quality which man has to cultivate within himself, childhood represents one of the central motives of world literature. For example, great stress was laid on it in *The Book of Mencius* which is a classic of Chinese philosophy cited by Zhao Yuanren in the following epigraph to the first Chinese translation of *Alice*: 大人者，不失其赤子之心者也.[322] Due to the vagueness of number semantics in classical Chinese, this phrase allows for different interpretations, reading the nouns in it either in singular or in plural, e.g. "The great man is the one who does not lose the child in his heart." or "The great man is the one who does not lose the hearts of his children." The second reading represents a political wisdom and refers to the calculating mind of an official who cannot allow himself to lose the hearts (the loyalty) of his subordinates. By contrast, the first reading – and I am quite confident that Zhao Yuanren had this first reading in mind when putting it at the beginning of his *Alice*-translation – is completely different, for any calculation is alien to it. It rather addresses a mental quality which a cultivated man should carefully preserve within himself and suggests a sincere, direct and earnest approach to the world. Perfectly in line with this idea of childhood is still another epigraph which Jan B. Gordon

321 From a letter of Anton Chekhov to Grigorij Rossolimo, 21 January 1900, Антон Павлович Чехов, *Собрание сочинений в 12 томах, т. 12, Письма* 1893–1904, Москва: Худ. Литература 1964, с. 353.

322 *Mengzi* 孟子, in: Zhu Xi 朱熹 (Comp.), *Sishu zhangju jizhu* 四书章句集注, Beijing: Zhonghua shuju 2008, p. 292.

took from Jules Michelet's *Le people* (1846) to introduce a study on the concept of childhood in Carroll's work:

> The child is the interpreter of the People. Rather, he is the People with their inborn truth before they become deformed, the People without vulgarity, without uncouthness, without envy, inspiring neither distrust nor repulsion. Not only does the child interpret the People, he also justifies and exonerates them in many things...No, childhood is not merely an age or a degree in life, it is the People, the innocent People.[323]

Both epigraphs which are intended to reproduce in a short symbolic form the essence of the *Alice*-books (Zhao Yuanren) and the idea of childhood peculiar to the Victorian prose (Jan B. Gordon), are concerned with the perception of childhood as a measure of man's inner integrity, greatness and purity. This philosophical approach makes it again necessary to raise the question as to how exactly the *Alice*-books are to be understood within the large corpus of children's literature. It would be no exaggeration to say that since their first publication this question has remained among the most fiercely debated issues in Carroll studies and that, in every particular case, the solutions proposed for it depend on different understandings of *childhood*. Among other things, reflections on this question concern the probable reactions of children who would read these books. As early as 1865, an anonymous reviewer of *Alice* voiced the opinion that these reactions could not be but repellent: "We fancy that any real child might be more puzzled than enchanted by this stiff, overwrought story."[324]

Some one hundred years later, having studied real children's reception of the *Alice*-books, Roger L. Green came up with a more cautious answer to this question: in childhood, the age to which reading Carroll proves especially appealing is that between four and eight years which is followed by the only decade in the readers' lives – i.e. between the age of eight and eighteen years – in which the books lose their attractiveness.[325] In Green's opinion, *Alice* cannot be regarded as a typical representative of children's literature but rather as a book that has gradually become a classic for the adult.[326] A similar observation has also been made by Jan B. Gordon in the essay mentioned above: whereas *Alice* never ceases

323 Jan B. Gordon, "The Alice Books and the Metaphors of Victorian Childhood" (1971), in: Robert Phillips (ed.), *Aspects of Alice*, New York: Vintage Books 1971, pp. 93–113, here p. 93.

324 A review of Alice's Adventures in Wonderland (by Anonymous), from "Children's Books" (1865), in: Robert Phillips (ed.), *Aspects of Alice*, New York: Vintage Books 1971, pp. 83–84, here p. 84.

325 Roger Lancelyn Green, "Alice" (1960), in: Robert Phillips (ed.), *Aspects of Alice*, New York: Vintage Books 1971, pp. 13–38, here p. 32.

326 Roger Lancelyn Green, *op. cit.*, p. 31.

to impress the adult public, it usually meets with indifference among children.[327] Therefore, Gordon regards the *Alice*-books as *decadent* products for adult reading rather than as children's literature.[328] By *decadent*, I believe, he may have meant the loss of many typically adult qualities that is required for accepting Carroll: of a distanced perception of the world, of a solid and healthy self-consciousness which is never subject to doubts and always wishes to be respected by others, of invulnerability, etc. Understood this way, without any negative connotations, the predicate *decadent* has also been applied to *Alice* by Walter de la Mare in whose eyes the ideal recipient of this text is "the child that is left in us"[329] and in Virginia Woolf's short masterpiece of literary criticism "Lewis Carroll's Crystallized Childhood" (1939), this idea has received arguably the deepest aesthetical and psychological elaboration.

That Carroll's books greatly appeal to analytical minds of the grown-ups, has been observed by a number of critics, e.g. by Gilbert K. Chesterton who – in *The Library of the Nursery* (1901) – prefers to see children enjoy the pleasures of making mud-pies rather than read *Alice* which, in his view, should be reserved for sages and grey-haired philosophers.[330] A similar opinion has also been expressed by the German author Ingeborg Boltz in her description of a great variety of intellectuals within Carroll's fans, including mathematicians, philosophers, psychoanalysts, etc.[331] The very special feature in the essay by Virginia Woolf is that she has found the way to explain what exactly is so intellectually appealing about the childhood idea in *Alice*:

> It is the world of sleep; it is also the world of dreams. Without any conscious effort dreams come; the white rabbit, the walrus, and the carpenter, one after another, turning and changing one into the other, they come skipping and leaping across the mind. It is for this reason that the two Alices are not books for children; they are the only books in which we become children. President Wilson, Queen Victoria, *The Times* leader writer, the late Lord Salisbury – it does not matter how old, how important, or how insignificant you are, you become a child again. To become a child is to become very literal; to find everything so strange that nothing is surprising; to be heartless, to

327 Jan B. Gordon, *op. cit.*, p. 94.

328 Jan B. Gordon, *op. cit.*, p. 94.

329 Walter de la Mare, "On the *Alice* Books" (1932), in: Robert Phillips (ed.), *Aspects of Alice*, New York: Vintage Books 1971, pp. 57–65, here p. 64.

330 "It is not children who ought to read the words of Lewis Carroll; they are far better employed making mud-pies." Gilbert K. Chesterton, "The Library of the Nursery" (1901), in: G. K. Chesterton, *Lunacy and Letters*, London: Sheed & Ward 1958, p. 26.

331 Ingeborg Boltz, "*Alice's Adventures in Wonderland*: Eine Kuriosität der viktorianischen Kinderliteratur", in: Christa Jansohn (Ed.), *In the Footsteps of Queen Victoria: Wege zum Viktorianischen Zeitalter*, Berlin: LIT 2003, pp. 279–299, here p. 286.

be ruthless, yet to be so passionate that a snub or a shadow drapes the world in gloom. It is to be Alice in Wonderland.[332]

Woolf's expression "to become literal" suggests deep connections between the language of a child (even if childhood is understood here as a mental state rediscovered by adults) and the perception of the world. This literalness is possible only if no protective distance is maintained between oneself and others so that one perfectly resonates with the world and does not need to resort to any kind of meaning transfer. The direct, immediate, and highly personal approach to the outside world which is characteristic of it accounts for the extreme vulnerability with which the literal mind instinctively reacts to the slightest manifestations of violence, arbitrariness and injustice. In Woolf's essay, this psychological inclination of the literal is presented from its gloomy side. Yet it may also be understood in a broader sense, as an acute sensitivity which is as naturally manifested in joy as in grief. In the present context, it is worth pointing out that "to become literal" stands not only – ironically – for a metaphor that captures the psychological essence of *Alice* but is also crucial for Carroll's language design. In a number of episodes, the immediateness of Alice's resonating with the world is presented by the author both as a linguistic event and as a source of joy. Consider the following scene from Chapter XI *Who Stole the Tarts?* in which Alice becomes witness of how a cheering guinea-pig is being disciplined in the hall of justice:

"I'm a poor man, your Majesty," he (the Hatter) began.
"You're *a very poor speaker*," said the King.
Here one of the guinea-pigs cheered, and was immediately suppressed by the officers of the court. (As that is rather a hard word, I will just explain to you how it was done. They had a large canvas bag, which tied up at the mouth with strings: into this they slipped the guinea-pig, head first, and then sat upon it.)
"I'm glad I've seen that done," thought Alice. "I've so often read in the newspapers, at the end of trials, 'There was some attempt at applause, which was immediately suppressed by the officers of the court,' and I never understood what it meant till now."[333]

Alice's joy at her sudden realization of the meaning of "to suppress an attempt at applause" arises from the fact that the metaphor is neutralized and turned into the literal, i.e. the plain and simple meaning of "to suppress" is "to put under

332 Virginia Woolf, "Lewis Carroll's Crystallized Childhood" (1939), in: *Alice's Adventures in Wonderland: A Critical Handbook*, ed. by Donald Rackin, Belmont: Wadsworth Publishing Company 1969, pp. 265–267, here p. 266.

333 *Alice*, pp. 119–120.

press" and as such it is as applicable in Alice's imagination to abstract objects like "attempt" as it is to the guinea-pigs. What is more, this deactivation of the figurative, which is a direct linguistic experience of "becoming literal", is emphasized by the author: Carroll anticipates Alice's difficulties with the figurative meaning of the word (*to suppress an attempt*) and uses it first in the literal meaning. As a result, the scene may be regarded as a case of the authorial play with the reader: not only is Alice watching what is going on with the guinea-pig, but she also seems to react to the commentary given by the author, as if she were reading or listening to the story and provided with a reader aid for *to suppress*. The aid is conceived of according to the same rules that made the boy in Chukovsky's book miss the vapor above the sea at sunset, which again illustrates the unity of word and object in children's perception. How difficult this way of approaching the figurative and literal may occasionally prove for the adult mind, can be illustrated by an example from the previously mentioned essay by George Pitcher *Wittgenstein, Nonsense, and Lewis Carroll*. The episode in which the guinea-pig is being suppressed before Alice's eyes inspired Pitcher to the following reflections:

> It is not clear what is to be made of the second paragraph (i.e. Chapter XI 'There was some attempt at applause, which was immediately suppressed by the officers of the court.') Did Alice think she understood what the phrase "suppressing the people" (i.e. those who attempt to applaud at the end of trials) means? If so, she was wrong – for such people are not generally put head first into large canvas bags and sat upon – and then the point of the passage would be to show just how drastic her misinterpretation of the ostensive definition was. Or, to read the passage more literally, did Alice rather think she understood what "suppressing an attempt" (e.g. at applause) means? If so, she was wrong again: for even if she knew what suppressing a guinea-pig was, it would not follow that she knew what suppressing an attempt at applause was. Indeed, on her understanding of the phrase "suppressing a guinea-pig," the phrase "suppressing an attempt at applause" is nonsensical, for attempts cannot be put into bags and be sat upon.[334]

What is particularly surprising about this piece of philosophical criticism is that it is exactly the unity of word and object that is so central to Carroll's literalness which is critically addressed and corrected by Pitcher's "more literal" interpretation: In his view, it would be impossible to take the scene in which the animal is depicted as *suppressed* as a fitting illustration of the same verb's ability to refer to abstractions (e.g. *an attempt at applause*.) This may testify to a high degree of impermeability of *Alice* for the adult analytical mind which insists on a funda-

334 George Pitcher, "Wittgenstein, Nonsense, and Lewis Carroll", in: *The Massachusetts Review*, Vol. 6, No. 3 (Spring-Summer 1965), pp. 591–611, here pp. 598–599.

mental discontinuity between the literal and the figurative and refuses to acknowledge any pictorial affinity between them. The logic of all the corrections to which he exposes Alice's language behavior is not difficult to understand. It addresses a child as a being that per definition is prone to make mistakes and thus directly opposes the essential quality of rediscovered childhood described by Woolf: the capacity to become literal.

One further example of this quality on which Carroll laid great stress by designing Alice's language behavior may be found in the following passage from Chapter IX "The Mock Turtle's Story":

> "When *I'm* a Duchess," she (Alice) said to herself (not in a very hopeful tone, though), "I wo'n't have any pepper in my kitchen *at all*. Soup does very well without – Maybe it's always pepper that makes people hot-tempered," she went on, very much pleased at having found out a new kind of rule, "and vinegar that makes them sour – and chamomile that makes them bitter – and – and barley-sugar and such things that make children sweet-tempered I only wish people knew *that*: then they wouldn't be so stingy about it, you know –"[335]

Here, again, the language provides Alice with a number of cues which prove helpful for understanding both the world and the human psychology. And again similarly to the first example, Carroll's presentation of the unity of words and objects is achieved by deconstructing the metaphorical meaning: hot-tempered, sour, bitter, sweet, – all these adjectives are turned into the literal and made responsible for some corresponding qualities of human disposition. Since due to these sudden discoveries the world appears to Alice much more logical than before, she is again greatly pleased at her new insights.[336]

In all the above examples, the language discoveries rest logically on induction, i.e. it is Alice's personal experience of some definite referents which proves to be their ultimate source. Without these referents, e.g. the guinea-pig that is put into a bag (*suppressed*) or the pepper in the Duchess' kitchen (*hot-tempered*), no discoveries of this kind would have been possible. For this reason, the joy which Alice feels at her new linguistic ideas is constantly connected to the joy about the world around her. In Chapters IX and X, she encounters two characters that

335 *Alice*, p. 94.

336 For similar language discoveries by 'real' children and their great delight at the discovered new rules see Steven Pinker *Words and Rules*, p. 192. For a much larger phenomenon of the so-called *overregularization*, i.e. children's extension of regular grammatical patterns to irregular words, see Gary F. Marcus, Steven Pinker (et al.), *Overregularization in Language Acquisition*. Monographs of the Society for Research in Child Development, Chicago: Univ. of Chicago Press 1992, 57 (4, Serial No. 228.)

personify an exact reversal of this attitude to the language and a negation of all the logical rules to which Alice resorts in exploring reality: the Mock Turtle and the Gryphon. From the point of view of literalness and childhood, they therefore deserve a close scrutiny.

It is not coincidental that Alice is introduced to them by the Queen: The language experience made by Alice during her conversations with the Mock Turtle and the Gryphon anticipates the main motif of the concluding chapters of the book in which the Queen plays one of the leading parts – that of arbitrariness. Already the first impression gained by Alice from listening to the Mock Turtle's sighs turns out as a deception, for the reasons of his grief are promptly laid bare by the Gryphon as follows: "It's all his fancy, that: he hasn't got no sorrow."[337] Thus, it is the lack of motivation, the emptiness of verbal expression, the absence of any real reference that determine the language behavior of the Mock Turtle (and, as is shown shortly afterwards, of the Gryphon as well.) Precisely as is the case with his tears, his words do not result from any actual experience of the world but rather from a pure improvisation the main principle of which – in marked contrast to Alice's literalness – is an arbitrary play with word meanings. This new and unexpected way of going about words confronts Alice with great difficulties. For example, from the very beginning, she tries to understand why something should be designated by a word without reference ("Why did you call him Tortoise, if he wasn't one?"[338]) and thus displays a conviction that language use has to be motivated in reality. Yet her curiosity is immediately rebutted by sheer arbitrariness and rudeness:

> "We called him Tortoise because he taught us," said the Mock Turtle angrily. "Really you are very dull."
> "You ought to be ashamed of yourself for asking such a simple question," added the Gryphon.[339]

In the further course of the conversation, the mistrust and rudeness with which Alice is treated by her new acquaintances constantly increase:

> "Yes, we went to school in the sea, though you mayn't believe it –"
> "I never said I didn't!" interrupted Alice.
> "You did!" said the Mock Turtle.
> "Hold your tongue!" added the Gryphon, before Alice could speak again.[340]

337 *Alice*, p. 100.
338 *Alice*, p. 100.
339 *Alice*, p. 100.
340 *Alice*, p. 101.

Alice stoically withstands the rudeness and does not react to it by any single word. Yet what she is absolutely not able to tacitly accept is how easily the logic is offended and the language is deformed, e.g. in the Mock Turtle's depiction of the courses he once attended at school:

> "French, music, and washing – extra."
> "You couldn't have wanted it much,' said Alice: 'living at the bottom of the sea."
> "I couldn't afford to learn it," said the Mock Turtle with a sigh. "I only took the regular course."
> "What was that?" inquired Alice.
> "Reeling and Writhing, of course, to begin with," the Mock Turtle replied. "And then the different branches of Arithmetic – Ambition, Distraction, Uglification, and Derision."
> "I never heard of 'Uglification,'" Alice ventured to say.[341]

Alice's observation that *washing* must have been superfluous at the bottom of the sea is absolutely logical. Yet the Mock Turtle evades a direct answer to it by discarding any referential connection between washing and water to which Alice alludes. It is only by means of this arbitrary act of language use that he is able to counter her remark. The inserted "of course" in his enumeration of school disciplines increases the absurdity of his story: it appeals to the ability of his interlocutors to follow the logic of his narration, although there is actually not much logic to be found in it. The Mock Turtle's words display an open act of verbal violence: its arbitrariness is based on a free creation of links between words that in reality lack any connection (deriving *Ambition*, *Distraction*, *Derision* from *Addition*, *Subtraction*, *Division*) as well as by coining new words (*Uglification*.) For confessing that she has never heard of Uglification before, Alice is accused of being a "simpleton."[342] This point of critique is inasmuch justified as compared with the language habits practiced by the Mock Turtle and the Gryphon, Alice's belief in language rules may strike as naïve and childish: she trusts in the conventionality of meaning and expects the others to share the same attitude. Yet even if most verbal creations and deformations produced by her interlocutors make her feel completely puzzled and she continues listening to them patiently in the hope of an explanation to come, she never fails to recognize arbitrariness which results in open violations of logic, as, e.g. in the following episode from Chapter IX:

341 *Alice*, p. 101.
342 *Alice*, p. 101.

"And how many hours a day did you do lessons?" said Alice, in a hurry to change the subject.

"Ten hours the first day," said the Mock Turtle: "nine the next, and so on."

"What a curious plan!" exclaimed Alice.

"That's the reason they are called lessons," the Gryphon remarked: "because they lessen from day to day."

This was quite a new idea to Alice, and she thought it over a little before she made her next remark. "Then the eleventh day must have been a holiday?"

"Of course it was," said the Mock Turtle.

"And how did you manage on the twelfth?" Alice went on eagerly.

"That's enough about lessons," the Gryphon interrupted in a very decided tone. "Tell her something about the games now."[343]

With her last question, Alice hits upon a serious logical mistake in the Mock Turtle's account: She is correct in pointing out that the number *twelve* should introduce a new first day, i.e. a new series, yet according to the free etymology of the noun "lesson", the series is conceived as having ten units only and not twelve. The abrupt change of subject by the Gryphon immediately after Alice's question underscores the obvious weakness of similar etymological experiments. If at the beginning of the chapter Alice is greatly pleased at having discovered a rule, according to which it is *pepper* that makes people *hot-tempered*, this discovery is not based on breaking with logic but rather on her personal observations of what she takes for real correspondences between psychological traits and qualities of taste. And this is exactly the kind of causality which is completely alien to the etymologies of the Mock Turtle who dismisses any reference of words to the real experience as well as the conventionality of semantics. That this position necessarily results in a negation of literalness and therefore represents an exact opposite of rules following which Alice learns the world around her, becomes particularly obvious in an episode from Chapter X in which the Mock Turtle produces a phrase which earlier, in Chapter VII, was pronounced by Alice herself, "I mean what I say"[344]:

"If I'd been the whiting," said Alice, whose thoughts were still running on the song, "I'd have said to the porpoise 'Keep back, please! We don't want *you* with us!'"

"They were obliged to have him with them," the Mock Turtle said: "no wise fish would go anywhere without a porpoise."

"Wouldn't it really?" said Alice in a tone of great surprise.

343 *Alice*, p. 103.

344 *Alice*, p. 73.

"Of course not," said the Mock Turtle, "why, if a fish came to *me*, and told me he was going a journey, I should say 'With what porpoise?'"

"Don't you mean 'purpose'?"

"I mean what I say," the Mock Turtle replied in an offended tone.[345]

The words "I mean what I say" which echo the events from Chapter VII raise a number of associations between the Mad Tea Party and Alice's encounter with the Mock Turtle and the Gryphon. In both of these instances, it is Alice's trust in intimate connections between words and objects of reality which is being challenged and in both cases the communication eventually fails. However, whereas at the Mad Tea Party language is not completely divorced with reality and the critique against Alice for whom saying what she means and meaning what she says is essentially the same is based on a play with figurative meanings, i.e. an area in which she does not yet feel at home, the situation into which the same phrase is inscribed in Chapter IX is much more dramatic: The Mock Turtle's "I mean what I say" has nothing whatever in common with sincerity and honesty suggested by Alice's phrase in Chapter VII but arises from an outspoken subjectivism which demands – like it will later be described by Carroll as peculiar to Humpty Dumpty's language habits – that meanings of words should exclusively depend on what a speaker wants them to mean. Understood this way, "porpoise" and "purpose" should not even be consonant, which is the basis of Carroll's wordplay, but either of them – as any other word in any language – can stand for anything if it accords with the speaker's intentions. No longer are there any stable links between words and referents, and the conventionality of semantics is totally substituted for by the irrational. As the highest possible manifestation of verbal violence, this time, "I mean what I say" turns against the man's ability to become literal. For the first time in Carroll's story, the language of childhood thus hits upon its probably most unrelenting adversary and is faced with the threat of a complete annihilation.

VII.II

The above episodes in which Alice is greatly pleased at having suddenly realized some hidden correlations between language and reality confront translators with the necessity to search for similarly tangible bridges between the figurative and the literal as they have been created by Carroll. These bridges should be taken from the conventions of one's lexicon and represent set semantical units with which

345 *Alice*, pp. 108–109.

any language user would be as familiar as English speakers are with the semantics of, e.g. *to suppress*, activating the idea of a weight which can be applicable to both physical (e.g. *a body*, *a guinea-pig*) and abstract objects (e.g. *an attempt.*) In the languages under study, similar correspondences are as a rule quite easy to find and particularly impressing are those versions in which some new images have been added to the story making its development take quite unexpected turns.

For the trial scene from Chapter XI, most translators found fitting semantical means for a more or less exact rendition of *to suppress*: *unterdrücken* in German (A. Zimmermann, p. 81; K. Hansen, p. 101), *tanya* 弹压 in Chinese (Zhao Yuanren, p. 157; Chen Fuan, p. 189), *подавить* in Russian (V. Nabokov, p. 103; N Demurova, p. 248), *sopprimere* in Italian (T. Pietrocòla-Rossetti, pp. 167–168), *toriosaeru* 取り押さえる in Japanese (Shōno Kōkichi, p. 173.) Compared with these versions, the following rendition provided by C. Enzensberger (p. 116) may be regarded as innovative: "Bei dieser Antwort brach eines der Meerschweinchen in Hochrufe aus und wurde von den Gerichtsdienern stracks unterbunden…Sie knüpften den Sack zu." ("Hearing this answer, one of the guinea-pigs burst out into cheers and was stopped by one of the ushers…They tied the bag up.") Here, it is the picture of a cord by which to tie up the bag that is triggered in the reader's imagination by the verb *unterbinden* (*to stop*): since *binden* has the meaning of *to tie up*, in this German version, Alice may easily recognize that a simple cord with which the guinea-pig is tied up in the bag would generally also be enough to suppress an attempt at applause.

When searching for fitting ways to express the semantics of *to suppress*, it is also important to bear in mind the emotional reaction of Alice to the scene in which it is used. This would seem to be among the primary criteria by which to judge about the quality of a new text. From this perspective, another felicitous innovative rendition of the episode has been provided by Zachoder (p. 108): "Морская свинка выдворена (в мекшок, за окно, подергали за веревку и Морская Свинка весело выскочила во двор…)" ("The guinea-pig was expelled (from the court)…It was put into a bag, then thrown out of the window. They drew the cords to open the bag and the guinea-pig sprang out cheerfully into the courtyard.") What gets completely lost in this back translation is the motivation of the Russian noun *courtyard* (*двор*) which is semantically closely linked to the verb *to expel* (*выдворить*, lit.: *put out into the court.*) This wordplay on the side of the translator fits well the original in terms of the emotions expressed in it: the guinea-pig is as cheerful after it is expelled from the court as during the trial, which in no way contradicts Alice's joy at seeing what has happened to it. Consider, by contrast, a French version by Paul Sueur[346] in which this joy appears

346 No page numbers.

much less plausible: "un des cochons d'Inde applaudit, et fut immédiatement étouffé." ("One of the guinea pigs applauded and was immediately suffocated.") This rendition makes use of an association chain (*the bag* vs. *to suffocate*) which is quite in line with the semantics of the original and therefore may be regarded as a fitting reproduction of a bridge from the literal to the figurative (*suppressing a guinea-pig* vs. *suppressing an attempt at applause*), however, the emotional effect of pleasure which should be triggered by it is rather improbable.

Yet in terms of quality, still more problematic seem to be the translations in which the pivotal linguistic event of the episode, i.e. the transposition of the literal (*to put under press*) into the metaphorical (*to suppress*) and, vice versa, a recognition of the metaphorical by means of the literal, has been reduced or completely ignored. Consider the following Italian version by Oddera (p. 107) in which *to suppress* is rendered by the verb *tacitare* (*to make silent*): "A questo punto uno dei porcellini d'India applaudí e venne immediatamente tacitato dai cancellieri... Vi sono stati tentativi di applausi, immediatamente tacitati dai cancellieri." ("At this point one of the guinea pigs applauded and was immediately made silent by the ushers...There were attempts at applause which were immediately made silent by the ushers.") Since *tacitare* could hardly be understood as a figurative expression when referring to *attempts at applause*, a more fitting rendition would be by *sopprimere* as used by T. Pietrocòla-Rossetti. The same problem is evident in Chinese versions by Zhu Haoyi (p. 156) and Ma Teng (p. 104): both use the verb *zhizhi* 制止 (*to check*, *to restrain*, *to put a stop to smth.*) that lacks any figurative meaning. Therefore, in contrast to the above mentioned versions provided by Zhao Yuanren and Chen Fuan, it is made completely incomprehensible for their readers what makes Alice feel pleased at her language discovery and what exactly has been discovered after all.

As for the second episode under study, the passage from Chapter IX in which a similar interplay of the figurative and the literal is used to confirm Alice in her realization of the unity of language and the world, since it contains a series of different images, its translators are confronted with yet more difficulties. And again, some renditions display great resourcefulness introducing a number of images that are new to the original, as, e.g. that of Zhao Yuanren (p. 117):

> "也许人家性急都是因为吃胡椒的缘故。"她说着觉得发明了一个新理，很高兴，她就接下去道，"心酸大概是喝了酸梅汤的缘故——命苦大概是吃了黄连的缘故——还有——还有小孩儿的脾气甜甜的，大概是吃了大麦糖那些东西的缘故。"("Maybe it's because of eating pepper that people get anxious," she said, feeling glad at having found out a new principle. She went on: "And one gets sorrowful drinking the sour

dark plums drink, and eating goldthread makes people unhappy, and – and – it's for eating barley-sugar that children get sweet-tempered.")

In the original, the image of *pepper* which is the first unit of the series is of a particular importance: it provides Alice with a key for seeing correspondences between taste qualities (*hot*) and qualities of character (*hot-tempered.*) All the other units follow the same semantical rule of building associations between taste and psychology: *sour* vs. *vinegar*, *bitter* vs. *chamomile*, etc. However, in Zhao Yuanren's rendition, no image is introduced to trigger a similar chain of associations, since *hujiao* 胡椒 (*pepper*) cannot directly be related to the mental state referred to by *xingji* 性急 (*anxious.*) It is only the second unit in his series which truly reproduces the source of Carroll's wordplay by juxtaposing *xinsuan* 心酸 (*sorrowful*, lit.: *a sour heart*) and *suan mei tang* 酸梅汤 (*sour dark plums drink*), i.e. making the language (*suan* 酸 (sour)) display direct correlations with things in reality. That the first unit fails to demonstrate the same mechanism of steering Alice's and the reader's associations, makes Zhao's rendition of the passage not really successful. Zhu Haoyi's version (p. 121) illustrates the same problem, since it does not contain any image to set off the necessary association chain: "说不定人们的脾气会那么暴躁就是因为胡椒的关系。" ("Maybe it's because of pepper that people get nervous.") Although *baozao* 暴躁 may be back-translated by *hot-tempered*, this rendition would by no means be mandatory so that here, again, there is no directly visible semantical connection between the corresponding images. The same thing holds good for the Chinese renditions prepared by Ma Teng (p. 81) and Chen Fuan (p. 139) both of whom equally refuse to reconstruct Carroll's bridge connecting language to the world and the figurative to the literal. Yet Chinese offers quite practicable means of reproducing this idea. Consider, e.g. the semantics of *la* 辣 (*spicy*) and words containing this character and referring to some corresponding psychological traits or mental states, such as 泼辣 *pola* (*grumpy*, *bad-tempered*, *severe*), 心黑手辣 *xin hei shou la* (*black-hearted and cruel*), 辣乎乎 *lahuhu* (both *spicy* and *a bitter experience*), etc. Therefore, the above mentioned Chinese renditions may be regarded as ones in which the extension of the original semantics (by adding new images like *eating goldthread which makes people unhappy*) is accompanied by a simultaneous reduction of it, which is by no means motivated by the nature of Chinese or some deficits in its semantics.

Among Russian translations of the passage, the ones produced by Nina Demurova and Vladimir Nabokov deserve special attention. Although some of the units in their series are also new to the original, they truly reproduce the basic rule of Carroll's wordplay and make perfectly recognizable for Russian readers what kind of discoveries Alice is making here. Consider the following version by Demurova (p. 204):

> "От перца, верно, и начинают всем перечить..." Алиса очень обрадовалась, что открыла новое правило. "От уксуса – куксятся, – продолжала она задумчиво, – от горчицы – огорчаются, от лука – лукавят, от вина – винятся, а от сдобы – добреют. Как жалко, что никто об этом не знает...Все было бы так просто. Ели бы сдобу – и добрели!" ("Pepper makes people contradict everyone." Alice was quite happy at having discovered a new rule. "Vinegar makes sulky," – she went on thoughtfully. – "Mustard makes unhappy, onions make dishonest, wine makes people confess and buns make good-hearted. It's such a pity nobody knows about it. Otherwise everything would become so simple! People should eat buns and get good-hearted!")

All the deviations from the original are motivated by the semantics of Russian. Whereas the associative links between images in the original are not marked at the formal level and are rather suggested by the respective qualities of taste (*hot, sour, bitter, sweet*), in Demurova's version, they rest on the consonance of unrelated words: *перец* (*pepper*) vs. *перечить* (*contradict*), *уксус* (*vinegar*) vs. *куксятся* (*get sulky*), *вино* (*wine*) vs. *виниться* (*to confess*), etc. Although all the combinations of images are more or less coincidental and mutually unrelated, the semantical correlations discovered between them by the Russian Alice (e.g. between *wine* and *guilt* suggested by *to confess*) are strikingly convincing. Since in designing her wordplay Demurova simultaneously uses two different sources, i.e. both semantical associations and word's sound, the principle of correspondences between language and reality discovered by her Alice may be regarded as a further progression of the rule introduced by Carroll. Although none of the units from the original series (*hot, sour, bitter, sweet*) has been translated directly, the message of the passage has been absolutely truly reproduced and Alice's joy at her discovery appears also quite plausible.

On his part, Nabokov (p. 78) follows in his rendition of the passage the original exactly: "Быть может, именно благодаря перцу люди делаются так вспыльчивы...А уксус заставляет людей острить, а лекарства оставляют в душе горечь, а сладости придают мягкость нраву..." ("It's maybe exactly because of pepper that people get hot-tempered...And vinegar makes their tongues sharp, and medicines leave behind spiritual bitterness and sweets make people sweet-tempered.") The associational links between images are triggered by purely semantical means, e.g. *перец* (*pepper*) corresponds to *вспыльчивость* (*hot temper*) and evokes in the consciousness of the Russian reader the image of a "glowing mouth" (*пылает во рту*) which is exactly the same kind of bridge connecting the literal and the figurative as the hot taste of pepper in the original.

The methods of rendering Alice's discovery illustrated above on some Chinese and Russian examples can be observed in all of the languages under study. For example, in his Japanese version, Shōno Kōkichi (p. 133) proceeds like most of his Chinese colleagues and provides no image that would trigger in the reader's perception a chain of associations similar to that of the original:

> 人がかっかとおこるのは、いつもたぶんコショウのせいなのよ…酢のせいでみんなはすねるし ― カミツレはにがいから、にがい顔になるし ― それに ― それに子どもたちがやさしい気だてになるのは、水あめやなんかのせいよ。(It's maybe always because of pepper that people lose their temper… People get sulky because of vinegar, and because chamomile is bitter, people's faces get sorrowful, and – and – the reason children get mild-tempered is because they drink *mizuame* sirup.)

Semantically, *kakka to okoru* かっかとおこる (*getting angry*, *losing one's temper*) has nothing to do with *koshō* コショウ (*pepper*.) Yet all the other units in the series constitute image pairs that, similarly to those provided by Demurova, are consonant (e.g. *su* (*vinegar*) vs. *suneru* (*to sulk*)) and, though not really mutually related, follow the logic of Alice's discovery and appear as correlating images. As for the first unit in the series, similarly to what is the case with the above mentioned Chinese versions, the refusal to reproduce the wordplay of the original does not arise from some deficit of Japanese semantics. On the contrary, the translator could have found quite appropriate ways of rendering it, e.g. by *karai* 辛い (*hot* (*spicy*), and also: *severe*), and thus constructing the same conceptual link between the literal and the figurative as in the English original. It is noteworthy that by refusing to search for adequate means of recreating the mechanism of Carroll's wordplay and by rendering it by the exact semantical equivalents of *pepper* (*koshō*) and *hot-tempered* (*kakka to okoru*), the translator ironically moves away from the original, for the corresponding words in Japanese cannot capture the interplay between the literal and the metaphoric. On the other hand, it may also strike as a paradox that having chosen to reproduce the pairs of images by semantical units that are completely new to the language of the original, Demurova, by contrast, gets much closer to its message. The same may be said, e.g. about the following German version by C. Enzensberger (p. 90):

> "Wenn *ich* einmal Herzogin bin", sagte sie sich (wenn auch nicht sehr zuversichtlich), "kommt mir keinerlei Pfeffer in die Küche. Suppe schmeckt auch ohne – und vielleicht ist es immer nur der Pfeffer, wenn die Menschen scharfzüngig werden…" ("When I'm

a Duchess," said Alice, though not in a very sure tone, "I shall not have any pepper in my kitchen. A soup can be delicious without any pepper in it – it's maybe because of pepper that people get a sharp tongue.")

The translator's inventiveness which results in bridging the literal and the metaphorical is manifested in the choice of *scharfzüngig* (*sharp-tongued*) for *hot-tempered*: though it is not really an exact rendition, it enables Enzensberger's Alice to make the same discovery of the relations between language and the world as it is conceived by Carroll.

Considering the fact that this passage is positioned at the beginning of Chapter IX shortly before Alice's conversation with the Mock Turtle and the Gryphon in which verbal arbitrariness figures as the central subject, a question which necessarily arises is in what way the language rule discovered by Alice is different to the excessive freedom pertaining to the language practice of her interlocutors. After all, Alice's discovery might also be interpreted as a free invention of non-existent links between words and objects of reality. Yet exactly this is not the case: Alice's idea is based on her experiences made in the Duchess' kitchen and therefore cannot be regarded as arbitrary. Immediately before making her discovery, Alice remembers the hot disposition of the Duchess: "Alice was very glad to find her (the Duchess) in such a pleasant temper, and thought to herself that perhaps it was only the pepper that had made her so savage when they met in the kitchen."[347] None of the translations discussed in the present study has neglected that Alice's discovery is actually rooted in her experience: neither those who proceed similarly to Zhao Yuanren and do not recreate the triggering effect produced by the first unit in the series (*pepper – hot – hot-tempered*), nor those who closely follow the original. Alice's recollection of the Duchess' hot temper is always reproduced, e.g. as *xingji* 性急 (*anxious*, Zhao Yuanren), *вспыльчивый* (*hot-tempered*, Demurova), *kakka to okoru* かっかとおこる (*getting mad/angry*, Shōno Kōkichi), etc. By doing so, the translators call to the reader's mind the opposition between Alice's careful approach to language which requires that words should have real and clear reference, and the arbitrariness peculiar to the Mock Turtle's / the Gryphon's language habits.

Different to Alice, the verbal strategy practiced by the Mock Turtle and the Gryphon is alien to literalness and is aimed not at proving the unity between words and objects but, on the contrary, at making the language split away from reality and lose the capacity to function as a dependable means of communication. They represent a principle demanding that the reference of words should

347 *Alice*, p. 94.

be discarded completely, which is also alluded to by the Queen shortly before Alice is introduced to them:

> "Have you seen the Mock Turtle yet?" "No," said Alice, "I don't even know what a Mock Turtle is." "It's the thing Mock Turtle Soup is made from," said the Queen.[348]

The definition provided here by the Queen is no definition in the strict sense of the term, since it does not contain any information concerning the essence of the described being or the qualities making it appear distinct from other individuals and kinds, and is limited to pointing to its possible applicability. Shortly afterwards, Alice learns from the Mock Turtle that his essence is suggested by his name, i.e. by the falsity which makes him dissimilar to both turtles that exist in reality and – in a broader sense, as a program – to anything real in general. *Mockery* is thus the basic principle that governs his language, and since this word constitutes the name and the essence of the Mock Turtle, its reproduction proves to pose great difficulties for translators: an adequate rendition requires searching for a name which would make this figure appear as a false turtle and at the same time reveal the idea behind his language behavior by directly referring to *mockery*, *derision*, and *disdain*. The only translation in which I was able to find a direct fitting word suggesting both of these meanings is the Japanese version by Seriu Hajime (p. 175) who renders the Mock Turtle's name by *kamemodoki* カメモドキ (*a pseudo-turtle*), *modoki* meaning *pseudo* and referring to a comic secondary character within a theatre performance whose task is to make fun of the protagonists. In other Japanese versions available to me, although the idea of falsity is obviously suggested by the corresponding words, the semantics of mockery (derision, ridicule) is missing, as, e.g. in Shōno Kōkichi's (p. 139) text in which the name is rendered by *niseumigame* ニセ海ガメ (*a pseudo-sea-turtle*) which is a compound consisting of *nise* (*mimic, pseudo*) and *umigame* (*sea turtle*.) In his Russian rendition, Nabokov (p. 78) plays with the sound of words in creating the name *Чепупаха* (Čepupaha.) This solution seems felicitous as it is suggestive of two different Russian nouns: *черепаха* (čerepaha = *turtle*) and *чепуха* (čepuha = *nonsense*.) Among Chinese versions, the probably most noteworthy rendition of the name has been provided by Zhao Yuanren (p. 123) in his word-creation Sujiayu 素甲鱼 (lit.: *a turtle for vegetarians*) in which the idea of falsity is suggested by *su* (*vegetarian*), yet nothing reveals here any connection with mockery. Probably the most original – and the most bulky – of all the versions of the name are the Russian ones created by Ščerbakov (p. 133) and Solovjova (p. 189), who, respectively, render it by *Черепаха-Телячьи-Ножки* (Čerepaha-Teljačji-Nozhki,

348 *Alice*, p. 98.

i.e. *a Turtle with the legs of a calf*) and by *Черепаха из телячьей головки* (Čerepaha iz teljačej golovki, i.e. *a Turtle made of a calf-head.*) In these last cases, the fantasy of the translators might have been triggered either by the fact that in English, *mock turtle* is associated with *mock turtle soup* (i.e. a soup made from a calf's head) or by the illustrations provided to Carroll's story by John Tenniel (1820–1914) who depicted the Mock Turtle as a turtle with a calf's head and calf's legs.

Compared with the challenges faced by the translators in rendering the language rule discovered by Alice (the bridge between the literal and the figurative) and in searching for an adequate name of the Mock Turtle in their language imagination, the arbitrariness peculiar to the language of the Mock Turtle and of the Gryphon in Chapters IX and X did not pose for them any significant problems. In all the versions under study, the practice of divorcing language with conventions and reference could be easily recreated. In one particular point, most versions demonstrate a great degree of unity: Since searching for semantical means to make words break with reality suggested a creative ("nihilist") approach to the conventions within one's own lexicon, the related passages are the ones that are probably the most distanced from the semantics of the original. What follows are a number of illustrations of word-plays provided by different translators for the four cases of arbitrariness introduced in the first part of this chapter:

I. "We called him Tortoise because he taught us," said the Mock Turtle angrily. "Really you are very dull!"

In Shōno Kōkichi's version (p. 144), "Tortoise" is rendered by *zenigame* (*a spotted turtle.*) The *spots* (*zeni*) make think of small Japanese coins with a whole in the middle, which provides the semantical motivation of the compound *zenigame*, lit.: *coin* (zeni)-*turtle*. For the Japanese translator, this semantical finding proves particularly felicitous as *zeni* represents an almost exact graphic and phonetic reversal of *nise* (*pseudo*) taken by him for the name of the Mock Turtle. The answer given to the question why the old teacher was called "Tortoise" if he was not one in reality, is rendered as follows (p. 144): 「その先生はゼニに目がなかったからですよ。」 ("It's because the teacher was mad after money // was very fond of money.") The wordplay is based on separating and reversing the syllables of *game* (*turtle*) and reading *ga-me* as *me-ga* (*nakatta*) which means *had no eyes*, a Japanese idiomatic expression for *love(d) something passionately*. The blindness under which the Mock Turtle's old teacher suffers in this Japanese version of *Alice* is paralleled by different negative qualities in other renditions, e.g. in the Italian version by T. Pietrocòla-Rossetti (p. 140), it is his inability to speak correctly: "La chiamavamo Tartaruga perchè c'insegnava a tartagliare." ("We called him Tortoise because he taught us to stutter.") This invention arises from the consonance of *tartaruga* (*tortoise*) and *tartagliare* (*to stutter*.) And in Zhao Yuanren's (p. 127) imagination, it is an extreme forgetfulness that is made characteristic of the old Tortoise: "我们管这老甲鱼叫老忘，因为他老忘记了教我们的工课。你怎么这么笨？" ("We called him Mr. Forgetful, because he always forgot to give us lessons. How can you be so stupid?") The link connecting the words *old tortoise* (*lao jiayu*) and *forgetful* (*lao wang*) is the semantics of *lao* which in the first case refers to the figure's age (*old*) and in the second – to his strong proclivity to forget things (*lao* meaning *always*, *ever*, *usually*.)

Yet metamorphoses experienced by the old teacher in different renditions are not always negative. For example, in Nabokov's version (p. 84) he appears as a young octopus: "Мы звали его Молодым Спрутом …потому, что он всегда был с прутиком." ("We called him a young Octopus because he always went along with a small twig.") The young age arises from Nabokov's invention that makes the teacher be accompanied by *a small twig* (*с прутиком*), words that are consonant with *Спрутик* (*a small/ a young octopus*.) And the metamorphosis which the Tortoise undergoes in Ščerbakov's (p. 120) rendition concerns both his gender and kind: the teacher appears here as *a female beet* (*Жучиха*): "Жучихой…Ведь она же учила нас." ("A Female Beet…because she taught us.") This wordplay is also based on consonant forms *a female beet* (*zhuchiha*) and *actually taught* (*zhe uchila*.) As for the teacher's size, the probably biggest reincarnation of the Tortoise that has ever arisen from translators' imagination may be found in the version by Zachoder (p. 94) who makes him appear as *a Sea Dragon with the Soul of an Anaconda*:

> Учителем был сущий Змей Морской. В душе – Удав! Между собой мы его называли Питоном.
> – А почему вы его так называли, раз он был Удав, а не Питон?
> – Он был Питон! Ведь мы – его питонцы.
> ("Our teacher was a real Sea Dragon, with the soul of an Anaconda. Among us we called him a Python."
> "Why did you call him a Python, and not an Anaconda?"
> "He was a Python, since we were his pupils.")

In this case, again, the back-translation of the passage does not make any sense in English, unless it is provided with a commentary on the semantical devices on which the wordplay rests. The key to this Russian word-play is the invention of the noun *питонцы* (*pitonzy*): it evokes associations with young pythons and sounds like *питомцы* (*pupils, alumni.*) The Mock Turtle's break with semantical conventions is in this case again as evident as the inventiveness of the translator who has created a word that does not exist in Russian and that for this very reason perfectly suits the Turtle's mocking rhetoric.

If in the last Russian rendition, the element inhabited by the Mock Turtle's teacher is the same as in the original (*water, the Sea*), in the French version by Paul Sueur it is substituted for *land*: "Nous l'appelions tortue terrestre parce qu'elle nous enseignait surtout la géologie..." ("We called her a land-turtle, because she taught us primarily Geology.") This translation is different from all the others mentioned above insofar as its word-play is motivated not phonetically, resting on similarities of the words' pronunciation, but purely semantically by bridging the terms *terrestre* (*terrestrial*) and *géologie* (*Geology*.)

Finally, the Chinese rendition prepared by Chen Fuan (p. 151) should also be mentioned, since it represents a rare case in which the original passage is reproduced literally: "我们叫它乌龟，因为它教我们书..." A back-translation of this Chinese sentence would result in exactly the phrase written by Carroll, yet, if the translator had not provided the passage with a commentary explaining the phonemic affinity of *Tortoise* and *taught* in English, the phrase would be completely incomprehensible for Chinese readers. This may serve as a new illustration of the fact that an attempt to achieve the maximum closeness to the semantics of the original almost automatically results in the maximum distance from anything reminiscent of the original word-play.

II. "French, music, and washing – extra."

> "You couldn't have wanted it much," said Alice: "living at the bottom of the sea."
> "I couldn't afford to learn it," said the Mock Turtle with a sigh. "I only took the regular course."
> "What was that?" inquired Alice.
> "Reeling and Writhing, of course, to begin with," the Mock Turtle replied. "And then the different branches of Arithmetic – Ambition, Distraction, Uglification, and Derision."
> "I never heard of 'Uglification,'" Alice ventured to say.[349]

In the Chinese version provided by Ma Teng (p. 85), this passage reads as follows:

> "法文、音乐、洗衣。"
> "既然你们住在海底，那也不需要洗衣裳的。"爱丽丝说。

349 *Alice*, p. 101.

"我不能学它，" 素甲鱼叹了一口气说，"我只学正课教的东西。"
"那么你们的正课是什么呢？" 爱丽丝问道。
"开始当然先学习'毒'和'泻'" 素甲鱼回答说， "接下去我们开始学习各门算术：假法、剪法、丑法、厨法。"
"我还从来没有听说过'丑法'，" 爱丽丝大着胆子说…
("French, music, and washing cloths."
"As you were living at the bottom of the sea, you would not have needed to wash cloths."
"I couldn't learn it," said the Turtle for Vegetarians[350] with a sigh. "I learned only the regular courses."
"And what were these regular courses?" asked Alice.
"At the beginning, 'poisoning' and 'pouring,' of course," said the Turtle for Vegetarians.
"Then we began learning the different branches of Arithmetic: Falsification, Annihilation, Uglification, and Cookery."
"I never heard of 'Uglification,'" Alice ventured to say.)

The translator follows the original series of subjects and for every of them he comes up with a word which sounds similarly, i.e. *du* 毒 (*poisoning*) for *du* 读 (*reading*), *xie* 泻 (*pouring*) for *xie* 写 (*writing*), *jiafa* 假法 (lit.: *the Art of Falsifying*) for *jiafa* 加法 (*addition*), etc. The only exception is the invented noun *choufa* 丑法 (*uglification*): it does not display much affinity with the pronunciation of *chengfa* 乘法 (*multiplication*) and the word coinage is motivated by the wish to get as close as possible to the semantics of the original, which again results in moving away from it, since this rendition fails to provide the complete series of arithmetic operations alluded to by the Mock Turtle.

All the translations under discussion demonstrate a struggle for an adequate expression, which underscores the importance of linguistic imagination as the only available source of means to approach the spirit of the original. By what significant changes in the development of the narration this search is occasionally accompanied, may be illustrated by Zachoder's version (p. 95) in which the Gryphon addresses Alice with the following critical remark: "Да уж, воображаю, какие вы там получаете поверхностные знания! У нас мальчиков – и тех учат гораздо глубже! А уж кто хочет по-настоящему углубиться в науку, тот должен добраться до самого дна! Вот оно и называется Законченное Низшее Образование!" ("I can imagine how superficial the education in your school must be! In our place, even boys receive much deeper knowledge! And those who want to be really immersed in learning have to get to the very depth. That's why it is called the accomplished lowest education!")

350 In rendering the name of the character, Ma Teng follows Zhao Yuanren's version.

III *"And how many hours a day did you do lessons?" said Alice, in a hurry to change the subject.*

"Ten hours the first day," said the Mock Turtle: "nine the next, and so on."
"What a curious plan!" exclaimed Alice.
"That's the reason they are called lessons," the Gryphon remarked: "because they lessen from day to day."
This was quite a new idea to Alice, and she thought it over a little before she made her next remark. "Then the eleventh day must have been a holiday?"
"Of course it was," said the Mock Turtle.
"And how did you manage on the twelfth?" Alice went on eagerly.
"That's enough about lessons," the Gryphon interrupted in a very decided tone. "Tell her something about the games now."[351]

In terms of its language design, the key event in this passage is the free etymology provided by the Mock Turtle for the noun *lessons*, his break with logic and Alice's pointing to the mistake, upon which the subject is promptly changed by the Gryphon. In order to illustrate the diversity of strategies applied here by translators, two Russian versions are presented for comparison. N. Demurova (p. 218) has provided the following reading:

– А долго у вас шли занятия? – спросила Алиса, торопясь перевести разговор.
– Это зависело от нас, –отвечал Черепаха Квази. – Как все займем, так и кончим.
– Займете? – удивилась Алиса.
– Занятия почему так называются? – пояснил Грифон. – Потому что на занятиях мы у нашего учителя ум занимаем... А как все займем и ничего ему не оставим, тут же и кончим. В таких случаях говорят: «Ему ума не занимать.» Поняла?
Это было настолько ново для Алисы, что она неевольно задумалась.
– А что же тогда с учителем происходит? – спросила она немного спустя.
–Может, хватит про уроки, – вмешался решительно Грифон. – Расскажи ей про наши игры...
("And how long were your lessons?" asked Alice, eager to change the subject.
"It depended on us," answered the Turtle Quasi. "As soon as we borrowed (occupied) everything, (the lessons) were finished."
"Borrowed (Occupied)?" said Alice in an astonished tone.
"Why do they call them lessons?" the Gryphon remarked. "Because taking lessons we borrow (occupy) the intelligence of our teacher. And as soon as we have borrowed

351 *Alice*, p. 103.

everything he possesses, we are finished. In such cases they say: 'He has no more intelligence to borrow.' Do you understand?"

It was such a new idea for Alice that she could not help thinking it over.

"And what becomes of the teacher in this case?" she asked after a while.

"Perhaps it's enough about lessons," the Gryphon interrupted her in a decided manner. "Tell her about our games.")

Now consider the rendition provided by V. Nabokov (p. 86–87):

"А сколько в день у вас было уроков?" спросила Аня, спеша переменить разговор.

"У нас были не уроки, а укоры," ответила Чепупаха. "Десять укоров в первый день, девять – в следуюий и так далее."

"Какое странное распределение!" воскликнула Аня.

"Поэтому они и назывались укорами – укорачивались, понимаете?" заметил Гриф.

Аня подумала над этим. Потом сказала: "Значит, одиннадцатый день был свободный?"

"Разумеется," ответила Чепупаха.

"А как же вы делали потом, в двенадцатый день?" с любопытством спросила Аня.

"Ну, довольно об этом!" решительным тоном перебил Гриф. "Расскажи ей теперь о своих играх."

("And how many lessons did you have a day?" Anja asked, eager to change the subject.

"We had reproaches rather than lessons," answered Čepupaha. "Ten reproaches the first day, nine – the second, and so on."

"What a strange plan!" exclaimed Anja.

"That's why they are called reproaches, they got shorter, do you understand?"

Anja thought about it for a while and said: "It means that the eleventh day was free?"

"Of course it was," answered Čepupaha.

"And how did you manage after that, on the twelfth?"

"Enough about it!" the Gryphon interrupted in a decided manner. "Tell her about your games now.")

In itself, the free etymology of *lessons* does not pose for the translators any difficulties. In her rendition, Demurova plays with the polysemy of the verb *zanimat* (*to borrow / to occupy*) and uses the idiomatic expression *Ему ума не занимать* (lit.: *He does not need to borrow intelligence*, which means: *He is a very intelligent person*.) On his part, Nabokov's word-play is based on the consonance of *uroki* (*lessons*), *ukory* (*reproaches*), and *ukorachivatsja* (*to get short*.) The problem which becomes apparent by comparing these renditions does not result from semantical innovations and the introduction of images that are missing in the original but concerns rather the reproduction of the idea with which the free etymology of *lessons* is invested in the story. Nabokov follows Carroll's pattern by reproducing two numeric series – one of ten and one of twelve units – that do not coincide. Thus, both the Mock Turtle's break with logic and Alice's reaction to it are recreated in a way that is completely comprehensible for Russian readers. Hence, whereas in the version by Demurova which chronologically is a much later production, this crucial point in the conversation is totally overlooked and the Mock Turtle's etymology appears to arise from a pure joy at experimenting with words, Nabokov's translation strategy may be interpreted as an attempt to truly reproduce the idea of the text and to pay maximum attention to all patterns of action in the original, no matter how complicated they might appear to the readers. In Demurova's version of the passage, Carroll's text has been significantly simplified, adapted for children's reading and one of the central motives of the book which ironically gets entirely obscured due to this strategy is childhood, that is, the inherent tension between literalness and arbitrariness and the exact motivation of the figures' language behavior.

Yet the refusal to reproduce the psychological motives characteristic of the figures' language in this passage is rather a rare case. In most versions under study, the translators have tried to use some appropriate means of rendering its logic, as, e.g. A. Zimmermann (p. 69) who resorted in her word-play to the homophony of the verbs *leeren* (*to empty*) and *lehren* (*to teach*) or Zhao Yuanren (p. 131) whose rendition is based on splitting the compound *duoshao* 多少 (*how many*, literally: *many few // much little*) into two parts and thus exactly recreating the Mock Turtle's mathematical argumentation by making *lessons* be *many* (*duo*) at the beginning and *few* (*shao*) at the end. In these renditions, the Mock Turtle's violation of logic is made as obvious as in Nabokov's text and the passage represents two fundamentally opposite attitudes to language: one of arbitrariness owing to which both referentiality and rationality are eagerly dismissed from language (the Gryphon / the Mock Turtle) and one that lays great stress on the necessity for a rational motivation of words and on their clear backing to reality (Alice.)

IV. "If I'd been the whiting," said Alice, whose thoughts were still running on the song, "I'd have said to the porpoise, 'Keep back, please! We don't want you with us!'"

> "They were obliged to have him with them," the Mock Turtle said: "no wise fish would go anywhere without a porpoise."
> "Wouldn't it really?" said Alice in a tone of great surprise.
> "Of course not," said the Mock Turtle, "why, if a fish came to *me*, and told me he was going a journey, I should say 'With what porpoise?'"

> "Don't you mean 'purpose'?"
>
> "I mean what I say," the Mock Turtle replied in an offended tone.[352]

There is more than one reason for regarding this episode as a particular one. First, it contains significant intratextual links that remind the reader of other stages in the development of the story, e.g. Alice's "If I'd been the whiting" echoes her "When *I'm* a Duchess" from the beginning of Chapter IX. Both sentences underscore Alice's inclination of putting herself in someone else's position, of trying to think and to feel the way the others do, to understand the motives of their actions. And equally important is the link between the Mock Turtle's remark "I mean what I say" and the same words pronounced by Alice in Chapter VII. As mentioned above, when produced by the Mock Turtle, these words suggest extreme subjectivity and arbitrariness and have nothing in common with Alice's approach to language and reality. Yet from the point of view of translation practice, this episode also proves to be quite a special case, for there are a large number of *Alice*-versions from which it has been completely omitted. For example, it has been cut out by A. Zimmermann (p. 72), V. Nabokov (p. 92), T. Pietrocò-la-Rossetti (p. 151), H. Bué (p. 157.) Of course, the readers of these versions will not be likely to re-discover the intratextual associations mentioned above. Consider, by contrast, the following Japanese rendition of the passage prepared by Tada Kōzō (pp. 140–141):

> 「わたしが鱈だったら」と、まださっきの歌のことを思っていたアリスは言いました。「海豚に言ってやったことよ。『すまないけど近よらないで。いっしょはおことわりよ!』って。」「いっしょでなくちゃならなかったんだよ」とにせ海亀が言いました。「賢い魚ならどこに行くにも海豚といっしょだよ」「ほんとにそう?」とアリスは、たいそうおどろいた口調で言いました。「もちろんさ」とにせ海亀は言いました。「そら、魚がわしのとこにやって来て、旅行に出かけますヽと言えばわしだって『何がおいるか』』って言うだろうさ。」「『おいりか』って言うのじゃないの?」とアリスは言いました。「わしの言うとおりさ」とにせ海亀がむっとした口調で答えました。
>
> ("If I'd been the whiting," said Alice, who was still thinking about the song she had just heard, "I'd have said to the dolphin: "I'm sorry, but please keep back. I/we don't want to be together with you." "But they must have been together with him," said the False Turtle. "Any clever fish should share his company, wherever they go." "Really?" asked Alice in a very surprised tone. "Yes, of course," said the False Turtle. "Look, if a fish came to me and told me that it was going a journey, I should say: "Do you (need some) dolphin?" Alice said, "Would you not rather say: "Do you need (it)?" "I would say exactly what I have just said," answered the False Turtle in an offended tone.)

352 *Alice*, pp. 108–109.

The probably most serious difficulty confronted by the translators of this passage is the rendition of the consonant nouns *purpose* and *porpoise*, for which Tada Kōzō finds an elegant solution: In the Mock Turtle's use, "Nani ga o iruka" makes the noun *iruka* 海豚 (*dolphin*) appear as related to the modal verb *iru* 要る (*to need.*) That the last verb cannot arbitrarily be interpreted as part of a *dolphin* (*iruka*), is an observation by which Alice corrects the Mock Turtle's free invention. The Mock Turtle's offended reaction to Alice's remark has to call to the translator's (and to the reader's) minds Alice's statement from Chapter VII: "I mean what I say." From the technical point of view, the re-creation of this intratextual connection should not pose for translators any difficulties comparable with the rendition of the word-play *purpose/porpoise*. Nevertheless, Tada Kōzō fails to reproduce this connection and makes the Mock Turtle pronounce a sentence which is completely different to his rendition of Alice's words in Chapter VII, p. 89: わたし言うことは思ってることだわ "What I say is what I think." It is remarkable that in this failure he is by no means alone. Consider some other renditions of this phrase:

Chapter VII	Chapter X
Alice: "I mean what I say..."[353]	The Mock Turtle: "I mean what I say."[354]
Zhao Yuanren, p. 87 我想的就是我说的 (I think as I say)	Zhao Yuanren, p. 139 我本来说的就是末！ (What I have said *is* correct, that's it!)
Chen Fuan, p. 103 我说的就是我想的 (What I say is what I think.)	Chen Fuan, p. 169 我怎么说就是怎么个意思 (It means what I say.)
Ma Teng, p. 61 我说的就是我想说的 (What I say is what I want to say.)	Ma Teng, p. 93 我知道我自己所说的意思。 (I know the meaning of what I say.)
Teutsch, p. 74 Ich meine – ich wollte sagen – Es kommt doch auf dasselbe heraus, oder? (I mean – I wanted to say – after all, it's the same, isn't it?)	Teutsch, p. 112 Du siehst, ich spreche nie die Unwahrheit! (You see, I never tell lies.)

353 *Alice*, p. 73.
354 *Alice*, p. 109.

Oddera, p. 63
...intendo quello che dico
(I mean what I say.)

Oddera, p. 96
Voglio dire quello che ho detto!
(I want to say what I have just said.)

D'Amico, p. 70
...dico quello che voglio dire
(...I say what I want to say)

D'Amico, p. 98
...voglio dire quello che dico
(I want to say what I say)

Giglio, p. 171
Vi dico quello che credo...
perché io quello che credo dico...
(I tell you what I believe...because
it's what I believe that I say...)

Giglio, p. 247
(No translation)

Battistutta, p. 60
...almeno ... cioè ... voglio dire...
è la stessa cosa
(At least...well...I want to say it's the
same.)

Battistutta, p. 97
Voglio dire quello che dico.
(I want to say what I say.)

Demurova, p. 174
...я всегда думаю то, что говорю.
(I always mean what I say.)

Demurova, p. 226
(No translation.)

Zachoder, p. 77
...что я говорю, то и думаю...
(What I say is what I think...)

Zachoder, p. 100
(No translation.)

Ščerbakov, p. 89
Я...я скажу, что я имею в виду, то есть я
имела в виду, чо скажу...
(I...I will say what I mean, that is, I meant
I would say...)

Ščerbakov, p. 130
Что я думал, то я сказал.
(I said what I meant.)

Sueur (n.n.)
...je pense ce que je dis.
(I mean what I say.)

Sueur
Je veux dire ce que je dis.
(I want to say what I say.)

Among the rare exceptions in which the original link is truly reproduced, are the German versions by Kurt Hansen (pp. 61, 91) and Christian Enzensberger (pp. 70, 105), both of whom render "I mean what I say" in Chapters VII and X by exactly the same wording: "Ich meine, was ich sage." as well as the French version by Jean-Pierre Bermann (pp. 153, 229: "je veux dire ce que je dis.") The translators' careful attention to the detail enables them to recreate the language event which is pivotal to this particular episode and which introduces the reader into the main theme of the concluding chapters of the book, i.e. the negation of literalness, sense, and reason.

Conclusion

The examples of Carroll's creative language use that have been in the focus of investigation in this chapter may be regarded as demonstrating two diametrically opposed approaches: that of verbal arbitrariness, on the one hand, and one of childlike trust in the literal which is closely connected to the idea of unity between words and objects, language and reality. The principal difference between these attitudes accounts among other things for different ways of an imaginative use of words: Whereas the strategy of arbitrariness is aimed at destroying language, Alice's fantasy, on the contrary, carefully seeks to preserve it. In psychological studies on the language of childhood, scholarly judgments on children's fantastic bridging of words and objects are often conceived as corrections of *creative mistakes*[355] and *illegitimate inventions*[356] and are based on the adults' lexicon as well as on the rules of grammar as valid standards of legitimacy. Quite a different perception of language findings produced by children is displayed by those who interpret each of these discoveries not as a failure but rather as a chance, i.e.

355 Ruth A. Berman, "Developmental Perspectives on Transitivity: A Confluence of Cues", in: Yonata Levy (Ed.), *Other Children, Other Languages: Issues in the Theory of Language Acquisition*, Hillsdale: Lawrence Erlbaum Associates 1994, pp. 189–241, esp. the section "Creative Errors and Other Later Strategies", pp. 223–227. The chapter title "Kids Say the Darnedest Things" from Steven Pinker's *Words and Rules* (pp. 189–210) is quite reminiscent of Alice's exclamation "Curiouser and curiouser!" and provides a careful and sympathetic analysis of similar creative errors, which can be illustrated by the manner in which it is introduced: "Grammatical errors like *bleeded* and *singed* have long epitomized the innocence and freshness of children's minds. The errors are acts of creation, in which children lift a pattern from their brief experience and apply it with impeccable logic to new words, unaware that the adult world treats them as arbitrary exceptions." (S. Pinker, *op. cit.*, pp. 189–190.)

356 For example, Eve V. Clark, "Lexical Innovations: How Children Learn to Create New Words", in: Werner Deutch (Ed.), *The Child's Construction of Language*, London: Academic Press 1981, pp. 299–328, here p. 301.

as a means of spiritually enriching the language. Agathon Keber who enthusiastically observed the language creations of German children of his time belongs to this last group of scholars. His observations inspired him to the following judgment: "Diese Produkte der Naivität, leider alle zur Vernichtung bestimmt, sind oft so originell, so sinnig, so treffend, daß jede Sprache bei ihrer Kindersprache in die Kur gehen könnte, theils zur Ausmerzung sinnloser Willkürlichkeiten des Sprachgebrauchs, theils zur Bereicherung."[357] ("All these products of naïvety that are unfortunately destined to disappear one day are so original, so spirited, and so accurate, that every language should use the language of its children as a cure against arbitrary nonsense and as a source of enrichment.")

357 Agathon Keber, *Zur Philosophie der Kindersprache. Gereimtes – Ungereimtes*, Halle: Verlag von Georg Schwabe 1868, p. 44.

VIII. The Language of Violence

VIII.I

As discussed in the previous chapter, the Mock Turtle's language behavior and its motto, according to which it means what it says, are based on a free invention of both the signified and the signifiers on the basis of accidental phonemic similarities between words. This arbitrariness insists on its right to exist with dictatorial determination: not able to allow any objections, it openly defies conventions and challenges rationality[358]. In the two concluding chapters of the first *Alice*-book, the motive of language violence comes rapidly to a head and culminates in the symbolic overcoming of the Wonderland-dream, i.e. in Alice's waking up and getting free from the powers of radical arbitrariness with which she was continuously confronted during her vision. The delirium in which she, although having little prospect of success, makes a steady effort to achieve mutual understanding based on rationality, thus comes to an end. Despite the idyllic conclusion of the story in the scene of a peaceful conversation between Alice and her elder sister, it is absolutely conceivable that, by designing this delirium plot, it was not only a child that Carroll intended to awaken in the hearts of his readers, but also an acute intuition of far more obscure dimensions of the human soul. Salvador Dalí (1904–1989) has dedicated to this book a cycle of illustrations[359] which powerfully re-create the course of the delirium and the helplessness of the rational in the face of the unconscious. That the great master of surrealism could be inspired to this piece of art, testifies to Carroll's infallible psychological precision and intuition. It would hardly be an exaggeration to say that the *Alice* books anticipated some of the most crucial events in Europe's spiritual development at the dawning of the twentieth century. The rise of surrealism was one among them. Although it is not very probable that Carroll could have perceived notable sympathies with this movement which proclaimed madness to be among the most fundamen-

358 Cf. the language of patients with "Thought-Disorders" explored by Sherry Rochester and James Robert Martin in their monograph *Crazy Talk: A Study of the Discourse of Schizophrenic Speakers*, New York: Plenum Press 1979, among other things, the observations concerning these patients' using "high proportions of unclear reference, relative to other speakers" as well as about persons listening to them "having to search for identifications which are promised but not provided." (Rochester/Martin, *op. cit.*, p. 201.)

359 Among recent editions of *Alice*, these illustrations are contained in *Alice's Adventures in Wonderland. 150th Anniversary Edition*, Princeton: Princeton Univ. Press 2015.

tal human rights[360], he surely foresaw the upcoming of the spiritual powers that caused its eventual global success. One of its key figures, whose psychological portrait is strikingly close to that of the Mock Turtle, was Jean-Pierre Brisset (1837–1919), elected *the prince of all masters of thought*[361] by the French avant-gardists in 1913 and the author of *La Science de Dieu ou la Création de l'Homme* (*The Science of God and the Creation of Man*, 1900.)

Among the main insights Brisset's was his conviction about the amphibian origin of man whose direct ancestor – the frog – may still be easily observed and admired in the marshes and ponds of our modern world and can provide us with useful information concerniung the beginnings of humanity. Not only is one of the arguably greatest questions of philosophy as to the "What", or *Quoi*, as it is – still – called in French, said to attest to man's amphibian past, but much more than that, the whole of the human language, even if Brisset addresses primarily the language of the French, conceals within his theory an infinite quantity of hidden evidence about man's origins. Consider the following passage in which he deciphered some of these hidden messages for his contemporaries in *the Science of God*:

> Voyons où ces ancêtres étaient *logés*: *l'eau j'ai* = j'ai l'eau ou je suis dans l'eau. *L'haut j'ai* = je suis haut, au-dessus de l'eau, car les ancêtres construisirent les premières loges sur les eaux. *L'os j'ai* = j'ai l'os ou les os; on les mangeait où l'on était logé. L'ancêtre était carnivore.[362] (Let's see where these ancestors were living (*logés*): water I have (*l'eau j'ai*) = I have water (*j'ai l'eau*). The top I have (*L'haut j'ai*) = I'm on the top (*je suis haut*), above the water because the ancestors constructed the first lodges above waters. The bone I have (*L'os j'ai*) = I have a bone or bones (*j'ai l'os ou les os*); they ate them at the place where they were living. The ancestor was carnivorous.)

Brisset's historical discoveries are based on a rule called by him *the Great Law or the Language Key* (*la Grande Loi ou la Clef de la Parole*.) According to this law, all ideas that are pronounced identically as the same series of sounds, are of the

360 See, for example, one of the manifests of Surrealism, Salvador Dalí's "Declaration of the independence of the imagination and the rights of man to his own madness", in: *Art Digest*, 1939, vol. 13, no. 19, p. 9.

361 For details, see Maximilian Gilleßen "Der Wortschatz der Sümpfe", in: Maximilian Gilleßen, Anton Stuckardt (Eds.), *Jean-Pierre Brisset, Fürst der Denker, Eine Dokumentation*, Berlin: zero sharp. 2014, pp. 9–116, here p. 46. Gilleßen's essay provides a vivid biographical (and psychological) sketch of Brisset as well as a thorough examination of causes for Brisset's success among surrealists.

362 Jean-Pierre Brisset, *La Science de Dieu ou la Création de l'Homme*, in: Marc Décimo (ed.), Jean-Pierre Brisset, Œuvres complètes, Paris: Les presses du reel 2001, pp. 697–885, here p. 704.

same origin and refer to the same object[363]. In the above quotation, he illustrated how much knowledge may be gained alone from a correct examination of the word *logés* (*situated*), beginning with the ancestors' life in waters up to their having been carnivorous. Similarities in sound which are said to attest to the identity of ideas hidden behind them are furthermore taken as referring to the same reference, even when the respective words come from different languages, as, e.g. French and Chinese:

> La Loi ci-dessus est une loi de la parole et non une loi de la langue française; elle s'applique à toutes les langues et à tous les dialects en particulier. Elle s'applique à l'ensemble de tout le langue humain. Si donc on trouvait réuni dans le chinois du peuple de la Chine, ou en toute autre langue, une suite de sons resonant à l'oreille comme: *les dents la bouche*, il y aurait entre ces quatre mots et ce qu'exprimerait avec ces mêmes sons la langue étrangère, un rapport certain, mathématique, une origine commune que l'esprit d'analyse de la parole pourrait retrouver, en remontant au besoin, au point unique qui est le créateur des hommes et des esprits.[364] (The above Law is a law of language in general and not (only) of French; it is applicable to all languages and to all dialects in particular. It is applicable to the whole of human language. If one found in Chinese of China's people or in any other language a phonic sequence which would resonate in the ear like *les dents la bouche*, there would be between these four words and those expressed in a foreign language by means of the same sounds a clear mathematical relation, a mutual point of origin which could be recovered by the spirit of language analysis, going back – if necessary – to the unique initial point, i.e. to the creator of men and spirits.)

Any reader willing to follow this train of thought, would promptly recognize the ideal affinity as well as the mutually shared reference peculiar to words like *baby* (in English) and 卑鄙 (pronounced "beibi", meaning *base, contemptible*) in Chinese, *rana* (*frog*) in Italian and *рана* (*rana*, meaning *wound*) in Russian, 豚 (*buta* meaning *pig/pork*) in Japanese and *Butter* (*butter*) in German, etc. Yet, for Brisset, the phonemic similarities between such expressions are not the only source of evidence about man's amphibian origin. Further information may, e.g. be gained from studying the semantics of languages that conserve in their lexicon sayings referring to one of man's ancestor's favorite foods – the fly: as, for example, the German expression "zwei Fliegen mit einer Klappe schlagen" (lit.: *to kill two flies with one flap*.) The useful ability referred to by this saying is paralleled by the wisdom of the Italian ancestor that is preserved in the idiom "In bocca chiusa non entrò mai mosca" (lit.: *no fly has ever entered a shut mouth*.) Brisset

363 J.-P. Brisset, *op. cit.*, p. 702.
364 J.-P. Brisset, *op. cit.*, p. 703–704.

does not hesitate to present similar sayings as corroborating his theory that traces the distant past of man:

> Qu'on ne croie pas que la petitesse de la mouche la garantît contre la bouche de forts ancêtres, car les nègres de l'Ouganda, avons-nous lu, se nourrissent encore d'insectes, de sauterelles, de moucherons qu'ils capturent au moyen de filets promenés vivement dans l'air[365]. (One should not believe that the smallness of a fly could protect it from the mouth of the strong ancestors because, as I have read, the Negroes of Uganda still eat insects, grasshoppers and midges which they catch by means of nets, scattered energetically through the air.)

The causal link produced here by Brisset between his theory of man's amphibian past and the culinary habits currently shared by the inhabitants of Uganda, the self-confidence with which his "car" ("because") is being pronounced are reminiscent of the matter-of-factness with which the Gryphon and the Mock Turtle explain the etymology of *lesson* to Alice:

> "That's the reason they are called lessons," the Gryphon remarked, "because they lessen from day to day." This was quite a new idea to Alice, and she thought it over a little before she made her next remark. "Then the eleventh day must have been a holiday?" "Of course it was," said the Mock Turtle.[366]

Both cases refer to linguistic discoveries that insist on being taken seriously as irrefutable truths. Mock Turtle's "of course it was" is similar to the ever recurrent signals in Brisset's work by which the reader is reminded of there being no doubt about the correctness of his arguments: he presents his theory as *indisputable* ("est vrai d'une vérité ineclutable"[367]), his linguistic observations are called to be *as sure as mathematics* ("un rapport certain, mathématique"[368]), the arguments by which he supports his idea of the origin of man's language and, in particular, of French are said to possess *a fascinating clarity* ("d'une clarté éblouissante"[369]), and the language law discovered by him – to be marked by *an invincible strength* ("est de toute rigueur inattaquable."[370]) The frequency with which all these signals are used testifies to a continuous acute intuition of hidden enemies who would have the cheek to contradict. And again like the Gryphon and the Mock

365 J.-P. Brisset, *op. cit.*, p. 710.
366 *Alice*, p. 103.
367 J.-P. Brisset, *op. cit.*, p. 703.
368 J.-P. Brisset, *op. cit.*, pp. 703–704.
369 J.-P. Brisset, *op. cit.*, p. 706.
370 J.-P. Brisset, *op. cit.*, p. 704.

Turtle who feel threatened whenever Alice displays the least signs of her trust in logic and language conventions, the author of *The Science of God* never frees himself from the iron grip of similar opponents. Occasionally, these are explicitly mentioned by name as in the following passage:

> Les ancêtres vivaient donc dans les eaux, mares et marais; ils y étaient doués de la parole et y créaient notre langue française actuelle, qui continuera à être parlée sur la terre jusqu'à la fin des siècles. C'est à nos ancêtres, les dieux marins, que nous devons notre parole, et non point aux mercenaires romains, comme voudraient l'établir les traîtres à la patrie qui allèrent au devant de César et de ses légions et lui aidèrent à établir sa domination...[371](Thus, our ancestors lived in waters, ponds and marshes. They possessed language abilities and created our contemporary French language which will continue to be spoken on Earth till the end of time. It's to them – to our ancestors, the see gods, – that we owe our language and not to the Roman mercenaries, as the traitors to the fatherland would have it, who ran to meet Caesar and his legions and helped them establish their rule...)

The verb établir (*to confirm, to prove*) is referred here first to the falsified evidence by which, according to Brisset, his spiritual opponents seek to prove that French descended from the Latin of the Roman Empire rather than from the language of frogs. For him, there could be no doubt about the fact that such heretic ideas in support of a language believed by him to be an artificial construct can mean nothing but a betrayal of the homeland as well as a conspiracy against man's real ancestor. Brisset's work is intended to expose the traitors and to furnish evidence of what in his eyes represents the ultimate truth:

> La grenouille et l'homme sont les deux seuls animaux ayant deux pieds et deux mains placés de la même manière. Il est certain que c'est là une preuve irrefragable de notre commune origine avec nos grenouilles actuelles: une preuve de l'origine de l'homme que son créateur lui avait cachée pour un temps.[372] (Frog and man are the only two animals whose two feet and two hands are placed in the same manner. It is certain that this is an irrefutable proof of our common origin with contemporary frogs. This proof of man's origin was for some time concealed from him by man's creator.)

Yet the irrefutable evidence rests entirely on the linguistic fantasies (*logés // l'eau j'ai*, etc.) of Brisset himself who persistently insists on their being objective, indisputable and universally valid. The obviously subjective observations about lan-

371 J.-P. Brisset, *op. cit.*, p. 706.

372 J.-P. Brisset, *op. cit.*, p. 706.

guage produced by him are not merely irrational but also highly militant: they are intended as a declaration of war against all those conspirators who do not accept the idea of frog as man's ancestor. Thus, compared with the Gryphon and the Mock Turtle, the irrationality peculiar to Brisse't language behavior is much more comprehensive: his principal aim is, namely, not just to assert himself before a challenging conversation partner but also to demand justice and to act as a judge.

This posture, owing to which anything rational is completely disbanded and one's self – with all the arbitrariness peculiar to it – is given the role of the only medium for determining the truth, corresponds exactly to some trends dominating the spiritual atmosphere of the modern world which were anticipated by Carroll's intuition in the concluding chapters of *Alice in Wonderland*. The central theme of these chapters is the enactment of the highest of all possible levels of verbal and mental arbitrariness, i.e. open violence. Other than in chapters IX and X which also focused on the issue of arbitrariness, here, Carroll addresses an imminent threat to human existence as one of its worst possible consequences. Chapter XI "Who Stole the Tarts?" introduces a long court trial which is called to determine the innocence or guilt of the Knave of Hearts accused of having committed the following crime:

> The Queen of Hearts, she made some tarts
> All on a summer day:
> The Knave of Hearts, he stole those tarts,
> And took them quite away![373]

At the formal level, the accusation anticipates the only piece of evidence against the Knave which is a poem written by an anonymous author to an anonymous addressee and which begins as follows:

> They told me you had been to her.
> And mentioned me to him:
> She gave me a good character,
> But said I could not swim...[374]

In terms of their contents, the two verses reproduced above do not have anything in common, which underscores the absurdity pertaining to the trial. The only thing that is shared by both poems is that in both of them personal pronouns

373 *Alice*, p. 116.
374 *Alice*, p. 127.

are used. However, whereas in the accusation the pronouns display a clear identity (*she/the Queen*; *he/the Knave*), those in the evidence poem have no clear reference and therefore cannot serve as proving anything on rational grounds. The King's order with which he addresses the jury immediately after the accusation is pronounced: "Consider your verdict!" is yet another confirmation of the irrationality reigning in the court. All the episodes following this order demonstrate the same degree of absurdity. Having learned from the Rabbit that it is not yet time for considering the verdict, the King begins to question the witnesses, the first of them being the figures from Chapter VII – the Hatter, the March Hare and the Dormouse. It is neither clear why they come into question as witnesses at all, nor does the first question by which the King addresses them "When did you begin?" suggest any connection with the trial. All of them give different answers (*fourteenth, fifteenth, sixteenth of March*), which – again for some mysterious reason – seem to be important for the judge, since he asks the jurymen to write them down. And the reaction of the jurymen to this request is also rather enigmatic: "the jury eagerly wrote down all three dates on their slates, and then added them up, and reduced the answer to shillings and pence.[375]"

What follows, is a short conversation between Alice who begins growing large rapidly and the Dormouse sitting next to her:

> "I wish you wouldn't squeeze so," said the Dormouse, who was sitting next to her. "I can hardly breathe."
> "I can't help it," said Alice very meekly: "I'm growing."
> "You have no right to grow *here*," said the Dormouse.
> "Don't talk nonsense," said Alice more boldly: "you know you're growing too."[376]

Of all the events that happen during the trial, the above scene is the only one in which the word *right* is used and yet, as Alice correctly recognizes, it is used – surprisingly – out of place. By associations, it could evoke the idea of justice as the principal aim of the whole trial, but exactly this is not the case: the pronounced word does nothing whatever to do with what is going on at the court, which once again underscores its sheer absurdity.

Questioning the first witnesses proves to be to no avail. The next witness to be questioned is the cook of the Duchess. In this case, it is also strange that she has been summoned to provide evidence. Things that happen afterwards come thick and fast and display the same general characteristics of the court trial, i.e. the lack of rationality. The cook resolutely refuses to give evidence, yet

375 *Alice*, p. 117.
376 *Alice*, p. 118.

she answers one of the judge's questions by saying that tarts are mostly made of pepper. This is promptly corrected (or completed) by a detail provided by the Dormouse ("Treacle"), which, in turn, makes the Queen lose her temper and come up with a series of commands reminiscent of the rapid fire of a machine-gun: "Collar that Dormouse! Behead that Dormouse! Turn that Dormouse out of court! Suppress him! Pinch him! Off with his whiskers!"[377] After a general disquiet caused by this in the hall of justice, the witness turns out to have disappeared, which makes the King feel surprisingly relieved, reacting to it by the short "Never mind."[378] The chapter concludes with Alice being called to be the next witness, as irrational an act as anything that has happened during the trial before. Alice is the only figure in Chapter XI who is able to think and act rationally, the behavior of all the rest being motivated purely by emotions: by fear (the Hatter), anger and relief (the King), hysteria (the Queen), sulk (the Dormouse), cheerfulness (the guinea-pigs), etc.

The issue of irrational (absurd) judgment is continued in the concluding Chapter XII "Alice's Evidence." Involuntarily, Alice who has just grown large upsets the jurymen and it takes some time before they get back to their seats. The first action produced by them thereupon is once again marked by a lack of rationality:

> As soon as the jury had a little recovered from the shock of being upset, and their slates and pencils had been found and handed back to them, they sat to work very diligently to write out a history of the accident, all except the Lizard, who seemed too much overcome to do anything but sit with its mouth open, gazing up into the roof of the court.[379]

Immediately after this incident, the King sets out to examine Alice's evidence and the first thing which becomes apparent during this procedure is the King's inability to act rationally for one simple reason, which is that for him – the judge – there is not so much difference between an affirmation and a negation:

> "What do you know about this business?" the King said to Alice.
> "Nothing," said Alice.
> "Nothing *whatever?*" persisted the King.
> "Nothing *whatever,*" said Alice.
> "That's very important," the King said, turning to the jury. They were just beginning to write this down on their slates, when the White Rabbit interrupted: "*Un*important,

377 *Alice*, p. 121.
378 *Alice*, p. 121.
379 *Alice*, p. 124.

your Majesty means, of course," he said in a very respectful tone, but frowning and making faces to him as he spoke.

"*Un*important, of course, I meant," the King hastily said, and went on to himself in an undertone, "important-unimportant-unimportant-important-" as if he were trying which word sounded best."[380]

Thus, it is not so much the evidence but rather the King's impression about which word sounds best that turns out to be crucial in examining what is important and what – not. Looking at the helpless jurymen who seem to doubt about which of these two words – important or unimportant – has to be recorded in the session report, Alice thinks to herself that "it doesn't matter a bit", thus providing the only evidence available at the trial for the existence of rational means of judgment. This mental decision of what in Alice's eyes is definitely unimportant is followed by a heated dispute between arbitrariness (personified by the royal couple) and rationality (defended by Alice):

(The King): "Rule Forty-two, "All persons more than a mile high to leave the court." Everybody looked at Alice.

"*I'm* not a mile high," said Alice.

"You are," said the King.

"Nearly two miles high," added the Queen.

"Well, I shan't go, at any rate," said Alice; "besides, that's not a regular rule: you invented it just now."

"It's the oldest rule in the book," said the King.

"Then it ought to be Number One," said Alice.[381]

Similarly to Chapter IX in which the etymology of the noun *lesson*, freely invented by the Gryphon, was easily set aside by Alice's mathematical and logical skills, here, she is equally quick at seeing through and at exposing the arbitrary nature of the King's way of reasoning. The conflict comes to a head in the next episode in which the alleged piece of evidence (the above mentioned poem, full of pronouns with no reference) is discussed. Formally, it is a continuation of the trial examining the Knave's guilt, yet the essence of what is happening concerns rather the violent nature of the King's judgments and the resistance of rationality which Alice opposes to it:

380 *Alice*, pp. 124–125.
381 *Alice*, p. 125.

(Alice): "*I* don't believe there is an atom of meaning in it."... "If there is no meaning in it," said the King, "that saves a world of trouble, you know, as we needn't try to find any.[382]

The trial ends with Alice's refusal to accept the validity of the Queen's demand "Sentence first – verdict afterwards." Alice's eventual triumph over the absurd, her realization that her opponents are but a pack of cards and therefore not able to harm her, happen after the highest of all possible manifestations of violence expressed in the Queen's command: "Off with her head!"[383] Alice's waking up from her dream which concludes the story is therefore primarily a symbolic event: it is a confirmation of her own identity, of the principles to which she sticks, of the value of rationality by which she succeeds in overcoming arbitrariness and violence.

The most dramatic element in Alice's experiences described in the concluding chapters is probably not so much the nonsensical quality peculiar to the court trial but rather the ambivalence that is displayed as pertaining to the concepts of *evidence* and *right*: whereas for Alice something can become evident only on the basis of facts and logic (e.g. "Then it ought to be Number One"), the King does not require any objective principles for regarding something as evident, i.e. as enough to prove or to negate someone's guilt or innocence. By saying "that saves a lot of trouble", as earlier by trying to find out which of the words "unimportant" or "important" makes a better sound, he does not only accept the senselessness of this kind of evidence but regards it as a source of a particular emotional and even aesthetic enjoyment. This ability makes him also similar to the prince of the French avant-gardist thinkers who was engaged in a fascinated contemplation of the man's ancestor by examining numerous pieces of – equally purely subjective – evidence (*preuves*):

Le son de la voix et la modulation du chant de la grenouille ont déjà quelque chose d'humain. Ses yeux, son regard sont semblables aux nôtres; et aucun animal ne possède une grâce corporelle, du talon au cou, qui le rapproche autant de celle du corps humain: peu de personnes même ont cette partie aussi élégante.[384] (Already the sound of its (the frog's) voice and the modulations of its song have something human. Its eyes, its gaze are similar to ours. And no animal possesses a bodily grace – from heel to neck – with which it approximates the grace of the human body. Even among men there are only few who display such elegance.)

382 *Alice*, p. 128.
383 *Alice*, p. 129.
384 J.-P. Brisset, *op. cit.*, p. 718.

A detailed study of the fascination exerted by Brisset upon the vanguard artists of his time – first of all upon surrealists – as well as an investigation of deep spiritual affinities between Brisset's visions and formal trends predominating among his contemporaries are provided by Maximilian Gilleßen in his essay "Der Wortschatz der Sümpfe" ("The Vocabulary of the Marshes", 2014.)[385] In regard to Gilleßen's psychoanalytical interpretation of Brisset, among other things from the perspective of Freud's *Der Witz und seine Beziehung zum Unbewußten* (*Jokes and their Relation to the Unconscious*, 1905), it should be remarked that personally for Brisset there was nothing in the least funny about the subject discussed in *The Science of the God*. On the contrary, in spite of all the sentimentality pertaining to his description of the frog's beauty – or maybe exactly owing to this sentimental stance – he takes his discussion absolutely seriously and insists on the irrefutable correctness of all the evidence (*preuves irrefragables*) provided in this work. Here, the appropriation of an acute consciousness of what is right and wrong by the forces of the irrational manifests itself with the same clarity as in Carroll's episode in which the Dormouse proclaims that Alice has no right to grow in the hall of justice. The fact that Brisset was met with so much sympathy among surrealists can largely be explained by their aspirations of the future triumph of the irrational over logical thinking. Dalí was among the first to recognize in similar aspirations a fruitful ground for a new promising aesthetical program and in his manifesto great stress was laid exactly on the concept of *right*. The idea of *the rights of the irrational* which was proclaimed in the title of this manifesto (lit. *the rights of man to his own madness*) was explained in its main text, among other things, in the following slogan: "It is man's right to decide that lukewarm telephones are disgusting, and to demand telephones that are as cold, green and aphrodisiac as the augur-troubled sleep of the cantharides."[386] The green aphrodisiac telephone was conceived as part of a spiritual programme that was not unsimilar to one in which man was declared to be a direct descendant of the frog. One of the essential differences between these two thinkers is, of course, that Dalí was quite conscious of the unconscious as well as of his own active role as an artist. In his personal spiritual delirium[387] he easily recognized the vast potential for

385 Maximilian Gilleßen, *op. cit.*, pp. 84–100.

386 Salvador Dalí, "Declaration of the independence of the imagination and the rights of man to his own madness" (1939), in: *Art Digest*, Vol. 13, no. 19, p. 9.

387 A detailed discussion of *delirium* as a general spiritual condition of Europe in the early 20th century is provided by Herbert Thüring in his essay "Die Sprache im Bann, im Bann der Sprache: Zur Genealogie des Sprachdeliriums um 1900 (Gottfried Benn, Heymann Steinthal, Paul Emil Flechsig", in: Maximilian Bergengruen, Roland Borgands (eds.), *Bann der Gewalt: Studien zur Literatur- und Wissensgeschichte*, Göttingen: Wallstein Verlag 2009, pp. 469–504.) Among the most important causes of this delirium, Thüring discusses the elevation of psychology into the status of an exact science, a wide-spread conviction, according to which ethics had come to be

aesthetic elaboration, whereas Brisset was completely engulfed in the obscure forces of his visions, convinced of their objective nature and not willing to hear of anything irrational pertaining to their nature. In other words, Brisset may be considered a personification of that vital source from which the great theoretician of surrealism deduced his wisdom: the madness. After all, not for nothing did Dalí address the unconscious as the final aim of surrealism, proclaim the necessity for getting free from reason, and discuss logic as a spiritual gaol.[388]

The irrational forces with which Alice finds herself confronted during the court trial are most evident in one particular quality characteristic of other figures' way to think, speak, and act: their automatism. The King's "Never mind" is automatically produced after the cook disappears, the jurymen automatically write down a report of having been upset by Alice, the witnesses automatically pronounce the numbers *fourteenth*, *fifteenth*, and *sixteenth* as pieces of evidence, Alice is automatically accused of being more than a mile high, etc. In all these cases, any causality is made impossible, which is the main reason why the communication between Alice and the rest of the figures fails. This also reveals one potent affinity with surrealism: It was not by chance that one of Dalí's programmatic writings, "El Surrealismo", begins as a praise of what its author calls "a mental automatism"[389] and emphasizes that one of the primary driving forces of the surrealist movement is nothing but "a dictate of thinking that is beyond

explained in terms of such a psychology, and the eventual complete dissolution of the concept of *soul* within the functions of brains ("die restlose Auflösung der Seele in Funktionen des Gehirns", H. Thüring, *op.cit.*, pp. 491–493.)

388 Salvador Dalí, "El Surrealismo" (1935), in: *Revista Hispánica Moderna*, No. 3 (Apr. 1935), pp. 233–234, here p. 234. Cf. the statements produced by Kazimir Malevič in 1915/1916: "Разум – каторжная цепь для художника" ("Reason is a prison chain for an artist", in: Kazimir Malevič, *Sobranie sočinenij v pjati tomah*, Moskva: Galileja 1995, Vol. I, p. 26); "Вся бывшая и современная живопись до супрематизма, скульптура, слово, музыка были закрепощены формой натуры и ждут своего освобождения, чтобы говорить на своем собственном языке и не зависеть от разума, смысла, логики, философии, психологии…" (*Ibid.*, p. 27: "All the arts of the past and present have been imprisoned by natural forms and are now waiting for a liberation, in order to speak their own language and to get free from reason, sense, logic, philosophy, psychology…"); "За ненадобностью я отказываюсь от души и интуиции." (*Ibid.*, p. 56: "I'm throwing my soul and intuition away on the scrap-heap. of redundancy.") I disagree with Nikolay Firtič's generalizing interpretation of similar statements as being "quite in tune with Carroll" (Nikolay Firtič, "Poetika neobyčnogo" ("The Poetics of the Strange"), in: Nikolay Firtič (Ed.), *Mir Alisy: Poetica neobyčnogo v litrerature i iskusstve XIX – XX vv.*, St Petersburg: Apollon 2017, pp. 5–39, here p. 34). While it is certainly true that Malevič – very much like Dalí – addresses a specific source of artistic inspiration which reaches far beyond any rational norms and laws, it is hardly correct to regard the *Alice*-books as celebrating the unconscious and discarding the laws of reason. The fact that at various instances in Carroll's text these laws are acutely challenged does not mean that they are being discarded, either by Alice or by the author.

389 "Automatismo psíquico", Salvador Dalí, "El Surrealismo", p. 234.

any control by reason, aesthetics, or morality."[390] The impossibility of a consensus between Alice and the inhabitants of Wonderland as it is described in Chapters XI and XII seems to rest exactly on a similar dictate of automatic thinking so that it would not be precipitated to recognize in Carroll's text a telling confirmation of what Walter Benjamin once wrote on the surrealist psychology:

> Wo liegen die Voraussetzungen der Revolution? In der Änderung der Gesinnung oder der äußeren Verhältnisse? Das ist die Kardinalfrage, die das Verhältnis von Politik und Moral bestimmt und die keine Vertuschung zuläßt. Der Sürrealismus ist ihrer kommunistischen Beantwortung immer näher gekommen. Und das bedeutet: Pessimismus auf der ganzen Linie. Jawohl und durchaus. Mißtrauen in das Geschick der Literatur, Mißtrauen in das Geschick der Freiheit, Mißtrauen in das Geschick der europäischen Menschheit, vor allem aber Mißtrauen, Mißtrauen und Mißtrauen in alle Verständigung: zwischen den Klassen, zwischen den Völkern, zwischen den Einzelnen.[391] (What are the preconditions of the revolution? Is it the change of mentality or that of external conditions? This is the capital question which determines the relationship between politics and ethics and which does not allow any cover-up. Surrealism is moving increasingly closer to the Bolshevik answer. And that means: pessimism all along the line, positively and completely. It is a distrust of the fate of literature, a distrust of the fate of freedom, a distrust of the fate of European humanity, but first of all it is a distrust, distrust and distrust of any communication: between classes, between nations, between individuals.)

As suggested by Benjamin's words, by advocating independence of one's fantasy from the control of reason, aesthetics and morality, the surrealism eventually hinders any communication and mistrusts any actual or potential opponent who would muster up courage and refuse to share the products of its imagination. In Brisset's work, this attitude is visible in his militant defense of the man's ancestor. On his part, Dalí directly addresses the psychological implications of his artistic movement, whenever he comes to speak about it as a source of traumas or as *the most dangerous mental poison*.[392] And in the concluding chapters of *Alice in Wonderland*, the dictate of the automatic thinking culminates in the Queen's command to behead Alice.

---

390 "dictado del pensamiento, fuera de todo control ejercido por la razón, fuera de todo control estético o moral", *ibid.*, p. 234.

391 Walter Benjamin, "Der Sürrealismus" (1929), in: Walter Benjamin, *Gesammelte Schriften*, II. 1, Rolf Tiedemann, Hermann Schweppenhäuser (Eds.), Frankfurt am Main: Suhrkamp. 1977, pp. 295–310, here p. 308.

392 Salvador Dalí, "El Surrealismo", p. 234.

It is quite comprehensible that in his investigation of what at first sight might seem to be among the most harmless expressions of the surrealist *dialectics of intoxication* (*Dialektik des Rauschs*), Walter Benjamin associates them with a presentiment about *a morning before a battle or after a victory*.[393] Looking back on the political arena in the decades that followed after the publication of his essay on surrealism in 1929, the real identity of all those battles, victories and defeats captured by Benjamin's intuition may easily be determined: No other modern era has politically been as heavily dominated by the primate of automatic thinking as during the rise of Nazism and for an analysis of its linguistic habits Carroll's text proves to provide illuminating perspectives.

For the best of my knowledge, parallels between the *Alice*-books and the spiritual atmosphere under the Nazi reign are relatively seldom drawn. Yet alone the parody written by James Dyrenforth and Max Kester during the rise of Nazism *Adolf in Blunderland: A political parody of Lewis Carroll's famous story* (1939) may be regarded for many reasons as groundbreaking. The following passage in which the trial scene of the last two chapters of *Alice in Wonderland* is imitated in order to provide a vivid picture of the current political agenda of that time, may illustrate the conversational mode characteristic of the whole parody:

> **Queen.** Give your evidence, Flatterer. And don't be nervous, or I'll send you to a Concentration Camp.
> **Flatterer.** (*Trembling*) I'm a poor man, your Heartlessness.
> **Queen.** That's nonsense! You have a fine house in Berlin, haven't you?
> **Flatterer.** (*Considering*) Well, I'm not so poor as I was before I joined the *Party*, of course.
> **Queen.** You'd be a complete fool if you were. What do you know about this heresy?
> **Flatterer.** All I know, since I joined the Party, is, the Fuehrer is always right. His slightest wish is my law. And the greatest joy a German can know is to give up his fat for his Fuehrer.
> **Grafvon.** (*Sotto voce*) Really, Adolf, you're growing alarmingly.
> **Adolf.** It's those inspiring words. They're *always* a tonic to me. You've no idea how *big* it can make you feel to realize that all your people are eating dry bread for you.[394]

Alice appears here as Adolf, the Mad Hatter – as the Mad Flatterer (i.e. Konrad Henlein), the Queen of Hearts – as the Queen of Heartlessness (i.e. Heinrich Himmler)[395], etc. For the readers of the parody it must have been obvious what

393 Walter Benjamin, "Der Sürrealismus", p. 299.

394 James Dyrenforth and Max Kester, *Adolf in Blunderland: A political parody of Lewis Carroll's famous story*, London: Muller 1940, pp. 54–55.

395 For more details about the real prototypes of this parody, see the essay by Jörg Thunecke "Malice in Wonderland: James Dyrenforth and Max Kester's Political Satire *Adolf in Blunderland*

party was meant joining which the Flatterer is said to have accumulated his riches and whose identity was alluded to by the people *eating dry bread* for Adolf. The words of the Flatterer who openly proclaims that all he knows is that the Fuehrer is always right are a fitting illustration of the main principle of automatic thinking. The inspiration referred to by Adolf in the last replica is one of the most frequently recurrent motives in the parody alluding to the megalomania of Nazism, as is also the case, e.g. with the following remake of the crocodile-poem:

> How doth the Nazi crocodile
> Improve his Lebensraum,
> By teaching Germans how to heil
> In all lands that allow 'em!
> How cheerfully he breaks their thrall
> To little nations' laws,
> And grabs them, gold and lands and all,
> With his insatiate jaws!
> How happily he drags them in
> To join his robber band,
> Then says to Mr. Chamberlain,
> "This is my last demand!"[396]

Of course, the parody is to be understood as a grotesque and it may appear strange that Alice is given in it the role of Adolf. Yet, as Jörg Thunecke remarks in his commentary to this text, its humor was not directed against Carroll or Alice but rather against a third party, which made its satire become an effective political tool[397]. In regard to Nazism derided in this text, it seems still more important that Carroll's *Alice*-books in themselves possess enough potential to be interpreted as a critique of this ideology. The motives of arbitrary language and thought, of a self-estrangement, of a defense of reason against the proliferating forces of the irrational that are central to them make it plausible that the only period in the German modern history in which no new *Alice*-translations appeared was the Nazi era. Franz Sester who was among the first to provide a new rendition of it after the collapse of the Nazi regime displayed an acute awareness of a huge ideological gulf between Carroll's world and Nazism when he wrote in his *Preface*:

(1939)", in: Victoria Hertling, Wulf Koepke (Et al., eds.), *Hitler im Visier: Literarische Satiren und Karikaturen als Waffe gegen den Nationalsozialismus*, Wuppertal: Arco Verlag 2005, pp. 251–274, esp. pp. 256–257.

396 James Dyrenforth and Max Kester, *op. cit.*, p. 17.

397 Jörg Thunecke, op. cit., p. 256.

> Nichts ist dem Engländer unerträglicher als hohes Pathos, theatralisches Auftreten, Größenwahn, aber nichts liegt ihm auch ferner als Selbstverachtung und übertriebene Demütigkeit; er überschätzt im allgemeinen weder sich noch andere, aber er hat ein gesundes Selbstbewußtsein und billigt dieses auch seinen Mitmenschen zu... Diese Erziehung zum "Sinn für Humor" ist in dem Buche Alice im Wunderland zu finden. Das Buch ist eine Lektüre für Kinder von Familien, in denen die individuelle Freiheit eine sehr große ist, und wo das Kind nicht zum kritiklosen Gehorsam und nicht zum Herdengeist erzogen wird.[398] (Nothing is more unbearable for an Englishman than elevated pathos, staginess, and megalomania and nothing is so foreign to his nature as self-contempt and exaggerated humbleness; he does not overestimate himself or others, and yet he possesses a sound self-esteem which he presupposes in other people as well...The *Alice* book bears testimony to the cultivation of a sense of humor. The book is a (recommendable) reading for children of the families in which individual freedom is held in high esteem and which do not allow their children to develop blind submissiveness and herd mentality.)

Reading *Alice* was quite openly promoted by Sester as pertaining to the German national agenda[399] of his time: all the qualities for which he praised the English in the above quote were to call to the consciousness of his compatriots some patterns of correct moral behavior and to critically reflect on all the psychological characteristics of the Nazi past. His critique against blind submissiveness and herd mentality may well be interpreted as a praise of Alice's ability to oppose the forces of the irrational and to wake up from her delirium.

Dangers inherent in the mental automatism, i.e. in the dictate of automatic thinking which is beyond any rational control, were indeed vividly captured by Carroll's intuition, so that it is quite comprehensible that the translator recommended reading *Alice* in order to overcome mental attitudes that had dominated the recent past. Yet the parallels shown by Sester in his *Preface* would seem to refer not only to some abstracted psychological qualities but also to the language in which mental automatism directly manifested itself. The second – practical – part of the present chapter which is to focus on some of the predominant linguistic patterns in Carroll's Chapters XI/XII and in the language of their translations, is not intended as an all-encompassing catalogue of the traits characteristic

398 Sester, Franz, "Vorwort", *Alicens Abenteuer im Wunderland*, Düsseldorf: Drei Eulen 1949, pp. 7–8, here p. 7.

399 For more details concerning the use of *Alice* translations into German as a means of denazification after the Second World War, see the essay by Emer O'Sullivan "Englishness in German translations of Alice in Wonderland", in: Luc van Doorslaer, Peter Flynn, Joep. Leerssen (Eds.), *Interconnecting Translation Studies and Imagology*, Amsterdam: John Benjamins Publishing 2015, pp. 87–107.

of the language of violence. Structurally, it follows the analytics of rhetorical means provided by Felicity Rash in her monograph *The Language of Violence: Adolf Hitler's Mein Kampf* (2006, pp. 191–242), among other things, a frequent use of grammatical superlatives, e.g. "teuerstes Blut" ("the most precious blood"), "die aufpeitschendste" ("the most exciting"[400]); of superlatives referring to size and amount: "das Gift kübelweise in das Volk hineingeschüttet" ("the poison poured into the people by bucketfuls"), "jämmerlich zwergenhaft" ("miserable and dwarfish"[401]); of a morphological and semantic repetition: "zu althergebracht, zu abgedroschen, dann wieder zu überlebt" ("too old-fashioned, too hackneyed, too out-of-date"[402]); of aggressive and apocalyptic vocabulary: "Kampfesmut" ("courage to fight"), "Unterjochung" ("subjugation"[403]); of sarcasm: "das durchschnittliche Spatzenhirn einer deutschen, wissenschaftlich natürlich höchst gebildeten Schreiberseele" ("the average sparrow brain of a German scribbler, equipped, it goes without saying, with a high scientific education"[404]), etc. As a matter of fact, the analysis of the violence rhetoric as it is manifested in Carroll's text is called to provide only a total impression of the respective style and is not understood as an attempt to reconstruct a life-size picture of the language of violence: none of the stylistic or rhetorical means taken alone can serve as its exact copy. It is rather the density of formal traits which matters, i.e. a formal hypertrophy characteristic of this language, of its endless repetitions and exclamations that never stop threatening those who venture to resist the dictate of automatic thinking.

VIII.II

Already before the begin of the trial Alice is quite surprised about the behavior of the jurymen who are busy with writing something on their slates without there being anything worth recording. As the Gryphon explains to her, they are putting down their own names for fear they should forget them at the end of the trial. The stupidity of this act impresses Alice so much that she is not able to control herself and exclaims: "Stupid things!"[405] Her surprise does not lessen after seeing that her exclamation has immediately been written down by all the jurymen. The automatism with which they act is introduced not as a minor detail

400 Felicity Rash, *The Language of Violence: Adolf Hitler's Mein Kampf*, New York/Berlin/Bern: Peter Lang 2006, p. 191.
401 *Ibid.*, pp. 193–194.
402 *Ibid.*, p. 198.
403 *Ibid.*, p. 203.
404 *Ibid.*, p. 233.
405 *Alice*, p. 115.

of the trial scene but represents rather the focus of what is happening and especially remarkable in this respect is the behavior of Bill after its pencil is removed by Alice who is terribly annoyed by its squeaking noise:

> She did it so quickly that the poor little juror (it was Bill, the Lizard) could not make out at all what had become of it; so, after hunting all about for it, he was obliged to write with one finger for the rest of the day; and this was of very little use, as it left no mark on the slate.)[406]

Rendering the automatism peculiar to the actions of the jurymen, including Bill, did not confront translators with any remarkable difficulties so that by comparing different Chinese, French, Italian, etc. versions no significant differences can be observed between them and the original. The first noticeable divergences may be seen in the renditions of the words produced by the judge who displays a special taste for imperatives, as, e.g. in his addressing the first witness – the Hatter:

> "Take off your hat," the King said to the Hatter.
> "It isn't mine," said the Hatter.
> "*Stolen*!" the King exclaimed...[407]

This conversation is also marked by automatic thinking: whereas the Hatter automatically – without any perceivable reason – calls the King's attention to the fact that the pronoun *your* in his address may among other things refer to the identity of a future potential owner of the hat, of someone who one day would buy it from the Hatter, the King deduces from the Hatter's words equally automatically that the hat is stolen. The reason why the communication does not work in this particular episode is the possibility of different interpretations of the semantics of the pronoun *your* and therefore it is clear that translators who recognized this and focused in their renditions on the semantics of the corresponding pronouns in their languages are the closest to the English original, as, e.g. V. Nabokov (p. 101):

> "Сними свою шляпу," сказал Король Шляпнику. "Это не моя," ответил Шляпник. "Украл!" воскликнул Король. ("Take off your hat," the King said to the Hatter. "It's not mine," replied the Hatter. "Stolen!" the King exclaimed.)

406 *Alice*, p. 115.
407 *Alice*, p. 117.

By the way of contrast, examples in which the pronoun has not been translated at all are provided in the Italian version by Bruno Oddera and in the Japanese by Tada Kōzō:

> Bruno Oddera (p. 104): "Togliti il cappello," disse il Re al Cappellaio. "Non è mio," rispose il Cappellaio. "Lo ha rubato!" esclamò il Re. ("Take off the hat," the King said to the Hatter. "It's not mine," replied the Hatter. "He stole it!" the King exclaimed.)

> Tada Kōzō多田幸蔵 (pp. 153–154):
> 「帽子をとれ」と王さまは帽子屋に言われました。「わたくしのものではございません」と帽子屋が言いました。「盗品だな！」と王さまは叫ばれて etc. ("Take off the hat," the King said to the Hatter. "It's not mine, your honor," replied the Hatter. "It's a stolen good!" the King exclaimed.)

The reflexive pronoun "ti" (lit.: *to you*) in "togliti" does not in any way suggest the idea of ownership. The readers of both versions are sure to have difficulties of understanding, for the translators did not reproduce the word play to which the semantics of *your* is central in the original, so that the answer of the Hatter loses its logic. If the translators had decided to provide their texts with corresponding pronouns, e.g. "il tuo" ("your") in "Togliti il tuo cappello" or "anata no" ("your") in "あなたの帽子をとれ", their versions might have become easier to understand, yet they would not sound quite natural as the language habits in Italian and Japanese do not require the use of possessive pronouns in similar contexts. The same is true of the Russian habits. Nabokov decides to use a pronoun in a situation in which none is normally used: "Сними шляпу" ("Take off the hat") sounds more natural than "Сними свою шляпу" ("Take off your hat".) The obvious problem faced in this case by the translators is a conflict between naturalness and comprehensibility. Quite a special case of solving this problem is represented by Zhao Yuanren's (p. 153) rendition:

> 那皇帝对那帽匠道，"脱掉你的帽子！" 那帽匠回道，"帽子是我的。" 那皇帝嚷道，"偷来的！(The King said to the Hatter: "Take off your hat!" The Hatter replied: "The hat is mine." The King shouted: "It is stolen!")

Here, the translator poses a great puzzle by providing a quite natural Chinese equivalent for "your" ("ni" 你) but at the same time omitting the negation in the Hatter's answer. For all I know, the only possibile interpretation of the King's reaction to it should be something in line with Pierre-Joseph Proudhon's conviction about "ownership being theft." Whether Zhao Yuanren had similar thoughts in mind while preparing his translation or, maybe, the omission of "not" is better explained simply by a lack of attention on the part of the translator, cannot be conclusively determined. Yet by no means could this curious rendition be interpreted as due to some deficit of Chinese, since negations in similar cases (c.f. "帽子不是我的") are absolutely natural.

The conversation that takes place between the King and the Hatter may be regarded as a typical example of the language of violence: it reveals both an – automatic – easiness with which the aggressive vocabulary is deployed by the King and his pleasure at his power as it is expressed in his sarcastic address of the Hatter. The aggressive vocabulary in itself, e.g. in phrases like "Give your evidence," said the King; "and don't be nervous, or I'll have you executed on the spot, etc." does not pose any translation problems. Yet rendering the King's sarcasm and the Hatter's confusion is not as simple, since it largely depends on reading – and reproducing – numerous instances of playing with words, e.g.:

> "Give your evidence," the King repeated angrily, "or I'll have you executed, whether you are nervous or not."
> "I'm a poor man, your Majesty," the Hatter began, in a trembling voice, "and I hadn't begun my tea – not above a week or so – and what with the bread-and-butter getting so thin – and the twinkling of the tea –"
> "The twinkling of *what*?" said the King.
> "It *began* with the tea," the Hatter replied.
> "Of course twinkling *begins* with a T!" said the King sharply. "Do you take me for a dunce? Go on!"[408]

In this episode, the King's sarcasm is aimed to expose the stupidity of the Hatter: that the word "twinkling" begins with a "t" is self-evident and therefore needs no mentioning in the court. The misunderstanding is based on the Hatter's meaning the noun "tea" which is understood by the King as the letter "t." This word play turned out to be particularly challenging for translators into Chinese, since there are no letters in its writing, and as was the case with many other examples discussed above, the renditions that are the most difficult to understand are those in which the translators seek to be the closest to the original, reproduce an exact copy of the passage by lexical means that are completely alien to the linguistic habits of the Chinese and refrain from providing any comments concerning the reason of the misunderstanding in the original, as, e.g. the following version by Chen Fuan (p. 187):

408 *Alice*, pp. 118–119.

"开头是茶水亮晶晶，" 帽匠答道。"亮晶晶这词当然是' T '字开头的！" 国王严厉地说 etc. ("It began with a sparkling tea," said the Hatter. "Sure that the word *liangjingjing* (*sparkling*) begins with the letter T," replied the King sternly.)

Since *liangjingjing* 亮晶晶 (*sparkling*) neither begins with a sound similar to "t", nor is it in any way similar to the letter "T" used by the translator, the meaning of this rendition is completely obscure for Chinese readers. Now consider for comparison a solution provided by Zhao Yuanren (p. 155):

那皇帝道，"说出你的证据来，要不然就无论你害怕不害怕，总归要把你杀掉。"
"陛下我是个穷人——我不过刚才起头喝我的茶，——喝了没有一个礼拜出头——而且说起那面包越弄越薄——而且那茶又要查夜——"
那皇帝道，"什么东西查夜？"
那帽匠道，"查夜先从茶起头。"
那皇帝厉声地道，"自然茶叶是茶字起头，你当我傻子吗？再说下去。"
(The King said: "Give your evidence, or I'll execute you, whether you are afraid or not."
"Your Majesty, I'm a poor man – I was only just about to begin my tea – I hadn't been drinking for above a week – besides the bread was getting thin – besides while drinking tea I had to hold a night vigil –"
"What do you mean by *night vigil*?"
"A night vigil begins with tea."
The King said in a stern voice: "Of course, the word *tea-leaves* begin with the character *tea*, do you take me for a fool? Go ahead.")

Zhao's solution rests upon contrasting the homophones *chaye* 查夜 (*a night vigil*) and *chaye* 茶叶 (*tea-leaves*). Since any Chinese reader would easily recognize the phonemic closeness of these word compositions written in different characters, the misunderstanding between the King and the Hatter is made here as plausible as in the original.

In contrast, translating the passage into languages with alphabetic writing is not accompanied by any significant problems: usually, translators provide combinations of two words beginning with the same letter, e.g. Ch. Enzensberger (p. 115: *taumeln* (*stagger*) / *Tee* (*tea*)), A. Zimmermann (p. 80: *Teller und Töpfe* (*plates and pots*) / *Tee* (*tea*)), T. Pietrocòla-Rossetti (p. 166, *la testa* (*head*) / *il tè* (*tea*), etc. Somewhat different are in this respect the versions provided by H. Bué and V. Nabokov:

H. Bué (pp. 172–173):

"…et les *dragées* du thé…"
"Les *dragées* de quoi?" dit le Roi.
"Ça a commencé par le thé," répondit le Chapelier.
"Je vous dis que dragée commence par un d!" cria le Roi vivement. "Me prenez-vous pour un âne ? Continuez!"
("And the tea-drag*é*es…" "What drag*é*es?" said the King. "It began with a tea," replied the Hatter. "And I say that (the word) *dragée* begins with a D!" the King shouted excitedly. "Do you take me for a dunce? Continue!")

Here, the King exposes the Hatter's stupidity by pointing out that he does not know how to spell the noun *dragées* and by correcting his mistake. On his part, Nabokov (p. 102) does not resort to the orthography as the source of the word play and provides a solution which rests on a purely semantic improvisation:

– Дай свои показания, – грозно повторил Король, – иначе будешь казнен, несмотря на твое волнение.
– Я бедный человек, ваше величество, – залепетал Шляпник, – только что я начал пить чай, а тут хлеб, так сказать, тоньше делается, да и в голове стало сыро.
– Можно обойтись без сыра, – перебил Король.
– А тут стало еще сырее, так сказать, – продолжал Шляпник, заикаясь.
– Ну и скажи так, – крикнул Король. – За дурака что ли ты меня принимаешь!
("Give your evidence," repeated the King sternly, "or you'll be executed, in spite of your nervousness."
"I am a poor man, your Majesty, I was just beginning to drink my tea, when my bread became smaller and smaller and I got wet (*сыро*) in my head."
"Can you leave the cheese (*сыра*) aside, please?"
"And then I got still wetter (*сырее*.)"
"You could have said so earlier. Do you take me for a dunce?")

The word play is based on the consonance of *syro* (*wet*) and *syra* (Gen. case of *syr* = *cheese.*) Although any reader of Russian would easily recognize the cause of the misunderstanding, the expression "got wet in the head" does not make any sense and the King's remark to it is equally completely enigmatic. Probably Nabokov intended to provide here a piece of nonsense which, however, did not prove quite successful, as the word play between "got wet in my head" and "leave the cheese aside" will not work in Russian: whereas *syr* (*cheese*) is a masculine noun, *stalo* (*syro*) ("*got* (*wet*)") is a verb with a neuter inflection, which makes a confusion of them rather unlikely. By contrast, a much more elegant translation was provided by Nabokov in a further episode from the dialogue in which the King continues giving vent to his sarcasm:

> "If that's all you know about it, you may stand down," continued the King.
> "I can't go no lower," said the Hatter: "I'm on the floor, as it is."
> "Then you may *sit* down," the King said.[409]

In the reproduced passage, the King's conviction regarding the Hatter's poor quality as a speaker is amply proven by the fact that he obviously is not familiar enough with the semantics of the verb *to stand down*. The lenient and sarcastic *sit down* is not used as a mere explanation of a word which has erroneously been interpreted by the Hatter but rather as an attempt to mute him by making his confusion complete. V. Nabokov (p. 103) renders this episode as follows:

> "Если тебе больше нечего сказать," продолжал Король, "можешь встать на ноги."
> "Я и так стою, только одна из них согнута", робко заметил Шляпник.
> "В таком случае встань на голову", отвечал Король.
> ("If you have nothing more to say, you may stand up," continued the King.
> "But I *am* standing, your Majesty. Only one of my legs is bent," replied the Hatter shyly.
> "You may stand on your head, then," said the King.)

Nabokov deploys his favorite style by a completely free rendition of the semantics of the original, yet the psychological effect achieved by his language use – the awkwardness of the Hatter exposed by the King's sarcasm – is true to the original. Nabokov refrains, for example, from translating *stand down* at all and uses *stand up*, which suggests that in his version the witness is kneeing before the King. The King's concluding remark permitting the Hatter to *stand on his head* has as little to do with the semantics of the original as that of *standing up*, yet again the effect produced by it is close to that of the original: the witness has been muted and his examination is over.

In view of the complexities pertaining to a true reproduction both of the semantics of a word play (*stand down* vs. *sit down*) and of the psychological effect produced by it, Nabokov's version may be considered illustrating the happy medium. Much easier would have been again to lay down one's arms and to cut out

409 *Alice*, p. 120.

the complicated passage altogether, which has been the case, e.g. with Pietrocòla-Rossetti's (p. 168) rendition. By contrast, a much more difficult strategy was chosen by those translators who tried to save both the semantics *and* the effect of the original word play. A. Zimmermann's and Zhao Yuanren's texts may serve as examples of this choice. Consider the rendition prepared by Zimmermann (p. 81):

> "Wenn dies Alles ist, was du zu sagen weißt, so kannst du abtreten," fuhr der König fort. "Ich kann nichts mehr abtreten," sagte der Hutmacher: "ich stehe so schon auf den Strümpfen." "Dann kannst du abwarten, bis du wieder gefragt wirst," erwiderte der König. ("If that's all you know, you can stand down," the King continued. "But I couldn't cede anything else (to you), because I'm already standing on my socks," said the Hatter. "Then wait till you are asked again," the King said.)

Two manoeuvres proved helpful for this German rendition: the polysemy of the verb "abtreten" (*stand down / cede* smth. to so.) and the observation that in the original the Hatter actually takes his shoes off (as indicated in the later scene of his leaving the court.[410]) As he is introduced as lacking his shoes, in Zimmermann's text this detail is suggestive of the Hatter's poverty and inability to cede anything to the King. On the contrary, in Zhao Yuanren's rendition (p. 157) the word play is reproduced by grammatical means:

> 那皇帝道，"假如你知道的就是这一点儿，你就退下去罢！"那帽匠道，"我不能再下去嘞，因为象这样我已经站在地板上嘞。"那皇帝答道，"那么你就坐下去。" (The King said: "As this is all you know about it, you may stand down." The Hatter said: "I cannot go no lower because I'm already standing on the floor." The King replied: "Sit down then.")

This rendition is among the closest to the original: Zhao makes use of the direction complement *xia* 下 (*qu* 去) which, similarly to *down* in English, is quite naturally attached both to the verb *tui* 退 (*recede*) and to *zuo* 坐 (*sit.*)

The three above episodes from the conversation between the judge (the King) and the witness (the Hatter) may be regarded as characteristic of the whole trial process that is dominated by the forces of the irrational: it is the dictate of automatic thinking which every time steers the language in a particular direction, intentionally and systematically disregarding what the interlocutor might actually mean by his word usage, in order to confound and eventually to mute him. Within this kind of communication, it is not so much the linguistic competence which matters but rather the distribution of power positions: the

410 *Alice*, p. 120: "the Hatter hurriedly left the court, without even waiting to put his shoes on."

King does not display any interest in drawing parallels between the words of the witness and the trial case in order to determine the guilt or the innocence of the accused Knave. Instead the primary target of his sarcasm seems to be an effective annihilation of the witness by language. Remarkable is the intensity with which the same formal means are used again and again to underscore the King's sarcastic self-confidence, e.g. by stating that the hat is stolen, that *twinkling* of course begins with a *T*, etc. All these statements are called to expose the Hatter's inability to speak, to unmask his stupidity, to emphasize his pettiness. By doing so, the King's awareness of his personal superiority steadily increases, thus nurturing his megalomaniac self that drives him to sarcasm and makes him persistently fall back on some never changing speech patterns.

The uncontrollable dictate of violent thinking is also characteristic of the Queen. Maybe in no other scene is the formulaic quality of her aggressive language as obvious as in the reaction to the Dormouse's sleepy remark that tarts are made of treacle:

> "Collar that Dormouse!" the Queen shrieked out. "Behead that Dormouse! Turn that Dormouse out of court! Suppress him! Pinch him! Off with his whiskers!"[411]

The sheer quantity of the imperatives as well as of the punitive actions with which she comes up in a rush is impressing. Since no word play accompanies this unique manifestation of violence, still another impressing thing is how few translations of this passage are close to the original. Most of them have shortened the text by reducing either the number of the imperatives or that of the exact actions ordered by the Queen. For example, in the German rendition by H. Scheu-Riesz, the original sequence consisting of six units is reduced to one of four and there is only one exclamation mark used in the whole passage:

> "Man soll dieses Murmeltier erwürgen," schrie die Königin, "man soll es abstechen, man soll es hinauswerfen. Hinaus mit ihm!" ("The Dormouse is to be strangled," the Queen shouted, "it is to be stabbed and thrown out. Off with it!")

Among renditions which reproduce the exact number of the imperatives yet minimize the diversity of the Queen's orders are the Japanese ones provided by Tada Kōzō (pp. 159–160) who uses here the verb *toriosaeru* 取り押さえる (*to subdue*) twice to render both *collar* and *suppress* and by Shōno Kōkichi (p. 221) who similarly deploys one word *chongireru* ちょんぎれる (*chop off*) to stand for both *to behead* and *off with his whiskers*; cf. the Chinese translation by Zhao Yuanren

411 *Alice*, p. 121.

(p. 159) in which *qu diao* 去掉 (*off with*) is used twice: "Qu diao ta de tou!" 去掉他的头！ ("Off with his head!") // "Qu diao ta de huzi!" 去掉他的胡子！ ("Off with his whiskers!") Purely hypothetically it could be assumed that by reducing units in the long sequence of the Queen's imperatives the translators may have pursued the aim of neutralizing the aggressiveness of her language and thus to adapt the book for children's reading. On the other hand, there are also a number of translations which go a good deal beyond a true reproduction of the Queen's speech and display a maximum of creative imagination due to which the Queen appears even more sophisticated in her brutal fantasies than in the original. In this respect, a particularly high degree of inventiveness has been triggered by the last imperative: "Off with his whiskers!" While rendering this command, many translators went into detail as to the exact way in which the whiskers could effectively be removed, e.g. B. Teutsch uses the image of *cutting off* (p. 126: "Schneidet ihm den Schnurrbart ab!" – "Cut off his whiskers!") and A. Zimmermann – that of *burning off* (p. 82: "Brennt ihm den Bart ab!" – "Burn off his whiskers!") Sometimes the play of fantasy took a different turn and made translators think of other bodily parts of which the Dormouse might be deprived in punishment, e.g. V. Nabokov has substituted *whiskers* for *ears* (p. 104: "Отрезать ему уши!" – "Cut off his ears!") and B. Zachoder – for the tail (p. 109: "Оторвать ей хвост!" – "Tear off her tail!")

Shortly after this episode, when the dust raised by the Queen's rage has settled and the court becomes quiet enough to proceed, turning to the only available piece of evidence – the already mentioned poem with unidentifiable pronouns – the King once again provokes the Queen's hot temperament by asking her whether she – like the female person mentioned in the poem[412] – has ever had fits:

> "...you never had *fits*, my dear, I think?" he said to the Queen. "Never!" said the Queen, furiously, throwing an inkstand at the Lizard as she spoke. (The unfortunate little Bill had left off writing on his slate with one finger, as he found it made no mark; but he now hastily began again, using the ink, that was trickling down his face, as long as it lasted.) "Then the words don't *fit* you," said the King, looking round the court with a smile. There was a dead silence. "It's a pun!" the King added in an angry tone, and everybody laughed.[413]

412 *Alice*, p. 127: "My notion was that you had been / (Before she had this fit) / An obstacle that came between / Him, and ourselves, and it."

413 *Alice*, p. 129.

This new outbreak of rage with which the Queen reacts to the King's provocative question makes the emphasis of the narration in the story again be laid on the automatism peculiar to the thinking and acting of its figures: the automatism with which the inkstand is thrown at Bill is immediately followed by that of Bill's writing. And again, the irrationality of the language of violence is underscored: not only is the victim of the Queen's rage fully accidental (theoretically, the inkstand could have been directed at anyone present at court), the King's remark that the words do not fit the Queen also resist any rational control, since the Queen, in spite of her assertion ("Never!"), has yet again clearly demonstrated how prone she actually is to have fits. The pun based on the semantics of *fit* confirms the King's ability to make words unfitting even then when they quite obviously fit as well as his psychological attitude towards the audience: everybody has to react to his words exactly in accord with his intended meaning and should there be someone to miss his point, the King's authority is quick enough to force the respective person into laughing. There is probably no other passage in the whole book in which his dictatorial posture appears as clearly as in the imperatively pronounced: "It's a pun!"

To reproduce this passage, the translators have again a variety of different strategies at their disposal: logically arguably the easiest way to make the King appear as a dictator is to refrain from using a pun exactly when he insists on having used one. This way was chosen, e.g. by Chen Fuan (p. 205) who renders the King's reaction to the Queen's rage as: 那么这句话跟你无关 ("Then the words don't suit you // don't apply to you.") No word play is used here and the expression chosen for *fit* (无关 *wuguan*) does not suggest any reference to the Queen's mental state. By contrast, a more complicated strategy has been chosen by those who tried to recreate Carroll's pun, e.g. V. Nabokov (pp. 111–112):

> "ты, кажется, никогда не падала в обморок, моя дорогая", обратился он к Королеве. "Никогда!" рявкнула с яростью Королева… "В таком случае это не совпадает", сказал Король, с улыбкой обводя взглядом присутствующих. Гробовое молчание. "Это – игра слов!" сердито добавил он, и все стали смеяться. ("I don't think you have ever had a fainting fit, my dear," he said to the Queen. "Never!" bawled the Queen, furiously…"Then the words do not in the faintest apply to you," the King said, looking around with a smile. There was a dead silence. "It's a pun!" the King added angrily and everybody laughed.

In this episode, Nabokov plays with the semantics of *падать в обморок* (*to faint*, lit.: *to fall into a faint*) and *совпадать* (*coinside*, *apply to sb.*, lit.: *to fall together*.) Yet this word play is not as easy to recognize in Russian as it is in the original, which is why the silence in the hall that follows after the King's phrase in this version is all the more comprehensible. Another innovation on the part of Nabokov was to specify the Queen's fit as one of *a faint*: by creating a bridge between the verbs *to faint / to coincide* on which the King's pun is based Nabokov evokes a psychological contrast between impotence (faint) which the Queen is assumed to be prone to display and the power with which she is actually invested at the court. Since by her repeated outbreaks of rage the Queen reveals anything but a faint disposition, the psychological pattern evoked by Nabokov's language in this episode proves significantly different to that of the original.

That a reproduction of an English pun in other languages is usually accompanied by distancing oneself from the semantics of the original may be illustrated by a number of further renditions of this passage, e.g. by Demurova (p. 258) who makes the Queen not only throw an inkstand at the Lizard but also order that it be beheaded, which is necessitated by the composition of her Russian pun: "ты у нас рубишь *с плеч*, а не сплеча" (lit.: "you'd rather let heads roll than shoot from the hip"); by Enzensberger (pp. 123–124) who plays with the semantics of the consonant German words *verschroben* (*eccentric, odd*) and *verschrieben* (*mistakes made in spelling*): "Dann hat er sich verschrieben" ("He must have spelled it wrongly."); by Oddera (p. 115) who equally resorts to a phonemic play of words *attacchi di furia* (*fits of rage*) and *attaccare* (*to attack*): "Allora, se non hai mai avuto attacchi, la poesia non può attaccare te." ("Well, if you have never had fits of rage, the poem can do no harm to you."), etc.

Finally, one more episode from Chapter XII should be mentioned here which follows directly after the King's comment ("It's a pun!") In it, Alice gets free from the delirium of the court trial and for the last time during her journey through Wonderland demonstrates her ability to resist the forces of the irrational:

> "Let the jury consider their verdict," the King said, for about the twentieth time that day.
> "No, no!" said the Queen. "Sentence first – verdict afterwards."
> "Stuff and nonsense!" said Alice loudly. "The idea of having the sentence first!"
> "Hold your tongue!" said the Queen, turning purple.
> "I won't!" said Alice.
> "Off with her head!" the Queen shouted at the top of her voice.

Repetition compulsion peculiar to the language of violence manifests itself in both the King's and the Queen's speech. It perfectly agrees with their regular behavior patterns: while the King never gets tired of addressing the jurymen by the same form of request, the Queen is not patient enough to wait till the verdict is pronounced and insists on the sentence being first. By comparing various translations of this relatively simple passage, one can easily see that – probably due to the increased emotionality of the culmination scene – the translators seldom limited themselves to providing an exact reproduction of the text and resorted instead to significant innovations. For example, the number *twenty* referring to the frequent recurrence of the King's request to the jury was rendered by Enzensberger (p. 124) as "etwa zehn" ("for maybe the tenth"), by Oddera (p. 115) as "dodici" ("the twelfth"), and by Kononenko – "уже в сотый раз за этот день[414]" ("for the hundredth time that day.") Depending on how much repetition the translators believe the King to be able to produce, the exact degree to which the grotesque is extended in their versions – and therefore the exact number semantics – varies. Variations are seen even in the depiction of the complexion of the enraged Queen: Seriu Hajime (p. 237) makes her turn *murasakiiro* むらさき色 (*purple, violet*), Tada Kōzō (p. 172) takes the *bright red/crimson* 真っ赤 (*makka*), Enzensberger (p. 124) – *krebsrot* (*lobster-red*) and Chen Fuan (p. 205) – *greenish blue* (*qing* 青.) Yet maybe nowhere else does the total impression that has been recreated in these various versions depend as much on the creative force of the translator's imagination as in the rendition of the Queen's furious command "Sentence first – verdict afterwards." Along some quite neutral renditions in which these words have been reproduced exactly, e.g. by Tada Kōzō (p. 172), Seriu Hajime (p. 237) and Shōno Kōkichi (p. 188), all of whom make *senkoku* 宣告 (*sentence*) be followed by *hyōketsu* 評決 (*verdict*), special attention deserve the versions provided by Enzensberger (p. 124) "Zuerst die Strafe, dann das Urteil!" ("Punishment first – verdict afterwords!") and by Nabokov (p. 112): "Сперва казнь, а потом уж приговор." ("Execution first – verdict afterwards!") Here, it is no longer a reversal of the usual sequence in which two formal official acts are pronounced at court but rather the highest possible increase with which blind violence wishes to assert itself. It needs no sanctions, no legal basis, and is openly directed against its greatest opponent personified in Alice: a hope in reason, justice and undersanding.

Conclusion: The Language of Violence – A Source of Fun or Horror?

One of the main experiences of Alice at the end of her journey through Wonderland is a new complete failure of communication with its inhabitants. She proves unable to accept the rules which recquire that conventions should be substitut-

414 The only source available for me to access this Russian translation by Andrej Kononenko ("Alisa v strane čudes") was a digital version in the internet under the following link: http://www.wonderland-alice.ru/translations/kononenko/?curPos=12.

ed for arbitrariness, clarity – for obscurity, sympathy – for violence, and that the final aim of communicating with others be understood as a militant assertion of oneself. In the above investigation of linguistic mechanisms peculiar to the rhetoric of violence in Carroll's text, arguably the most prominent among their formal features proved to be an excessive repetitiveness, imperativeness, and aggression. Ironically, the primary aesthetic effect of the language of violence is fun, i.e. figures that are associated with it appear as a butt of ridicule and whoever reads their parts – in spite of all their aggressiveness or maybe exactly due to it – is rather likely to smile than to be horror-stricken. For example, the long sequence of the Queen's imperatives beginning with "Collar this mouse! Behead this mouse!" may be perceived as comic, for it is concluded by imagining punitive actions (*to suppress, to pinch, off with his whiskers*) that are much less bloody-minded that the beginning ones. For this reason, the formal hypertrophy of this kind of language is burlesque rather than horrible: it is not so much the figure to be punished that is standing in the focus of the reader's attention but the Queen who is unable to control herself. In this particular instance, the comic effect is enhanced by the intratextual association that arises between one of the Queen's imperatives (*to suppress*) and an episode from Chapter XI in which Alice witnesses how a cheering guinea-pig becomes *suppressed* by the court-officers and feels extremely glad for having at last learned the meaning of this complicated verb. Another factor which significantly curbs the brutality of the language of violence is that, different to Alice, the reader of the story never forgets that Alice's opponents are but a pack of playing cards and therefore do not deserve to be feared. Nevertheless, both in terms of psychology (megalomania, aggression, sarcasm) and at the formal level (arbitrariness, a formal hypertrophy, repetitiveness, imperativeness), the characteristic patterns of the language of violence in Carroll's work have much in common with those that dominated the spiritual atmosphere of the first decades of the 20th century. For this reason, the power of the irrational as it was captured in *Alice* may certainly be interpreted as an intuition of the delirium which would later dominate aesthetics (surrealism) and politics (totalitarian languages.) The paradox pertaining to the language effect produced by *Alice* (i.e. the comic vs. the brutal/the tragic) opened for its translators two alternative ways to follow: either to diminish the grotesque dimension, to minimize all the features of the text which would appear not fitting for children's reading, or to exactly reproduce the realm of the irrational and, by doing so, clearly suggest to their audiences all those complexities that have to be taken into account when interpreting Carroll's work against the spiritual background of the modern world.

IX. McTaggart's Paradox: Time and the Parity of Tenses

"All in the golden afternoon // Full leisurely we glide..." These lines from a poem by which Carroll introduces his book refer the reader to a specific event from the past: to a day in July 1862 when for the first time he told the *Alice*-story to the Liddell sisters in order to entertain them during a boat trip. Here, the morphological form of the verb *to glide* has the semantics of historic present, calling to mind an episode from the past as if it were still vividly present. Simultaneously, this recollection anticipates a story which the reader of the book has to learn immediately after the poem's end, that is, the poem also addresses the future, referring both to the adventures of Alice in Wonderland and, by extension, to the infinity of generations to come that will become familiar with her story. However, as I will try to show in this chapter, this symbolical merging of tenses, when the past, present, and future seem to become one, paradoxically also demonstrates the reality of time.

Probably in no other part of Carroll's book does the relationship between time and reality feature as prominently as in the story's framework: Having awoken from her dream, Alice tells the story to her older sister who instantly begins to think about the future and to picture to herself how, having grown up, Alice might one day tell wonderful stories to her own children and make their eyes shine with excitement. The particular quality which in the eyes of the sister would help Alice sustain harmony in her future life, is the ability to "keep ... the simple and loving heart of her childhood."[415] Childhood is thus also a category which is conceived at different temporal levels, i.e. as the actual childhood of Alice (the present), that of her children (the future), and a childhood which is supposed to be preserved within her heart after growing up (the past in the future.) Yet, again, by making these levels run together, Carroll does not make any of them lose their individual reality so that all of them retain their distinct positions on the temporal scale. Time is by no means conceived of as an illusion, as something that is inexorably flowing away into nothing, but rather as a complementary existential relationship between past, present, and future. Within this conception, *childhood* appears as a focal category which is opposed to what Carroll calls a *dull reality*[416]: a down-to-earth perception of the present as the only tangible dimension of existence.

415 *Alice*, p. 132.
416 *Alice*, p. 7.

Reflections concerning the relationship between time and reality which so prominently feature in the narrative frame (the introductory poem and the conclusion of the story), sometimes reappear in the story itself, e.g. in an episode from Chapter V in which Alice is completely confused by the Caterpillar's seemingly quite simple question as to who she is: "I-I hardly know, sir, just at present – at least I know who I *was* when I got up this morning, but I think I must have been changed several times since then.[417]" It is nothing but the strange course of the time that makes her identity suddenly turn into quite a mystery. Yet the metamorphoses of self appear wondrous only when they are measured against the experience of time in everyday life: that all of a sudden she has gained the ability to grow huge and tiny within seconds makes time itself appear as one of the main sources of wonders throughout the story. Nevertheless, however great her confusion about all the sudden changes of size may appear, one thing which she still perfectly knows in this episode is who she was when she got up in the morning and it is not coincidental that the form *was* has been marked by the author in the above sentence. The tense morphology comes as a rescue to her since the world where she got up "this morning" is the only one in which she has a sure experience of spatial and temporal laws so that the past form makes it possible for her in the given situation to judge at least partly with certainty about her own identity. Compared with the above mentioned reflections of her older sister upon the course of time, this, of course, is a different kind of thinking about it since it is free of anything symbolic and of any abstractions which would make the past and present meet. Still the problem of time and of its relation to reality is as prominent here as in a number of other episodes in the book.

In the dialogue with the Caterpillar, the "at least I know who I was" is a means of self-protection with which language directly provides her: although she cannot conceal her embarrassment about all the changes she has to go through in Wonderland, there is one area which has remained completely real to her, i.e. the familiar world within her memory. It is not only the issue of time and reality which seems to be centrally concerned in episodes like this, but also one of time and tenses, the question as to how the temporal system of a language is related to time in physical and metaphysical senses. This last problem has been heatedly discussed in modern language philosophy and quite a prominent role in the related debates over the un/reality of time has played John E. McTaggart's (1866–1925) essay "The Unreality of Time" (1908.)

In McTaggart's hypothesis concerning the unreality of time, the crucial argument is the negation of reality of what he calls the A-series of events in which every single event has a definite position in the future, then moves away from it

417 *Alice*, p. 49.

first to become present and later turns into past[418]. Since, according to his theory, in absolute reality, among the primary qualities of time would be its parity, that is, all the three temporal levels would be supposed to exist side by side, the change of positions in the A-series causes a paradox, for these positions are mutually incompatible and no event can be said to be positioned simultaneously in the future, present, and past.

Among numerous recent studies dedicated to this paradox, Rögnvaldur D. Ingthorsson's monograph *McTaggart's Paradox* (2016) deserves special mentioning, for both its systematic approach to the problem and for the clarity of argumentation, a characteristic which significantly distinguishes its author from most scholars in this area. Ingthorsson emphasizes the great achievement McTaggart's as an idealistic proponent of metaphysics who especially nowadays, in the postmodern era in which the plurality of realities is so frequently postulated, deserves much attention. I believe that one of the most fascinating things about the whole discussion of the unreality of time by McTaggart and by Ingthorsson is that they both belong to the most vocal advocates of *one* absolute reality and objectivity. It may appear strange that here the discussion of them is called to elucidate the issue of time and tenses in Carroll's work as well as in its various translations: in the *Alice*-books, it is the direct experience which counts as the source of evidence for what is real or not, which in Ingthorsson's interpretation of McTaggart's thesis could at best convince only a naïve realist[419]. Yet the reading of Carroll is not understood here as a possible defense or as a negation of McTaggart's theory. What is of paramount importance for the present chapter is rather the variety of implications which in the modern philosophy of language have resulted from discussions on his theory in regard to tense. While I completely agree with the key argument in Ingthorsson's critique of McTaggart's hypothesis, namely, that its basic premise concerning the parity of future, present, and past is dubious, some points in his discussion of what meaning has been conceded by McTaggart to the issue of language and particularly to that of tenses, should be corrected. Whereas it is certainly true that McTaggart's work was produced before the *linguistic turn* and language did not play as crutial a role in his philosophy as in the philosophical works that appeared in the decades after his death, it is not correct to maintain that in McTaggart's argumentation language was not attributed any significance at all[420]. Consider, for example, the following passage from McTaggart's essay:

---

418 John Ellis McTaggart, "The Unreality of Time" in: *Mind, New Series*, Vol. 17, No. 68 (Oct. 1908), pp. 457–474, here p. 467.

419 Rögnvaldur D. Ingthorsson, *McTaggart's Paradox*, New York: Routledge 2016, p. 52.

420 Ingthorsson, *op. cit.*, p. 47: "He (McTaggart) is not asking what is implied by language itself, either by how it is popularly used or what its syntax or grammar implies, or what competent speakers take it to mean..."

> The characteristics, therefore, are incompatible. But every event has them all. If M is past, it has been present and future. If it is future, it will be present and past. Thus all the three incompatible terms are predicable of each event, which is obviously inconsistent with their being incompatible...It may seem that this can easily be explained. Indeed it has been impossible to state the difficulty without almost giving the explanation, since our language has verb-forms for the past, present, and future, but no form that is common to all three. It is never true, the answer will run, that M *is* present, past and future. It *is* present, *will be* past, and *has been* future. Or it *is* past, and *has been* future and present, or again *is* future and *will be* present and past.[421]

In this quote, McTaggart's argument essentially rests on observations of the temporal grammar in modern English and some linguists might regard it as naive that in these words the morphology of tenses in English is called to support universalistic claims as to the unreality of time. If he had considered other natural languages with underspecified tense morphology, he may have totally discarded tenses from his theory since languages in which one and the same verbal form is usually taken for the past, present, and future would obviously contradict it, at least at the formal level. Consider, e.g. the following Chinese rendition of the above phrase from *Alice* by Zhao Yuanren (p. 55): "我不大知道，先生，我现在不知道，－无论怎么，我知道我今儿早晨起来的时候是谁..." Here, no formal differentiation has been made between verbs referring to the present (I don't really know – wo bu da *zhidao*) and those referring to the past (who I *was* when I got up this morning – wo jin'er zaochen *qi lai* de shihou *shi* shui.) In itself, this absence of formal temporal markers cannot be taken as evidence of the reality of time, yet it clearly demonstrates that languages lacking a well-developed morphology of tenses are as able to differentiate between the semantics of the past, present, and future, as languages like English, in which this semantics is made explicit by verbal forms. In terms of the relationship between time and tenses, Chinese may be regarded as an extreme case since it displays no temporal morphology. At the end of this chapter I am going to draw on some predominant standpoints towards the issue of time in Chinese linguistics, yet, as the above quote from McTaggart's essay suggests, in approaching the issue of time and tense, it would first of all be necessary to turn to languages with a well developed temporal morphology.

In the modern philosophy of language, one of the predominant views that have been expressed in discussions of McTaggart's hypothesis is marked by a strongly skeptical approach to tenses, as is, for example, the case with the works of David H. Mellor and Peter Ludlow. Already the title of Mellor's monograph

421 McTaggart, *op. cit.*, p. 468.

Real Time (1981) suggests the position adopted by its author: contrary to McTaggart, time is interpreted here as real. The category which, in turn, is considered unreal is tense: "Tense, it will turn out, is not being banished altogether, merely replaced where it belongs – in our heads."[422] In Mellor's opinion, those who would not follow this advice would be committing themselves to the risk of a great confusion, misinterpreting their personal sensations as reality. On his part, Yuval Dolev challenges Mellor's view according to which tensed relations are entirely dependent on tenseless ones and for this reason cannot be regarded as pertaining to reality:

> ...understanding a tenseless explanation turns on already possessing tensed language. In ordinary language this mix manifests itself in the presence of tense in sentences describing tenseless relations: we say that the American Revolution occurr*ed* before, or preced*ed* the French Revolution, or that Kennedy *was* assassinated in 1963, or that it is raining at the time in which this very sentence is being uttered.[423]

By showing how strongly our conceptions of reality actually depend on linguistic tenses, Dolev relativizes that unbreachable gulf that in Mellor's theory separates the mind ("the dwelling place of the subjective tense"[424]) and the world of real time. On his part, Peter Ludlow has argued that this dependency may eventually result in serious misconceptions. This is one of the major ideas of his monograph *Semantics, Tense, and Time: An Essay in the Metaphysics of Natural Language* (1999), a work which by far surpasses even the radicalness of Mellor. Ludlow introduces it by critically distancing himself from Benjamin Lee Whorf's famous *Language, Thought, and Reality* (1956), referring the reader first to the following quotation:

> I find it gratuitous to assume that a Hopi who knows only the Hopi language and the cultural ideas of his own society has the same notions, often supposed to be intuitions, of time and space that we have, and that are generally assumed to be universal. In particular, he has no general notion or intuition of TIME as a smooth flowing continuum in which everything in the universe proceeds at an equal rate, out of a future, through a present, into a past; or, in which, to reverse the picture, the observer is being carried in the stream of duration continuously away from a past into a future.[425]

---

422 David H. Mellor, *Real Time*, Cambridge: Cambridge University Press 1981, p. 92.

423 Yuval Dolev, "The Tenseless Theory of Time: Insights and Limitations", in: *The Review of Metaphysics*, Vol. 54, No. 2, Dec. 2000, pp. 259–288, here p. 280.

424 Yuval Dolev, *op. cit.*, p. 273.

425 Benjamin Lee Whorf, *Language, Thought, and Reality*, Cambridge (Massachusetts): The MIT Press 2012, p. 73, quoted by Ludlow, Peter, *Semantics, Tense, and Time: An Essay in the Metaphysics of Natural Language*, Cambridge, Mass.: MIT Press 1999, p. xiii.

The word *reality* in the title of Whorf's book is for him as important as for McTaggart. However, his conception of reality is quite dissimilar to that of McTaggart since, according to Whorf, in different cultures, reality is structured in radically different ways, which is constantly reflected in the respective languages. In the above quotation, the pronoun *we* is quite consciously used by him to represent Western civilization which has developed concepts of time and space that differ from the conceptual equipment of the Hopi. His theory does not suggest that the Hopi language is free from temporal relations. What he means instead is that these relations significantly differ from, say, those in English. In order to achieve understanding between these languages of what regards their aspectual and temporal categories, it is primarily required to become familiar with the cultural other, among other things, with its metaphysical concepts. For example, he provides the following comment to a Hopi phrase that has the literal meaning of "it stops getting eaten": "Without knowing the underlying Hopian metaphysics, it would be impossible to understand how the same suffix may denote starting or stopping."[426]

Ludlow does not engage himself in a detailed analysis of what in Whorf's opinion represents differences in the metaphysics of the Hopi and the English and he even admits that Whorf's main thesis, according to which language structures the reality, is basically correct.[427] Yet paradoxically, right after this benevolent remark, he negates the importance of structural differences in languages for the construction of reality. In Ludlow's eyes, differences in natural languages are "superficial at best"[428], which leads him to the following conclusion concerning the reality: "It follows that humans all share the same reality."[429] The main personal thesis which he proposes in his book is the following: "More to the point, I doubt that we actually have a "general notion or intuition of TIME"...I

426 Benjamin Lee Whorf, *op. cit.*, p. 78. A careful reader would notice that it is not a total negation of tense which is highlighted by Whorf, but rather significant differences in the world-view structures, which, among other things, can be observed in the conceptualization of time in Hopi and in English. Whorf himself discusses three tenses of Hopi (*op. cit.*, pp. 65–66: "factual, or present-past, future, and generalized or usitative".) Ekkerhart Malotki, whose seminal study *Hopi Time: A Linguistic Analysis of the Temporal Concepts in the Hopi Language* (Berlin: Mouton Publishers 1983) was a direct critical response to Whorf's language relativity thesis, is also acutely aware of the actual existence of such differences. See, for example, his discussion of "how deeply his (Hopi's) thinking has been affected by English thought" (Malotki, *op. cit.*, pp. 620ff.)

427 Ludlow, *op. cit.*, p. xiii.

428 Ludlow, *op. cit.*, p. xiii.

429 Ludlow; *op. cit.*, p. xiv.

am quite sure that we have "no words, grammatical forms…that refer directly to what we call 'time.'"[430]

By this radical negation of direct semantical and grammatical relations in English and some other Indo-European languages to the temporal concepts of the past, present, and future, he intends to provide a personal contribution to metaphysics. After all, the major aim of his analysis of the semantics of natural languages is no more and no less than gaining "insight into the metaphysics of time."[431] However, on closer scrutiny, his study reveals that temporal semantics is relevant to him only from the point of view of grammatical ambiguity. For example, in English, the present perfect is sometimes used after the conjunction *since* to mean continuity ("I've been in England since January 1", been there continuously[432]), yet occasionally it may also refer to actions with interruptions ("I've been in (to) England since January 1", been there once or more[433].) Since this particular tense which is normally associated with the semantics of the past in fact does not always display a clear reference to the past, by pointing it out, Ludlow thinks to provide enough reason for denying its temporal reference in general. Discussing similar cases of temporal ambiguity, Ludlow aims at banishing the category of tense from the linguistic discourse altogether:

> Perhaps we can go one step further and exorcise the talk of temporality from what we sloppily call "temporal adverbs," "temporal anaphora", "tense morphemes" and so on. This might sound crazy, but in a sense it is entirely natural, since many natural languages don't have tense morphemes anyway. We need not look to unfamiliar languages such as Hopi. English doesn't have a genuine future-tense morpheme; rather, it relies on modals to do (or so we think) the work of a future-tense morpheme. As we move from English to other languages, we find that future-tense morphemes …are always suspicious looking. In Romance languages, they appear to have modal elements packed within them. Purported past-tense morphemes are no less suspicious, usually being nothing more than aspectual markers. The standard view supposes that we are using modals and aspectual markers to express future tense and past tense (hence, to express things about the future and the past), but why should we suppose that? Why not suppose we are just using modals to express modality…and aspectual markers to express aspect?[434]

430 Ludlow; *op. cit.*, p. xiv.
431 Ludlow; *op. cit.*, p. xiv.
432 Ludlow; *op. cit.*, p. 127.
433 Ludlow; *op. cit.*, p. 127.
434 Ludlow; *op. cit.*, pp. 156–157.

The reasons why Ludlow suggests a critical revision of some of the traditional grammatical categories of natural languages are in themselves quite clear. After all, he is not the first to point to instances of a simultaneous interaction between different categories which may produce a confusing impression on the philosophers of language. Otto Jespersen has, for example, demonstrated how modals are used in English to express the future[435], and in his classical study on the category of aspect, Bernard Comrie has provided various examples of a strong interrelation between aspect and tense in a number of languages. The extent to which this grammatical phenomenon has progressed is, among other things, reflected in his terminology, e.g. in terming tense *situation-external time* and aspect *situation-internal time*[436]. I believe that the problem with Ludlow's thesis is rather that the category which is traditionally termed *tense* and which he seeks to reduce to modality and aspect cannot so easily be divested of temporal semantics. The temporal use of perfective and imperfective verbs in Russian may serve as a good illustration of a close interaction between semantics and grammar: whereas the perfective verbs never refer to the present, the imperfective ones can be used in all tenses. On the other hand, whenever two related perfective (e.g. *прочесть, to read through*) and imperfective (e.g. *прочитывать, to read through*) verbs are used in the past or in the future tense, they always express different temporal semantics, which would perfectly correspond to Comrie's use of terms, since the *internal situation*, i.e. an action which does not depend semantically on the time in which a sentence is produced, will be understood as completed only in cases with perfective verbs. Even languages that do not possess a similar fixed aspectual opposition of verbs, demonstrate a close reciprocal relationship between tense and aspect. Consider, e.g. Gilbert Ryle's contrasting of *task verbs* and *achievement verbs* in English, differences in the logical behavior between *kicking* and *scoring*, *treating* and *healing*, *hunting* and *finding*, *clutching* and *holding fast*, *listening* and *hearing*, *looking* and *seeing*, *travelling* and *arriving*. As Ryle puts it, "in applying an achievement verb we are asserting that some state of affairs obtains over that which consists in the performance."[437] Thus, the logic of the achievement verbs is in the implication of a finis, a conclusion, which makes them quite similar to the perfective verbs in Russian.

In terms of temporal semantics, the following observation of Ryle is worth mentioning: "To begin with, seeing and hearing are not processes. Aristotle points out, quite correctly (*Met*. ix, vi. 7–10) that I can say 'I have seen it' as soon

435 Otto Jespersen, *The Philosophy of Grammar*, Chicago: The University of Chicago Press 1992 (1924), p. 260.

436 Bernard Comrie, *Aspect: An Introduction to the Study of Verbal Aspect and Related Problems*, Cambridge: Cambridge University Press 1976, p. 5.

437 Gilbert Ryle, *The Concept of Mind* (1949), New York: Penguin Books 1976, p. 143.

as I can say 'I see it.' To generalize the point that I think he is making, there are many verbs part of the business of which is to declare a terminus."[438] In other words, in the present tense, the idea of a terminus (a finis) which is expressed by verb *to see* may be interpreted as relativizing the semantics of the present, which is why it can easily be replaced with perfect tense forms (i.e. the semantics of the past underscores the declaration of a terminus.) Zeno Vendler goes even one step further and regards similar uses of achievement verbs in the present tense in general as historic present:

> in cases of pure achievement terms the present tense is almost exclusively used as historic present or as indicating immediate future. "Now he finds the treasure (or wins the race, and so on)" is not used to report the actual finding or winning, while the seemingly paradoxical "Now he has found it" or "At this moment he has won the race" is.[439]

All perfective verbs in Russian display a similar logic and their grammatical behavior may be interpreted as still more radical since they cannot be used in the present tense at all. Similar cases may also be found in German. Consider, e.g. the verb *abkochen* (*to boil off*) which only seldom refers to the present. Its semantic domain is rather in the past and in the future (cf. the corresponding perfective verbs in Russian *отварить, вскипятить.*) Situations in which it is used in the present tense are nevertheless quite common, yet they mostly refer rather to the future (e.g. "Jetzt/gleich kochen wir die Milch ab.", cf. "Now, we'll boil the milk." in English.)

This apparent contradiction between a definite perception of the temporal position of an event (i.e. the temporal semantics) and the choice of a particular grammatical tense is exactly the point at which Ludlow targets in negating the existence of temporal semantics: in the above examples, for one and the same situation, the present tense would be used in German, but the future tense – in English. Yet in spite of his critique, it would be difficult to deny that in both languages the action is equally positioned in the future, i.e. for any German speaker, the future semantics in the above example will be as clear as the future semantics in the corresponding English sentence for the speakers of English.

In his critical reflections concerning temporal semantics of natural languages, some of the examples drawn on to illustrate incongruities between semantics and grammar are taken from Italian. Since an English sentence like "I am going to the theater tomorrow" would be translated into Italian in the present tense

438 Gilbert Ryle, *Dilemmas*, Cambridge: Cambridge Univ. Press 1954, pp. 102–103.

439 Zeno Vendler, "Verbs and Times", in: *The Philosophical Review*, Vol. 66, No. 2, Apr. 1957, pp. 143–160, here p. 147.

("Vado al teatro domain"), whereas the future tense is often used to express possibility "Saranno le otto" ("I think it is about eight o'clock *now*", referring to the present), Ludlow suggests it would be reasonable to dismiss the conventional idea according to which the grammatical present has something in common with the semantics of the present time and the future tense – with the future semantics. The conclusion which he reaches in the end is the following:

> We moved from the assumption that there must be a future and a past to the conclusion that there must be linguistic elements that allow us to speak about such things. Perhaps this philosophical assumption has become a procrustean bed in which we categorize things as temporal elements, when to a Martian linguist with no knowledge of western philosophy of time, these elements would look like ordinary modals and aspectual markers.[440]

The metaphysics of natural languages announced by Ludlow in the title of his book reaches in the above quote its culmination: time is declared to be something external to language, a category which is imposed upon it from philosophy. By these words, he actually proposes a two-fold negation, one of the temporal semantics and one of western philosophy of time

While Ludlow's conclusions may rightly be regarded as extremely far-reaching, his observations of incongruities between semantics and grammar of time actually rest on rather sporadic examples (like the two Italian sentences mentioned above.) In what follows, I would like to produce a closer and more systematic analysis of similarly complex, seemingly incongruous cases in *Alice* as well as in the translation languages that have a well-developed morphology of tenses.

As I have tried to demonstrate at the beginning of this chapter on the examples of the temporal semantics of the verb *to glide* and of the conceptualization of time (the idea of *childhood*) in the narrative frame of Carroll's text, choosing a definite grammatical tense to refer to temporal semantics which is different to what is normally associated with this tense (e.g. the present tense – for past and future events) does not necessarily result in a contradiction. The conceptual interconnectedness of grammatical tenses is rather a factor which directly affects temporal semantics and enables the realization of highly complex links between morphology and semantics. This complexity is by no means confusing or chaotic. On the contrary, on closer examination, the manner in which grammatical tenses converge reveals quite a transparent pattern: the choice of the present or of the future tense for events in the past by no means results in the semantics of the past becoming in some way ambiguous, the same thing holds good for

440 Ludlow, *op. cit.*, p. 157.

choosing past morphology to refer to the present or with taking future tenses to express the idea of the past.

Looking back on the debates concerning the un/reality of time, and once again raising the question as to the possibility of freeing tenses – at least partially – from the blame of subjectivity and of showing their clear reference to reality, one of the perspectives which may prove to be particularly illuminating for discussing this complex issue is provided by a theorist of language who, for the best of my knowledge, has not yet been drawn on by the philosophers of time: Walter Benjamin. Benjamin's reflections on a close mutual relation between languages as "a continuum of metamorphoses" ("Kontinuum von Verwandlungen"[441]), and as a unique convergence act which demonstrates that languages are "not strangers to one another" ("einander nicht fremd"), but rather that they come most closely together in their intentions[442], his ideas concerning "(a) pure language" ("eine reine Sprache") as a sum of these intentions[443], i.e. as an objective category which is the only fathomable source of any good translation, may be regarded as the implicit theoretical background for the whole of my following attempt in defense of the semantics of tenses and of their relation to reality.

The Semantics of the Present

Quite common are situations in which Carroll uses the habitual present in the form of wh-clauses, e.g in the following phrase of Alice in Chapter IV: "I know *something* interesting is going to happen, **whenever I eat** or **drink** anything."[444] Formally, French, German, and Italian are close to English in using similar forms of temporal morphology. Consider the following examples:

> J.-P. Berman (p. 85): "Je sais que, chaque fois que je **bois** ou **mange** quoi que ce soit, à coup quelque chose d'intéressant va se produire." A. Zimmermann (p. 22): "Ich weiß, etwas Merkwürdiges muss geschehen, sobald ich **esse** oder **trinke**..." B. Oddera (p. 36): "So che accadrà di certo qualcosa d'interessante, qualsiasi cosa **possa** mangiare o bere..."

441 Walter Benjamin, "Über Sprache überhaupt und über die Sprache des Menschen" (1916), in: Walter Benjamin, *Gesammelte Schriften*, Rolf Tiedemann, Hermann Schweppenhäuser (Eds.), Vol. II.i, Frankfurt am Main: Suhrkamp 1977, pp. 140–157, here p. 151.

442 Walter Benjamin, "Die Aufgabe des Übersetzers" (1921), in: Walter Benjamin (Transl.), Preface to Charles Baudelaire, *Tableaux Parisiens*, Heidelberg: Richard Weissbach 1923, pp. VII–XVII, here pp. IX.

443 *Ibid.*, p. XI.

444 *Alice*, p. 39.

Leaving aside for the moment the future semantics of "to be going to" and putting the focus first on the corresponding verbs for *to eat/ to drink*, each of the above examples reproduces exactly the temporal semantics of the original present tense: *bois/mange*, *essse/trinke*, *possa mangiare o bere*. Consider, by contrast, some Russian versions of the sentence:

> Ščerbakov (p. 59): "Каждый раз, как только я что-нибудь **выпью** или **съем**, происходят очень интересные вещи." Zachoder (p. 57): "Я уж знаю: **стоит** мне что-нибудь **съесть** или **выпить**, – обязательно случится что-нибудь интересное". Demurova (p. 124): "**Стоит** мне что-нибудь проглотить, как тут же происходит что-нибудь интересное. Olenič-Gnenenko (p. 75): "Я знаю, всякий раз, когда я что-нибудь **ем** или **пью**, случаются интересные вещи."

In the above renditions, Ščerbakov, Zachoder and Demurova have reproduced the verbs in question by corresponding perfective verbs (*выпить/съесть*), whereas Olenič-Gnenenko has taken the imperfective counterparts (*есть/пить.*) It would seem that the perfective verbs come nearer to the needs of the original, for *something* interesting (in Alice's phrase) is a direct result of her *eating/drinking* and by using the perfective verbs the translators have provided the sentence with additional dynamic. However, as mentioned above, a perfective verb in Russian cannot be used in the present tense, as *eat/drink* are used in the original. The solution to the problem found by Zachoder and by Demurova is the following: they link both verbs with the imperfective *stóit* which has the semantics of a temporal conjunction (*as soon as*) and is used in both versions quite naturally in the present tense.

Ščerbakov's version offers a still more elegant solution: the perfective verbs in the dependent clause are used in the future tense *выпью / съем*, which enables the translator to reproduce the dynamic of the action and to avoid the usage of the rather formal *stóit*. From the point of view of the relation between tense and (extra-linguistic) time, it is worth mentioning how natural the rendition of the main verb (*происходят – happen*) is in the present tense, although it is conceived as a result of actions in the future tense (*выпью / съем.*) Here, future morphology does not suggest the idea of a future event and refers unequivocally to the present, or, more specifically, to a general rule, to something that is likely to happen at any time, or *whenever*, as it is put in the original. Still another possibility of rendering the temporal clause in Russian would be by putting both perfective verbs in the past, without in any way affecting the semantics of the present, by the conjunction "*что бы ни*" (*whatever*): "Что бы я ни выпила или ни съела, происходят очень интересные вещи." ("Whatever I drink or eat, something interesting is going to happen.") Consider Ščerbakov's translation of another phrase from Chapter V: "Whoever **lives** there," thought Alice, "it'll never do to come upon them *this* size: why, I should frighten them out of their wits![445]" Ščerbakov (p. 76) offers the following rendition: "Кто бы здесь ни **жил**, – подумала Алиса, – нельзя являться к ним при моем собственном росте. Они же с ума сойдут от страха." A back-translation of the phrase would be an exact copy of Carroll's passage, yet in terms of the tense morphology it is again worth pointing out how natural the past tense in Russian reproduces the semantics of the present: the past form *zhil* is required by the grammatical norms after the particle *ni*. Moreover, it is important to note that in this particular case the verb *zhit* (*to live*) is imperfective, so that in other grammatical environments it can quite naturally be used in the present tense, yet not in constructions like *kto by ni*, in which the idea of the present can be expressed strictly by a past form.

Incidentally, something that would hardly be imaginable in the morphology of Russian is the use of the future tense for suppositions referring to the present, which is quite a common temporal pattern in German, French, and Italian. Consider the episode from Chapter IV in which Alice, having heard strange sounds in the chimney of the Rabbit's house, supposes that Bill is approaching her: "This is Bill."[446] In Enzensberger's version (p. 43), the present is rendered by the future tense: "Das wird Egon sein." In all the other German renditions that I have studied, by contrast, the present tense has been used, exactly as in the original. However strange it may seem, in all the Italian versions that I have consulted, the phrase has also been rendered in the present tense "Questo è Bill", although the future tense (*futuro semplice* "Sarà Bill") would probably much better reflect the actual grammatical habits of the Italians. The same thing holds good for the French renditions: although there are striking parallels in the use of the epistemic future in French, Italian, and German, I could not find one single instance of its use in French in this context[447]. Contrary to Ludlow's critique, in situations in which this particular form of the future is used in German, French, and Italian (cf. "Saranno le otto"), there can be no doubt about the temporal semantics expressed by it: such suppositions refer mostly to the present time. A comparison of competing grammatical forms for the expression of suppositions, e.g. of the conditional mood and the future tense in Italian and in German, reveals for both languages the same regularity: in an actual context, the future tense is used

445 *Alice*, p. 58.

446 *Alice*, p. 44.

447 Cf. Bué, p. 52: "Voilà Jacques sans doutes"; Berman, p. 93: "C'est Bill"; Sueur: "Voilà Bill." For a comparison of the epistemic futur in Italian and French, see Andrea Rocci, "L'interprétation épistémique du futur en italien et en français: une analyse procédurale", in: *Cahiers de Linguistique Française*, Vol. 22, 2000, pp. 241–274.

(for example, "Es wird Bill sein", in German, since somebody is actually climbing up the chimney in this episode), whereas in hypothetical contexts, the preference would be for the conditional mood. Consider the following examples for this rule in Italian from R. Solarino's *Imparare dagli errori*: "Bussano: – chi sarà" ("Someone is knocking at the door: who could it be?" – not "sarebbe") vs. "Che cosa direbbe tua madre?" ("What would your mother say?")[448]

A contradictio in adiecto represents, as I believe, the designation "non-temporal use of tenses" which, e.g. Otto Jespersen has applied in describing the semantics of the preterit forms when referring to unreality, impossibility, found in wishes and conditional sentences.[449] The term "non-temporal" suggests the idea of timelessness, while in wishes and in conditional sentences it is usually totally clear what temporal semantics is meant by the speaker. Consider, for example, the following translations of Alice's phrase from Chapter I: "Well, I wouldn't say anything about it, even if I fell off the top of the house!"[450]

> Zimmermann (p. 4): "Ich würde nicht viel Redens machen, wenn ich selbst von der Dachspitze hinunter **fiele**!" Nabokov (p. 7): "Если бы я даже с крыши **грохнулась**, я и тогда бы не пикнула." Ščerbakov (p. 30): "С крыши **свалюсь** – и **не охну**!" Zachoder (p. 40): "Может, даже с крыши слечу и не **пикну**!"

Whereas Zimmermann and Nabokov have rendered the conditional clause by preterit forms (*fiele / grohnulas*), Ščerbakov and Zachoder have preferred more categorical forms in the future tense: *svaljus / ne ochnu // slechu / ne piknu*. Yet in both cases the reader will be quite aware of the fact that in this episode Alice is reflecting upon what might be a likely result of her decision in the future, rather than imagining a timeless situation or one referring to the past. The conditional mood used by Nabokov requires that the verb be used in the preterit tense,

448 Rosaria Solarino, *Imparare dagli errori*, Napoli: Tecnodid 2009, p. 115. Solarino defines the epistemic future form in Italian as "una congettura su un contesto situazionale vero, relativa cioè a un evento che sta avvenendo realmente" ("an opinion expressed in a real situational context, referring to an event which is actually happening", *ibid.*, pp. 114–115.) For a more detailed analysis of the epistemic future in Italian, see Pier Marco Bertinetto, *Tempo, aspetto e azione nel verbo italiano*, Firenze: L'Academia della Crusca 1986, pp. 491–498. Bertinetto (p. 495) interprets this particular use of the future tense as addressing a present situation with uncertainty, which is typical of discussing any future events. For a discussion of *will*, the epistemic future in English (e.g. *Mary will be at the opera now.*) and the problem of interrelations between tense and modality see Philippe De Brabanter, Mikhail Kissine, Saghie Sharifzadeh, "Future tense vs. future time: An introduction", in: P. De Brabanter, Mikhail Kissine (et al., eds.), *Future Times, Future Tenses*, Oxford: Oxford University Press 2014, pp. 4–16.

449 Otto Jespersen, *The Philosophy of Grammar*, p. 265.

450 *Alice*, p. 13.

yet for the reader this grammatical form is not in any way suggestive of the past. Consider some translations of another relevant example which is a wish-sentence from Chapter I: "Dinah, I wish you were down here with me!"[451]

> Zimmermann (p. 4): "ich **wollte**, du wärest hier unten bei mir." // Enzensberger (p. 12): "Suse, liebe Katze, ich wollte, du **wärest** hier unten bei mir!" Nabokov (p. 8): "если бы ты **была** здесь со мной!" Demurova (p. 80): "Ах, Дина, милая, как жаль, что тебя со мной **нет**!" Ščerbakov (p. 32): "Дина, миленькая, вот бы ты **падала** вместе со мной!"

In all the above translations, except for that by Demurova, the wish-sentence is rendered in the conjunctive mood, i.e. the verbal stems are all preterit (in the German versions, even the "I wish" has been put in the preterit.) In Ščerbakov's rendition ("Dinah, dear, I wish you were falling together with me!"), the verb of the wish-sentence is different to the original, yet its temporal semantics has been reproduced exactly. As for the rendition provided by Demurova ("Dear Dinah, it's such a pity you are not here with me."), although the verb is used here in the present tense, this version may be regarded as an exact semantic equivalent for all Russian renditions in which the verb stands in the preterit form, that is, the morphological pattern (either the past or the present) does not bear on the reader's clear interpretation of the temporal semantics of the present.

The Semantics of the Past

Exactly like the future perfect tense in English may express suppositions concerning events from the past (e.g. "He will have arrived by now"), similar forms are used in German and in Italian: in German, it is the *Futur II* tense ("Er wird angekommen sein.") and in Italian it is the *futuro anteriore* ("Sarà arrivato.") Unfortunately I could not get hold of any German or Italian translations in which these two rather antiquated morphological future forms would have been used to express the semantics of the past. By contrast, a grammatical pattern which can much more easily be drawn on for this purpose, may be found in numerous renditions of English passages containing a sequence of tenses, i.e. whenever in the original narration two or more subsequent actions in the past are introduced by two or more verbs in the past tenses, as, for example, in the following passage from Chapter I: "...she (Alice) **had** plenty of time as she went down to

451 *Alice*, p. 14.

look about her, and to wonder what **was** going to happen next."[452] Consider first three translations of this phrase into French:

> Berman, p. 27: "…elle **eut** tout le temps, pendent sa chute, de regarder autour d'elle et de se demander ce qui **allait** se produire ensuite."
> Sueur: "…elle **eut** beaucoup de temps pour regarder autour d'elle et de se demander ce qui **allait** se passer après."
> Bué, p. 3: "…elle **eut** tout le loisir, dans sa chute, de regarder autour d'elle et de se demander avec étonemment ce qu'elle **allait** devenir."

The exact equivalence between the *futur proche dans le passé* in French and the "was going to" in English represents quite a lucky case in the translation practice. In all the three renditions above, this form of the past has been used: on the one hand, the preterit form *allait* allows an exact reproduction of the original semantics of the past (the positioning of two events in the past from the narration perspective), on the other hand, it is also an exact copy of the temporal morphology in the original. Totally different to it are, e.g. translations of the passage into Russian which does not offer any similar morphological possibilities. Consider the following examples:

> Nabokov (p. 6): "вполне хватало времени осмотреться и подумать, что **может** дальше случиться"; Ščerbakov (p. 30): "подумать о ближайшем будущем"; Zachoder (p. 40): "что ее **ждет** впереди"; Demurova (p. 72): "подумать, что же **будет** дальше"; Olenič-Gnenenko (p. 24): "гадать, что **произойдет** дальше."

In none of the above Russian versions is the past morphology rendered by a past form of the corresponding verbs: in Ščerbakov's text, the verb is substituted by a noun (*to think about the next future*), Nabokov and Zachoder put the verbs in the present tense (*mozhet / zhdjot*), whereas Olenič-Gnenenko uses the future tense (*budet / proizojdjot*.) Unlike the conditional mood which requires past tense morphology, in the objective clause that follows the infinitive *podumat'* (*to think*), it is possible to use all the three tenses, so that the phrase could have been translated in the past tense as well, e.g. as: "подумать, что могло случиться дальше" ("to think what could happen next.") Yet, again, for all the three possible choices of temporal morphology, the perception of temporal semantics is exactly the same: the sentence will be interpreted as referring to the past, even when the verb is put in the present or in the future tense.

452 *Alice*, p. 12.

This chapter began by the discussion of a line from Carroll's introductory poem in which the verb is symbolically put in the present tense, referring to events from the past: "Full leisurely we *glide*". Consider still another example of the historic present used in an episode from Chapter IV in which Bill, having luckily survived his flight from the chimney in the Rabbit's house, recounts his adventure to his friends:

> Well, I hardly know, – No more, thank'ye, I'm better now – but I'm a deal too flustered to tell you – all I know is, something **comes** at me like a Jack-in-the-box, and up I **goes** like a sky-rocket![453]

The historic present tense is sometimes also labelled 'narrative' or 'dramatic' present: its use makes events from the past – like the forms *comes / up I goes* in Bill's story – appear particularly spectacular. An exact reproduction of this form may be found in the German rendition by Enzensberger (p. 43): "Also, ich weiß selbst kaum – genug jetzt, es geht mir schon wieder besser – ich bin nur noch so aufgeregt, kann noch gar nicht recht erzählen – ich weiß nur noch, plötzlich **geht** von unten etwas auf mich **los** wie ein Springteufel, und schon **zisch ich ab** wie eine Leuchtrakete!" In all the languages under study, the present tense may similarly be used here to underscore the dramatic effect of the narration. By contrast, what would seem to be a specific characteristic of Russian grammar is the possibility to use the future tense for the same purpose, i.e. as the narrative future. Consider the following rendition of the passage by Zachoder (p. 60): "Ничего-то я не разобрал, ка-аа-аак оно **шандарахнет** меня, так я и **полетел** оттуда турманом." (Literally: "I couldn't figure anything out, when something ***will strike*** me and I *flew off* like a bullet.") What in the back-translation is totally ungrammatical in terms of temporal morphology is completely natural in Russian: the alternation between past and future forms serves the same aim as that between past and present forms in the original and in the above German version. And here, again, the temporal semantics of the past is by no means affected.

In terms of temporal semantics, the present perfect forms represent quite a special category since they make the semantics of the past merge with that of the present and this temporal ambiguity has received lots of scholarly attention. I have already mentioned some ideas expressed by Ryle and Vendler regarding the semantic convergence of time in the past and present forms of the achievement verbs: it is possible to say "I have seen it" as soon as one can say "I see it", so that the present form in the latter sentence may be interpreted as historical present. And yet it is remarkable how differently the conceptualization of temporal

453 *Alice*, p. 44.

convergence has progressed in different languages. As early as at the beginning of the 20th century, Otto Jespersen wrote the following observations concerning this phenomenon in his *The Philosophy of Grammar*:

> ...the perfect tends to become a mere preterit, though the tendency is not equally strong in all languages. English is more strict than most languages, and does not allow the use of the perfect if a definite point in the past is meant, whether this is expressly mentioned or not. Sentences containing words like yesterday or in 1879 require the simple preterit...On the other hand, Germans will often say: *Waren Sie in Berlin?* where an Englishman would have to say: "Have you been in Berlin?" When an Englishman hears a German ask: "Were you in Berlin?" his natural inclination is to retort: "When?"[454]

More than one hundred years have passed since Jespersen published these observations, yet in general nothing has changed about the relatively free use of the perfect by the Germans and, contrastively, about the great sensitivity of the English to the temporality expressed by the perfect and the preterit forms. This is easily seen in comparing the frequent instances in which the perfect has been used by German translators to render the preterit forms of the original. Consider the following renditions of the King's question to the Hatter from Chapter XI: "When did you begin?"[455]

> Zimmermann (p. 79): "Wann hast du damit angefangen?"; Enzensberger (p. 113): "Wann hast du denn angefangen?" Teutsch (p. 121): "Wann haben Sie damit angefangen?"

As these examples suggest, the use of the perfect after the interrogative "wann?" in German is as natural as that of the preterit in English. Consider also some counterexamples where the perfect form of the original "I've had such a curious dream!"[456] (Chapter XII) has been reproduced in German by the preterit and, in the version by B. Teutsch, even by the past perfect:

> Enzensberger (p. 125): "Ach, und ich hatte so einen seltsamen Traum!"; Teutsch (p. 135): "Ach, und ich hatte so was Komisches geträumt!" Hansen (p. 110): "Oh, ich hatte so einen seltsamen Traum!"

Although some translators into German have used the present perfect tense (e.g. Zimmermann, p. 89: "O, ich habe einen so merkwürdigen Traum gehabt!"), the

454 Otto Jespersen, *The Philosophy of Grammar*, pp. 270–271.
455 *Alice*, p. 117.
456 *Alice*, p. 130.

general frequency of rendering this phrase by the preterit testifies to a much looser connection between the present and the past in the German perfect compared with its English counterpart.

Jespersen regards the perfect as a variety of the present and not of the past, which he illustrates by the use of the adverb *now* in: "Now I have eaten enough."[457] (Cf. in German: "Nun habe ich genug gegessen.") This is a somewhat controversial view and many readers would be likely to doubt its validity, yet theoretically it could be supported by various translations in which the semantics of the present in the original has been reproduced by means of the perfect tense. Consider, as an example, the following Italian and French renditions of the sentence "The Dormouse is asleep again."[458] from Chapter VII:

> Oddera (p. 65): "Il Ghiro si è addormentato di nuovo."; Petricòla-Rossetti (p. 98): "Il Ghiro è tornato a dormire."; D'Amico (p. 71): "Il Ghiro si è riaddormentato."; Giglio (p. 173): "Ecco, il Ghiro s'è addormentato un'altra volta."; Bué (p. 103): "Le Loir est rendormi."; Berman (p. 157): "Le Loir est à nouveau endormi."

On the other hand, although the frequency with which the present has been rendered by the perfect tense in the above versions may appear striking, there are also instances of rendering it by the present (cf. Battistutta (p. 61): "Il Ghiro dorme di nuovo.") On the whole, the perception of the temporal semantics associated with the perfect forms in the languages under study may be regarded as reflecting a balance between the past and the present. This can also be corroborated by comparing the following renditions of the Queen's question to the gardeners from Chapter VIII: "What *have* you been doing here?"[459]:

> Enzensberger (p. 83): "Was war denn *hier* wieder los?"; Bué (p. 121): "Qu'est-ce que vous faites donc là?"; Giglio (p. 197): "Che cosa facevate, qui?"; Ščerbakov (p. 106): "Вы что здесь делали?"; Nabokov (p. 71): "Чем вы тут занимались?"; Zachoder (p. 86): "Отвечайте: что вы тут делаете?"

In these versions, the temporal semantics is introduced either by means of past morphology (the preterit forms in the versions by Enzensberger, Ščerbakov, Nabokov, Giglio) or by the present tense (the versions by Bué and Zachoder.) Unlike the previously discussed cases in which a form of the past is used to express the idea of the present (e.g. in "Кто бы здесь ни **жил**" for "whoever lives here") or, vice

457 Otto Jespersen, *op.cit.*, p. 269.
458 *Alice*, p. 75.
459 *Alice*, p. 87.

versa, in which present forms refer to events from the past (e.g. "and up I goes like a sky-rocket"), here, the traditional terms for tenses prove to be in complete accord with the actual temporal semantics: the past forms stand for the idea of the past, and the present ones – for that of the present.

As these examples reveal, to a certain extent the temporal semantics of the present perfect tense in English is perceived by the translators as ambiguous, as being both past and present and in this quality different to the corresponding semantics in the target languages which require the use of either a past or a present form. Of course, this ambiguity becomes all the more visible when it is observed in its relation to the allness of translations or, to use once again the expression of Walter Benjamin, to the infinite "continuum of metamorphoses" ("Kontinuum von Verwandlungen") within the one pure language.

The Semantics of the Future

Compared to other tenses, one that meets with most skepticism among linguists is the future tense. As I have shown elsewhere, the future form in Italian which is occasionally used to express suppositions concerning the present (e.g. "Saranno le otto"), raised Ludlow's suspicions as to its ability to express the temporal semantics of the future in general. A similar criticism, though in a different context, has been made by the American linguist John White about the future morphology in German. According to him, the use of the simple future tense (Futur I, i.e. constructions in which the verb *werden* is combined with infinitive forms of other verbs) indicates "a very formal and stilted speech", whereas the use of the present tense for future semantics will be a sure sign of "the prevailing, cultivated, colloquial German."[460] However, even if in both languages the future tense morphology is often used to refer to the present it does not mean that future semantics has become absolutely alien to it. To demonstrate this, I would like to draw on some Italian and German renditions of the following passage from Chapter I: "Well, I'll eat it", said Alice, "and if it makes me grow larger, I can reach the key; and if it makes me grow smaller, I can creep under the door, so either way I'll get into the garden..."[461]

---

460 John White, ""Die gebildete Umgangssprache" and Our College Grammars: The German Present Tense in Future Meaning", in: *The German Quarterly*, Vol. 17, No. 3, May 1944, pp. 131–134, here p. 132.

461 *Alice*, p. 18.

Oddera, p. 17: "Bene, la **mangerò** – disse Alice – e se mi **farà** crescere, **riuscirò** ad arrivare alla chiave, e se mi **farà** diventare piú piccola, **potrò** strisciare sotto la porta, cosí, in un modo o nell'altro **andrò** nel giardino…"; D'Amico, p. 24: "Be', io la **mangio** – disse Alice – così se mi **fa** cresscere, **arrivo** a prendere la chiave; e se mi **fa** diminuire, **potrò** strisciare sotto la porta. In un modo o nell'altro **riuscirò** a entrare nel giardino…"; Enzensberger, p. 17: "wenn er mich größer **macht**, **kann** ich zu dem Schlüssel hinaufreichen, und wenn er mich kleiner **macht**, kann ich unter der Tür durchkriechen. In den Garten komme ich so oder so."; Kurt Hansen, p. 14: "Wenn er mich größer **macht**, **kann** ich den Schlüssel erreichen, wenn er mich kleiner **macht**, **kann** ich unter der Tür hindurchkriechen. So **werde** ich auf jeden Fall in den Garten **gelangen**…"

The first Italian version above clearly illustrates how natural the use of future morphology (*futuro semplice*) is in Italian for expressing the semantics of the future: all the verbs in the passage (*mangerò*, *farà*, *riuscirò*, ecc.) have been rendered in the future tense. In the second version, by contrast, present (*mangio*, *arrivo*, *fa*) and future (potrò, riuscirò) forms are counterbalanced. In the corresponding German versions, the lesser use of the future morphology is first of all due to the grammatical norm which requires that in conditional clauses introduced by *wenn* (*if*) the verb should be put in the present tense. Yet in different grammatical environments, the future tense can be quite naturally used in German, as is illustrated by Hansen who does not shy away from rendering the last phrase by "werde … gelangen" (lit.: *will get*.) Although in both Italian and German the present morphology and that of the future represent two competing forms for expressing future semantics, in situations that involve a sure supposition about future events, the use of the future tense will be much more likely than of the present. Consider the following renditions of another passage from Chapter IV: "How surprised he'll be when he finds out **who I am**. But **I'd better** take him his fan and gloves."[462]

Enzensberger (p. 36): "Der **wird** aber Augen **machen**, wenn er **merkt**, wer ich bin! Aber den Fächer und die Handschuhe will ich ihm doch lieber holen."; Hansen (p. 29): "Wie überrascht **wird** er **sein**, wenn er **merkt**, wer ich bin! Aber es ist am besten, wenn ich ihm seinen Fächer und seine Handschuhe **hole**…"; Oddera (p. 34): "Come si **stupirà** quando **verrà** a sapere chi sono! Ma **farò** meglio a portargli il ventaglio e i guanti…"; T. Pietricòla-Rossetti (p. 42): "Ei s**arà** molto sorpreso quando scopri**rà** chi io sia. Ma è meglio recargli il ventaglio e i guanti…"; D'Amico (p. 40): "Chissà la sorpresa quando scoprirà chi sono! Intanto però sarà meglio che gli porti il ventaglio e i guanti…"; Giglio (p. 101): "Come resterà sorpreso quando saprà chi sono. Ma è meglio che il

462 *Alice*, p. 38.

ventaglio e i guanti glieli porti." (Cf. the use of a past (sic) tense in the Russian version by Ščerbakov (p. 59): "Вот бы он **удивился**, когда **узнал** бы, кто я на самом деле!")

Aside from the instances of using present forms in temporal and conditional clauses after *wenn*, which is required by the grammar rules, in the rest of the above German examples the semantics of the future has been rendered mostly by the future tense, which by no means sounds formal or stilted. In the Italian versions, the predominance of the future morphology is still more evident, which is due to the fact that – unlike German – Italian grammar allows the use of the future tense in temporal and conditional clauses.

In terms of the relationship between temporal semantics and tense morphology, the last quotation from *Alice* is particularly interesting since all the three tenses are used in it to refer to the future: the future (he'*ll be*), the present (when he finds out) and the past (I *had* better / I'd better.)

The intentional and forward-looking form *I **had** better* in English and the use of a past form in the Russian conditional "Вот бы он **удивился**" in Ščerbakov's rendition both seem perfectly suitable to conclude the present chapter on the ways in which all tenses are *semantically* interconnected: what is probably most striking about the morphological forms of natural languages is that tenses that conventionally are termed *future*, *present*, and *past* reveal quite a paradoxical semantical behaviour, that is, every single of them is actually used to refer to *any* temporal semantics. This parity of grammatical tenses may be regarded as a real and firmly tangible counterpart to the controversial idea concerning the parity of times in McTaggart's paradox. The fact that the paradox of the semantical behavior of tenses does not result in any confusion concerning the semantics of time and that in most cases it is, on the contrary, quite clear how an event is positioned on the chronological scale with respect to the speech (or the narration) time strongly testifies to the objectivity and reality of tenses.

Two languages that have featured prominently in all the other chapters of this book have not been discussed in the present chapter: Japanese and Chinese. This was motivated by the following reasons. The temporal morphology of Japanese verbs is limited to two morphemes – *ru* and *ta* the use of which does not reveal the variety of mutual connections between tenses and temporal semantics as one that may be observed in languages with a complex temporal morphology. As for Chinese, since it does not have any temporal morphology at all[463] it does

463 Cf. the wide-spread opinion according to which Chinese is a "tenseless" language in such studies as Clara S. Smith's "Time With and Without Tense", in: Jacqueline Guéron, Jacqueline Lecarme (eds.), *Time and Modality*, Dordrecht: Springer 2008, pp. 227–249 and Jo-Wang Lin's,

not offer much material that would be relevant to the present chapter, i.e. the question as to how temporal semantics is reflected in the *forms* of verbs. However, the fact that these languages occasionally also reveal complex ambivalent connections between temporal semantics and temporal grammar (in Chinese – at the syntactical level) that are similar to those discussed above, may be regarded as further evidence of the reality of pure language in which, to use Benjamin's words again, intentions of all human languages coalesce.[464]

"Time in a Language without Tense: The Case of Chinese", in: *Journal of Semantics*, Vol. 23, 2005, pp. 1–53. This, however, is not a universally shared attitude. See, for example, the reservations expressed by Jiun-Shiung Wu in "Tense as a Discourse Feature: Rethinking Temporal Location in Mandarin Chinese", in: *Journal of East Asian Linguistics*, Vol. 18, No. 2, May 2009, pp. 145–165, p. 146: "In this paper, the definition of tense is extended to refer to temporal location in general. Under this extended definition of tense, it is possible that every language has tense because expressing the temporal location of situations is a universal need."

464 For Japanese, see, for example, the occurrences of *-ta-forms* (past) referring to the present and the future and, vice versa, of – *ru-forms* (present/future) referring to the past. This phenomenon has been in the focus of Kayako Hirata's dissertation *Temporal Properties in Japanese*, Ann Arbor: UMI 1987. While I agree with most observations made in this study, many instances of the ambivalent semantic behavior of Japanese tenses which are drawn on by its author could prove insightful in further critical discussions of this subject. See, for example, the interpretation of "Basu ga kita!" ("The bus has come.") as "The bus is coming." (p. 15) The author states that "by native speakers' intuition, it is judged to be associated with present interpretation of a time model" (*ibid.*), saying at the same time that it would be possible to interpret the phrase as referring to past: "The bus has come" or "The bus came" (*ibid.*, fn. 4.) Some other illustrations of the same kind are the expressions "Katta, katta!" interpreted as "We're winning" (p. 16) or "Wakatta!" as "I understand it." While it is certainly true that all these expressions may be interpreted as referring to the present, the past semantics of the morpheme – *ta* is not completely neutralized in them. Cf. the above discussion of "I see" / "we're winning" by Ryle and Vendler, where the present forms of the achievement verbs are interpreted as historic present. The interpretation of some analogous Japanese cases provided by Hirata may corroborate this view: semantics of the past does not disappear in Japanese, but rather merges with that of the present. For Chinese, I mean first of all the grammatical particle "le" which is equally able to function as a marker of perfect referring to the past and as a change-of-state aspectual marker referring to *both* the past and future.

References

Primary Sources

Carroll, Lewis, *Alice's Adventures in Wonderland* and *Through the Looking Glass* (*The Annotated Alice*), Martin Gardner (Ed.), London: Allen Lane / The Penguin Press 2000.

Translations

Chinese

Ailisi meng you qi jing 爱丽斯梦游奇景, Taibei: Taiwan dongfang chubanshe 2002.

Chen Fuan 陈复庵 (Tr.), *Alisi man you qi jing ji* 阿丽思慢游奇境记, Beijing: Zhongguo duiwai fanyi chubanshe 1981.

Guan Shaochun 管绍淳 (Tr.), Zhao Mingfei 赵明菲 (Tr.), *Ailisi qiyu ji* 爱丽丝奇遇记, Ürümci: Xinjiang renmin chubanshe 1981.

Ma Teng 马腾 (Tr.), *Ailisi meng you xianjing* 爱丽丝梦游仙境, Beijing: Lianhe chuban gongsi 2016.

Zhu Haoyi 朱浩一 (Tr.), *Ailisi meng you xianjing* 愛麗絲夢遊仙境, Taibei: Emily Publishing Company 2016.

Zhu Hongguo 朱洪国 (Tr.), *Ailisi man you qi jing ji* 艾丽思慢游奇境记, Chengdu: Sichuan shaonian ertong chubanshe 1987.

Zhao Yuanren 赵元任 (Tr.), *Alisi man you qi jing ji* 阿丽思慢游奇境记 (1921), Beijing: The Commercial Press 1988.

French

Berman, Jean Pierre (Tr.), *Les Aventures d'Alice au pays des merveilles*, Paris: Pocket 2017.

Bué, Henri (Tr.), *Aventures d'Alice au pays des merveilles*, Londre: Macmillan and Co. 1869.

Sueur, Laurent Paul (Tr.), *Les Aventures d'Alice au pays des merveilles*, Wrosłav: Amazon 2015.

German

Enzensberger, Christian (Tr.), *Alice im Wunderland*, Frankfurt am Main: Insel-Verlag 1963.

Hansen, Kurt (Tr.), *Alice im Wunderland*, Hamburg: Richard Hermes Verlag 1948.

Scheu-Riesz, Helene (Tr.), *Liese im Wunderland*, Wien: Konegen 1921.
Teutsch, Barbara (Tr.), *Alice im Wunderland*, Hamburg: Cecilie Dressler Verlag 1989.
Zimmermann, Antonie (Tr.), *Alice im Wunderland* (1869), Altenmünster: Verlag Jürgen Beck 2015.

Italian

Battistutta, Luigina (Tr.), Alice nel Paese delle Meraviglie, Pordenone: Edizioni C'era una volta…1995.
D'Amico, Masolino (Tr.), Alice: Le Avventure di Alice nel Paese delle Meraviglie; Attraverso Lo Specchio E Quello Che Alice Vi Trovò. Milano: Mondadori 1978.
Giglio, Tommaso (Tr.), Alice nel Paese delle Meraviglie, Milano: Rizzoli 1966.
Oddera, Bruno (Tr.), Alice Nel Paese Delle Meraviglie, Milano: Mondadori 1997.
Pietrocòla-Rossetti, Teodorico (Tr.), Le avventure d'Alice nel paese delle meraviglie, Londra: Macmillan and Co. 1872.

Japanese

Ishii Mutsumi 石井睦美 (Tr.), *Fushigi no kuni no Arisu* 不思議の国のアリス, Zürich: BL Publishing 2008.
Seriu Hajime 芹生一 (Tr.), *Fushigi no kuni no Arisu* ふしぎの国のアリス, Tokyo: Kaiseisha 1979.
Shōno Kōkichi 生野幸吉 (Tr.), *Fushigi no kuni no Arisu* ふしぎの国のアリス, Tokyo: Fukuinkan bunko 1971.
Tada Kōzō 多田幸蔵 (Tr.), *Fushigi no kuni no Arisu* 不思議の国のアリス, Tokyo: Obunsha 1975.
Waki Akiko 脇明子 (Tr.), *Fushigi no kuni no Arisu* 不思議の国のアリス, Tokyo: Iwanami shoten 1998.
Yamagata Hiro'o 山形浩生 (Tr.), *Fushigi no kuni no Arisu* 不思議の国のアリス, Tokyo: Asahi shuppansha 2003.

Russian

Demurova, Nina (Tr.), Нина Демурова, *Алиса в стране чудес* (*Alisa v strane čudes*), Moskva: Studija "4+4" 2013.
Kononenko, Andrej (Tr.), Андрей Кононенко, *Алиса в стране чудес* (*Alisa v strane čudes*) (1998–2000), http://www.wonderland-alice.ru/translations/kononenko/?curPos=12.

Nabokov, Vladimir (Tr.), Владимир Набоков, *Аня в стране чудес* (*Anja v strane čudes*) (1923), Ann Arbor: Ardis 1982.

Olenič-Gnenenko, Aleksandr (Tr.), Александр Оленич-Гнененко, *Алиса в Стране чудес* (*Alisa v Strane čudes*) (1940), St. Petersburg: Gumanitarnaja Akademija 2018.

Ščerbakov, Aleksandr (Tr.), Александр Щербаков, *Приключения Алисы в стране чудес* (*Priključenija Alisy v strane čudes*), Moskva: Chudozhestvennaja literatura 1977.

Solovjova, Poliksena (Tr.) Поликсена Соловьева, *Приключения Алисы в стране чудес* (*Priključenija Alisy v strane čudes*), St. Petersburg: Tropinka 1909.

Zachoder, Boris (Tr.), Борис Заходер, *Приключения Алисы в Стране чудес* (*Priključenija Alisy v Strane čudes*), Moskva: Detskaja literatura 1983.

Secondary Sources

Abrahams, Roger D.; Babcock, Barbara A., "The Literary Use of Proverbs", in: The *Journal of American Folklore*, Vol. 90, No. 358, 1977, pp. 414–429.

Arnswald, Ulrich, Jens Kertscher, Matthias Kroß (Eds.), *Wittgenstein und die Metapher*, Berlin: Parerga 2004.

Asher, Nicholas; Morreau, Michael, "What Some Generic Sentences Mean", in: Gregory N. Carlson, Francis Jeffry Pelletier (Eds.), *The Generic Book*, Chicago: The University of Chicago Press 1995, pp. 300–338.

Auden, Wystan Hugh, "Today's 'Wonder-World' Needs Alice", in: Robert Phillips (ed.), Aspects of Alice: Lewis Carroll's Dreamchild as Seen through the Critics' Looking-Glasses, New York: Vintage Books 1971, pp. 3–12.

Bale, Alan; Jessica Coon, "Classifiers Are for Numerals, Not for Nouns: Consequences for the Mass/Count Distinction", in: *Linguistic Inquiry*, 2014, Vol. 45, No. 4, pp. 695–707.

Barrett, E. Boyd, "Can There Be Tolerance without Understanding?", in: *The Journal of Religion*, Vol. 9, No. 1, 1929, pp. 20–37.

Baum, Alwin N., "Carroll's 'Alices': The Semiotics of Paradox", in: *American Imago*, Vol. 34, No. 1, 1977, pp. 86–108.

Benjamin, Walter, "Die Aufgabe des Übersetzers" (1921), in: Walter Benjamin (Transl.), Preface to Charles Baudelaire, *Tableaux Parisiens*, Heidelberg: Richard Weissbach 1923, pp. VII–XVII.

Benjamin, Walter "The Task of the Translator", in: *Illuminations*, Harry Zohn (Tr.), Hannah Arendt (Ed.), New York: Harcourt Brace Jovanovich 1968, pp.69–82,

Benjamin, Walter, "Der Sürrealismus: Die letzte Momentaufnahme der europäischen Intelligenz" (1929), in: Walter Benjamin, *Gesammelte Schriften*, II. 1, Rolf Tiedemann, Hermann Schweppenhäuser (Eds.), Frankfurt am Main: Suhrkamp 1977, pp. 295–310.

Benjamin, Walter, "Über Sprache überhaupt und über die Sprache des Menschen" (1916), in: Walter Benjamin, *Gesammelte Schriften*, Rolf Tiedemann, Hermann Schweppenhäuser (Eds.), Vol. II.i, Frankfurt am Main: Suhrkamp 1977, pp. 140–157.

Berman, Ruth A., "Developmental Perspectives on Transitivity: A Confluence of Cues", in: Yonata Levy (Ed.), *Other Children, Other Languages: Issues in the Theory of Language Acquisition*, Hillsdale: Lawrence Erlbaum Associates 1994, pp. 189–241.

Berretta, Monica, "Problemi testuali della traduzione: casi di ambiguità anaforica in Alice nel paese delle meraviglie", in: Daniela Calieri, Carla Marello (Eds.), *Linguistica Contrastiva*, Publicazioni della Società di Linguistica Italiana 20, Roma: Bulzoni 1982, pp. 229–254.

Bertinetto, Pier Marco, *Tempo, aspetto e azione nel verbo italiano*, Firenze: L'Academia della Crusca 1986.

Birkenmaier, Willy, "Die Funktion von *odin* im Russischen", in: *Zeitschrift für slavische Philologie*, Vol. 39, No. 1, 1976, pp. 43–59.

Bisang, Walter; Wu Yicheng, "Numeral classifiers in East Asia", In: *Linguistics* 2017, Vol. 55 (2), pp. 257–264.

Bloomfield, Leonard, *Language*, New York: Holt, Rinehart and Winston 1933.

Boltz, Ingeborg, "Alice's Adventures in Wonderland: Eine Kuriosität der viktorianischen Kinderliteratur", in: Christa Jansohn (Ed.), *In the Footsteps of Queen Victoria: Wege zum Viktorianischen Zeitalter*, Berlin: LIT 2003, pp. 279–299.

Brisset, Jean-Pierre, *La Science de Dieu ou la Création de l'Homme*, in: Marc Décimo (ed.), Jean-Pierre Brisset, *Œuvres complètes*, Paris: Les presses du réel 2001, pp. 697–885.

Brown, Cecilia, *Alice hinter den Mythen: Der Sinn in Carrolls Nonsens*, Paderborn: Wilhelm Fink 2015.

Brown, Daniel, *The Poetry of Victorian Scientists: Style, Science and Nonsense*, Cambridge: Cambridge University Press 2013.

Cammarata, Adele, "Italians Love *Alice*!", in: John A. Lindseth (Ed.), *Alice in a World of Wonderlands: The Translations of Lewis Carroll's Masterpiece* 2015, Vol. 1, pp. 310–315.

Carroll, Lewis, "Alice on the Stage", in: *The Theatre* (1887), Harold Bloom (Ed.), *Lewis Carroll's Alice's Adventures in Wonderland* (*Bloom's Modern Critical Interpretations*), New York: Chelsea House Publications 2006.

Carroll, Lewis, *Symbolic Logic* and *The Game of Logic*, Mathematical Recreations of Lewis Carroll, New York: Dover Publications 1958.

Chekhov, Anton, *Rano!* (*Early!* 1887), in: *Sobranije sochinenij*, Vol. V, Moskva: Hud. Literatura 1962.

Chekhov, Anton, Zhitejskaja meloč (*Quite an Everyday Trifle*, 1886), in: Anton Checkov, *Sobranije sočinenij*, Vol. IV, Moskva: Hud. Literature 1962.

Chekhov, Anton, *Selected Stories*, ed. by Cathy Popkin, tr. by Hugh Aplin, New York: W. W. Norton & Company 2014.

Chekhov, Anton, *Sobranije sočinenij v dvenadzati tomach*, Vo. 12, *Pisma* 1893–1904, Moskva: Hud. Literatura 1964.

Chen Shou 陳壽, *San guo zhi* 三國志 (*Records of the Three Kingdoms*), Beijing: Zhonghua shuju 1973.

Cheng, Lisa Lai-Shen; Rint Sybesma, "Bare and not so Bare Nouns and the Structure of NP", in: *Linguistic Inquiry*, Vol. 30, No. 4, 1999, pp. 509–542.

Chesterton, Gilbert K., "The Library of the Nursery" (1901), in: G. K. Chesterton, *Lunacy and Letters*, London: Sheed & Ward 1958.

Chierchia, Gennaro, "Plurality of Mass Nouns and the Notion of 'Semantic Parameter'," in: Susan Rothstein (Ed.), *Events and Grammar*, Dorderecht: Kluwer Academic Publishers 1998, pp. 53–103.

Chukovsky, Kornej, *From Two to Five*, tr. by Miriam Morton, Berkeley: Univ. of California Press 1971.

Clark, Beverly Lyon, "Nabokov's Assault on Wonderland", in: J. E. Rivers and Charles Nicol (Eds.), *Nabokov's Fifth Arc: Nabokov and Others on His Life's Work*, Austin: University of Texas Press 1982.

Clark, Eve V., "Lexical Innovations: How Children Learn to Create New Words", in: Werner Deutch (Ed.), *The Child's Construction of Language*, London: Academic Press 1981, pp. 299–328.

Comrie, Bernard, *Aspect: An Introduction to the Study of Verbal Aspect and Related Problems*, Cambridge: Cambridge University Press 1976.

Corbett, Greville G., *Gender*, Cambridge: Cambridge University Press 1991.

Corbett, Greville G., "Gender in Russian: An Account of Gender Specification and its Relationship to Declension", in: *Russian Linguistics*, Vol. 6, 1982, pp. 197–232.

Corbett, Greville G., "Gender in Slavonic from the Standpoint of a General Typology of Gender Systems", in: *The Slavonic and East European Review*, Vol. 66, No. 1, 1988, pp. 1–20.

Crump, Thomas, *The Anthropology of Numbers*, Cambridge: Cambridge Univ. Press 1992.

Dalí, Salvador, "Declaration of the independence of the imagination and the rights of man to his own madness", in: *Art Digest*, 1939, vol. 13, no. 19, p. 9.

Dalí, Salvador, "El Surrealismo" (1935), in: *Revista Hispánica Moderna*, No. 3 (Apr. 1935), pp. 233–234.

Dascal, Marcelo, "Defending Literal Meaning", in: *Cognitive Science*, Vol. 11, No. 3, 1987, pp. 259–281.

Dascal, Marcelo, "The Language of Thought and the Games of Language", in: Michael Astroh, D. Gerhardus, and G. Heinzma (Eds.), *Dialogisches Handeln: Eine Festschrift für Kuno Lorenz*. Heildeberg: Spektrum Akademischer Verlag, pp. 183–191.

Davidson, Donald, "A Nice Derangement of Epitaphs" in: Donald Davidson, *Truth, Language, and History*, Oxford: Clarendon Press 2005, pp. 89–108.

Davidson, Donald, "What Metaphors Mean", in: Donald Davidson, *Inquiries into Truth and Interpretation*, Oxford: Clarendon Press 1984, pp. 245–264.

De Brabanter, Philippe, Mikhail Kissine, Saghie Sharifzadeh, "Future tense vs. future time: An introduction", in: P. De Brabanter, Mikhail Kissine (et al., eds.), *Future Times, Future Tenses*, Oxford: Oxford University Press 2014, pp. 4–16.

De la Mare, Walter, "On the *Alice* Books" (1932), in: Robert Phillips (ed.), *Aspects of Alice*, New York: Vintage Books 1971, pp. 57–65.

Demmerling, Christoph, *Sinn, Bedeutung, Verstehen: Untersuchungen zu Sprachphilosophie und Hermeneutik*, Paderborn: Mentis 2002.

Demuurova, Nina M., "O perevode skazok Karrolla", in: *Ijulskij polden zolotoj: Statji ob anglijskoj detskoj knige*, Moskva: Izdatelstvo URAO 2000, pp. 87–123.

Dolev, Yuval, "The Tenseless Theory of Time: Insights and Limitations", in: *The Review of Metaphysics*, Vol. 54, No. 2, Dec. 2000, pp. 259–288.

Douglas, Mary, *Purity and Danger: An Analysis of Concepts of Pollution and Taboo*, London: Routledge 2002.

Dyrenforth, James; Kester, Max, *Adolf in Blunderland: A political parody of Lewis Carroll's famous story* (1939), London: Muller 1940.

Düringsfeld, Ida von, *Sprichwörter der germanischen und romanischen Sprachen, vergleichend zusammengestellt*, Leipzig: Herman Fries 1872.

Edwardes, Martin P. J., *The Origins of Self: An Anthropological Perspective*, London: UCL Press 2019.

Farber, Jerry, "Towards a Theoretical Framework for the Study of Humor in Literature and the Other Arts", in: *The Journal of Aesthetic Education*, Vol. 41, No. 4, 2007, pp. 67–86.

Feng Zongxin, "*Alice* in Chinese Translation", in: John A. Lindseth (Ed.), *Alice in a World of Wonderlands: The Translations of Lewis Carroll's Masterpiece*, 3 Volumes, New Castle: Oak Knoll Press 2015, Vol. 1, pp. 187–198.

Firtič, Nikolay, "Poetika neobyčnogo", in: Nikolay Firtič (Ed.), *Mir Alisy: Poetica neobyčnogo v litrerature i iskusstve XIX – XX vv.*, St Petersburg: Apollon 2017, pp. 5–39.

Flescher, Jacqueline, "The Language of Nonsense in Alice", in: *Yale French Studies*, No. 43, 1969, pp. 128–144.

Flonta, Teodor, *A Dictionary of English and Romance Languages Equivalent Proverbs*, București: Teopa 1992.

Gaipa, Mark; Scholes, Robert, "On the Very Idea of a Literal Meaning", in: Reed Way Dasenbrock (Ed.), *Literary Theory after Davidson*, University Park, Pa.: Pennsylvania State Univ. Press 1993, pp. 160–179.

Gill, Jerry H. (Ed.), *Wittgenstein and Metaphor*, Washington D. C.: Univ. Pr. of America 1981.

Gilleßen, Maximilian; Stuckardt, Anton (Eds.), *Jean-Pierre Brisset, Fürst der Denker, Eine Dokumentation*, Berlin: zero sharp 2014.

Givón, Talmy, "On the Development of the Numeral 'One' as an Indefinite Marker", in: *Folia Linguistica Historica* II/1 1981, pp. 35–53.

Gordon, Jan B., "The Alice Books and the Metaphors of Victorian Childhood" (1971), in: Robert Phillips (ed.), *Aspects of Alice*, New York: Vintage Books 1971, pp. 93–113.

Gorishneva, Elena, *The Variety of Functions of the Numeral and Infinitive Marker 'one' in Bulgarian and Russian*, Herne: Gabriele Schäfer Verlag 2016.

Green, Roger Lancelyn, "Alice" (1960), in: Robert Phillips (ed.), *Aspects of Alice*, New York: Vintage Books 1971, pp. 13–38.

Guéron, Jacqueline, Jacqueline Lecarme (Eds.), *Time and Modality*, Dordrecht: Springer 2008.

Halliday, Michael A. K., "Representing the Child as a Semiotic Being (One Who Means)" (1998), in: M. A. K. Halliday, *The Language of Early Childhood*, London/New York: Continuum 2004, pp. 6–27.

Heath, Peter, *The Philosopher's Alice*, New York: St. Martin's Press 1974.

Heine, Bernd, *Cognitive Foundations of Grammar*, Oxford: Oxford University Press 1997.

Hennelly, Mark M., "Alice's Adventures at the Carnival", in: *Victorian Literature and Culture*, Vol. 37, No. 1, 2009, pp. 103–128.

Hirata, Kayako, *Temporal Properties in Japanese*, Ann Arbor: UMI 1987.

Holmes, Roger W., "The Philosopher's *Alice in Wonderland*" (1959), in: Phillips, Robert (Ed.), *Aspects of Alice*, New York: Vintage Books 1971, pp. 159–174.

Homer, *The Odyssey*, Walter Shewring (Tr.), Oxford: Oxford Univ. Press 1980.

Huxley, Francis, *The Raven and the Writing Desk*, London: Thames and Hudson 1976.

Ide, Sachiko, "Women's Language as a Group Identity Marker in Japanese", in: Marlis Hellinger and Hadumod Bußmann (Eds.), *Gender Across Languages, The linguistic representation of women and men*, Amsterdam/Philadelphia: John Benjamins Publishing Company 2003, Vol. 3, pp. 227–238.

Ingthorsson, Rögnvaldur D., *McTaggart's Paradox*, New York: Routledge 2016.

Jespersen, Otto, *The Philosophy of Grammar* (1924), Chicago: The University of Chicago Press 1992.

Jiang, L. Julie, "Marking (In)definiteness in Classifier Languages", in: *Bulletin of Chinese Linguistics*, Vol. 8, 2015, pp. 319–343.

Keber, Agathon, *Zur Philosophie der Kindersprache. Gereimtes – Ungereimtes*, Halle: Verlag von Georg Schwabe 1868.

Kincaid, James R., "Alice's Invasion of Wonderland", in: *Publications of the Modern Language Association*, Vol. 88, No. 1, 1973, pp. 92–99.

Krifka, Manfred, "Common Nouns: A Contrastive Analysis of Chinese and English", in: Gregory N. Carlson, Francis Jeffry Pelletier (eds.), *The Generic Book*, Chicago: The University of Chicago Press 1995, pp. 398–411.

Lecercle, Jean-Jacques, "'Bégayer la langue' – Stammering Language", in: *L'Esprit Créateur*, Vol. 38, No. 4, 1998, pp. 109–123.

Lecercle, Jean-Jacques, *Philosophy of Nonsense: The intuitions of Victorian nonsense literature*, London: Routledge 1994.

Lecercle, Jean-Jacques, Response to Angelika Zirker, "Alice was not surprised", in: *Connotations*, Vol. 17, 2007/2008, pp. 281–286.

Lecercle, Jean-Jacques, *The Violence of Language*, London: Routledge 1990.
Legge, James, *The Works of Mencius*, Hong Kong: Hong Kong University Press 1960.
Levorato, Alessandra, *Language and Gender in the Fairy Tale Tradition: A Linguistic Analysis of Old and New Story Telling*, Basingstoke: Palgrave Macmillian 2003.
Lin, Jo-Wang, "Time in a Language without Tense: The Case of Chinese", in: *Journal of Semantics*, Vol. 23, 2005, pp. 1–53.
Lindseth, John A. (Ed.), *Alice in a World of Wonderlands: The Translations of Lewis Carroll's Masterpiece*, 3 Volumes, New Castle: Oak Knoll Press 2015.
Liu Fugen 刘福根, *Hanyu lici yanjiu* 汉语詈词研究 (*A Study of the Abusive Language in Chinese*), Hangzhou: Zhejiang renmin chubanshe 2008.
Ludlow, Peter, *Semantics, Tense, and Time: An Essay in the Metaphysics of Natural Language*, Cambridge, Mass.: MIT Press 1999.
MacKay, Donald G.; Konishi, Toshi, "Personification and the Pronoun Problem", in: *Women's Studies Int. Quarterly* 1980, Vol. 3, pp. 149–163.
Malevič, Kazimir, *Sobranie sočinenij v pjati tomah*, Moskva: Galileja 1995.
Malotki, Ekkerhart, *Hopi Time: A Linguistic Analysis of the Temporal Concepts in the Hopi Language*, Berlin: Mouton Publishers 1983.
Marcus, Gary F.; Steven Pinker (et al.), *Overregularization in Language Acquisition*. Monographs of the Society for Research in Child Development 57 (4, Serial No. 228), Chicago: Univ. of Chicago Press 1992.
May, Leila S., "Wittgenstein's Reflection in Lewis Carroll's *Looking Glass*", in: *Philosophy and Literature*, Vol 31, 2007, pp. 79–94.
McCabe, Janice; Fairchild, Emily; Grauerholz, Liz (et al.), "Gender in Twentieth-Century Children's Books: Patterns of Disparity in Titles and Central Characters", in: *Gender and Society*, Vol. 25, No. 2, 2011, pp. 197–226.
McManus, Denis, "Austerity, Psychology, and the Intelligibility of Nonsense", in: *Philosophical Topics*, Vol. 42, No. 2, 2014, pp. 161–199.
McTaggart, John Ellis, "The Unreality of Time", in: *Mind, New Series*, Vol. 17, No. 68 (Oct. 1908), pp. 457–474.
Mellor, David H., *Real Time*, Cambridge: Cambridge University Press 1981.
Michelet, Jules, *Le peuple*, Paris: Comptoir des Imprimeurs-Unis 1846.
Momma Yoshiyuki, "*Alice* in Japanese: Named One of 'The Best 100'", in: John A. Lindseth (Ed.), *Alice in a World of Wonderlands: The Translations of Lewis Carroll's Masterpiece* 2015, Vol. 1, pp. 316–319.
Moyal-Sharrock, Danièle, "The Good Sense of Nonsense: a reading of Wittgenstein's *Tractatus* as nonself-repudiating", in: *Philosophy*, Vol. 82, No. 319, Jan. 2007, pp. 147–177.
Nières-Chevrel, Isabelle, "The French Translations of *Alice*: From an Ambivalent Literary Reception to a Masterpiece of Universal Literature" (Tr. by Justine Houyaux), in: John A. Lindseth (Ed.), *Alice in a World of Wonderlands: The Translations of Lewis Carroll's Masterpiece* 2015, Vol. 1, pp. 239–248.

O'Sullivan, Emer, "Englishness in German translations of *Alice in Wonderland*", in: Luc van Doorslaer, Peter Flynn, Joep Leerssen (Eds.), *Interconnecting Translation Studies and Imagology*, Amsterdam: John Benjamins Publishing 2015, pp. 87–107.

O'Sullivan, Emer, "Miss Zimmermann and Her Successors: German Versions of *Alice in Wonderland*", in: John A. Lindseth (Ed.), *Alice in a World of Wonderlands: The Translations of Lewis Carroll's Masterpiece* 2015, Vol. 1 pp. 259–269.

Otten, Terry, "After Innocence: Alice in the Garden", in: Edward Guiliano (Ed.), *Lewis Carroll: A Celebration. Essays on the 150th Anniversary of the Birth of Charles Lutwidge Dodgson*, New York: Clarkson N. Potter 1982, pp. 50–61.

Perlmutter, David M., "On the Article in English", in: Manfred Bierwisch and Karl Erich Heidolph (Eds.), *Progress in Linguistics: A Collection of Papers*, The Hague/Paris: Mouton 1970, pp. 233–248.

Phillips, Robert (Ed.), *Aspects of Alice*, New York: Vintage Books 1971.

Piaget, Jean, *The Language and Thought of the Child*, London: Routledge 1926.

Pinker, Steven, *Words and Rules*, New York: Basic Books 1999.

Pitcher, George, "Wittgenstein, Nonsense, and Lewis Carroll", in: *The Massachusetts Review*, Vol. 6, No. 3 (Spring-Summer 1965), pp. 591–611.

Preyer, Willian Th., *Die Seele des Kindes: Beobachtungen über die geistige Entwicklung des Menschen in den ersten Lebensjahren*, Leipzig: Grieben 1890.

Pulleyblank, Edwin G., *Outline of Classical Chinese Grammar*, Vancouver: UBC Press 1995.

Pusch, Luise F., "Von Frauenflüchtlingen und Männerleichen", in: Luise F. Pusch, *Die Frau ist nicht der Rede wert*, Frankfurt am Main: Suhrkamp 1999.

Rackin, Donald, *Alice's Adventures in Wonderland and Through the Looking-Glass: Nonsense, Sense, and Meaning*, Twayne's masterwork studies, No. 81, New York: Twayne Publishers 1991.

Rackin, Donald, "Alice's Long Journey to the End of Night", in: Rackin, Donald (Ed.), *Alice's Adventures in Wonderland. A critical Handbook*, Belmont: Wordsworth Publishing Company 1969, pp. 339–361.

Rash, Felicity, *The Language of Violence: Adolf Hitler's Mein Kampf*, New York/Berlin/Bern: Peter Lang 2006.

Rocci, Andrea, "L'interprétation épistémique du futur en italien et en français: une analyse procédurale", in: *Cahiers de Linguistique Française*, Vol. 22, 2000, pp. 241–274.

Rochester, Sherry; Martin, James Robert, *Crazy Talk: A Study of the Discourse of Schizophrenic Speakers*, New York: Plenum Press 1979.

Rother, James, "Modernism and the Nonsense Style", in: *Contemporary Literature*, Vol. 15, No. 2, 1974, pp. 187–202.

Rothstein, Susan, "Counting and the Mass/Count Distinction", in: *Journal of Semantics*, Vol 27, 2010, pp. 343–397.

Rothstein, Susan, *Semantics for Counting and Measuring*, Cambridge: Cambridge University Press 2017.

Ryle, Gilbert, *Dilemmas*, Cambridge: Cambridge Univ. Press 1954.

Ryle, Gilbert, *The Concept of Mind* (1949), New York: Penguin Books 1976.

Said, Edward W., *Orientalism: Western conceptions of the Orient*, London: Penguin Books 1978.

Sale, Roger, *Fairy Tales and After: From Snow White to E. B. White*, Harvard: Harvard University Press 1978.

Sester, Franz, "Vorwort", *Alicens Abenteuer im Wunderland*, Düsseldorf: Drei Eulen 1949, pp. 7–8.

Sewell, Elizabeth, *The Field of Nonsense* (1952), London: Dalkey Archive Press 2015.

Sharvy, Richard, "Maybe English Has No Count Nouns: Notes on Chinese Semantics. An Essay in Metaphysics and Linguistics", in: *Studies in Language*, 1978, Vol. 2, No. 3, pp. 345–365.

Sheridan, Richard B., *The Rivals*, London: Benn 1979.

Shibamoto Smith, Janet S., "Gendered Structures in Japanese", in: Marlis Hellinger and Hadumod Bußmann, *Gender Across Languages, The linguistic representation of women and men*, Amsterdam/Philadelphia: John Benjamins Publishing Company 2003, Vol. 3, pp. 201–226.

Shibles, Warren A., *Wittgenstein, Language and Philosophy*, Dubuque: Kendall Hunt 1970.

Sigalow, Emily; Fox, Nicole S., "Perpetuating Stereotypes: A Study of Gender, Family and Religious Life in Jewish Children's Books", in: *Journal for the Scientific Study of Religion*, Vol. 53, No. 2, June 2014, pp. 416–431.

Skuratovska, Liudmila I.; Maria I. Isakova, "*Alice* in Russian: A Metamorphosis", in: John A. Lindseth (Ed.), *Alice in a World of Wonderlands: The Translations of Lewis Carroll's Masterpiece* 2015, Vol. 1, pp. 461–466.

Smith, Clara S., "Time With and Without Tense", in: Jacqueline Guéron, Jacqueline Lecarme (eds.), *Time and Modality*, Dordrecht: Springer 2008, pp. 227–249.

Solarino, Rosaria, *Imparare dagli errori*, Napoli: Tecnodid 2009.

Steiner, George, *After Babel: Aspects of Language and Translation*, Oxford: Oxford Univ. Press 1975.

Stern, Clara; Stern, William, *Die Kindersprache*, Darmstadt: Wissenschaftliche Buchgesellschaft 1975.

Sutherland, Robert D., *Language and Lewis Carroll*, The Hague/Paris: Mouton 1970.

Tabakowska, Elzbieta, "Point of View in Translation: Lewis Carroll's *Alice* in grammatical wonderlands", in: Chloe Harrison, Louise Nuttall (et al., eds.), *Cognitive Grammar in Literature*, Amsterdam/Philadelphia: John Benjamins Publishing Company 2014, pp.101–116.

Talmage, Catherine J. L., "Literal Meaning, Conventional Meaning and First meaning", in: *Erkenntnis*, Vol. 40, No. 2 (Mar., 1994), pp. 213–225.

Talmage, Catherine J. L., "Davidson and Humpty Dumpty", in: *Nous*, Vol. 30, No. 4 (Dec., 1996), pp. 537–544.

Thunecke, Jörg, "Malice in Wonderland: James Dyrenforth and Max Kester's Political Satire *Adolf in Blunderland* (1939)", in: Victoria Hertling, Wulf Koepke (Et al., eds.), *Hitler im Visier: Literarische Satiren und Karikaturen als Waffe gegen den Nationalsozialismus*, Wuppertal: Arco Verlag 2005, pp. 251–274.

Thüring, Herbert, "Die Sprache im Bann, im Bann der Sprache: Zur Genealogie des Sprachdeliriums um 1900 (Gottfried Benn, Heymann Steinthal, Paul Emil Flechsig)", in: Maximilian Bergengruen, Roland Borgands (eds.), *Bann der Gewalt: Studien zur Literatur- und Wissensgeschichte*, Göttingen: Wallstein Verlag 2009, pp. 469–504.

Tigges, Wim, *An Anatomy of Literary Nonsense*, Amsterdam: Rodopi 1988.

Tinto, Edoardo, *Verso la filosofia della grammatica*, Roma: Libreria Editrice Universitaria 1953.

Vendler, Zeno, "Verbs and Times", in: *The Philosophical Review*, Vol. 66, No. 2, Apr. 1957, pp. 143–160.

Venuti, Lawrence, *The Translator's Invisibility: A History of Translation* (1995), London/ New York: Routledge 2008.

Vetrov, Viatcheslav, "The World's Countability: On the Mastery of Divided Reference and the Controversy over the Mass/Count Distinction in Chinese", in: *Monumenta Serica* 2022 (forthcoming.)

Von Humboldt, Wilhelm, *Lettre à M. Abel-Rémusat, sur la nature des formes grammaticales en général, et sur le génie de la langue chinoise en particulier*, Paris: La Librairie Orientale de Dondey-Dupré 1827.

Von Humboldt, Wilhelm, *Über die männliche und die weibliche Form* (1795), in: Wilhelm von Humboldt, *Werke*, Albert Leitzmann (Ed.), Berlin: B. Behr's Verlag 1903, Vol. I, pp. 335–369.

Wagner, David, "The uses of nonsense: Ludwig Wittgenstein reads Lewis Carroll", in: *Wittgenstein-Studien*, Vol. 3, No.1, 2012, pp. 202–216.

Wagner, Susanne, *Gender in English Pronouns: Myth and Reality* (PhD Dissertation), Freiburg im Breisgau 2003.

Weaver, Warren, *Alice in Many Tongues: The Translations of Alice in Wonderland*, Madison: The Univ. of Wisconsin Press 1964.

White, John, "'Die gebildete Umgangssprache' and Our College Grammars: The German Present Tense in Future Meaning", in: *The German Quarterly*, Vol. 17, No. 3, May 1944, pp. 131–134.

White, Roger M., "Literal Meaning and 'Figurative Meaning'", in; *Teoria*, Vol. 67, No. 1, 2001, pp. 24–59.

Whorf, Benjamin Lee, *Language, Thought, and Reality*, Cambridge (Massachusetts): The MIT Press 2012.

Wierzbicka, Anna, "'Oats' and 'Wheat': The Fallacy of Arbitrariness", in: John Hayman (Ed.), *Iconicity in Syntax: Proceedings on a Symposium on Iconicity in Syntax*, Amsterdam/Philadelphia: John Benjamins, 1985, pp. 311–342.

Wittgenstein, Ludwig, *Culture and Value*, Ed. G.H. von Wright, Oxford: Blackwell 1998.

Wittgenstein, Ludwig, *Philosophische Grammatik*, in: Ludwig Wittgenstein, *Schriften*, Vol. 4, Rush Rhees (Ed.), Frankfurt am Main: Suhrkamp 1969.

Wittgenstein, Ludwig, *Philosophical Investigations*, Tr. by G. E. M. Anscombe, Oxford: Basil Blackwell 1953.

Wittgenstein, Ludwig, *Preliminary Studies for the "Philosophical Investigations" Generally Known as The Blue and Brown Books*, Oxford: Basil Blackwell 1969.

Wittgenstein, Ludwig, *Tractatus Logico-Philosophicus*, London: Routledge 1955.

Woolf, Virginia, "Lewis Carroll's Crystallized Childhood" (1939), in: Donald Rackin (Ed.), *Alice's Adventures in Wonderland: A Critical Handbook*, Belmont: Wadsworth Publishing Company 1969, pp. 265–267.

Wu, Jiun-Shiung, "Tense as a Discourse Feature: Rethinking Temporal Location in Mandarin Chinese", in: *Journal of East Asian Linguistics*, Vol. 18, No. 2, May 2009, pp. 145–165.

Wu Yicheng; Adams Bodomo, "Classifiers ≠ Determiners", in: *Linguistic Inquiry*, Vol. 40, No. 3, 2009, pp. 487–503.

Zhang, Niina Ning, *Classifier Structures in Mandarin Chinese*, Berlin: Walter de Gruyter 2013.

Zhang Qunxing, "Creation for Fidelity – Zhao Yuanren's Translation of Lexical Nonsense in *Alice's Adventures in Wonderland*", in: *International Journal of Comparative Literature and Translation Studies*, Vol. 5, No. 1 2017, pp. 71–79.

Zhu Xi 朱熹 (Ed.), *Si shu zhang ju ji zhu* 四書章句集注, Beijing: Zhonghua shuju 2008.

Zirker, Angelika, "'Alice was not surprised'": (Un)Surprises in Lewis Carroll's Alice-Books", in: *Connotations*, Vol. 14.1–3, 2004–2005, pp. 19–37.

Index